Writers for Young Adults

Writers for Young Adults

Ted Hipple

Editor

SUPPLEMENT 1

CHARLES SCRIBNER'S SONS
New York

Charles Scribner's Sons
1633 Broadway
New York, NY 10019

Library of Congress Cataloging-in-Publication Data

Writers for young adults / Ted Hipple, editor.
     p. cm.
    Summary: Contains articles on writers whose works are popular with young
adults, including contemporary and classic authors.
    IBSN 0-684-80618-5; Supplement to set ISBN 0-684-80474-3.
    1. Young adult literature, American—Bio-bibliography—Dictionaries. 2. Young
adult literature, English—Bio-bibliography—Dictionaries. [1. Authors, American.
2. Authors, English. 3. Young adult literature.] I. Hipple, Theodore W.
PS490.W75
810.9'9283'03
  [B] —DC21   97-6890
                                                 CIP
                                                 AC

1 3 5 7 9 11 13 15 17 19 20 18 16 14 12 10 8 6 4 2

Printed in the United States of America.

The paper used in this publication meets the minimum requirements of the American National Standard for Information Sciences—Permanence of Paper for Printed Library Materials, ANSI Z39.48-1992.

Contents

Illustration Acknowledgments

K. A. Applegate: Photo Credit: Mike Haberman Photography.
Jane Austen: Prints and Photographs Collection, Library of Congress. Engraving of Jane Austen portrait by Evert A. Duyckink.
Michael Cadnum: Photo by: Dave Thomas.
Sharon Creech: Photo credit: Matthew Self.
Karen Cushman: Photo credit: Fred Mertz.
Paul Fleischman: Photo credit: Becky Mojica.
Nancy Garden: Photo credit: Midge Eliassen.
Mel Glenn: Photo courtesy of Mel Glenn.
Adele Griffin: Courtesy of Hyperion Books for Children
Jim Haskins: Photo courtesy of William Morrow & Company.
Karen Hesse: Photo courtesy of Scholastic, Inc.
Lou Kassem: Photo credit: Gene Dalton.
Stephen King: Photo credit: Virginia Sherwood/ABC, Inc.
David Klass: Photo courtesy of Scholastic, Inc.
Annette Curtis Klause: Photo courtesy of Random House, Inc.
Ronald Koertge: Photo credit: Judith Heinrichs.
Trudy Krisher: Photo credit: Larry Burgess.
A. C. LeMieux: Courtesy of The Westport News/Helen Neafsey photographer.
Carolyn Meyer: Photo Credit: Kim Jew Photography.
Arthur Miller: Prints and Photographs Collection, Library of Congress.
Margaret Mitchell: Margaret Mitchell House & Museum.
Kyoko Mori: Photo credit: Katherine McCabe.
Donna Jo Napoli: Photo by Barry Furrow.
Rodman Philbrick: Photo by Andrew Edgar. Courtesy of Scholastic, Inc.

Preface

by Ted Hipple

To edit a book and then to wonder about its reception is necessarily to delay gratification. Answers to questions about whether reviewers will comment favorably about the book, whether potential buyers will purchase it, and, most importantly, whether readers will value it, must be deferred. Publishing takes time, months really, after much of the editor's work is completed. Then reviewers, buyers, and readers render their judgments by their actions and comments, and inferences can be made about those judgments. Finally, however, this process is worked through and the evidence is in; the time for gratification—or despair—is at hand.

Thus, when Sylvia Miller of Scribners told me that *Writers for Young Adults* had done very well with reviewers, buyers, and readers, I felt highly pleased. Buyers, mostly school and public librarians, have purchased the books in numbers that significantly exceeded expectations. And these purchasers have reported to us how much their readers, mostly young adults and their mentors, have liked the three volumes. The success of *Writers for Young Adults* is, at bottom, the success of numerous others: the 114 contributors, each of whom wrote about 2,500 words about one or more authors, 129 in all, whose works are commonly read by young adults.

Anyone who has ever read a collection, an anthology, can easily understand how its editor faced decisions laden with anticipated criticisms about omissions ("How could you possibly have left so and so out of your selection of authors?") and commissions ("What in heaven's name prompted you to include so and so?"). Full disclosure mandates my admitting that there were some of these sorts of questions, but very few. So, when Sylvia called and said, "We're thinking of doing a supplement. Are you interested in editing it?" I answered quickly, "You bet I am."

Here was a chance to go to some of the contributors for new essays and also to go to new contributors, to ask them to write about authors who, for space reasons, just barely missed the cut the first time around or about authors whose recent emergence into the forefront of young adult literature made their inclusion this time an easy choice. It was a chance again to examine schoolhouse literature curricula to see if those authors we called "classic" in the first three volumes, authors like Shakespeare or Mark Twain or Robert Frost, should now be accompanied by other classic authors whose works are widely read in middle school and junior and senior high school English language arts classes.

For this supplement I again asked contributors to focus their writing about their authors for an intended audience of young people. A reference book about writers read—and often revered—by young adults, should itself be accessible to young adults. Imagine, I suggested to the contributors, an eighth or ninth grader (or sixth or eleventh) who reads, say, *Out of the Dust* by Karen Hesse and wants to know more about her, more about her life, more about her books. And that young person goes to the library, gets this book, and reads your essay. I want him or her to be able to understand what you have said and be inspired to read more. The contributors achieved this goal admirably; young people will find in these pages essays they will understand. Yet the essays are also sufficiently sophisticated that older readers—teachers, librarians, parents—will discover much that is insightful and useful.

That decision on including Karen Hesse, by the way, was easy. Other decisions about whom to include, whom to exclude, were more difficult; I knew I needed help. So again I went to colleagues in the field of young adult literature and asked for suggestions. I supplied them with the table of contents of the first three volumes and asked them, simply, "Who now? We have space for thirty-nine writers. Which ones?" They were extraordinarily helpful, taking their task seriously, talking in turn with other colleagues of theirs, asking young people or their teachers and librarians about favorite authors. We, these colleagues and I, shared recommendations. We debated. And, finally, I had the thirty-nine authors the supplement would cover and, soon, too, the contributors who would write what we came to call "bio-crits" about these authors, essays of about 2,500 words that were part biography, part criticism.

Once more, I opted for non-formulaic essays. The divergence of methods of approach and of writing styles that proved so exciting in the initial volumes should, I assumed, prove just as exciting in this one. I think it has.

Now in your hands, the product is ready again for the judgment of reviewers, buyers, and readers. As I felt with the first set, I am again elated with the results of all of our labors, not least among them those of the Scribner people, like Sylvia Miller and her associate Laura Smid, both of whom truly went the second mile on this project. They read each and every contribution themselves; they read my reactions to those contributions; they commented on both contributions and reactions, all the while making good essays better. Sylvia and Laura were superb. I owe them much and I thank them.

What remains for me in this introduction to the supplement is the opportunity to make a few remarks about its contents. I begin with the "classic" authors. Though the term "young adult literature" admits of many definitions, a fairly common one, and, I think, a good one is that it is literature written *for* young adults. That is, the author of such literature envisions a reader who is between the ages of ten or eleven and sixteen or seventeen. Clearly, authors like Jane Austen, Arthur Miller, Walt Whitman, and Thornton Wilder do not fit that mold. Yet examine any school literature program and you will find *Pride and Prejudice, Death of a Salesman, Leaves of Grass,* and *Our Town* prominently studied. These authors are widely read by young readers—in the case of *Our Town,* their reading is often accompanied by their playing roles on school stages of that oft-produced play—and clearly merit their inclusion in a reference work like this one.

Equally justifiable is the inclusion of Margaret Mitchell, who, it is true, wrote but one book. But what a book it was! A colleague who teaches university freshmen says that she can bank on at least 50 percent of her students having read *Gone With the Wind* and at least 75 percent having seen the movie, some of them many times.

Stephen King, R. L. Stine, and Christopher Pike share, in their novels, an affinity for what some call "bizarre" plots, those on the edge, ones that perhaps overstretch our credulity. But note their enormous popularity with younger (and with older) readers. These authors had to be included in this volume.

Recent Newbery Award winners are here: Sharon Creech, Karen Cushman, Cynthia Rylant, Karen Hesse, Paul Fleischman, Louis Sachar. They have earned what many regard as the most prestigious award in the business of writing for young people, and these six join other Newbery winners whose bio-crits appear in the first three volumes.

Enough. The supplement is completed. I await the gratification—or the lack of it. But I do so knowing full well that I was merely the putter-together of the efforts of a lot of really able people, the authors of novels and plays and poems read by young people and the contributing writers who wrote about the authors and their novels and plays and poems. As with Sylvia and Laura, I owe them much and I thank them. If this volume reaches the levels of success achieved by the first three, it will be owing to the excellence of these two groups—the authors and the contributors—and their large commitment to young people.

I think again we have a volume we can all be proud of. And may I say (hope?) that if a second supplement is in the cards, I have begun my list of candidates for inclusion.

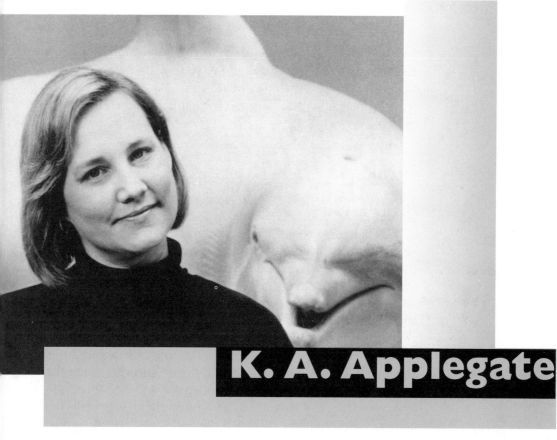

K. A. Applegate

(1956–)

by David Gill

The writer sits at the keyboard, typing out the words of her latest novel. Suddenly, her fingers begin to change. The nails grow longer and turn into talons, and feathers shoot out from her eyebrows. Wings take the place of arms, completing her transformation into a hawk. She continues writing, and just as suddenly, her form changes again. The wings recede, replaced by four legs as big as tree trunks. Her nose grows from a beak into a long, gray trunk, and ears the size of throw-rugs pop out of the sides of her head. Seconds later, she changes a third time. The trunk shrinks back into her face, and her mouth turns into a snout full of white fangs. Fur sprouts all over her body, and she howls with delight as she finishes the scene. Finally, the writer returns to her ordinary human form, K. A. Applegate.

But Katherine Alice Applegate is no ordinary writer. The author of over one hundred books, she is the creator of the spectacularly successful Animorphs, a series that has over 15 million books in print and has been made into a popular television show on Nickelodeon. Applegate has legions of fans, receiving over one hundred messages a day from loyal readers, and each eagerly awaits the next book in the series. Like her morphing characters, who can shift at will from one animal form to another, Applegate has undergone something of a metamorphosis herself.

Turning into a Writer

Applegate was born in 1956 in Michigan and has lived in Texas, Florida, and California. By her own admission, she enjoys extreme changes: She once moved from Florida to Minneapolis, Minnesota, for a change of scenery. She claims, tongue in cheek, that she was a model child: "I always did my homework, always got straight A's and did the dishes without being asked twice," she said in one of several interviews she has given. "Also, I loved animals—well, at least the part about loving animals is true!"

tongue in cheek with insincerity or exaggeration

Her first story, called "Alice the Peccary," was about a pig. She wrote it in the sixth grade, and it isn't surprising that the main character was an animal. Applegate and her three siblings were raised with animals all around them—she calls it a menagerie—including cats, gerbils, and dogs. Based on this environment, she thought she would make either a good veterinarian or a good writer. Though she worked as a vet's assistant during high school, "doing everything from cleaning out cages to assisting in surgery," she decided to become a writer. A writer, she realized, could socialize with any "animal under the sun—and perhaps a few from a galaxy down the road."

peccary a nocturnal animal related to pigs

Like many writers, she had other occupations before her career took off. "I went through a series of jobs," she says, "typing (badly), waiting tables (also badly), and taking care of plants (many of which did actually survive)." However, no matter what job she was doing, she knew she wanted to be a writer. Nevertheless, she put off writing for awhile, until she realized that being a writer took commitment and discipline. "It turns out," she admits, "that in order to become a writer, you actually have to start writing."

Though she has a college degree, she has had no formal training as a writer. To become a writer, Applegate discovered that she first had to be a reader: "The best training for a writer is to be a reader. The more you read, the better." As a writer, she learns her craft from reading other authors. For young readers, she recommends a variety of authors, such as Charles

Dickens or Jules Verne. She is especially fond of J. R. R. Tolkien's *Lord of the Rings* (1965).

"You literally cannot," she says, "read a book that doesn't teach you something, no matter how minor, about writing. Adult book, kid's book, mystery, science fiction, literary novel, classic, it doesn't matter: if you read and pay attention you'll learn something about writing."

Lightning in a Bottle: The Animorphs

Though she had published over a hundred other books, which ranged from Disney pop-up books to adult romance novels, Applegate was looking for a way to reach the middle grade audience. One day she was sitting in her apartment in Florida when the idea of the Animorphs struck her. Originally called the Changelings (before it was "morphed" by the publisher, Scholastic), Animorphs is the story of five teens who have been chosen to save Earth from an evil race called the Yeerks.

In a nutshell, the teenagers—Rachel, Tobias, Jake, Marco, and Cassie—are mall rats selected by a dying member of an alien race, the Andalites, to defend Earth from another race of aliens, the Yeerks. Yeerks are sluglike creatures who invade a person's brain through the ear. Once there, they control the person, who becomes a "Controller." This helps the Yeerks to control the human population. To help the human kids defeat the Yeerks, the Andalite passes on the ability to "morph" into other species, thus the name "Animorphs."

Every book in the series tells the ongoing story of the Animorphs' battles with the Yeerks. Each of the five humans takes turns narrating the books, and their points of view shape how the story is told. Marco, a Hispanic, tells his stories with side comments and wisecracks. Tobias, who is trapped in a morph of a hawk (because he stayed in morph past the two-hour time limit), has a calmer, more retrospective voice. The other three humans add their perspectives, as does Ax, an Andalite who later joins forces with the Animorphs and has his own point of view.

What makes Animorphs so special (and so successful)? Some critics, such as Mark West in *The Five Owls* (1998), think that it is Applegate's ability to "get into the heads" of the animals she describes. When Tobias morphs into a hawk, for example, Applegate allows her readers "to see the world as a

There is an article about Charles Dickens in volume 1. There is an article about J. R. R. Tolkien in volume 3.

Jules Verne (1828–1905) was a French novelist who wrote early science fiction works, including *Twenty Thousand Leagues Under the Sea.*

narrating telling a story

point of view the position or perspective from which the story is told

retrospective commonly surveying the past

shrew a small animal
with a long, pointed
snout, related to moles

rehabilitation
restoration to good
health

thermal rising body of
warm air

unconventional out
of the ordinary

hawk might see it—to soar on the warm breezes and hurtle toward the ground to make a kill." Other animals require her to describe the world in different ways. When Rachel turns into a shrew in one episode, the paralyzing fear the shrew instinctively feels almost gets her killed. Applegate spends many hours researching animals to get this effect. Besides using her own library, she talks to zoologists and curators at zoos. "The zoo guys are the best," she says on the Scholastic website devoted to her books, "because they observe the animals all day long."

To write about Tobias becoming a hawk, she visited a falconer and vet at a rehabilitation center for birds. Her research led to the following passage from *The Predator* (1996):

> **We flew. Not side by side, because that would have looked suspicious. Hawks and eagles don't exactly fly in formation like geese. We kept a hundred yards apart. But with our incredible vision and thought-speak, we might as well have been next to each other. We rose higher and higher on the thermals, then thermal-hopped. . . . Flying is as wonderful as you'd think. It has problems, too, like anything else. But oh man, on a warm day with the mountains of fluffy white clouds showing the way to the thermal updrafts, it's just wonderful.**

No matter how much research Applegate does, she depends on her writer's instincts to fill out the details: "Climbing into the head of an animal is like climbing into the head of another human being," she explains. "It becomes pure imagination."

Characters: Coming to Life

So what does it take to climb into the head of another human being? What does Applegate do to create characters so vivid that her readers think of them as real people even friends? Maybe it's the way she approaches her readers. She wanted to write for the middle grade audience, the junior high set that she has called "the best readers on the planet." She finds this group open to new ideas and willing to accept unconventional characters. Her own unconventional characters may begin as photographs of real people, ones that help her form a concrete image of the character she wants to write about. Then she sketches out a form for the character and writes a catch phrase that summarizes them in a few words. For example, her phrase for Jake was "regular guy turned reluctant hero," a description that allows her to describe him consistently. But she doesn't stop there. To keep track of five humans, a couple of Andalites, and a host of Yeerks, she has developed categories, such as Age, Looks, Personality, Role in the Group, and Role in the Series. She can take up three single-spaced pages filling out the rest of the data including likes and dislikes, families, grade in school, and so forth.

It can be difficult keeping up with so much information, especially because Animorphs is published monthly. Applegate keeps what she calls "a series bible," a collection of information about the series, the plots of the novels, and the above-mentioned biographical information about each character. This helps her to maintain continuity from book to book. Even so, sometimes she does make mistakes, something she calls a KASU (Katherine Applegate Screw Up).

Like real people, characters sometimes don't stay the same. They change over time, act differently in new situations, and despite the author's best intentions, interact with other characters, causing them to change, too. Rachel, says Applegate, started out as "brave and beautiful." She has stayed that way, but over time, her character has developed more depth, gaining a sense of humor and a love for battle. Applegate wonders if maybe "Rachel is getting caught up in the thrill of battle and losing sight of what she's fighting for. . . . I know it sounds hokey, but after awhile the characters seem to be running themselves, with me just kind of watching and going 'hmmmm.' " That may explain why many readers who e-mail Applegate often address their letters to the characters, not to the author.

hokey corny

Other Books, Other Voices

Applegate did not start out as a science fiction author, and she did not write for a middle school audience. Her first children's book, *The World's Best Jinx McGee,* was published in 1992. It is the story of Jinx, the fastest runner in second grade until a new girl with faster legs shows up. Five years later, she followed with another children's story, *Jack Rabbit and the*

Beanstalk (1997). This book adds a new twist to the beanstalk folktale. Jack becomes Jack Rabbit, a curious bunny who tricks the giant at the top of the stalk. Applegate authored several books for the Disney Company, using their animated characters. She wrote several Little Mermaid novels and teamed up with various illustrators for books that featured Mickey Mouse, Aladdin, Jasmine, and the Pirates of the Caribbean.

Like her morphing characters, Applegate makes a habit of changing her identity. Many writers find a niche that makes them comfortable, but she seems to thrive on variety. In 1992, Applegate also began publishing romance novels, making a name for herself as one of a handful of young adult romance writers. Her Ocean City series features several books about teenagers in love, as did two of her other series, Boyfriends Girlfriends and Summer. By adult standards, they were pretty tame, but her readers found them charming, and she developed a strong following among adolescent girls. She followed these series with several other romance novels.

When it was time to do a short story, she teamed up with other young adult romance writers for the short story collection *See You in September* (1995). Even with the success of the Animorphs, she continues to publish in the romance genre—her mass market Making Out series debuted in 1998. Again like a leopard that can change its spots, Applegate switched to nonfiction. Her biography about two African American generals in the armed forces, *The Story of Two American Generals: Benjamin O. Davis, Jr. and Colin L. Powell,* came out in 1995.

Dealing with Success

How has outrageous success changed Applegate's life? Not much, except for a move from Minneapolis to Illinois. She continues to write at a prolific pace, spending about three hours of actual writing at the keyboard every day. Those three hours, though, require "three hours of thinking and research, three hours of shopping and another three hours of complaining about one thing or another." Writing requires her to expend energy, and though she enjoys her job, it is not always easy work. Some books, usually every tenth one or so, are difficult to write, and she wonders if she will ever finish. But finish she does.

Readers often ask Applegate which animal she would morph into, if given the chance. "I would like to morph into a dolphin," Applegate has said. "I've spent time with dolphins

niche place or position best suited to a person

General **Benjamin O. Davis, Jr.** (1877–1970) was the first African American general in the U.S. Army.

General **Colin L. Powell** (1937–), also a general in the army, was the first African American to be appointed chairman of the Joint Chiefs of Staff.

prolific producing a large amount

and their trainers. I love their beauty and their sense of freedom." She lives a very private life, shunning personal publicity, preferring to let her books do the talking for her. Most of her contact with fans is on the Animorphs website, where she occasionally hosts on-line conferences, answering readers' questions about books, writing, and of course, characters.

With increased attention, though, comes increased criticism. Not all critics are immediately impressed with Animorphs. Because it is a series, Applegate must supply background about the continuing story in every issue. While this informs new readers, it makes her prose feel formulaic. Also, Applegate's descriptions do not vary much from one novel to the next, and the characters themselves have not developed since the first issues. Another lament some readers have is Applegate's overuse of fads, alluding to fashion trends and teenage popular culture in every chapter. Some critics, such as Christine Hepperman in *Horn Book,* were skeptical about this "extraterrestrial-among-us craze." Initially Hepperman found the alien conspiracy and teenage morphing too contrived, but in time, she, like many Animorphs readers, "became caught up in Applegate's gutsy . . . attempts to imagine" the world through the eyes of animals.

prose writing without regular rhythm; ordinary writing

Down the Road

The Animorphs series started in 1996. An immediate success, it has replaced R. L. Stine's Goosebumps as the number one-selling series, with over twenty books already published. Over 15 million books are in print. Like many hit television shows, the series has spawned spin-offs, including the Andalite Chronicles and The Hork-Bajir Chronicles. Nickelodeon has adapted Animorphs into a weekly television series, aging the characters a couple of years. Although Applegate is not involved in writing the television series, the producers have generally stayed close to the plots of the early novels.

There is an article about R. L. Stine later in this volume.

As for the future of the series, Applegate remains mum. She admits to signing on for thirty more books (making Animorphs continue to at least number 54), as well as other spin-offs. "Seems like an awful lot," she says, but with millions of readers with huge appetites for Yeerks and Andalites, how can she stop?

plot the deliberate sequence of events in a literary work

Many readers wonder, what will happen in those next books? What direction will the series take? Will the Yeerks be defeated, and if so, how? "Hah," says Applegate, "like I'm going to tell?" She keeps it close to the vest, refusing to reveal anything about plots to come, and tells fans to keep reading "because I am going to do my best to surprise you, scare you, and amaze you."

If you like K. A. Applegate, you might also like Jane Yolen.

Selected Bibliography

WORKS BY KATHERINE APPLEGATE

Animorphs Novels

The Encounter (1996)

The Invasion (1996)

The Message (1996)

The Predator (1996)

The Visitor (1996)

The Alien (1997)

The Andalite Chronicles (1997)

The Andalite's Gift (1997)

The Android (1997)

The Capture (1997)

The Change (1997)

The Forgotten (1997)

The Reaction (1997)

The Secret (1997)

The Stranger (1997)

The Decision (1998)

The Departure (1998)

The Discovery (1998)

The Escape (1998)

Hork-Bajir Chronicles (1998)

In the Time of Dinosaurs (1998)

Megamorphs #2 (1998)

The Pretender (1998)

The Solution (1998)

The Suspicion (1998)

The Threat (1998)

The Underground (1998)
The Unknown (1998)
The Warning (1998)
Alternamorphs: The First Journey (1999)
The Attack (1999)
The Experiment (1999)
The Exposed (1999)
The Extreme (1999)

Romance Novels

My Sister's Boyfriend (1992)
The Unbelievable Truth (1992)
Boardwalk (1993)
Fireworks (1993)
Love Shack (1993)
Ben's in Love (1994)
Bonfire (1994)
Claire Gets Caught (1994)
Heat Wave (1994)
Jake Finds Out (1994)
Lucas Gets Hurt (1994)
Nina Won't Tell (1994)
Ocean City Reunion (1994)
What Zoey Saw (1994)
Zoey Fools Around (1994)
July's Promise (1995)
June Dreams (1995)
Ocean City Forever (1995)
See You in September (1995)
Shipwrecked (1995)
Swept Away (1995)
Summer: August Magic (1995)
Beaches, Boys, and Betrayal (1996)
Listen to My Heart (1996)
Sand, Surf, and Secrets (1996)
Sharing Sam (1996)

Summer: Christmas Special Edition (1996)

Summer: Rays, Romance, and Rivalry (1996)

Summer: Spring Break Reunion (1996)

Zoey Plays Games (1996)

Aisha Goes Wild (1999)

Chapter Books

The Boyfriend Mix-Up (1994)

Tales from Agrabah: Seven Original Stories of Aladdin and Jasmine (1995)

Children's Books

The World's Best Jinx McGee, illustrated by Cathy Pavia (1992)

The Haunted Palace, illustrated by Philo Barnhart (1993)

King Triton, Beware!, illustrated by Philo Barnhart (1993)

Disney's Christmas With All the Trimmings: Original Stories and Crafts from Mickey Mouse and Friends, illustrated by Phil Wilson (1994)

Jack Rabbit and the Beanstalk (1997)

Biography

The Story of Two American Generals: Benjamin O. Davis, Jr. and Colin L. Powell (1992)

How to Write to the Author

K. A. Applegate
c/o Scholastic, Inc.
555 Broadway
New York, NY 10012

You can also write to K. A. Applegate at the Animorphs website:
www.scholastic.com/animorphs

WORKS ABOUT KATHERINE APPLEGATE

Animorphs Page. Scholastic, Inc. 1 January 1999. *www.scholastic.com/animorphs*

Hepperman, Christine. "Invasion of the Animorphs." *Horn Book,* January/February 1998, pp. 53–56.

West, Mark I. "Of Gavin, Animals, and Animorphs." *The Five Owls,* November/December 1998, p. 29.

———. "Scholastic's Animorphs Series Has Legs." *Publisher's Weekly,* 3 November 1997, pp. 36–37.

Jane Austen

(1775–1817)

by Amy B. Maupin

Timeless, classic, romantic, suspenseful, witty, and fun: readers see many things in Jane Austen and her characters. Elizabeth Bennett, Elinor Dashwood, Mrs. Jennings, and Mr. Collins are characters whom Austen fans will recognize and know well, like their own best friends, at the mere mention of their names. Austen fans know her characters intimately because not only does the great British writer present them realistically, but she does so with color and completeness. Readers laugh at them, weep for them, and celebrate with them as they undergo all the things people must face when looking love straight in the eye. Whether you are thirteen years old or sixty-five, you can identify with the many emotions with which Austen's characters struggle. You can just as easily see yourself standing in a drawing room in an early nineteenth-century English manor as you can see the Bennett sisters standing there. In fact, you can visualize everything that Jane Austen describes, from the rolling English countryside to the pump rooms of historical Bath. You can

Bath, England was originally the site of Roman baths that were built on hot mineral springs. When the baths were rediscovered in 1755, they were revived as a spa, the **pump rooms** drawing water from the springs. Bath was the most fashionable place in England outside of London during the eighteenth and early nineteenth centuries.

imagine the beautiful lakes and gardens of the country as well as the bustling streets of London. The reader of an Austen novel sees all, hears all, and feels all. Perhaps that is why her works are still so widely read and have found their way to the movies.

Young girls and women alike may appreciate Austen more than their male peers because her protagonists are heroines who attain love and conquer the petty foolishness that society is so good at inventing. Through a woman's eyes, usually those of a very insightful and independent woman, the reader of Austen learns about the early nineteenth-century British class system, particularly about the middle class and its everyday dialogue and concerns. Through her writing, Austen was able to capture the essence of humanity in her day, and her depiction of human nature remains true today. Jane Austen is classic reading, and there are few who do not enjoy her works.

The Parson's Daughter

dialogue conversation between characters

Born on 16 December 1775, just half a year before America declared its independence, Jane Austen was welcomed at the rectory of Reverend George Austen and his wife, Cassandra. The Austen family made their home in the village of Steventon, in England's Hampshire County, where Mr. Austen served as parson.

rectory home of a rector, or parish clergyman

The Austens were by no means rich, but they were practical and well educated enough to be able to manage a comfortable household and provide a secure environment for their eight children: James, George, Edward, Henry, Cassandra, Francis, Jane, and Charles. They promoted literacy in every possible way, particularly in the reading of books and the writing of letters and poetry. A 1751 graduate of St. John's College, Oxford, George Austen was tall, handsome, witty, educated, sociable, and charming, and he took a special interest in educating his children. His reputation as a highly respected scholar gave him the social position and upper-class connections needed to provide his children with access to greater experiences than those of children of a typical country parson. George Austen wanted the most for his children; therefore, he enthusiastically encouraged his daughter Jane to write for publication. Many would have frowned upon this, as women were hardly recognized as independent professionals. Not only did Mr. and Mrs. Austen encourage intellectual growth, but George Austen naturally promoted a spiritual thirst that led to two of their sons becoming clergymen like their father and to Cassandra's engagement to a rector, though like Jane, she never married. Certainly the emphasis on religion and intellectual teachings in her childhood and adolescent years provided Jane with the inspiration for much of her writing.

Mrs. Austen was said to have been attractive and amiable, yet practical and intelligent. She, too, made significant contributions to the children's upbringing by introducing social graces and intellectual curiosity. She was especially fond of amateur theatricals and often entertained her family with witty charades and humorous verses.

verse here, poetry

Jane and her sister, Cassandra, much like Elizabeth and Jane Bennett of *Pride and Prejudice* (1813), were especially close. The two were sent away to school in Oxford when Jane was seven, but they stayed only a few months because of an outbreak of typhus fever, which both girls contracted. A couple of years later, the two sisters went to the Abbey School in Reading, where they studied for a year. When they returned home in late 1786, their father continued with their education. Jane began writing as early as age eleven, and it was not many years before she drafted her first novels.

typhus a sometimes fatal disease that is transmitted by body lice, fleas, and mites, occurring in crowded or poorly sanitized places

Jane's first writings consisted mostly of short parodies of the literature of the time, especially sentimental fiction. She also wrote comic burlesques, primarily for her family's entertainment. Her first pieces were quite short; by 1790, however, her literary talent began to surface. She completed six novels in her lifetime, but each went through extensive revision, and many were published long after their completion. *Northanger Abbey,* for example, probably written in 1798, was not published officially until 1818, after her death in 1817. (Austen's brother actually published *Northanger Abbey* and *Persuasion* at the end of 1817, though they are both dated 1818.) Her novels made her very little money, but they were later admired by men as notable as Sir Walter Scott, a famous novelist. He commented that she "had a talent for describing the involvements and feelings and characters of ordinary life which is to me the most wonderful I ever met with."

parody an exaggerated or satirical imitation (especially for purposes of ridicule)

burlesque a literary work that ridicules through gross exaggeration

Sir Walter Scott (1771–1832) was a Scottish writer, famous for his historical works such as *Ivanhoe* and *The Talisman.*

Austen's short life was largely spent visiting family and writing her books. She and Cassandra lived their entire lives with their mother and father, first at Steventon and then in Bath until her father's death in 1805. The Austen women next moved to Southhampton and finally to Chawton. To receive better medical care, Jane Austen was moved to Winchester just before her death on 18 July 1817. She was buried in Winchester Cathedral, a place that is visited by many of her loyal fans to this day.

Pride and Prejudice

First written between 1796 and 1797 (under the title *First Impressions*), *Pride and Prejudice* has remained the most popular of Jane Austen's novels and has even been called one of the most popular in the English language. Published in 1813, its appeal goes far deeper than the love story at its center. Austen's keen ability to describe people enables readers to meet the most vivid and memorable characters that they might ever encounter in a novel. The dialogue is funny, satirical, and truthful. Its opening line is one of the most famous in all literature: "It is a truth universally acknowledged, that a single man in possession of a good fortune, must be in want of a wife." We hear ourselves, our families, and our friends when we listen to the people in an Austen work. *Pride and Prejudice* is a novel about marriage and manners, but it is more than romantic comedy. The author's ingenious use of irony and witty dialogue make the themes work. The book is about reality and relationships—the good, the bad, and the ugly.

Mr. and Mrs. Bennett have five daughters: Jane, Elizabeth, Mary, Kitty, and Lydia. Their estate is destined to become the property of their foolish cousin Mr. Collins, a clergyman and their nearest male relative. Mrs. Bennett, equally silly and quite comical, is determined to find husbands for her daughters, none of whom have much sense themselves, except for Jane and Elizabeth. When word reaches their home that single and very rich Mr. Bingley has taken up residence at nearby Netherfield, hysterical excitement sweeps over the household in hopes that he will be a good match for the eldest, Jane. Indeed, the two do fall in love, but Mr. Bingley's snobbish sister Caroline and proud, wealthy friend Mr. Darcy, convince the love-stricken Bingley that Jane is of low connections and poor social standing, and that a match would not be advisable. But before Bingley goes away to London, Jane visits Netherfield and becomes ill. She is visited by her sister Elizabeth, whose unconventional manner takes the Bingley family and Mr. Darcy by surprise.

Elizabeth's first meeting with Mr. Darcy was a disagreeable one, to say the least, in that Darcy did not find her pretty

satirical ridiculing through sarcasm and irony

irony a situation in which the actual outcome is opposite or contrary to what was expected

enough to ask for a dance, an assertion that she herself over-heard. Upon meeting him at Netherfield, however, she actually becomes the object of his admiration, though she suspects nothing of the sort at the time.

Cleverly, and much to our pleasure, *Pride and Prejudice* takes turns and twists that engage readers to the point of addiction. Austen introduces Mr. Wickham, a handsome yet deceiving man, as a foil for Darcy. We find ourselves urging Elizabeth to swallow her own pride and unite once and for all with the haughty, but quite generous and likable Mr. Darcy, the same man whom Austen first made us detest. As Austen carefully unfolds the truths about her characters, she demonstrates the way people inevitably judge one another. She makes us understand the difference between perception and reality. Austen's insights make *Pride and Prejudice* worthy of more than one reading. Our flaws are humorously acted out by the likes of Mr. Collins and his patron, Lady Catherine de Bourgh. We cannot resist the temptation to laugh out loud at the snobbery, the foolish flamboyance, or the insincerity that the insightful Elizabeth Bennett herself recognizes. We can only learn, as she does, that life is filled with pride and prejudice.

foil a person who, by contrast, highlights the qualities of another character

inevitably unable to be avoided

flamboyance extravagant showiness

Sense and Sensibility

Elinor Dashwood has sense. She is reasonable, rational, and responsible. She practices control with elegant composure. Her younger sister Marianne, however, is full of sensibility. That is, she is emotional, spontaneous, and very outspoken. Such contrasts in these Austen heroines set the stage for the theme of her title: we must balance ourselves with reason and passion, mind and heart, sense and sensibility.

Elinor and Marianne, with their mother and younger sister Margaret, are left homeless when their father dies and leaves the Norland estate to their half brother, John Dashwood. Mrs. Dashwood takes her family to Barton Park, where they rent a cottage from their relative Sir John Middleton. Elinor, who is in love with Edward Ferrars, John Dashwood's brother-in-law, secretly and painfully laments the move for fear of ending a relationship that was only just beginning before they left Norland. Although Marianne is also pained by their departure, she quickly recovers and is brought to the sheer joy and madness of love when she meets the handsome and brave Mr. Willoughby. While walking, she falls and sprains her ankle,

composure self-control

lament to feel sorrow or regret

and as the rain pours down, Willoughby rides by on his horse. When he discovers her, he carries her back to the cottage with the gallantry of a medieval knight. Her sense of emotion is so elevated by their budding romance, that she nearly becomes ill of heartbreak when Willoughby must go to London. Furthermore, Elinor's troubles multiply when she learns of a secret engagement between Edward Ferrars and Lucy Steele, an irritable and rather vulgar young girl who comes to stay with the Middletons. Naturally, the Dashwood sisters survive the trials and tribulations of love, and in the end, as in all Jane Austen novels, they get their men. Nevertheless, we are sometimes quite surprised by who the men are.

vulgar lacking in good taste

Sense and Sensibility, drafted in 1795 and revised at least twice some years later, was finally published in 1811 and was the first of Austen's works to be printed. It is a novel that satirizes sensibility, a very common theme in an Austen work. Jane Austen would like for us to see the absurd for what it really is and, likewise, understand the true value of being sensible and rational. But immature Marianne is not meant to be foolish like the ridiculous Mr. Collins or the silly Lydia; nor is Elinor meant to be so straight-laced and settled that she hardly seems to feel. Rather, *Sense and Sensibility* is to be understood as a call for us to be equally balanced between passion and reason.

Like *Pride and Prejudice, Sense and Sensibility* is engaging. Jane Austen novels are the kind that one takes to the reading chair on a cool, rainy day or on a long winter's night. They are the kind that we read over and over, just to get another glimpse of the handsome Mr. Darcy or the charming Marianne Dashwood. Austen has given us the perfect escape—the hills and lakes of England, the country cottages and the grand chateaus, and the seemingly complicated lives of a simple people. All six of her published novels have sustained the test of time, becoming favorites of many readers, both young and old. If one has not read an Austen novel, one has certainly seen an Austen novel. Thanks to Hollywood, Jane Austen has made it to the movies.

Jane Austen: Then and Now

Addicting might be the best way to describe the production of *Pride and Prejudice* (1995), as done by the British Broadcasting Corporation (BBC) and the Arts and Entertainment (A&E) television networks. While six fifty-minute episodes might seem like an eternity, it is unlikely that you will ever want the film to end. Brilliantly directed and perfectly cast, the movie follows the book almost exactly. To an Austen fan, it is sheer bliss; to a first-timer, it is the beginning of a new relationship. The 1995 production of *Pride and Prejudice* is not to be missed. Once you see it, you will probably want to see other Austen novels at the movies, though you might not find them as enticing as this one.

Another movie production of an Austen novel, *Sense and Sensibility,* won an Oscar for best adapted screenplay in 1995. Starring Hugh Grant, Emma Thompson, and Kate Winslet, the film increased popular interest in the British author's literature. Also making a comeback was *Emma* (1815). Produced in 1996, this movie brings to life the matchmaking and endearing Emma Woodhouse. The plot for *Emma* was also the basis for the movie *Clueless,* a much more contemporary version of the novel but hardly a match for the book.

All the Austen novels have been made into movies at some point. There are at least two productions of *Persuasion* (1817), another of Austen's more popular works. There are good movies, and there are better movies. Even so, most video rental stores have a collection of Jane Austen films on the shelves.

Another indication of Austen's enduring popularity is the Jane Austen Society of North America (JASNA), a nonprofit, volunteer organization that has more than 3,700 members in the United States and Canada (and a few in Europe, Australia, and the Middle East). According to Elsa A. Solender, the 1998 president of JASNA, the mission of this unique group "is to foster study, appreciation, and understanding of Jane Austen's works, life, and genius." In addition to publishing a newsletter called *JASNA News,* the society hosts annual general meetings in U.S. and Canadian cities for its members to gather, study, and enjoy fellowship. Furthermore, there are regional chapters that coordinate various activities such as celebrating Austen's birthday. They also publish *Persuasions,* a literary journal dedicated to Jane Austen scholarship.

Clueless (1995), an Amy Heckerling film, features Alicia Silverstone as Cher. A modern Emma in Beverly Hills, California, Cher attempts to play matchmaker for several couples.

The most recent film version of *Persuasion* was released in 1995, featuring Amanda Root as Anne Elliot.

To find out more about **JASNA,** visit the JASNA website at *www.jasna.org* or call 1-800-836-3911.

If you like the works of Jane Austen, you might also like the works of Louisa May Alcott, Charles Dickens, Sir Arthur Conan Doyle, Margaret Mitchell, and Laura Ingalls Wilder.

Selected Bibliography

WORKS BY JANE AUSTEN

Sense and Sensibility (1811)

Pride and Prejudice (1813)

Mansfield Park (1814)

Emma (1815)

Northanger Abbey (1817)

Persuasion (1817)

WORKS ABOUT JANE AUSTEN

Collins, Irene. *Jane Austen: The Parson's Daughter.* London: Hambledon, 1998.

Nokes, David. *Jane Austen: A Life.* New York: Farrar, Straus, and Giroux, 1997.

Poplawski, Paul. *A Jane Austen Encyclopedia.* Westport, Conn.: Greenwood Press 1998.

Tomalin, Claire. *Jane Austen: A Life.* New York: Alfred A. Knopf, 1997.

Michael Cadnum

(1949–)

by Patty Campbell

Wandering through the vast Opryland Hotel in Nashville in search of a meeting room, Michael Cadnum and I finally went out a side door to the lawn to get our bearings. "I like to go outside and go around and then come back in," he said—a perfect description of the way this writer approaches his subjects. Cadnum's style has been called oblique and enigmatic, and he delights in telling a story from the other, unexpected point of view—the sheriff of Nottingham instead of Robin Hood, for instance—or in speaking in the voice of someone we would not ordinarily find sympathetic—a self-centered young thief, or a boy who kills his best friend and hides the crime. "I find myself fascinated by these marginal characters and believe that they need advocates," he says. "Somebody to see through their eyes and to express what it is like to be that sort of person." It is a mark of the skill of this brilliant writer that he is able to make us understand these backdoor characters and eventually feel compassion for them.

Quotations from Michael Cadnum that are not attributed to a published source are from a personal interview conducted by the author of this article on 21 November 1998 and are published here by permission of Michael Cadnum.

oblique indirect in meaning

enigmatic puzzling, mysterious

point of view the position or perspective from which the story is told

Living the Characters

protagonist the main character of a literary work

mystical obscure, mysterious

In writing his young adult novels, Cadnum gets involved with his protagonists in an almost mystical way. "I become those characters. I'm so fully inside that character's life that I know things that I couldn't possibly personally understand," he says. When he was working on *Heat* (1998), a story about a young high diver, he sent his wife Sherina to buy a Speedo swimsuit for the fictional girl, and like an empty shadow it hung on his bulletin board where he could touch it whenever he needed to get closer to his character. An ancient slingstone on his desk helped transport him to the Middle Ages when he was writing *In a Dark Wood* (1998). "You have to see what you're writing about clearly with your whole nervous system," he explains, so that the reader, too, comes to inhabit the flesh and blood of the main character.

Waiting to Become a Writer

Michael and Sherina Cadnum have been married thirty years, through all the lean times when his promise as a novelist was unrecognized. He introduces her as "the person to whom all my books are dedicated." Although he graduated from the creative writing program at San Francisco State University with a master's degree in 1974 after earning a B.A. at the University of California at Berkeley, his first novel—an adult thriller titled *Nightlight*—was not published until 1990. Sherina's work as an English teacher allowed them to maintain their household, and Cadnum held a variety of part-time jobs over the years that would leave him relatively free to write. He was a shipping clerk in a furniture factory, an assistant at a real estate listing service, and a substitute teacher in the Oakland, California, inner city schools. For a time he ran a suicide prevention center in Alameda County, and one year while living in southern England he volunteered on an archaeological dig.

Cadnum was born on 3 May 1949 in Orange, California. He had always planned to be a writer, even as a boy growing up in the Orange County town of Costa Mesa in southern California. He liked riding his bicycle, being outdoors, and playing sports—although he wasn't very good at ball games and was always the last to be chosen for teams. But writing was his center. "When I was a child I would draw pictures of adventures before I could write. And then as I learned to write, I wrote stories in little notebooks. I wrote a novel when I was in sixth grade about a dinosaur that lived in a volcano, and every time the volcano erupted, which was fairly frequently, the dinosaur would wake up and come down and kill some villagers. And I remember my mother suggesting I write something cheerful." While he admits that superficially this was a dumb idea for a novel, he also muses, revealingly, "In a way, I was on to something. The idea of a thing that's hidden, waking up and coming out periodically to cause harm . . . the stories you go on to write as an adult have seeds in your early childhood."

superficially lacking deep or sincere character

The Poetry Connection

It was as a poet that Cadnum first appeared in print. From the time he was sixteen he wrote and published poetry, and he continues to do so. He has published half a dozen volumes of poems with various small presses, and his verse often appears in literary magazines. "I love writing poetry, and I do it almost daily, as a kind of a yoga, a discipline like a concert pianist practicing the piano every day. Half an hour of serious work is enough to keep you honed within your talent."

How has his affinity for poetry influenced his fiction writing? Cadnum claims he has never wanted to write a "poet's novel," a form that he feels can be dull. Creating a strong enough character and a powerful situation frees him to use his interest in visual images and lots of concrete detail to embellish the narrative. "Strong stories liberate a writer the way a strong tune frees a composer to do the work with the oboe and the harpsichord that he finds delicious."

One way that his bent toward poetry shows up in his fiction is through wonderful metaphors that bring an image sharply alive. For instance, we see a fierce falcon as "a knife with eyes" in *In a Dark Wood.* Bonnie Chamberlain, in *Heat,* watches her cat give birth and thinks, "The first kitten looked like a dark sock soaked in snot." In the same novel the sound of a deserted swimming pool as water gurgles in and out of the filter valves is "a sound like a dog lapping water very, very slowly." These figures of speech can be particularly satirical when applied to people. Bonnie's stepmother, wearing "a sherbet thing" looks like "someone auditioning for hostess at a pancake restaurant"; her mother's lawyer is a woman who resembles "Bugs Bunny without the ears."

satirical ridiculing through sarcasm and irony

Another more subtle way the poet in Cadnum appears in his young adult novels is in the obliqueness of his storytelling. Instead of flatly stating what a character is feeling, he gives us the sights and sounds and minor events around the moment that bring the emotion directly to the reader. Sometimes what isn't said is more important than the words that are actually there. Cadnum is interested in the things his characters cannot bring themselves to say because "they're right at the very limit of their pain threshold."

Calling Home: The Obliqueness of Cadnum's Storytelling

A magnificent example of this technique is the scene in *Calling Home* (1991) in which Peter strikes and accidentally kills his best friend Mead in an argument over the breaking of a bottle of cognac. He focuses intensely on picking up each little piece of broken glass, and our senses are completely filled with the glitter of candlelight on the fragments, their sharpness, and the heavy fragrance of the spilled liquor. Peter—and we—cannot bear to acknowledge the corpse that lies just out of the line of vision.

Peter goes home, leaving Mead's body in the cellar of the deserted house, and tells no one about it—not even himself. He goes on with his life around the edges of this great yawning hole of denial, and eventually begins to telephone Mead's parents and reassure them in the dead boy's voice. It becomes a way to bring Mead back to life for a moment in Peter's body: "A miracle. A dead person walking. And breathing, too, the old stiff lungs swelling like two grocery bags." In the telephone booth there is a fragmenting and distancing from reality as Cadnum anatomizes sensations instead of naming emotions: "Parts of the body want to run. The lower lip shivers and the thumb has a tremor in it."

Creating the illusion that Mead is alive gives Peter a reason to continue living, although he must more and more numb himself with alcohol to cope with the ordinary days: school, friends, his parents' divorce. Visiting his father, he wants to tell him about Mead "the way a drowning man wants to kick his way out of the trunk at the bottom of a river." But he can't. Yet, as the pressure builds, we know he must, and the suspense focuses on which of the people in his life he will choose to trust with his confession.

Calling Home, published in 1991, was Cadnum's first young adult novel. His unique talent was immediately recognized, and one critic labeled his work "Cormieresque," in recognition of its resemblance in style and spirit to *The Chocolate War* (1974) and other novels by the great young adult author Robert Cormier.

There is an article about Robert Cormier in volume 1.

Other Young Adult Novels

Cadnum's next young adult novel, *Breaking the Fall* (1992), shows the same spare, precise mastery of words in its exploration of addiction to danger. Stanley's angry mother accuses him of being "completely disengaged," and it's true, he feels dead inside, in danger of being caught up in the gray adult world. So when his charismatic friend Jared challenges him to try his game of housebreaking for fun, Stanley knows he's got to do it. The rules are to sneak silently into the bedroom where the homeowners are sleeping and take something of little value for proof. Stanley is terrified, much to Jared's contempt, but the adrenaline high makes him feel alive—until the day he gets caught. Cadnum evokes the thudding heart and breathlessness of fear vividly, and the animal terror of the chase, as well as the self-disgust that follows.

charismatic possessing extraordinary personal charm

These bored and desperately vulnerable kids of the upper middle class and their self-absorbed parents are the typical cast of a Cadnum young adult novel. Although he grew up in southern California, he now lives in Alameda, a town just across the Bay from San Francisco, and his novels reflect this northern California ambience with devastating accuracy. In his books, the characters are moneyed, educated people who have replaced traditional American materialism with stylish goals in the professions or the arts, often with the sacrifice of warmth and simplicity. Their kids take good schools, designer clothes, swimming pools, and new cars for granted, but hunger for guidance and meaning or smolder with unfocused rage. Cadnum says, "I'm interested in the problems of being upward and mobile. When you have parents who are lawyers, or who have tried to have interesting professions writing books or making videos, what pressure has this put on the family?"

He explores this question in several of his novels, such as *Taking It* (1995), in which Anna Charles lives with her high-powered trial lawyer father and has a tense relationship with

estranged hostile separation from someone previously close and friendly

irony a situation in which the actual outcome is opposite or contrary to what was expected

mentor a wise or trusted teacher

acquitted cleared of an accusation

embezzlement fraudulent use of another's money for one's own gain

her estranged mother, a successful television executive. To make life a little more interesting, and for other hidden reasons she doesn't understand, Anna pretends to steal things from stores. She enjoys giving the security people something to do—until they find a scarf she's never seen before in her purse. She goes on stealing things without meaning to, as her life slides out of control. Selfish and amoral, Anna flees for comfort and understanding to her brother Ted, who is working as a manual laborer for a landscape architect. But his lifestyle repels her. Snobbishly, she says, "Ted had one of those apartments where everything was out of date." She is unable to share his satisfaction in earning his own way and learning an honest trade, and betrays him by stealing his savings, driving furiously into the desert and crashing her car.

In a sense, Anna feels that her brother is living outside his proper class. Cadnum's adults are also often arrogant in their attitudes toward working-class people, embarrassed when trapped into social exchanges with people not of their background, people who don't know the rules of style and irony and "good taste." On the other hand, the young adult characters often yearn for the simple counsel and wisdom of working-class mentors. In *Edge* (1997), Zack's mother disapproves of his waitress girlfriend and her fake-cowgirl mother, while Zack respects and likes Chief, his boss at his spa delivery job. Zack has dropped out of school, and nurses a rage so uncontrollable that he gets into street brawls. When his father is shot and the assailant is acquitted, Zack's terrible anger leads him to retrieve the gun he had hidden earlier and lay in wait for the man.

The emotional insulation of Cadnum's characters is particularly apparent in *Edge,* the story of a young competitive diver who hits her head on the way down and struggles to find the courage to return to the high diving platform, as she must later struggle to come to terms with her adored father's conviction for embezzlement. In this book, and in most of Cadnum's young adult novels, people talk to each other in a sort of shorthand, with clipped sentences and long pauses, or they trade witty remarks without expressing anything real. They hold each other at arm's length verbally, as if conversation were a game. Why is it so hard for them to say what they are really thinking? "A very complicated question," Cadnum responds. He feels that partly this is an accurate reflection of a socio-economic style, partly it's because of the nature of these particular characters, and partly it's because communication goes beyond words—as in *Zero at the Bone* (1996), in which Cray tries to ease his parents' months' long vigil for a missing daughter by fixing them a homely dinner of macaroni and cheese.

The medieval novel *In a Dark Wood* is a very different kind of story, although full of Cadnum's brilliant metaphors and intense insight into character. Rich with the details of life in the Middle Ages, it takes the part of Geoffrey, Sheriff of Nottingham, a man at odds with his society as much as is his slippery adversary Robin Hood. Geoffrey is a compassionate, thoughtful man in internal conflict with a job that requires him to be a brutal administrator, to oversee torture and lead men to kill. He sees in Robin Hood a galling, embarrassing antagonist. The rapport that Geoffrey reaches with Robin Hood and with the warring parts of his own nature make this a subtle and satisfying novel.

Adult Novels

But is *In a Dark Wood* a young adult novel? Some critics posed this question, citing scenes of violence and sex, and—more relevant—the adult protagonist, as proof that this story is outside the genre, in spite of the fact that it was designated young adult by its publisher Orchard Books. But a look at Cadnum's eight novels actually published for adults shows that they are an entirely different kind of writing. Loosely categorized as horror (although Cadnum calls them "literary thrillers"), they are twice as long, full of occult mysticism and emotional excesses. The spare, restrained writing that makes his young adult novels so effective is a marked contrast to the more showy style of his adult thrillers.

Cadnum has also written short stories for adult anthologies, as well as a picture book, *The Lost and Found House* (1997), about a child coping with the upset of moving to a new home. He is currently working on a book set during the time of the Crusades.

While it should be obvious by now that Michael Cadnum's young adult novels are not for sissies—or for lazy readers—the rich literary feast he lays out for us is young adult writing at its finest.

metaphor a figure of speech in which one thing is referred to as something else; for example, "My love is a rose"

adversary opponent

antagonist hostile opponent

rapport harmonious connection

occult pertaining to magical arts and practices

If you like the novels of Michael Cadnum, you might also enjoy the novels of Robert Cormier, Aidan Chambers, and Chris Crutcher.

Selected Bibliography

WORKS BY MICHAEL CADNUM

Novels for Young Adults
Calling Home (1991)
Breaking the Fall (1992)
Taking It (1995)
Zero at the Bone (1996)
Edge (1997)
Heat (1998)
In a Dark Wood (1998)

Novels for Adults
Nightlight (1990)
Sleepwalker (1991)
Saint Peter's Wolf (1991)
Ghostwright (1992)
The Horses of the Night (1993)
Skyscape (1994)
The Judas Glass (1996)
Rundown (1999)

Children's Books
The Lost and Found House, illustrated by Steve Johnson and Lou Fancher (1997)

Poetry
The Morning of the Massacre (1982)
Wrecking the Cactus (1985)
Invisible Mirror (1986)
Foreign Springs (1987)
By Evening (1992)
The Cities We Will Never See (1993)

WORKS ABOUT MICHAEL CADNUM

Articles

Edgar, Kathleen J., Terrie M. Rooney, and Jennifer Gariepy, eds. *Contemporary Authors.* Detroit: Gale Research, 1996, vol. 151, pp. 93–95.

Jones, Patrick. "People Are Talking About . . . Michael Cadnum." *Horn Book,* March/April 1994, pp. 177–180.

Kooser, Ted. "A Few Attractive Strangers." *Georgia Review,* Fall 1990, pp. 503–505.

Selected Reviews

Caldiero, Wendy D. Review of *In a Dark Wood.* In *School Library Journal,* April 1998, p. 128.

Campbell, Patty. Review of *Calling Home.* In *Horn Book,* May/June 1994, pp. 358–361.

Clark, Phillip. Review of *Saint Peter's Wolf.* In *School Library Journal,* February 1992, p. 121.

Flowers, Ann A. Review of *In a Dark Wood.* In *Horn Book,* March/April 1998, p. 219.

Knoth, Maeve Visser. Review of *Taking It.* In *Horn Book,* January/February 1996, p. 77.

Peters, John. Review of *Edge.* In *Booklist,* 15 June 1997, p. 1684.

Phillips, Marilyn Payne. Review of *Heat.* In *School Library Journal,* September 1998, pp. 200–201.

Rausch, Tim. Review of *Edge.* In *School Library Journal,* July 1997, p. 90.

Rogers, Susan L. Review of *Breaking the Fall.* In *School Library Journal,* September 1992, p. 274.

Smith, Alice Casey. Review of *Zero at the Bone.* In *School Library Journal,* July 1996, p. 98.

Zvirin, Stephanie. Review of *Breaking the Fall.* In *Booklist,* 15 November 1992.

———. Review of *Heat.* In *Booklist,* August 1998, p. 1990.

How to Write to the Author

Michael Cadnum
c/o Viking Children's Books
345 Hudson Street
New York, NY 10014

Sharon Creech

(1945–)

by Jim Blasingame and John H. Bushman

A Journey Across America

"Huzza, huzza!" Gram Hiddle shouts as she wriggles her toes in the sand of Lake Michigan. In Sharon Creech's Newbery Medal–winning novel, *Walk Two Moons* (1994), "Huzza, huzza!" is Gram Hiddle's exclamation of awe and excitement over the beauty and wonder of America. *Walk Two Moons* follows thirteen-year-old Salamanca Tree Hiddle and her grandparents as they travel from Euclid, Ohio, to Lewiston, Idaho, for a very important rendezvous. The novel is actually several stories within one, all from the imagination of Sharon Creech. Creech herself went on a similar trip from Ohio to Idaho as a young girl in 1957 and was amazed at the raw beauty and variety of the geography as well as the diversity of the people. This trip later became the basis for her novel.

Quotations from Sharon Creech that are not attributed to a published source are from a personal interview conducted by the authors of this article on 10 February 1999 and are published here by permission of Sharon Creech.

Childhood and Family

Sharon Creech was born on 29 July 1945 in Cleveland, Ohio. She grew up in suburban Cleveland but spent much of her summers near Quincy, Kentucky, where her cousins, aunts, and uncles lived. Quincy was a special place to her, especially her cousins' farm outside of town, by the Ohio River. Quincy, Kentucky, would later become the fictitious Bybanks, Kentucky, where Creech's novels often begin. Bybanks appears in her very first young adult book, *Walk Two Moons.* Later her cousins' farm was the model for Zinny Taylor's family farm in *Chasing Redbird* (1997). Quincy and the people around there are "charged with significance" for Creech. It was a place where people all knew each other, a place untainted by the outside world.

untainted unspoiled

Creech's novels reflect many of her childhood experiences as the second oldest daughter growing up in a large family. With one older sister, three younger brothers, a multitude of cousins, aunts and uncles, and grandparents, she had a wealth of experience to draw from. The family in *Absolutely Normal Chaos* (1990) is very much like the "rowdy and noisy family" Creech herself grew up in, as noted in the 1997 HarperCollins book *Sharon Creech.* Often she did not consciously base her characters on family members but recognized afterward that she had been inspired by them. After *Walk Two Moons* was completed, Creech recognized two of her favorite people in her characters Gram and Gramps Hiddle, Salamanca's strong, independent, adventurous, and humorous grandparents. Gram and Gramps were inspired in part by Creech's sister, Sandy, and Sandy's husband, Jack. Jack has a wonderful sense of humor and can make a person laugh even after the blackest day, according to Creech. After the book was finished, Creech realized that the comical interplay between Gram and Gramps is very much like the way Sandy and Jack play off each other.

decipherable able to be understood despite indistinctness

stroke a sudden loss of consciousness because of an obstruction of an artery leading to the brain

Creech's father was the inspiration for Uncle Arvie in *Pleasing the Ghost* (1996). Uncle Arvie is a lovable ghost who appears to his nephew, Dennis, still speaking with the effects of the stroke he had. He speaks in nonsense words and phrases that are comical to the reader but decipherable to Dennis. Uncle Arvie comes to enlist Dennis' help in finishing something he hadn't quite finished in life. Creech's father, whose name was Arvel, also suffered a stroke, which left him unable to speak normally. Although this was very difficult for everyone, it was often quite humorous when Creech's father would say something so crazy that "even he would laugh at it."

Teacher, Mother, Writer

Creech received her B.A. from Hiram College in Ohio and her M.A. from George Mason University in Virginia, but she believes she learned the most about writing when she became a teacher. She doubts that she would have become a writer if she had not had the experience of teaching great books and interacting with students. This was where she learned what makes a good book, one that young people will connect with. She feels that she learned from teaching great works, such as those by Chaucer, Shakespeare, Fitzgerald and Hemingway, and also from the remarkable insights of her students. Creech was intrigued by their individual responses, which shaped her perception of what makes a good story.

Another profound influence on Creech's writing has been her experience as a mother. She describes the births of her two children, Rob and Karin, as two of the most important events in her life. Creech believes being a mother greatly influences the human aspect of her writing by teaching her humility and compassion. In addition, parenting emphasizes to her how important good teachers and good books are in the lives of children. She believes that good literature has the power to intrigue them and push them to think. For this reason alone, Creech knows that she would never submit inferior writing for possible publication when young adults need the very best in literature.

Creech became a teacher, realizing the need that children have to be accepted for who they are. Her philosophy of teaching includes recognizing each student as a unique individual and encouraging those personal qualities that set students apart rather than forcing them to conform. This philosophy is evident in a poem she wrote, "The Sun on the Bottom," about a first grader who creatively painted pictures with the sun at the bottom and the trees upside down at the top. That first grader was Creech's own son, Rob.

Creech's experience as a teacher convinced her that schools should not treat students as square pegs to be forced into round holes. Her appreciation for people as individuals is evident in her characters, many of whom are enjoyably eccentric. Creech says, "I particularly enjoy eccentric people and

Geoffrey **Chaucer** (1340–1400) was an English writer who wrote *The Canterbury Tales*. F. Scott **Fitzgerald** (1896–1940) was an American writer who wrote *The Great Gatsby* (1925).

There is an article about Ernest Hemingway in volume 2. There is an article about William Shakespeare in volume 3.

humility the state of being humble

eccentric odd and quirky

cultivate them as my friends because they add a bit of zing, sort of show you how to look at the world in a different way."

Her Characters

"Life is too short to spend it as a wimp!" Creech advises us all, and her protagonists always grow to be assertive, strong-willed, and independent by the end of their stories. She believes people have more control over their lives than they know. Sal, Zinny, Domenica, Mary Lou, and Dennis all begin with feelings that their lives are beyond their control. Creech points out that they gain control over their lives by growing to understand themselves.

The quest for self-understanding is common in Creech's novels. The quest may involve a journey across the country as in *Walk Two Moons* or the uncovering of a mysterious, lost highway as in *Chasing Redbird.* Creech believes that all people have an emotional need to know who they are and where they come from; for her, it surfaced at age thirteen, the approximate age of her protagonists. Creech's books often include adopted children who do not know their biological parents; she realizes that this may be frustrating for them, like a lost "key to yourself that you ought to have access to." Characters are stronger after resolving this need to know.

Creech has often discovered after finishing a novel, that her protagonists are composites of people in her life or individual facets of her own personality. Salamanca in *Walk Two Moons* is probably a composite of Creech and her daughter, Karin. Creech believes that she often unconsciously explores different parts of herself. In *Absolutely Normal Chaos,* Mary Lou Finney may represent Creech's "off-the-wall emotional side." In *Walk Two Moons,* Sal may represent the "more lyrical, soft, gentle, contemplative side." In *Chasing Redbird,* "Zinny . . . has that kind of earnest, seeking side" that has "to find the answer to the problem." In *Bloomability* (1998), Domenica "breaks out of her bubble" to represent the exuberance for life that Creech feels personally.

After moving to England to teach American and British literature, Creech met her husband Lyle Rigg, the headmaster of a private school. Later the family followed Lyle's career to a school in Switzerland. Creech values these experiences in Europe that introduced her and her family to a diversity of culture and people beyond what they could have experienced in

protagonist the main character of a literary work

facet aspect

the United States. She credits her desire for that kind of adventure to that long family trip from Cleveland to Idaho.

The Author's Works

Walk Two Moons won the Newbery Medal in 1995. In this book, the main character, Salamanca, tells us her story while trying to come to grips with it herself. Creech keeps this book engaging through interweaving subplots, each coming to its resolution when Salamanca reaches Idaho. The significance of past events must unfold as the story unfolds. Although we know Sal's destination is Idaho, it begs several questions: Why did her mother journey to Lewiston a year earlier, and why has she remained there? What does Sal hope to resolve there, and why are her grandparents determined to see that she gets there, even at the risk of their own lives?

Seemingly insignificant details turn out to be very meaningful at the end of the novel. For example, Mrs. Cadaver has an important connection to Sal's mother and even to Sal herself. The temporary disappearance of her friend Phoebe's mother is much more disturbing to Sal than we think, and for good reason. The significance of these and other events become crystal clear at the end.

Absolutely Normal Chaos is written from Creech's experience of growing up in a large family. When thirteen-year-old Mary Lou Finney hands in her summer journal assignment, she writes her teacher a note: "Here it is: my summer journal. As you can see, I got a little carried away. The problem is this, though. I don't want you to read it" (p. 2). A more enticing beginning has probably never been written. In addition to writing the journal, Mary Lou also must read Homer's *Odyssey*. She ends up paralleling events in the Greek epic with those of her family and friends, although she notes that unlike the Greeks, they have no Zeus or Athena "who can live forever and help people out of trouble" (p. 225). She grows to accept, as her father has told her, "that bad things happen sometimes to remind us we are mortal and to remind us to appreciate people more" (p. 225).

The need for adopted children to know their biological parents is an important issue in this book. When Mary Lou's cousin Carl Ray comes to live with the Finneys, the reason (to find a job) isn't a satisfactory explanation. Only after their neighbor, Mr. Furtz, dies will Mary Lou find out that he was

subplot a secondary series of events that is less important than the plot

Homer was an ancient Greek poet most famous for his epic poems the *Iliad* and the **Odyssey**. The *Odyssey* is the story of Odysseus' journey home after fighting for Greece in the Trojan War.

Zeus and **Athena** were gods in Greek mythology. Zeus was the ruler of the gods. Athena, the daughter of Zeus, was the goddess of war, wisdom, and arts and crafts.

actually Carl Ray's father, although neither Carl Ray nor the Finneys knew this while Mr. Furtz was alive.

One of the funniest events in the book occurs when Mrs. White makes an "almost hysterical" phone call to Mary Lou's mother (p. 29). Mrs. White's son Johnny has participated in Mary Lou's first kiss during a brief interlude between climbing trees and eating sandwiches. Mary Lou impulsively kissed Johnny and then "kissed him again, mainly to see if [she] could taste anything" (p. 28). Mrs. White is so upset she demands that Mary Lou never again go near her son who is "too innocent for some 'wild girl'" (p. 29). Mrs. Finney suggests waiting a few years before practicing kissing again. Creech's novel *Pleasing the Ghost* targets upper-elementary readers, although it has implications that are fairly mature. Nine-year-old Dennis is regularly visited by ghosts but never the one ghost he would most like to see: his dad's. When the ghost of Uncle Arvie appears, Dennis helps him finish a painting for Aunt Julia and shows her the chest of love letters and money Uncle Arvie had saved for her over the course of a lifetime.

This is a charming and funny story that only hints at the sadness Dennis feels over the loss of his father. Uncle Arvie has retained the nonsensical speech resulting from a stroke late in his life, and his **dialogue** is often very funny. When a would-be suitor comes to see Aunt Julia, the ghost of Uncle Arvie calls him a "beany, beany bud booger" and invisibly pinches him until he leaves in bewilderment (p. 69).

Chasing Redbird returns to Bybanks, Kentucky, where Zinny Taylor attempts a nearly impossible project. She discovers an ancient stone road buried under the sod behind their family farm and sets out to uncover and restore its entire length of twenty miles. The project is actually a **metaphor** as she unconsciously uncovers the meaning behind the events of her childhood, including the death of her cousin, Rose, and her Aunt Jessie.

At the age of four, Rose and Zinny had contracted whooping cough, but only Rose had died. Aunt Jessie and Uncle Nate seem to accept Zinny as a **surrogate** for their own lost child, but when Aunt Jessie dies, Zinny feels responsible. Zinny's memories of childhood have been partially blocked out and return only when her experiences along the ancient Chocton Trail bring back the past.

This is a multitiered story in which Zinny must deal with a painful past, a bewildering present, and an uncertain future.

dialogue conversation between characters

metaphor a figure of speech in which one thing is referred to as something else; for example, "My love is a rose"

surrogate one who acts as a substitute

These multiple conflicts seem unrelated, but they tie together very neatly and reach resolution simultaneously at the end. A number of mysterious places and objects are revealed but not explained until the conclusion: a secret cabin, a buried locket, and the ghostly presence that Zinny characterizes as a barely perceptible flash of red.

Bloomability comes from Creech's experience with private schools. The story is about thirteen-year-old Domenica Doone's year at an American school in Lugano, Switzerland. Dinnie, as she is called, comes from an American family best described as transient. When Dinnie is sent to live with her Aunt Sandy and Uncle Max in Lugano, she attends the school where Uncle Max is the headmaster and becomes a member of the extended family that the school population provides.

Living in twelve different states in thirteen years, Dinnie had come to think of herself as the permanent new kid, the one who was out of step. At the boarding school, however, she finds everyone is new and starting on equal footing. Students are not judged by appearance or wealth, and the gaps in her schooling are no problem either. The situation is so different that Dinnie find her "mouth was hanging half open most of the time" (p. 88).

Dinnie feels, at first, as if she has been kidnapped and taken to Lugano against her will, but a gradual transformation takes place. Before the end of the book Dinnie grows to love the close friends the boarding school atmosphere has encouraged, even some who are a little more prickly than lovable.

The title of *Bloomability* comes from one of Dinnie's friends, a Japanese student named Keisuke. He tends to create his own English words, one of which, "bloomable," he uses in place of "possible." As the teachers and students at Dinnie's school look back over a year of good experiences, they can see the wonderful "bloomabilities" the world has to offer.

The Present

Creech lives with her husband, Lyle, in New Jersey, where he is the headmaster of a private school and Sharon continues to write. Creech is an often-invited guest at national and regional conferences and literature festivals where she continues to whet the appetites of current and future readers. Her engaging personality and love of young people make her a favorite around the country.

perceptible capable of being noticed through the senses

transient passing through places with only brief stays in each place

If you like Sharon Creech, you might also like Sue Ellen Bridgers, Karen Hesse, Ursula K. Le Guin, and Richard Peck.

✍

How to Write to the Author

Sharon Creech
c/o HarperCollins
10 East 53rd Street
New York, NY 10022

Selected Bibliography

WORKS BY SHARON CREECH

Absolutely Normal Chaos (1990)

Walk Two Moons (1994)

Pleasing the Ghost (1996)

Chasing Redbird (1997)

Bloomability (1998)

WORKS ABOUT SHARON CREECH

Allen, Raymond, "Sharon Creech: 1995 Newbery Medal Winner." *Teaching PreK–8,* May 1996, p. 48.

Author Spotlight: Sharon Creech, HarperCollins Children's Books. New York: HarperCollins, 1997.

Creech, Sharon. "Newbery Medal Acceptance." *Horn Book,* July/August 1995, p. 418.

Rigg, Lyle. "Sharon Creech." *Horn Book,* July/August 1995, p. 426.

Sharon Creech, ACHUKA: Children's Books UK. Website address: *www.achuka.co.uk*

Sharon Creech, HarperCollins Children's Books. New York: HarperCollins, 1997.

Karen Cushman

(1941–)

by Rebecca Barnhouse

In *The Midwife's Apprentice* (1995), Alyce says, "I know what I want. A full belly, a contented heart, and a place in this world" (p. 81). Finding a name, a home, "a place in this world": these threads are woven through Karen Cushman's fiction as well as her life. Although she has been writing and reading since she was a child, Cushman was fifty years old before she began to write her first novel, *Catherine, Called Birdy* (1994).

The novel won numerous awards, including a prestigious Newbery Honor award, establishing Cushman in the pantheon of writers for young adults. So she wrote another novel, *The Midwife's Apprentice,* and it won even higher acclaim: the Newbery Medal. Cushman's husband Philip said in his article about her in the July/August 1996 *Horn Book* that "over the years she tried many different careers, from organic gardening to a job as administrator of a community arts program, from two masters degrees to a position as editor of the *Museum Studies Journal*" (p. 422). The Cushmans also raised a daughter, Leah. Although Cushman was always very good at what

prestigious honored or well-known

pantheon a group of people noted for outstanding ability or accomplishment she did, and despite "all the variety and action, something was still not right" (p. 422). Finally, however, with the publication of her novels, Karen Cushman had discovered who she was and what she could do in this world.

Finding a Place

In some cultures and historical periods, people have fewer choices about what they can do with their lives than many of Cushman's readers do. This was true for Cushman herself. In the 1960s, when she was going to college, the options available to her as a woman were more limited than they are now. At Stanford University she majored in classics (Greek and Latin), and later she went on to earn two master's degrees, one in museum studies and one in human behavior. But many more women her age became secretaries than scholars, and that's the kind of job Cushman took. She was working as a low-level administrator when she met her husband, who was a graduate student. It may be Philip whom we have to thank for *Catherine, Called Birdy* ever making it past the idea-stage. Cushman says she told her husband about an idea she had for a story. She often told Philip her ideas, but this time he stopped her and asked her to "write it down and read it to him. I think that was one reason I actually put words on paper," Cushman says in her interview with Judith Hendershot and Jackie Peck in the November 1996 *The Reading Teacher.* "And the result was Birdy" (p. 199).

Like Cushman herself, her characters have to overcome the obstacles set by their societies—and they have to live within those societies. Many problems have no easy solutions, and when she was writing *Catherine, Called Birdy,* Cushman wondered about what happens when you can't change a situation. Her answer? "All you can deal with is yourself." She applied that idea to the Middle Ages, "when children had much less value and power than they do now," and when it was even more difficult to change the way things are (p. 198).

In England in 1290, the setting of both *Catherine, Called Birdy* and *The Midwife's Apprentice,* girls couldn't do just anything they wanted to do. Your social class helped define what was expected of you. Birdy is a member of the upper class, so she must marry whomever her father tells her to marry. This expectation fuels the plot of the book: Birdy tries her best to outwit both her father and her suitors. She feels as caged as

plot the deliberate sequence of events in a literary work

suitor potential spouse

the birds she keeps in her room and longs for her freedom. Deep down, however, she knows that she must marry, and that she must abide by her father's wishes and the expectations of her society. Birdy's challenge is to accept the place her world allots her.

Alyce, the young homeless girl in *The Midwife's Apprentice,* is from a much lower social class than Birdy. In some ways, her choices are much narrower than Birdy's, but because she has no family to answer to and therefore fewer expectations placed upon her, in some ways she has more freedom than Birdy. She decides to stay with Jane Sharp, the village midwife, even though Jane is cruel and beats her. But living with Jane is better than trying to stay warm by burying yourself in a dungheap, and even an onion for dinner is better than no meal at all. Alyce is smart enough to realize that by watching and listening, she can learn to help Jane in her midwifery, and in so doing, learn how to become a midwife herself.

midwife one who assists women in childbirth

Lucy, the heroine of Cushman's third novel, *The Ballad of Lucy Whipple* (1996), lives 600 years and an ocean away from Birdy and Alyce, but she too struggles within and against societal confines. Lucy knows she belongs in dignified Massachusetts, where she grew up, but her mother moves the entire family to the very undignified Gold Rush town of Lucky Diggins, California. All Lucy wants is civilization; all she gets is the dirt and tobacco-spit of gold miners. That is, until she starts to pay attention to what the miners have to offer. Like Lucy, they aspire to something more than they have. And like Lucy, they must make do with the reality of Lucky Diggins. When Lucy finally realizes what the miners give her and what she herself can offer to the world, she also realizes that she doesn't need to go back east to find her place in the world. Lucky Diggins might turn out to be good enough, after all.

The most famous **Gold Rush** in U.S. history began with the discovery of gold at Sutter's mill in California in 1848. Thousands of people moved west in a short period of time hoping to strike it rich.

Like Lucy, Karen Cushman moved to California when she was young, and like Lucy, Cushman also learned to call it home. After growing up in Chicago, where she was born 4 October 1941 to Arthur and Loretta Lipski, Cushman's family moved to California when she was eleven. Except for a few years in Oregon, Cushman has lived there ever since.

Finding a Name

Throughout her novels Cushman's characters struggle not only to find a home and a place in the world. They also try to

theme central message about life in a literary work

define themselves by deciding what they want other people to call them. They struggle to find names. This theme is apparent in *The Ballad of Lucy Whipple.* Lucy names herself because her given name, California Morning Whipple, suits her even less than the state of California suits her. But anyone who has ever tried on a new nickname and had trouble getting people to use it knows exactly how Lucy feels. Even though she tells everyone her new name, it takes a long time for it to stick.

protagonist the main character of a literary work

Alyce, the protagonist of *The Midwife's Apprentice,* does not even have a name at the beginning of the book. She accepts the names people carelessly toss at her, such as Brat and Beetle. As she begins to gain a sense of herself as something other than a hungry stomach, she recognizes her need for a name. She tries on a few before she settles on Alyce. Like Lucy, Alyce has trouble making the name stick. "This business of having a name was harder than it seemed," she says. "A name was of little use if no one would call you by it" (p. 35). After Alyce has named herself, she names her friend the cat, Purr. When she meets a little boy known as Runt, who is as homeless as she once was, Alyce insists that he find a proper name. He chooses to be called Edward, after the king of England. Once he has a name, Alyce helps him find a home as well.

Unlike Alyce and Lucy, Birdy has names aplenty that are accepted by her family. Although her given name is Catherine, her nicknames are Little Bird and Birdy. Nevertheless, Birdy too experiments with names as she tries to decide who she is. For a little while, she decides that Aelfgifu, the name of an English queen, suits her better than Catherine, but her nurse laughs at her, and no one else will accept the name either.

Birdy also thinks up less-than-becoming nicknames for her suitors and her father. Her father, who is making her marry against her will, is the Beast; Shaggy Beard is the name she gives the man she is to marry. For Birdy, as for Alyce and Lucy, naming yourself or others is an important way of taking charge of a world that offers limited choices.

Researching the Past

gravitate to be drawn or attracted to something, especially by natural inclination

With two master's degrees and a job as a professor of Museum Studies at John F. Kennedy University, you can be sure that Cushman knows how to research a topic. When you hear about how she spent her childhood, you know that she gravitates naturally to research. In J. Sydney Jones's article in *Some-*

thing About the Author Cushman described the time she wanted to learn ballet. She got a book and read it to her friends, who "gripp[ed] the car door handles like a ballet bar as [Cushman] read to them what to do" (p. 44). All sorts of interests claimed the young Cushman—"the Civil War for instance, or . . . the physiology of the brain"—and she fed her hunger for each new subject by finding books in the library (p. 43). When it came time to find out how people lived long ago, Cushman knew just how to go about it.

For all three of her novels, Cushman had to do a lot of research. What did Birdy see when she put down the linen she was hemming and looked out the solar window? Cushman didn't only have to know what Birdy would see outside, she also had to know that a gentlewoman in medieval England would sit in a room called a *solar* hemming sheets made of linen. Cushman said in her interview with Elizabeth Madrid McKindley in the winter 1998 *The New Advocate* that she looked for the details of daily life—"I wanted to know what they used for toilet paper, not what battles were fought" (p. 3). Much of the research that went into *Catherine, Called Birdy* also informs *The Midwife's Apprentice,* but the second novel also required some specialized knowledge, such as what a midwife might carry in her basket and what kinds of remedies she might use for fever or for bleeding. Research into a very different place and time went into *The Ballad of Lucy Whipple*—California during the Gold Rush years of 1849–1852. But many of the questions remained the same: What did people eat? What were their houses (or tents or cottages) like? How did they talk? What kind of medicine did they use? How did they spend their days?

To find out, Cushman explained in her interview with Stephanie Loer on the Houghton-Mifflin website that she used history books as well as primary sources, or "first hand accounts of life and incidents in letter form, private journals, and personal papers." She also "read books about the manners, clothing, agriculture, foods, and even recipes of the period" (p. 2). It might take Cushman an entire day searching through books in the library to find a particular fact, and sometimes even after such a search, she didn't find out what she needed to know. Such detailed research is partly why *Catherine, Called Birdy* took three and a half years to write, while *The Midwife's Apprentice* only took nine months, since much of Cushman's research into England in the year 1290 had already been completed. *The Ballad of Lucy Whipple* took eighteen months to write and research.

Medical Knowledge

In all of her books, Cushman focuses some of her attention on forms of medical knowledge. It shouldn't surprise readers, then, to discover that Cushman's novel *Matilda Bone* (which in 1999 had no set publication date), is about a medieval bone-setter. In *Catherine, Called Birdy*, Birdy learns from her mother and from her own experimentation how to heal wounds and calm upset stomachs, one of the many tasks that fell to the lady of the manor. Birdy doctors her mother, who has a frightening pregnancy, and her father, who suffers from drinking too much ale, as well as the servants and villagers.

Alyce has no knowledge of healing until she becomes the apprentice to the midwife. Unlike Birdy, neither Alyce nor the midwife can read. They know the herbs they use by their smell and their look. Much of their craft comes from experience and experimentation, and Alyce learns that much of what a medieval midwife does is based on common sense. However, as Cushman reminds us in her author's note, "Medieval common sense knew nothing of germs, little of anatomy, and all too much of magic and superstition" (pp. 119–120).

Medical knowledge in an out-of-the-way place like Lucky Diggins, California, in 1850 was more like medieval medicine than modern medicine. When Lucy's brother falls ill, there is little more than peppermint tea and herb tonics to help him— along with mothering and prayer. No antiseptic hospitals with their complicated machinery were available in either Lucky Diggins or medieval England.

antiseptic free from contamination

Reading and Language

Like medical knowledge, reading and literacy also play a large role in Cushman's works. Birdy is unusual for her time period because her brother has taught her to read and write in Latin. Not very many girls in England in 1290 could read and write English, let alone Latin. It wasn't a very practical skill when your days were spent sewing and making soap and doctoring people. Birdy's story is written in the form of a diary. Perhaps it isn't very realistic for Birdy to have written her life story so coherently and

coherently clearly and intelligibly

so humorously as a diary, but it is realistic for her not to have a notebook in which to write it. Instead, she uses sheepskin and ink left over from her father's household accounts.

Unlike Birdy, Alyce is illiterate. Although she is scorned by the villagers because she is small and weak and has no one to protect her, she is never made fun of for not knowing how to read: none of the other villagers would have been able to read either. Alyce spends some time working at a tavern where a scholar is writing an encyclopedia. Over a long winter, he teaches Alyce her letters. But she doesn't run out to buy a book—books were far too expensive for a poor girl like Alyce. Even Birdy's household only contained two or three books. Since printing didn't come to England until 1476, all the books during Birdy and Alyce's time would have been copied laboriously by hand on parchment made from the skins of sheep, cows, or goats.

By the nineteenth century, however, printing and cheap paper made books much more easily available. Lucy reads voraciously and she treasures her books. More than anything from her old town in Massachusetts, she misses the library. The miners who live in and near Lucky Diggins share Lucy's books with her as an escape from the tedium of long, solitary days panning for gold. In the end, it's the idea of starting her own library that helps Lucy find her place in the world.

Language is an important element in the characterization of Lucy, Birdy, and Alyce. All three girls use specific kinds of language in an attempt to define themselves, in a similar way to how they find themselves through their names. Birdy would rather be a villager than a lady, and her oaths, such as *"Corpus bones!",* allow her to identify with the villagers instead of with her mother or other gentlewomen. Lucy adopts the language of the miners as she tries to fit into her surroundings—her favorite phrase is "Dag diggety!" Alyce's speech becomes gentler as people begin to speak more gently to her. She learns to use words other than oaths and swear words when she finds a home and a place in the world.

In her Newbery Medal Acceptance speech, Cushman talks about why she writes. "Writing is my niche, my home, my place in the world, a place I finally found, just as Alyce, the midwife's apprentice, found hers" (pp. 413–414). Cushman writes not just about thirteen-year-old girls named Birdy and Alyce and Lucy; she also writes about herself. "I am Alyce," she says, "who becomes truly alive only when she learns to smile

voraciously with excessive eagerness; avidly

tedium boredom

characterization method by which a writer creates and develops the appearance and personality of a character

niche place or position best suited to a person

and sing and tell stories to the cat" (p. 416). Like Alyce, Cushman found her place in the world through stories, and the world is richer for it.

If you like Karen Cushman's books that are set in the Middle Ages, you might also like Rosemary Sutcliff's *Knight's Fee* and *The Witch's Brat* and Nancy Garden's *Dove and Sword: A Novel of Joan of Arc.*

Selected Bibliography

WORKS BY KAREN CUSHMAN

Novels
Catherine, Called Birdy (1994)
The Midwife's Apprentice (1995)
The Ballad of Lucy Whipple (1996)

Speech
"Newbery Medal Acceptance." *Horn Book,* July/August 1996, pp. 413–419.

WORKS ABOUT KAREN CUSHMAN

Barnhouse, Rebecca. "Books and Reading in Young Adult Literature Set in the Middle Ages." *The Lion and the Unicorn,* September 1998, pp. 364–375.

Cushman, Philip. "Karen Cushman." *Horn Book,* July/August 1996, pp. 420–423.

Elliot, Ian. "Karen Cushman: Pursuing the Past." Online. Teaching K-8 Archives. *www.teachingk-8.com/archives/html/2_98outtakes1.html* 3 December 1998.

Hendershot, Judith, and Jackie Peck. "Interview with Newbery Medal winner Karen Cushman." *The Reading Teacher,* November 1996, pp. 198–201.

Jones, J. Sydney. "Cushman, Karen." In *Something About the Author.* Edited by Alan Hedblad. Detroit: Gale Research, 1997, vol. 89, pp. 43–47.

Loer, Stephanie. "Interview with Karen Cushman." Online. Houghton-Mifflin Website. *www.eduplace.com/rdg/author/cushman/question.html.* 3 December 1998.

Love, Amy Umland. "Karen Cushman: Flying Starts." *Publisher's Weekly,* 4 July 1994, pp. 39–40.

McKindley, Elizabeth Madrid. "Writing from the inside out: a 'chat' with Karen Cushman." *The New Advocate,* winter 1998, pp. 1–10.

Rochman, Hazel. "The *Booklist* Interview." *Booklist*, 1 and 15 June 1996, pp. 1700–1701.

Zornado, Joseph. "A Poetics of History: Karen Cushman's Medieval World." *The Lion and the Unicorn*, April 1997, pp. 251–266.

How to Write to the Author

Karen Cushman
c/o Clarion Books
215 Park Avenue South
New York, NY 10003

Paul Fleischman

(1952–)

by Pam B. Cole

Have you ever thought about your future career and considered the possibility of following in your father's footsteps? If so, you may enjoy reading about Paul Fleischman, son of Sid Fleischman, award-winning author of adventure stories for children. Sid Fleischman won the Newbery Medal for *The Whipping Boy* in 1987; Paul won the award two years later for *Joyful Noise: Poems for Two Voices* (1988) and has won numerous other awards, including a Newbery Honor for *Graven Images: Three Stories* (1982), a Golden Kite Award Honor for both *The Half-a-Moon Inn* (1980) and *Path of a Pale Horse* (1983), and the Scott O'Dell Award for historical fiction for *Bull Run* (1993).

Born 5 September 1952 in Monterey, California, the son of Albert Sidney (Sid) and Beth Taylor Fleischman, Paul's childhood was filled with the sound of story. As his father wrote, he read his books out loud to the family, chapter by chapter. Because of his father's influence, Fleischman found writing for children both an honorable and possible profession. He grew up in Santa Monica, attended the University of California at

There is an article about Scott O'Dell in volume 2.

Berkeley (1970–1972), and then later attended the University of New Mexico at Albuquerque (1975–1977). He has worked as a bagel baker, a bookstore clerk, and a proofreader. He currently lives in Pacific Grove, California, where he continues to write stories. He also travels throughout the country as a guest speaker/lecturer for numerous literary and educational forums.

Unlike many writers, Fleischman writes in a variety of genres—he has published novels, short stories, poetry, picture books, and nonfiction. His works are influenced by his keen interest in history and his passion for music. Music, Fleischman says, is his first love, and because of it he pays particular attention to the sound of his writing. His two volumes of poetry, *I Am Phoenix: Poems for Two Voices* (1985) and *Joyful Noise* reflect his attention to the sound of language as do novels such as *Bull Run, Seedfolks* (1997), and *Whirligig* (1998). Fleischman carefully chooses words and crafts phrases and sentences so that his writing has a musical quality. Picture books, poetry, and short stories make up the bulk of his earlier work, while novels dominate his later material.

Central to Fleischman's later work is the idea of community, or the coming together of individual people for some common goal or purpose. This theme occurs in *The Borning Room* (1991), a story about family togetherness and the continuity of life. It is echoed in *Bull Run,* when Northern and Southern voices describe the coming together of people to experience the first major Civil War conflict, and in *Seedfolks,* a novel in which a diverse group of people join in transforming a vacant city lot into a neighborhood garden. Fleischman also carries the theme into *Whirligig,* a story in which the protagonist learns the myriad ways in which we are connected and how our acts link us together. Our acts affect other people; how we act as a group and what happens when we do so becomes a central motif in these novels.

genre type of literature, such as science fiction or romance

keen intense

theme central message about life in a literary work

protagonist the main character of a literary work

myriad a great number; countless

The Borning Room

Through the life of an Ohio farm girl living during the Civil War era, Fleischman writes about the continual cycle of birth, living, and dying, and how as a part of that cycle we each carry with us "seeds" of our past history, which we pass on to later generations. The setting of the story is the borning room (a room set aside for births and deaths) of the Lott family. For young Georgina Lott, it is a room that echoes both joy and fear. As Georgina matures, she witnesses the birth of her siblings as well as the death of her grandfather and her own mother. She comes to value family and the lessons taught her by her elders. She marries as a young woman and delivers her own children in the borning room. As years pass, her father dies and so does her husband, Clement. Georgina recognizes and accepts her place and the places of her family members in the cycle of life. She comes to view living and dying as congruent states: " 'In the midst of life we are in death.' The opposite, I found, is true as well" (p. 88).

congruent in agreement or harmony

In addition to celebrating the cycle of life, the story also acknowledges heritage and the influence that family has over future generations. From her grandfather, for example, Georgina gains her beliefs about religion and spirituality, and from her mother she inherits her belief that she will marry and have children. Though *The Borning Room* is a warm story about family and relationships, the story raises an interesting question about how individuals create identity apart from their families. As a young child, Georgina watches her mother go through childbirth, she sees the pain of childbirth, fears having babies, and experiences the death of her own mother during childbirth. As years slip by, however, she grows into womanhood, discovers first love, and accepts that her life is identical to her mother's. She takes her place in the borning room, just as her mother did before her, first as a caretaker for the ill, then as a mother giving birth, and finally as an old woman.

Bull Run

This Scott O'Dell Award-winning historical novel is written to be performed as a reader's theater. Unique to this novel is a multi-character approach to relating the events of the first great battle of the Civil War. Sixteen diverse characters—young and old, male and female, African American and white, Southerners and Northerners—narrate the events in rotating chapters. Early chapters tell events that lead up to the first battle of the Civil War, and subsequent chapters detail episodes and events of the actual battle and its aftermath. Fifteen of the sixteen characters are fictional, though General McDowell is real. Through these voices, Fleischman reconstructs the realities and horrors of the first battle of Bull Run. These voices tell of

narrate to tell a story

the false dreams and the absurdities of battle glory, the grim realities associated with war, and the anguish of an immature country discovering truths about war.

A Fate Totally Worse than Death (1995)

Danielle, Tiffany, and Brooke are filthy rich and evil to the core. Jealous of Helga, an exquisite exchange student from Norway, they plot revenge against her. They become convinced that Helga is the ghost of Charity, an attractive girl whom they murdered. When the girls realize they are aging prematurely, they blame Helga for casting an evil spell on them and plan to kill Drew, a boy over whom Danielle obsesses, who was attracted to Charity. His death, they believe, will satisfy the ghost's need for revenge, thus freeing them from the awful spell. Success is not in the cards, however. Not only are they caught arranging the murder, but they also learn that they each received an injection of an aging potion from an elderly lady at the nursing home where they resented doing community service as part of their school curriculum.

A Fate Totally Worse than Death is a fast-paced farce, a completely unbelievable but funny look at the world of teenagers and high school culture. Fleischman exaggerates adolescent concerns (such as physical appearance, belonging, sexuality, and dating) with a pronounced sense of humor, pushing the story to the point of absurdity. And in doing so, he asks adolescent readers to laugh at some of life's absurdities and acknowledge the silliness that goes along with some forms of human behavior. Danielle is a perfect "dumb blonde" stereotype who is obsessed with boys and her physical appearance, and Tiffany and Brooke play equally stereotyped supporting roles. Their obsession with their physical appearance sends them out of control once they realize they are acquiring liver spots, gray hair, arthritis, and sagging breasts. Helga is unmatchable—not only ravishingly beautiful but also intelligent.

The Half-a-Moon Inn

In the style of Edgar Allan Poe, Fleischman creates a setting and mood that are haunting and suspenseful in this brief novel. Unaware that a blizzard is approaching, Aaron's mother sets out to Craftsbury in her wagon loaded with wool to trade in the mar-

---

The first battle of **Bull Run** in Manassas, Virginia, on 21 July 1861, was one of the early battles of the Civil War. After tired Union forces ran in wild retreat from the battle, Northerners realized that this war would not be over in three months, as many had predicted. Confederate confidence was boosted by their victory.

farce a light dramatic composition characterized by broad satirical comedy and a highly improbable plot

stereotype universal type; character that conforms to a preconceived and often oversimplified notion about a person or group

There is an article about Edgar Allan Poe in volume 3.

setting the general time and place in which the events of a literary work take place

ket, leaving twelve-year-old Aaron alone in their house near the ocean. When his mother fails to return at the appointed time, Aaron panics and sets out in a desperate search to find her. Lost and cold, he accepts a ride offered by a ragman and finds himself at the eerie Half-a-Moon Inn, where he is kidnapped by the owner, Miss Grackle. Since Aaron is mute, he is unable to tell anyone of his plight; he must obey the cruel and crafty Miss Grackle, who forces him into servitude. Aaron searches desperately for a way out. Though a short novel, *The Half-a-Moon Inn* is packed with suspense and mystery.

Saturnalia

The English who founded the American colonies in the 1600s were accustomed to having servants. Indentured servants from England, slaves from the West Indies, paupers, and criminals filled these positions; however, the demand far exceeded the number of available servants, forcing the English to look elsewhere for servants. American Indians sometimes filled these roles.

In this historical novel, Fleischman tells the story of William, a fourteen-year-old Narraganset boy who was taken from his family during King Philip's War. The story takes place six years after his capture. Though William leads a promising and peaceful life as a printer's apprentice, he longs for some connection with his past. After curfew, and risking the wrath of the local officials, William can be found in the streets, piping Narraganset songs on a flute made by his grandfather and searching for clues that can lead him to his lost brother and his Indian heritage.

Saturnalia is a story about racial prejudices and equality. The Currie family, to whom William is apprenticed, treats him as one of their own children: he is well educated, has plenty to eat, and has warm clothes to wear. Mr. and Mrs. Currie even celebrate the Saturnalia—a Roman holiday of general feasting and revelry in celebration of winter in which masters and servants trade roles. Their willingness to do so illustrates the respect they have for those who work beneath them.

Several characters serve as foils for the Curries. Mr. Baggot, the man whose job it is to take spiritual charge of several families, noting their attendance at church and the manner in which children are raised, hates William because he is Narraganset. When he visits the Currie household, he thinks: "How

indentured servant a person who signs a contract to work for someone for a specified length of time in exchange for maintenance and travel expenses

King Philip's War (1675–1678) was the most destructive Indian war in New England's history. King Philip, a chief of the Wampanoag Indians, became concerned that white settlers would destroy his people. He made plans to massacre all the white settlers in New England, but when the fighting started, he burned both white and Indian settlements. Philip was killed in 1676, though fighting continued for two more years.

apprentice one who learns by experience under the direction of a skilled craftsperson

foil a person who, by contrast, highlights the qualities of another character

avidly very eagerly

foreboding an uneasy feeling that something bad is going to happen

chastised reprimanded

foible flaw or short-coming

very English he [William] looks. . . . How avidly he reads. How well he speaks. How universally admired he is. And how black is his barbarous heart, he added. For beneath his linen shirt and his Latin, the viper wasn't English. He was an Indian" (p. 7). Mr. Baggot's contempt is so intense that he concocts plans to destroy William. When several attempts are thwarted, he accuses William of the murder of Mr. Rudd, an evil and dishonest eyeglass maker who starves and tortures his apprentices and happens by chance to take into apprenticeship William's uncle and cousin.

Both Mr. Baggot and Mr. Rudd have evil hearts; they believe in social class supremacy. The tone in which they are described and the mood surrounding their presence in the story is dark, somber, and heavy; however, not all the characters who believe in social class supremacy are described with such foreboding. Through the characters of Mr. Hogwood the wigmaker and his handsome young apprentice, Malcolm, Fleischman gives an otherwise bleak and somber novel a few good laughs.

Mr. Hogwood, who dresses above his station but detests others who do so, woos Madam Phipp, a rich widow whose hand in marriage would guarantee him social advancement. Unschooled in the ways of courtship, Mr. Hogwood accepts advice from Malcolm in courtship ritual. A charmer and scoundrel, Malcom ill advises and misrepresents Mr. Hogwood. Mr. Hogwood's dream of social success through marriage ends when, sporting his best attire, he ascends a tree at Malcolm's urging and enters Madam Phipp's room through a window. Here he is mistaken for a servant by a visually impaired Madam Phipp. He is humiliated and chastised before he makes his escape.

Though Fleischman treats prejudice and racial hatred seriously and with respect, he also gives the story a lighter twist by illustrating some of the silliness of "high" society and human foibles through the ridiculous and cartoonlike characters of Mr. Hogwood and Malcolm.

Seedfolks

One day Fleischman, while eating in a bagel shop, came across an article about a psychotherapist who uses gardening as therapy. According to the article, ancient Egyptians used to prescribe walking through gardens as a cure for the insane. Fleischman coupled that idea with his personal hunger for joining with others for some common purpose, a theme found elsewhere in his writing, and the plot for *Seedfolks* took shape.

A vacant lot transformed into a garden in Cleveland is the setting for this novel about diversity, personal growth, and sense of community. Thirteen dissimilar characters disclose the story of how an unkempt city lot becomes a beautiful neighborhood garden. The transformation begins when a nine-year-old Vietnamese girl takes lima beans out to a run-down lot and plants them in an effort to connect with the spirit of her father, a man she never knew. She tends them lovingly, and her work does not go unobserved. An elderly Romanian woman, Ana, and a white American man, Wendell, notice and are moved by her efforts. Wendell realizes there are many things about his life that he cannot change, but there are some things he can: "Can't bring the dead back to life on this earth. Can't make the world loving and kind. Can't change myself into a millionaire. But a patch of ground in this trashy lot—I can change that. Can change it big" (p. 12). Wendell brings a shovel home from work one afternoon, and the transformation begins.

Soon folks of all ages and cultures, for their own reasons, come to the abandoned lot and cultivate their own small gardens. Young and old, white, African American, Hispanic, Haitian, and Korean, strong and weak, rough, obsessed, timid and confident transform the once trashy lot into a kaleidoscope of colors and forms. In doing so, each character benefits from the healing powers of nature, is transformed in some personal way, and expresses a small piece of the larger fabric of life. The strangers who come together in the lot learn the value of unity and the power and strength that come with being a part of a larger community.

Whirligig

In this painful but healing story, we learn how human choices and actions affect other people and how relationships give us strength. Though we may see some of the consequences of our actions, we can never know *all* the consequences of our behavior. Brent Bishop is a high school student hanging on the edges of popularity. When humiliated at a party of rich

whirligig a figure or object that whirls or spins in the wind, such as a pinwheel

metaphor a figure of speech in which one thing is referred to as something else; for example, "My love is a rose"

dysfunctional characterized by impaired or abnormal functioning

kids, he jumps into his car drunk and drives away in a rage. When attempting to kill himself, he accidentally hits another car head on and kills its teenage driver. Brent survives, but he must deal with the aftermath of his actions. At the request of the dead girl's mother and as a way of escaping from his life, Brent sets out on a cross-country trip to build and set up whirligigs in Maine, California, Washington, and Florida—the four corners of the United States—in honor of the girl. Brent sets out feeling disconnected from life, and his first whirligig takes tremendous effort. It turns out to be simplistic, and he views it as a disappointment. Each subsequent whirligig, however, is more elaborate and becomes more meaningful for Brent, symbolizing his increasing awareness of both simple and complex ways in which people influence one another. Unbeknownst to Brent, each whirligig becomes a gift to another individual: the whirligigs bring love to a young girl in Maine and understanding to a confused street sweeper in Florida, change a controlling parent in Washington, and bring happiness to a California teenager. By the end of the journey, Brent has worked through his pain with the help of the people he has met along the way, and he is ready to re-enter his old life.

In this moving story, the whirligig becomes a symbol, a metaphor for human connection. Just as all parts of a whirligig are connected and work in unison, so do people. Without one another, we are dysfunctional; just as each piece of a whirligig sets in motion the other pieces, so do people give energy to one another, so do people soar when they work in harmony with those around them. Brent comes to this realization at the end of his adventures when he steps into a diner for food and sees music and dancing:

> Couples turned in circles, skirts rippling. Brent stared. It was a human whirligig, set in motion by music instead of wind. He sank into a chair and watched dance after dance. Suddenly, a young woman rushed up to him. "We need one more couple." She held out her hands.
> To his great amazement, he agreed. (P. 130)

The whirligig represents the multifaceted and often complex connections created by our lives and our acts.

I Am Phoenix: Poems for Two Voices and *Joyful Noise: Poems for Two Voices*

Though these two collections of poetry were written and published three years apart, both collections were written with the same premise. Fleischman structured each poem to be read aloud by two voices, one taking the left-hand column, the other taking the right-hand column. At times each voice speaks alone; at other times, both voices speak in unison. When read aloud, the poems have a musical quality and resound with a cheerful and reverent praise of birds and insects. The first collection, *I Am Phoenix,* celebrates the bird world—finches, condors, wrens, seagulls, egrets, owls, and numerous others come to life on the page. When the poems are read aloud, the birds sing, soar, rejoice, and parrate their own histories, qualities, and attributes. The second collection, *Joyful Noise,* celebrates the world of insects. Each poem in this Newbery Award-winning volume depicts the life of an insect. The poems alternate between funny and sad, loud and quiet, and busy and slow, depending on the characteristics of the insect or bird that is described.

Writing Style

Fleischman's writing is diverse in style, genre, and content. Despite this diversity, common themes and elements are evident: the power of community; connections and togetherness; historical events and time periods; and multiple characters as narrators. Unique to Fleischman's writing is the lyrical quality of not only his poetry, but also of his short stories and novels. His work is popular among young readers today and ranks among the best in children's and adolescent literature.

Selected Bibliography

WORKS BY PAUL FLEISCHMAN

Novels for Young Adults
  The Half-a-Moon Inn (1980)
  Path of the Pale Horse (1983)
  Rear-View Mirrors (1986)

If you like Paul Fleischman, you might also like Christopher and James Lincoln Collier and Ann Rinaldi.

Saturnalia (1990)

The Borning Room (1991)

Bull Run (1993)

A Fate Totally Worse than Death (1995)

Seedfolks (1997)

Whirligig (1998)

Short Stories

Graven Images: Three Stories (1982)

Coming-and-Going Men: Four Tales (1985)

Children's Books

The Birthday Tree (1979)

Rondo in C (1988)

Shadow Play (1990)

Time Train (1991)

Poetry

I Am Phoenix: Poems for Two Voices (1985)

Joyful Noise: Poems for Two Voices (1988)

Nonfiction

Townsend's Warbler (1992)

Copier Creations: Using Copy Machines to Make Decals, Silhouettes, Flip Books, Films, and Much More! (1993)

Dateline: Troy (1996)

WORKS ABOUT PAUL FLEISCHMAN

Burns, Mary. Review of *Joyful Noise: Poems for Two Voices*. *Horn Book,* May–June 1988, pp. 366–67.

Commire, Anne, ed. *Something About the Author.* Detroit: Gale Research, 1983, vol. 32, p. 71.

Commire, Anne, ed. *Something About the Author.* Detroit: Gale Research, 1985, vol. 39, pp. 72–73.

Copeland, Jeffrey. *Speaking of Poets 2: More Interviews with Poets who Write for Children and Young Adults.* Urbana, Ill.: NCTE, 1994.

Kovac, Deborah. *Meet the Authors: 25 Writers of Upper Elementary and Middle School Books Talk About Their Work.* New York: Scholastic, 1995.

Phelan, Carolyn. Review of *Joyful Noise: Poems for Two Voices. Booklist,* 15 February 1988, p. 1000.

Robb, Laura. "Talking with Paul Fleischman." *Book Links,* March 1997, p. 39.

Telgen, Diane, ed. *Something About the Author.* Detroit: Gale Research, 1993, vol. 72, pp. 68–70.

How to Write to the Author

Paul Fleischman
c/o HarperCollins
Children's Books
10 East 53rd Street
New York, NY 10022

Nancy Garden

(1938–)

by Joan F. Kaywell

W hen Nancy Garden was young, her father used to tell her—his only child—that a girl could do anything a boy could do if she worked hard enough at it. He also told her, however, that to get recognition she would have to do it twice as well. In life as well as in her writing, it is obvious that Nancy took her father's words to heart.

For a girl born in 1938 to a father of Italian descent and a mother of German heritage, growing up after World War II presented numerous challenges. Probably the three most profound influences on her approach to life, other than her parents' influence, were Nancy's maternal grandmother's sister, Tante Anna, affectionately called "Tanna"; her first- and second-grade teacher, Miss Peek; and the fact that her family frequently moved. She remembers feeling that as soon as she got settled in one place, they would pack up and leave to go to another. One reason had to do with her father's job with the American Red Cross, and another, with the actual housing shortage that followed World War II. Because men returning

Quotations from Nancy Garden that are not attributed to a published source are from personal interviews conducted by the author of this article between March 1999 and May 1999 and are published here by permission of Nancy Garden.

maternal related through the mother

The **Red Cross** is an organization that works to relieve human suffering in more than 135 countries. The name "Red Cross" comes from the organization's flag, which is a red cross on a white background. This is a tribute to Switzerland, where the Red Cross was founded in 1863.

from serving in the war had first choice of available housing, and since Nancy's father had been unable to serve because of his poor eyesight, there were times when the family had to relocate (sometimes with little notice) to accommodate the needs of returning soldiers. By the time she was ten, Nancy had lived in two different states and five different cities.

Reading and storytelling were stable pastimes, and they served her and her family well. Nancy recalls that her mother, Elisabeth Yens Garden, was a wonderful storyteller. She could take insignificant little incidents and make them fun, romantic, and memorable. Her "Mum" just didn't say that she heard a mouse in a cupboard but said she heard "scratch, scratch, scratch, PLOP-SPLASH; scratch, scratch, scratch, PLOP-SPLASH" to describe a mouse she had found trying to make its way out of a bowl of chicken soup! Tanna often visited and was a skilled oral reader who had unbelievable patience with Nancy as well as with animals. She would listen for hours on end as Nancy recalled movie plots and practiced memorizing lines of poetry for school. Her teacher, Miss Peek, also encouraged Nancy's make-believe stories and promoted her acting efforts. Even her father, Peter T. Garden, got into the act, making up his own stories. Nancy especially enjoyed the ongoing ones he made up about "Mr. Talkie," a man whose clothes told him whenever he put them on wrong; "The Flounderie," about a fish who talked a man out of eating him for supper; and "Josephine the Ostrich," the only one her father actually put into writing. The best part of it all was that reading and storytelling were always cooperative efforts.

Nancy Garden's writing career began with a poem she wrote when she was eight years old, and another passion was discovered when she befriended Sandra Scott at the age of twelve. Her relationship with Sandra, her life partner, didn't really take off until she turned sixteen, and Nancy did not pursue writing as her life's work until well after receiving her B.F.A. (1961) and M.A. (1962) from New York's Columbia University. Her first career was in theater, where she worked sometimes as an actress and sometimes as a lighting designer. Working in summer stock, she found another longtime friend, David Vosburgh. While pursuing her graduate degree, she taught part-time and supplemented her income by working in a newly formed insurance company. The latter experience, though brief, introduced her to Barbara Sueling and Winnette Glasgow, two women whose friendships with Nancy and San-

summer stock productions of regional theatrical companies presented during the summer

dra have lasted more than 35 years. Her first job in publishing earned her only $75.00 a week, but it taught her a lot about the craft of writing. She has since worked in various capacities: as an editor, freelance writer, teacher, and author. Her public speaking engagements range from speaking to children about writing to addressing adults about writing, censorship, and gay issues.

freelance work done independently, not for an individual employer

Nancy Garden is probably best known for her pioneering efforts in addressing the controversial topic of homosexuality in *Annie on My Mind* (1982), *Lark in the Morning* (1991), "Parents' Night" (1994), *Good Moon Rising* (1996), and *The Year They Burned the Books* (1999). She approaches this formerly taboo subject with tact and sensitivity, reaching her young readers with insights into an issue that is often uncomfortable for adolescents to discuss. Garden portrays gay teenagers positively in her books, not to "promote" homosexuality but to try to reduce the alarming percentage of homosexual teenagers who kill themselves. In *Good Moon Rising*, there are no foul language, no explicit sex, no slams against parents, and no violence. Nevertheless, this beautiful love story of two adolescent girls who meet and become romantically involved while rehearsing for their school play—Arthur Miller's *The Crucible*—has fueled much discussion around the country. While Jan and Kerry struggle to go slowly with their relationship so that they can understand and sort out their strong feelings, the character "Proctor" in *The Crucible* is quick to play judge and jury. One can find similar situations in Garden's own life.

censorship the suppression of something that one finds objectionable

There is an article about Arthur Miller later in this volume.

Annie on My Mind, another novel about a first homosexual relationship between two young women, has captured more than just accolades since its publication in 1982. This touching portrayal of young love in a homophobic society caused great controversy in several Kansas school districts. The novel was forced to face homophobia just as its two characters are. In 1993, Project 21, a gay organization that encourages the inclusion of accurate gay and lesbian literature in school libraries, donated copies of *Annie on My Mind* to 42 schools in the Kansas City area. A fundamentalist minister burned a copy of the book in front of the building that housed the Kansas City School Board, and soon the novel was removed from school libraries, some of which had had copies on their shelves for years. This blatant act of censorship burned in the hearts of the community.

accolade award or praise

fundamentalist referring to a member of a movement of Protestantism that stresses a literal interpretation of the Bible as the basis of Christian life and teaching

A group of students in Olathe, Kansas, along with their parents, sued the school superintendent and school board for violating their First and Fourteenth Amendment rights. Backed by the American Civil Liberties Union (ACLU) and the American Library Association (ALA), the suit went to the Federal District Court of Kansas, where Nancy Garden was asked to testify. After almost not being called to the stand, because one of the defendants' attorneys thought it unnecessary to hear from the author of the novel, Nancy defended her book's right to be on any American shelf. The court ruled that it was unconstitutional for *Annie* to be removed from school libraries—a victory for the students, the novel, and First Amendment rights.

This lawsuit prompted Nancy Garden's novel *The Year They Burned the Books* (1999). Although this book is not about the *Annie* case, Garden's firsthand experience with censorship lends itself well to this novel. She also expected to publish a book in the year 2000 called *Holly's Secret,* a touching middle-grade novel about a young girl who begins to question her life as the child of a lesbian couple and whether or not it is right for her.

Nancy Garden's realistic fiction is not limited to homosexual issues. She writes of racial tensions in *What Happened in Marston* (1971); alienation and drugs in *The Loners* (1972); the differences in opinion between people from two opposite socioeconomic groups in *Peace, O River* (1986); and the futility of war in her historical novel, *Dove and Sword: A Novel of Joan of Arc* (1995). Garden introduces young readers to the fascinating realm of fantasy in her Fours Crossing sequence: *Fours Crossing* (1981), *Watersmeet* (1983), and *The Door Between* (1987); and to the supernatural in books such as *Prisoner of Vampires* (1984); *My Sister the Vampire* (1992); *My Brother, the Werewolf* (1995) and the five books in her Monster Hunters series.

Nancy Garden has received many honors and awards. Despite being controversial, *Annie on My Mind* was selected as a 1982 Booklist Reviewer's Choice and a 1982 American Library Association (ALA) Best Book, and it is on the 1966–1986 Booklist Best of the Best List, the 1970–1983 ALA Best of the Best List, and ALA's 1994 list of Best Books for Young Adults for the Past 25 Years. It was also nominated in 1982 for ALA's Gay Book Award and for the Golden Kite Award. *Fours Crossing* was selected for the 1983–1984 William Allen White Award

Master List. *Dove and Sword* was on both the 1995 New York Public Library Books for the Teen Age and Children's Book Lists. *Good Moon Rising* won the 1996 Lambda Book Award in Children's and Young Adult Literature, was on the 1997 New York Public Library Books for the Teenage List, and was selected as a 1997 Notable Children's Trade Book in the Field of Social Studies.

Is the glass half empty or half full? We all know that the answer depends upon one's point of view. Imagine truth as a multifaceted prism that we are right smack up against when we are born. As we get older, we see more of the prism—or truth—but to do so we must get farther away from it. Our perception of what we see is colored by the reflections of our individual childhoods. If one is raised in an idyllic setting full of life, love, and positive experiences, then one sees the glass as half full. If, on the other hand, a person is raised with negative experiences, then the glass is perceived as half empty. Sometimes it takes a person who has experienced both to help each side of the extreme to understand what the other sees. Nancy Garden is like a hawk who sees the prism from up above—the glass has water in it, but how much is always relative to and dependent upon her purpose.

Garden believes that children are wonderfully receptive to new ideas and are fascinating individuals; that a person can be both happy and gay—these are not mutually exclusive terms; that being gay is not something people choose, but homosexuals fall in love just like heterosexual couples do; and that well-adjusted gay teachers are sorely needed as role models for homosexual teenagers having difficulty with their sexuality. Other people may believe that children need to be protected from "evil ideas"; that gay people are "sick" or criminal; that gay teachers try to "recruit" their students into homosexuality; and that homosexuals, therefore, should never be allowed to be around children. One will have to decide for oneself which set of beliefs views the glass as half empty or half full.

The topics of Garden's writings revolve around the issues that face adolescents every day. In one publication (Daniel and McEntire, 1999), Nancy wrote:

> **How I long for the day when no child yells 'Faggot!' or 'Dyke!' to another on a school playground or in the streets, when 'It's so gay' is no longer used as a put-down in school lunchrooms, and when no gay**

multifaceted having several aspects

idyllic lighthearted and carefree

or lesbian teenager fears for his or her life or safety, or thinks seriously of suicide in the darkness of the night. Sadly, as this century draws to a close, that day has not yet arrived. (P. 223)

Nancy Garden's books help youngsters talk about various issues, offering a perspective that helps readers be more at ease with controversial subjects while helping them to understand the obstacles that homosexual teenagers face. These novels are a beneficial addition and an important asset to every school library.

Nancy Garden resides in Carlisle, Massachusetts, with longtime friend and companion Sandra Scott and numerous animal friends.

If you like the historical works of Nancy Garden, you might also like the works of Christopher Collier and James Lincoln Collier and Ann Rinaldi. If you like Garden's stories about real-life issues, you might also like Marion Dane Bauer, Chris Crutcher, Bette Greene, Sandra Scoppettone, and Cynthia Voigt. If you like Garden's fantasy stories, you might also like Lois Duncan, Kathryn Lasky, and Ursula K. Le Guin.

Selected Bibliography

WORKS BY NANCY GARDEN

Novels for Young Adults and Younger Readers

What Happened in Marston, illustrated by Richard Cuffari (1971)

The Loners (1972)

Maria's Mountain, illustrated by Barbara Bascove (1981)

Favorite Tales from Grimm, retelling; illustrated by Mercer Mayer (1982)

Annie on My Mind (1982, 1988)

Prisoner of Vampires, illustrated by Michele Chessare (1984)

Peace, O River (1986)

Lark in the Morning (1991)

My Sister, the Vampire (1992)

My Brother, the Werewolf (1995)

Dove and Sword: A Novel of Joan of Arc (1995)

Good Moon Rising (1996)

The Year They Burned the Books (1999)

Fours Crossing sequence

Fours Crossing (1981)

Watersmeet (1983)

The Door Between (1987)

Monster Hunters series

Case #1: Mystery of the Night Raiders (1987)

Case #2: Mystery of the Midnight Menace (1988)

Case #3: Mystery of the Secret Marks (1989)

Case #4: Mystery of the Kidnapped Kidnapper (1994)

Case #5: Mystery of the Watchful Witches (1994)

Short Story

"Parents' Night." In *Am I Blue? Coming Out from the Silence.* Edited by Marion Dane Bauer. New York: Harper-Collins, 1994, pp. 127–145.

Nonfiction

Berlin: City Split in Two (1971)

Vampires (1973)

Werewolves (1973)

Witches (1975)

Devils and Demons (1976)

Fun with Forecasting Weather (1977)

The Kids' Code and Cipher Book (1981)

Adaptations

What Happened in Marston, adapted for television as an "ABC Afterschool Special" titled *The Color of Friendship* (1981)

Annie on My Mind, adapted for radio and broadcast by the BBC (1992)

Garden, Nancy. "Annie on Trial: How It Feels to be the Author of a Challenged Book." *Voice of Youth Advocates,* June 1996.

WORKS ABOUT NANCY GARDEN

Chelton, Mary K. "VOYA Interview with Nancy Garden." In *The VOYA Reader.* Metuchen, N.J.: Scarecrow Press, 1990, pp. 270–274.

Daniel, Patricia L., and Vicki J. McEntire. "Rights of Passage: Preparing Gay and Lesbian Youth for Their Journey into Adulthood." In *Using Literature to Help Troubled Teenagers Cope with Family Issues.* Edited by Joan F. Kaywell. Westport, CT: Greenwood, 1999, pp. 193–224.

Gallo, Donald R., ed. Nancy Garden. In *Speaking for Ourselves, Too: More Autobiographical Sketches by Notable Authors of Books for Young Adults.* Urbana, IL: NCTE, 1993, pp. 70–72.

Kaywell, Joan F. Review of *Good Moon Rising* by Nancy Garden. In *ALAN Review,* spring 1997.

Mitchell, Judith N. "Loving Girls." *ALAN Review,* fall 1982, pp. 32–34.

Rich, Susan. "Nancy Garden." *Twentieth Century Young Adult Writers,* First Edition. Edited by Laura Standley Berger. Detroit, MI: St. James Press, 1994, pp. 233–234.

Sleator, William. "*Annie on My Mind* by Nancy Garden." In *Censored Books: Critical Viewpoints.* Scarecrow Press, 1993, pp. 80–86.

Critical Essays

Hile, Kevin S., and Diane Telgen, eds. *Something about the Author.* Detroit: Gale Research, vol. 77, 1994, pp. 69–72.

McMahon, Thomas, ed. *Authors and Artists for Young Adults.* Detroit: Gale Research, vol. 18, 1996, pp. 105–112.

Metzger. Linda, ed. *Contemporary Authors, New Revision Series.* Detroit: Gale Research, vol. 13, 1984, p. 203.

Morad, Deborah J., ed. *Children's Literature Review.* Detroit: Gale Research, vol. 51, 1999, pp. 57–83.

Nakamura, Joyce, ed. *Something about the Author.* Detroit: Gale Research, vol. 8, 1989, pp. 79–98.

How to Write to the Author

Nancy Garden
c/o Farrar, Straus & Giroux
19 Union Square West
New York, NY 10003

Mel Glenn

(1943–)

by Teri S. Lesesne

"My life is an open book," jokes Mel Glenn. Born in Zurich, Switzerland, on 10 May 1943, Glenn possesses a well-developed sense of humor. This ability to see the lighter side of life serves him well. Glenn is a veteran high school English teacher whose passion is the language of poetry. Glenn uses that passion to motivate people to read more poetry. He also uses unusual twists to breathe new life into his writing. From poems about a wide range of high school students and teachers, to a murder mystery told entirely in poems, to a poetry collection about a history teacher who takes his class hostage on the last day of school, Mel Glenn's writing attracts an audience of readers who desire stories about their own lives. That is exactly what Glenn provides, and he provides this in an unusual format: poetry. Welcome to Mel Glenn and "the poetry zone."

Quotations from Mel Glenn that are not attributed to a published source are from personal interviews conducted by the author of this article between March 1995 and March 1999 and are published here by permission of Mel Glenn.

The Poetry Zone

Glenn is not at all reluctant to talk about his work. In a series of interviews, he described his approach to writing and his writing habits in some detail. When his writing is going well, Glenn says, it is "like a sky burst; there is no awareness of the clock," (*Emergency Librarian,* p. 58). Writing is essential to Glenn, who believes that each person has a unique talent waiting to be developed. His development as a writer can be traced back to his childhood. Glenn recalls being inspired by his father, a biblical scholar, who frequently wrote articles in Yiddish. Glenn vividly remembers sitting and watching his father write. Later, putting ideas onto paper proved to be rewarding for Glenn as well. Features for his college newspaper reflected his easy sense of humor and provided him a showcase for his burgeoning writing talents. Fellow classmates would stop him to tell him how much they had enjoyed reading his latest offering. That is when Glenn discovered that writing had some extrinsic reward also. He began to branch out with his efforts. Fascinated with sports, Glenn realized that, even if he could not be an athlete, he could write about sporting events. He covered basketball games for New York University at Madison Square Garden. The power of writing was already well known to Glenn as a college student. Writing was to be a tool Glenn would turn to often in life. Later, during a stint in the Peace Corps, Glenn kept a daily journal. This early dedication to putting words on paper serves him well today in his poetry.

Glenn now sets goals for his writing, trying to write one or two poems a day, taking whatever time is necessary to get them right. He prefers the tactile sensation of using a pencil and paper and later transcribing his work onto his outmoded computer, a machine he calls a "typewriter with a thyroid problem." Much of this writing is done at night; his days are spent teaching high school English at the school he attended as a student. Occasionally, during those late nights, Glenn enters "the poetry zone," a place where time does not exist, where words seems to come freely, and where poems find their way onto the page.

Classroom Antics

Glenn's literary firstborn is *Class Dismissed! High School Poems* (1982), a collection of poems about students in a ficti-

extrinsic from the outside; not usually accompanying

The **Peace Corps,** established in 1961, is a volunteer program of the U.S. government. Volunteers work in developing countries to improve living conditions and to train the local people to do the work the volunteers perform, such as construction or agricultural tasks.

tactile able to be touched

tious high school. Black and white photographs by colleague and friend Michael J. Bernstein accompany selections about new cars, stepfathers, mental retardation, grades, baseball, and a myriad of other topics on the minds of the students who are the subjects of the poems. So realistic are the poems that frequently readers believe that all Mel Glenn has done is collect the writing of high school students and put them into a book. The photographs, readers will assert, are actual pictures of the students who have written the poems. This delicious confusion confirms the fact that Glenn manages to capture the voices of real-life teens, their problems, their hopes, their dreams, their frustrations, and their deepest feelings. Teens do not speak with ONE voice; rather readers will hear voices of students who are at the head of the class, students who struggle for decent grades, students with learning disabilities, and students for whom grades are meaningless. The high school students criticize teachers, criticize the school system, and criticize life in general because they see the flaws, the illogical, and the irrational in the world around them. Glenn gives voice to many who have never had that power before. Perhaps that is why this book remains one of his favorites to this day.

Class Dismissed! was soon followed by three more collections of poems about high school students: *Class Dismissed II: More High School Poems* (1986), *Back to Class* (1988), and *My Friend's Got This Problem, Mr. Candler: High School Poems* (1991). The formula that worked so well for the first book became the basic pattern for each successive book: black and white photographs accompany poems about students one might reasonably expect to meet in the hallways of a typical high school in any city in any state. Not content to simply write yet another collection, though, Glenn continued to hone his skills, to try new directions in each one.

hone sharpen

Class Dismissed II followed in the footsteps of its predecessor, giving voice to another group of students. *Back to Class* featured more poems about teachers as well as high school students. This collection is also organized a bit differently, with poems describing students' experiences during the course of a school day going from class to class. Readers can meet Robert Winograd, a teacher who longs to be mistaken for a big time baseball player, or Neil Pressman, a fine arts teacher whose favorite creation is his 6-year-old son. In each of their classes we hear from several students; those poems do not comment so much upon the content of the individual classes and teachers but about any and all things on their minds at the moment. Problems with school, parents, and peers are all possible subjects in Glenn's collections. Sometimes a student gains insight into his or her problems. More often, there is no resolution, no neat solving of problems. This open-ended quality mirrors real life when easy answers are not always available. Students can ponder their situations, worry about the future, or complain about the present. However, the brief glimpse Glenn provides readers does not give them answers; rather these poems raise more questions. What will happen to this student? Will he confront his fears? Will she find success? Part of what makes Glenn's collections interesting to read is this ability for the poems to generate discussion and debate. There is no ONE right answer. Instead, each person, each character, must find his or her own way in life.

Mr. Candler, the title character from *My Friend's Got This Problem, Mr. Candler,* is a guidance counselor. Glenn's choice of main character for this collection also dictated its organizational scheme: the voices we hear in this book are the voices of the students who come into the counselor's office over the course of a week. Therefore, the book is divided into five sections, one for each day of the school week. As in the case of *Back to Class,* Glenn adds some new voices. The voices of parents are the new ones heard here. Sometimes the parents are warm and supportive, sometimes overly critical. Seeing their presence alongside that of their children provides even more insight into the angst and anger, sorrow and celebration of life. For example, Matthew Egan describes his father as someone who is never satisfied with his performance as a student. Readers might be inclined to dismiss this complaint until they meet Mr. Egan a few pages later complaining to Mr. Candler about his son's measly 90 percent overall average. Seeing the two poems, poised as counterpoints, brings more clarity to the characters and makes them more realistic. Students come into the counseling office for a variety of reasons. Occasionally, they are there simply for a friendly chat. More often, there are problems they wish to discuss with Mr. Candler.

Glenn's reputation as a poet who knows well the world of teens was secure with these four volumes. It was time to head in a new direction, to try something new with his writing.

angst anxiety or anguish

Whodunit?

The path Glenn chose for his next endeavor was one not navigated by another poet before. In *Who Killed Mr. Chippendale? A Mystery in Poems* (1996), Glenn presented readers with a murder mystery told entirely in poems. Mr. Chippendale is a high school English teacher, revered by some students, tolerated by others, and despised by a few. Each day, Chippendale runs along the school's track in an effort to stave off the middle age paunch. One day, a shot rings out and Chippendale falls to the ground dead; a bullet has nearly torn off his head. Who could have hated the teacher so much as to wish him harm? How will the students and faculty of the school respond to this tragedy? Glenn explores the answers to those questions and others in blank verse. Readers can read the official statement issued by the school principal, a person intent on keeping the situation out of the papers as long as possible. There is a mysterious character clad in a red hooded sweatshirt. Is he the murderer or simply a red herring? Glenn keeps the reader guessing until the end of the "novel." *Who Killed Mr. Chippendale?* was nominated for the prestigious Edgar Allan Poe Award for best juvenile mystery. This award, presented by the Mystery Writers of America, is given annually to works for adolescents and adults. Glenn felt honored even to receive the nomination, the first ever for a book of poems. The book was named to the American Library Association's Best Books for Young Adults list as well. With this critical praise and these nominations for awards, Glenn's writing had taken him in a new direction. What was the inspiration for such a change of course? Glenn explains that the beginning of the idea for this novel came from the opening scene of the movie *The Big Chill* in which somebody is being prepared for his funeral. The entire movie centers on a group of characters and their relationship with the deceased. Despite the multitude of characters, all of the story lines weave into one cohesive narrative. That is what Glenn strove to do in *Mr. Chippendale*. So, a new course was set. Where would Glenn venture next?

paunch protruding belly

blank verse poetry written in unrhymed iambic pentameter; each line alternates between unstressed and stressed syllables for ten syllables

red herring something that distracts attention from the main issue

The Big Chill (1983) starred Tom Berenger, Glenn Close, Jeff Goldblum, William Hurt, and Kevin Kline as former college radicals who reunite for a friend's funeral.

cohesive sticking together

Pushing the Envelope

Enter Room 114 in *The Taking of Room 114: A Hostage Drama in Poems* (1997). It is the last day of school and students are signing yearbooks and making plans for the summer. One by one they file into the last classes of their high school careers. One is Mr. Wiedermeyer's history class. As students approach the class, they notice some things are different. The door to the classroom is locked, and Mr. Wiedermeyer has a gun. Suddenly, instead of dreams about college and the future, students in this history class are faced with their own mortality. Mr. Wiedermeyer shows no sign of releasing the students any time soon, despite the efforts of administration and police. Why he has decided to commit this crime is not apparent at first. Nor are the students particularly interested in Mr. Wiedermeyer's motives; each is much more concerned with surviving this hostage situation. As they consider what has brought them to this point in time, readers are able to see these students as real characters who have grown and changed in their four years of high school. The organization for this volume presents a poem about each of the hostages and then flashes back with each student to their freshman, sophomore, and junior years. Mr. Wiedermeyer's character and the motivation for his unusual actions are also revealed through a series of poems, notes he sends through his locked door to the authorities. Once again, suspense is provided in great doses. Will Wiedermeyer injure or kill any students? Will he manage to survive? What will happen when and if the hostages are released? Glenn tells the entire story, giving readers insights into the minds and hearts of his characters. Perhaps, then, this is the hallmark of Glenn's work.

New Directions and Challenges

In *Jump Ball: A Basketball Season in Poems* (1997), Glenn turns to one of his other passions: basketball. This novel in poetic form opens with a weatherman forecasting a severe winter storm and advising listeners to avoid travel if at all possible. Then, the story reverts to an earlier time as eager Michael Jordan wannabes try out for the Tower High School Tigers' basketball team. In addition to hearing from the hopefuls, readers meet some of the local townspeople who are rabid fans, students who are involved with the team as manager's or cheerleaders, and a reporter discussing the Tigers' season. As the story progresses, readers learn that there has been an accident on those icy roads predicted by the weatherman: a school bus has skidded off the road. There are injuries, and students are being transported to area hospitals. Not all of the players whom readers have come to know in the poems will survive. Once again Glenn makes readers care about what will happen to the members of the team. They are not merely characters in a book; they are teens one might meet in any school in any town. This ability to create multidimensional characters who seem to live and breathe off the page is another defining characteristic of Mel Glenn's poetry.

Words of Encouragement

How can one coalesce Glenn's wide range of works into a few simple sentences? The best answer came directly from the source. Glenn points readers to a line from one of his favorite plays, *Death of a Salesman* (1949), by Arthur Miller, in which Willy Loman's wife cries out, "Attention must be paid." Teenagers, Glenn asserts, cannot be lumped into one group simply by nature of their age or maturity. Rather, others must learn to listen to all of the unique voices of teens, people who have "different concerns, problems, and aspirations." It is this ability to listen to all of the voices of the thousands of students who have passed through his classes which are most evident in Glenn's poems. Giving voice to this wide variety of voices is not easy, but Glenn still sits down every day to find that poem or two which will give voice to yet another character, a voice which will tell yet another story. Readers have much to look forward to as Glenn continues to push the envelope, nudging poetry out of its pigeonhole and thrusting it into the hands of more willing readers.

coalesce to come together as one

There is an article about Arthur Miller later in this volume.

Selected Bibliography

WORKS BY MEL GLENN

Novels for Young Adults
   One Order to Go (1984)
   Play-By-Play (1986)
   Squeeze Play: A Baseball Story (1989)

Poetry
   Class Dismissed! High School Poems (1982)
   Class Dismissed II: More High School Poems (1986)
   Back to Class (1988)

My Friend's Got This Problem Mr. Candler: High School Poems (1991)

Who Killed Mr. Chippendale? A Mystery in Poems (1996)

Jump Ball: A Basketball Season in Poems (1997)

The Taking of Room 114: A Hostage Drama in Poems (1997)

Foreign Exchange: A Mystery in Poems (1999)

How to Write to the Author

Mel Glenn
c/o Dutton Children's Books
345 Hudson Street
New York, NY 10014

WORKS ABOUT MEL GLENN

Hedblad, Alan, ed. *Something About the Author.* Detriot: Gale Researh, 1997, vol. 93, pp. 67–70.

Lesesne, Teri S. "The Poetry Zone According to Mel Glenn." *Emergency Librarian,* vol. 25, 1998, pp. 58–59.

Lesesne, Teri S. An Interview with Mel Glenn. In *Journal of Adolescent and Adult Literacy,* March 1997, pp. 502–506.

Adele Griffin

(1970–)

by Michael Cart

Ask novelist Adele Griffin if she wanted to be a writer when she was a girl and she doesn't hesitate before answering "No. I always used to say I was going to become an actress."

With a little gentle prodding from an interviewer, however, she admits—a bit ruefully—that her family might not agree. "Everyone points to this: every year from age eight to thirteen I wrote very long novels for my grandparents. I'd work on them all year until they were all over one hundred pages long. My grandmother still embarrasses me by bringing them out from time to time," she laughs.

Books were clearly an important part of Griffin's childhood not only as things to write but also as things to read. "No childhood memory is brighter to me than the beginning of school vacation," she recalls in an undated Hyperion promotional brochure. "My mom encouraged reading and she would take me on a special trip to our local bookstore and help me to select my summer reading. I went straight for the subject I

Quotations from Adele Griffin that are not attributed to a published source are from a telephone interview conducted by the author of this article on 2 March 1999 and are published here by permission of Adele Griffin.

Cherry Ames was the main character of a mystery series written by Helen Wells and Julie Tatham between 1943 and 1968. Cherry is a nurse.

The *Bobbsey Twins* and *Nancy Drew* series were created by the Stratemeyer syndicate. There is an article about Edward Stratemeyer in volume 3.

protagonist the main character of a literary work

A Little Princess is the story of a wealthy young girl in boarding school. When her father dies, she loses her money and becomes a servant to her former classmates. In ***The Lord of the Flies***, a group of schoolboys stranded on an island form a lawless society.

freelance work done independently, not for an individual employer

liked best: girls. I leaned toward princesses and orphans and was delighted if I found a book where the heroine was a combination of both."

Griffin was also an avid reader of series books, borrowing a stack from the public library every Friday. The Bobbsey Twins, Cherry Ames, and Nancy Drew were all favorites (not coincidentally, Nancy Drew is protagonist Lane's favorite reading in Griffin's first novel *Rainy Season* [1996]).

Other favorites? "I loved *A Little Princess* [by Frances Hodgson Burnett], which was sort of the standard girl's book but I also loved *Lord of the Flies* [by William Golding]! I went back and forth from monitored girls to lawless boys."

But, she recalls, "it was the voices of those storybook girls that have stayed with me. They speak from the secret place of childhood, a place I try to recapture in my own writing."

A Place to Recapture

Adele Griffin was born on 29 July 1970 in Philadelphia, Pennsylvania, the oldest of three children. Her father was an Army officer (like Lane's father in *Rainy Season*) and the family moved fairly often. Griffin recalls living in Rhode Island, California, Washington, D.C., and North Carolina but says that such routine relocation had no particular emotional impact on her childhood. More important is the fact that her parents divorced when Griffin was fifteen and she and her younger brothers, Robert and Geoffrey, moved with their mother, Priscilla Sands Watson, back to Philadelphia. There Griffin attended a private girls' school, as does Danny, the protagonist of her second novel *Split Just Right* (1997). And, like Danny, Adele was "a faculty child," her mother being the school's assistant principal. She went on to the University of Pennsylvania, where she graduated in 1993 with a major in English. Shortly after graduation she moved to New York. Why the Big Apple? "I decided that cities were good, especially since I'm such a bad driver. So I thought, why not the ultimate city?"

Since arriving in New York, Griffin has worked in publishing as a freelance reader for a major children's book publisher. She evaluates manuscripts that range the publishing spectrum—from picture books to young adult novels.

A Comfortable Place to Start

Has working in publishing had an impact on her writing? "I would say so," she answers. "Being in publishing gave me a chance to rediscover the classics. And it's put me in touch with the editorial process and with editorial discussions—it's a very lucky job that way." And then there is the reading of all those manuscripts. "Out of that," she says, "naturally grew the obvious 'I can do that . . . maybe!' thought."

She actually began writing "about a year" after she started working in publishing. "In mid-1995," she recalls, "I was working on a draft of *Rainy Season* when I met Margaret Raymo [of Houghton Mifflin]."

The meeting was serendipitous, because Raymo became the book's editor and *Rainy Season* was published in 1996.

"It was a comfortable place to start," Griffin says of her first novel, "though when I began, I didn't think it would actually turn into a book. It was more of an intense experiment. The book started as undeveloped feelings and came out in all these little pieces." When these "little pieces" began to come together, Griffin recalls, "I was so taken by surprise that I finished the book."

Though foreign to most readers, the novel's richly realized setting—the Panama Canal Zone—was familiar to the author. Following her parents' divorce, her father had settled in Central America, and Griffin visited him there as a teenager during school breaks. But more important to an understanding and appreciation of Griffin's novels, *Rainy Season* introduced themes that would appear in all of her later works: family, the psychological impact of emotional loss, secrets, and—perhaps most significant of all—the interplay of intense sibling relationships. "There's a level of trust between siblings that has to be very strong." Griffin asserts. "It's rooted in the strength of that long relationship."

In *Rainy Season* the loss is the death of Lane Beck's older sister, Emily, who has been killed in a car crash before the action of the novel begins. By mutual consent the Beck family keeps this a secret from their circle of acquaintances in the Canal Zone. Lane, who tells the story in her own first-person voice, keeps the death a secret from the reader too, referring to Emily as her former babysitter.

"I think of families as secret keepers," Griffin muses. "The family kinship is unique among relationships." Emily's death

serendipitous relating to the phenomenon of finding things when one is not seeking them

theme central message about life in a literary work

first-person the position or perspective of someone inside the story, using the pronoun "I"

chronic constant over a long period of time

has had a devastating emotional impact on Lane, who is twelve, and on her younger brother, Charlie, who is eleven. In Lane this is manifested as chronic anxiety. "I'm scared of everything," she says (p. 186). Charlie, on the other hand, is fearless and nothing is too scary for him to try. Unfortunately his behavior is becoming increasingly reckless and self-destructive. It will take another devastating accident to start the two siblings talking about their sister's death and with communication—and the breaking of the family's bond of silence—comes the promise of healing.

Griffin acknowledges that she and her brother Robert, who is only fifteen months younger than she is provided the real life models for Lane and Charlie. "Robert says he isn't Charlie," Griffin acknowledges. "But," she adds, laughing, "he doesn't have the last word, since I'm the author!"

The pattern of their relationship—in which the older sibling is the more parental and the younger, the more unstable—recurs in the brothers Cliff and Rock in *Sons of Liberty* (1997) and the sisters Holland and Geneva in *The Other Shepards* (1998). Geneva, though the younger, resembles Lane in that she reacts to the loss of her siblings by retreating into a world of fear and phobias. "Nobody's scared like me," she says (p. 13). This reaction is also borrowed from real life.

phobia an exaggerated or illogical fear of a particular object or situation

"Mine is a very phobic family," Griffin candidly acknowledges, "especially the women. It's a personal trait but shared by so many that I don't think I'm revealing anything too personal." This family characteristic manifests itself not only in her youthful characters but also—in *Sons of Liberty*—in the adult character of the Kindle brothers' mother, whose agoraphobia plagues her and perplexes and angers Rock.

Aside from Charlie in *Rainy Season,* the character in Griffin's novels who most defies this trait is Rock's best friend Liza. Fearless in the face of her stepfather's battering (which she tries to keep secret), she finally decides to run away from home and—with the help of the Kindle brothers—disappears into the anonymous city streets of New Haven, Connecticut.

anonymous lacking individuality or distinction

"I approached her very much from the outside," Griffin says. "She's very brave—nothing I'd personally understand nor is she modeled on any particular person. But there's always a girl in fifth to seventh grade who stands out because she's disruptive. You stand in awe of them . . . but very far away."

Griffin observes, "that type of character is always very satisfying to write." And to read about, too, apparently. "When I go into schools now, there's such a response to Liza—I hadn't anticipated this. Kids want to know what happened to her."

Being a Faculty Kid

After the intensely emotional experience of writing *Rainy Season*, Griffin says she needed a change of pace. Happily it was at this time that she met another editor, Donna Bray.

"We talked about books we had found to be funny," Griffin recalls, "and I started writing *Split Just Right* hoping that Donna would find it funny." Presumably she did, because she became the book's editor and it was published in 1997.

In her second novel Griffin continues her thematic exploration of family but this time, with a much lighter tone. Danny (short for "Dandelion"!) and her larger-than-life actress/drama teacher mother, Susan, comprise a two-person family. Danny's parents were divorced when she was still a baby—or so her mother has led her to believe. It will turn out that here again, the truth is hiding behind a closely guarded family secret.

Danny is a faculty kid, able to attend the tony Bradshaw School for Girls tuition free only because her mother is a member of the faculty. When her mother loses her part-time job as a television actress, however, their existence takes a precarious turn. Susan finds another part-time job as a waitress (keeping this a secret from her daughter), while Danny redoubles her efforts to win the thousand dollar-first prize in a writing contest. This in turn leads to a comic misunderstanding that will ultimately reveal the truth about her father.

Split Just Right is notable for having, in Susan, one of the two most vividly realized adult characters in Griffin's four novels—the other being George Kindle, the father in *Sons of Liberty*. Unlike George, however, Susan is altogether engaging and endearing in her theatricality, her love for her daughter, and her determination to preserve her family of "just two people."

"I wanted to create the feeling that this was an improvised family," Griffin observes, "that Danny's mother was going at it alone and that she was creating everything out of nothing. She took every opportunity and made it into as much as she could—that's how I've always perceived my own mom."

tony aristocratic in style or manner

precarious uncertain and potentially dangerous

Sons of Liberty

Griffin's third novel, a National Book Award finalist and an ALA Best Book for Young Adults, represents several significant departures. While continuing her thematic exploration of family issues, it is the only one of her four books to feature a male protagonist—Rock Kindle—and the only one that is not told in the first-person voice and the present tense. "Maybe I was being overly cautious writing in the third person," she says, "but to me 'I' is always the voice of a girl."

As for her departure from the present tense, one supposes it was a further—though subconscious—act of distancing. She would, after all, return to its use in her fourth novel, *The Other Shepards,* which has female protagonists.

Be that as it may, this distance in no way diminishes the emotional immediacy of this beautifully written and deeply felt novel. Thirteen-year-old Rock's struggle to come to terms with his father's tyranny and his own conflicted feelings about personal liberty completely engage the reader.

Sons of Liberty is also a wonderful example of how a writer's creative imagination transforms personal experience of emotional loss into art. In the end Rock, his mother, and his siblings stage their own personal revolution by climbing into the family car and driving away, leaving the martinet father behind. In Griffin's personal life, the situation was reversed: "My dad walked out on our family many times," she explains. "There were enough chaotic false starts that my brothers and mom and I lived in perpetual limbo. Getting past this loss and reshaping our family was a critical part of my adolescence."

Clearly the Kindles are taking their own first steps toward getting past loss. They are reshaping themselves as a different—and one hopes—more functional family.

After Sons

"After *Sons of Liberty,*" Griffin laughs, "I wrote this terrible story that no one ever saw; it was just so pretentious and awful that it got me back to thinking about what I might have wanted to read myself as a twelve year old. I sat down and made a list of all my favorite things in books: sisters, ghost stories, mysterious characters, city stories, stories containing

third person the position or perspective of someone outside the story

tyranny oppressive power

martinet strict disciplinarian

travel to a different and strange place, something unbearably tragic—all of this gave me *The Other Shepards,* a story I would have given to my twelve-year-old self as a present!"

Set in New York's Greenwich Village, this is another novel exploring how one family deals—or very nearly fails to deal— with overwhelming loss. It is the story of how the death of Holland and Geneva Shepard's three older siblings—the other Shepards of the title—haunts the two girls and their parents. The entire family is living a half-life in the shadow of this loss when a mysterious young woman named Annie shows up one day to begin the long-overdue process of healing.

Though there are clues to Annie's identity—some more obvious on a second reading—it is not until the end of the book that her real identity is revealed, though with sufficient ambiguity that many readers will conclude she is a ghostly incarnation of Holland and Geneva's older sister, Elizabeth. In fact, it is Griffin's intent that Annie should exist only in the girls' imagination, an invention of their psychological need for emotional healing.

ambiguity having the quality of being understood in more than one way

Be that as it may, Griffin agrees with an interviewer's suggestion that Annie is also something of an American Mary Poppins, a figure who appears out of nowhere and transforms a family by providing unusual and unexpected adventures. Annie has more heart than Mary Poppins, however, and helps restore the girls' capacity to feel. Sadly, though, it appears that their parents will continue to live an emotionally stunted life, having—as Geneva says—"used up all [their] love" on the other Shepards (p. 50).

Each of Adele Griffin's four novels is wonderfully individual yet all have in common an element that Griffin herself describes eloquently: "They are all autobiographical in the sense that their characters move from a state of baffled inertia to a kind of resolve; they will deal with loss in such a way that it might be absorbed into a more appropriate place so its enormity doesn't suffocate their future."

autobiographical related to the author's own life

inertia tendency to remain still or to avoid change

Clearly Griffin's own future as an author is filled with bright promise. Though her career is a scant three years old, she has already established herself as a major figure in young adult literature, a writer of great creative power and a particular gift for transforming human experience into unforgettable art. If *The Other Shepards* is a gift to herself, all of her books are wonderful gifts to her growing body of readers.

If you like Adele Griffin, you might also like Sharon Creech and Karen Hesse.

Selected Bibliography

WORKS BY ADELE GRIFFIN

Novels

Rainy Season (1996)

Sons of Liberty (1997)

Split Just Right (1997)

The Other Shepards (1998)

WORKS ABOUT ADELE GRIFFIN

Cooper, Ilene, Review of *The Other Shepards.* In *Booklist,* August 1998, p. 1999.

Edwards, Carol A. Review of *Split Just Right.* In *School Library Journal,* June 1997, p. 117.

Flynn, Kitty. Review of *Sons of Liberty.* In *Horn Book,* January/February 1998, p. 72.

Guarria, Carrie A. Review of *The Other Shepards.* In *School Library Journal,* September 1998, p. 203.

Lockwood, Lucinda. Review of *Rainy Season.* In *School Library Journal,* November 1996, p. 104.

Vasilakis, Nancy. Review of *Rainy Season.* In *Horn Book,* March/April 1997, p. 198.

Vasilakis, Nancy. Review of *Split Just Right.* In *Horn Book,* July/August 1997, p. 455.

Weischedel, Elaine Fort. Review of *Sons of Liberty.* In *School Library Journal,* November 1997, p. 118.

How to Write to the Author

Adele Griffin

c/o Hyperion Books for Children

114 Fifth Avenue

New York, NY 10011

Jim Haskins

(1941–)

by Suzanne Elizabeth Reid

As a prolific writer of more than one hundred works of nonfiction, the man Jim Haskins is often overshadowed by the volume of his writing and the impact of his subjects on modern culture. Born on 19 September 1941, to Henry and Julia (Brown) Haskins in the rural town of Demopolis, Alabama, James S. Haskins absorbed the values of literature and learning from his family and community early in his life. From his Aunt Cindy's unique versions of traditional European folktales where the Three Little Pigs met Hansel and Gretel, he learned originality, and from the storytelling of the black community, segregated from white mainstream educational and cultural institutions, he learned to listen to the cadence of language, particularly the African American voice which would inform his adult writing. Although stories of voodoo, magic, and make-believe abounded, and later appeared as subjects in his work, Haskins' early concern was sifting fact from fiction, information from story. In an essay for *Something About the Author Autobiography Series* (1987), Haskins explains: "I was born into a society in which blacks were in deep trouble if they for-

prolific marked by producing many works

segregated separated by discriminatory means because of race, class, or ethnic group

cadence rhythm in music and poetry

voodoo African religion involving ancestor worship and the use of charms and spells

got about the real world. For if they daydreamed and were caught off-guard, they could pay dearly" (p. 199). In the world of Haskins' youth, formal education provided about the only access to mainstream power; students succeeded in schools by using the language of facts and information.

Preference for Facts

Haskins' mother encouraged her son's interest in education, first by purchasing an encyclopedia series, one volume at a time, from the local supermarket. African Americans were barred from using the public library, but when Mrs. Haskins' white employer learned about James's intellectual ambitions, she checked out books for him on her own card every week. While this wide assortment of literature helped Haskins to develop his literary skills, his first loyalties remained to the language and tone of his first reading, the encyclopedia. In the segregated public schools Haskins attended, the teachers commanded great respect from the community for their devotion to educating their students beyond the scope of the outdated equipment, texts, and meager supplies provided by the county. Haskins remembers that his teachers made a point to emphasize the valuable role that black Americans played in U.S. history, a point which has become a major focus of his writing.

The **civil rights movement** of the 1950s, 1960s, and 1970s was a political campaign to gain civil rights for all people, particularly African Americans, regardless of sex, ethnicity, or color. Civil rights are the freedoms and rights that a person may have as a member of a community, state, or country, including the right to receive fair and equal treatment under the law, and the freedoms of speech, religion, and the press.

Participation in Civil Rights Movement

During his adolescent years, Haskins moved to Boston with his mother where he attended the academically challenging Boston Latin School. Although he was lonely among the largely white student population, he was a good student. After graduation, he entered Alabama State University in Montgomery, Alabama, where he became involved in the emerging civil rights movement, led by the young and charismatic Martin Luther King, Jr. Although his own involvement was nonviolent, Haskins was arrested during a march in downtown Montgomery and expelled from the university. After earning a degree in psychology from Georgetown University in Washington, D.C., in 1960, Haskins returned to Alabama State to complete a second bachelor's degree in history. He then went to the University of New Mexico where he earned a graduate degree in social psychology.

charismatic possessing extraordinary personal charm

A Teaching Career

After a brief foray in the business world as a stock broker in New York City, Haskins found his true calling as a teacher and writer. His classroom teaching has taken him from his first job in Harlem (1966–1968), to the New School for Social Research (1970–1972), to the Staten Island Community College of the City University of New York (1970–1977), to the University of Florida at Gainesville, where he has been professor of English since 1977.

Haskins' first teaching job was the source of his first publication, *Diary of a Harlem School Teacher* (1969), which records his daily concerns and frustrations of teaching at P.S. 92, where teachers often found it easier to let the children run wild than to deal with their overwhelming problems. One student told about an aunt who died alone in her apartment and was found with a leg chewed off by her German shepherd who had not been fed. Another student was shot to death on a neighboring street. By the end of the year, only nine of Haskins' original fifteen students remained in his class. Haskins ends his journal with a heartbreaking description of these students, ranging in age from nine to eleven and all labeled mentally retarded. How much of their potential may have been blighted by the grinding poverty, the daily dangers, and the overwhelming confusion of living in a drug-infested, broken-down ghetto? In his review of the book in the 8 February 1970 *New York Times Book Review,* critic Ronald Gross called this "the saddest book on education I have ever read, and its truth is in its sadness. . . . [the book is] a weapon—cold, blunt, painful" (pp. 6–7). Haskins himself had tried experimental methods, using newspaper articles and other current materials for reading texts to such an extent that his class reading scores were raised. But, he still sensed the heavy oppression his students faced and called for radical change in the traditional school system which has failed, and still does fail, to adequately serve residents of American inner cities.

Writing for Young Adults

After the publication of this powerful book, Haskins was invited to write books for young adults. Eager to fill the voids he had felt as a child without informational books about black people and their histories, Haskins began his prolific career as

Martin Luther King, Jr. (1929–1968) was the most important leader of the civil rights movement in the United States during the 1950s and 1960s. He stressed nonviolence as a means of resisting discrimination, but was often the target of violence, finally becoming the victim of an assassin on 4 April 1968.

foray short excursion into something outside one's accustomed field

blighted decayed; ruined

ghetto part of a city in which members of a minority group live

undergird to form the foundation of

racism hatred for or intolerance of another race

"I have a dream that one day this nation will rise up and live out the true meaning of its creed: 'We hold these truths to be self-evident; that all men are created equal. . . .' And when this happens . . . all of God's children . . . will be able to joins hands and sing . . . 'Free at last! Free at last! Thank God Almighty, we are free at last!' "
—from "I Have a Dream" speech

an author with *Resistance: Profiles in Nonviolence* (1970), which describes the history of passive resistance up to Martin Luther King, Jr., and *A Piece of the Power: Four Black Mayors* (1972). Fueled by an avid curiosity, an excellent educational background which allowed him to explore a number of unrelated topics, and the will to spend many hours researching new areas, the teacher/author soon found himself writing histories and biographies about witchcraft, voodoo, business, theater, sports, entertainment, civil rights, and economic and social issues. In all his books, Haskins uses details and facts about historical events, but he also includes information about individual participants and their backgrounds to show his readers the whole picture.

Fighting Prejudice by Erasing Ignorance

In *Who Are the Handicapped?* (1978), Haskins explains how the natural curiosity of children about physical differences is a healthy attitude which should be encouraged rather than hushed up. Prejudice is caused by not knowing about a physical difference or an ethnic or racial difference. Haskins believes that learning as much as possible about other people could erase prejudice. Ignoring or avoiding people or situations which are unfamiliar causes separation, misunderstanding, and loneliness. This philosophy of fighting prejudice with education undergirds all of Haskins' writing; his best books are full of individual details and facts organized to help his readers understand how they fit in a larger historical pattern. His style is straightforward, concise, and efficient; he lets readers draw their own conclusion from the information he provides.

One excellent example is *The March on Washington* (1993), a lucid account of perhaps one of the greatest days in U.S. history, when 250,000 citizens gathered in an orderly peaceful protest against the injustice of racism. Haskins places this day in the context of civil rights movements from 1909 to 1990, describing the organization, the competition among participants, the inspiring words of the "I Have a Dream" speech by Martin Luther King, Jr., and the drudgery of cleaning up afterward. He provides the whole story with inspiring and intriguing detail. Other works documenting the struggle for civil equality include *Resistance: Profiles in Nonviolence, Ralph Bunche: A Most Reluctant Hero* (1974), *I Have a*

Dream: The Life and Words of Martin Luther King (1992), *The Day Martin Luther King, Jr. Was Shot: A Photo History of the Civil Rights Movement* (1992), and *I Am Rosa Parks* (1997) in conjunction with Rosa Parks herself.

Haskins also writes about other ethnic groups. *The New Americans: Vietnamese Boat People* (1980) and *The New Americans: Cuban Boat People* (1982) explore the struggles of immigrants escaping lands troubled by political unrest and poverty, who are often disappointed to find rejection and un-employment after their dangerous and exhausting trip. *The Filipino Nation: A Concise History of the Philippines* (1982), a three-volume series, traces the fascinating progress of a coun-try dominated by several foreign cultures. In the Count Your Way series of more than fifteen volumes, Haskins uses the numbers from one through ten written in different languages as a basis for historical and cultural information about areas in-cluding China (1987), Russia (1987), the Arabian countries (1987), Africa (1989), India (1990), Greece (1996), and Brazil (1996), all published by Carolrhoda. On the first page of *Count Your Way Through the Arab World,* Haskins explains how Arabic is the language spoken in twenty-two countries, mostly Islamic. The remainder of the book provides short pas-sages about Bedouins, folktales, the Koran, praying and a prayer clock, camels, the Kaaba in Mecca, eight ways to define your cousins, the Muslim market, and sand dunes. The reader learns all this information, which is illustrated by Dana Gustafson, and also learns to count to ten in Arabic! The other books are just as varied in their subject matter.

Biographies

Haskins is perhaps best known for his biographies. He has written about numerous African American leaders in a variety of fields. His books trace the lives of writer Langston Hughes (1973) and politicians Adam Clayton Powell (1974); Shirley Chisholm (1975); Malcom X (1975); Barbara Jordan (1977); Andrew Young (1979); Thurgood Marshall (1992); Colin Pow-ell (1992); Bayard Rustin (1997); and Pinckney Benton Stewart Pinchback (1973), the first black governor. Haskins celebrates the toughness and determination of African Americans in his many books about entertainers. He writes about Diana Ross of the Supremes (1980); dancer Katherine Dunham (1982); Donna Summer (1983); Bill Cosby (1988); Richard Pryor

Ralph Bunche (1904–1971) was the director of the Trustee-ship Division of the United Nations and an American statesman. In 1950 he became the first African American to win the Nobel Prize for Peace.

Rosa Parks (1913–) is an African-American woman who refused to give up her seat on a bus to a white passen-ger in Montgomery, Alabama, in 1955. Her refusal helped bring about the civil rights movement that led to the desegregation of buses.

Bedouins nomadic Arabs

Koran sacred book of Muslims

The **Kaaba in Mecca** is the most sacred shrine of Islam. Mus-lims everywhere turn toward the Kaaba when they pray.

The movie *The Cotton Club* stars Richard Gere, Diane Lane, and Gregory Hines.

Scatman Crothers (1910–1986) was one of the first African-American entertainers to work in white-only clubs. He also acted in many movies, including *One Flew Over the Cuckoo's Nest* (1975) and *The Shining* (1980).

(1984); Lena Horne (1983); Nat King Cole (1990), Queen of the Blues Dinah Washington (1987); Bill Robinson, also known as Mr. Bojangles (1988); and Spike Lee (1997). One of Haskins' most famous books, *The Cotton Club* (1977) is the basis of the movie *The Cotton Club* (1984), which portrayed the irony of blacks performing in clubs where they were not allowed as guests. *Black Dance in America: A History Through Its People* (1990) traces the history of African dance beginning with the horrible practice of "dancing the slaves" on shipboard to keep them healthy before their sale in the Americans to the traditional steps and moves that so deeply affected all American dancing. *Scatman: An Authorized Biography of Scatman Crothers* (1991), written with Helen Crothers, details the incredibly mean-spirited walls of abuse and insult which African Americans had to pierce in the beginning of the twentieth century. Often Haskins' research about African Americans before the 1950s was difficult, because earlier journalists and historians considered blacks too unimportant to write about—like cats and dogs. Much information about African American life has been retained more through oral histories than by written record, and Haskins had to spend many hours listening to people whose lives were somehow connected to these earlier figures.

Haskins has written relatively few books about sports heroes, because their stories are already known, and he wanted to introduce other kinds of role models for young people. Those he did write include a survey, *From Lew Alcindor to Kareem Abdul Jabbar* (1972), and biographies about soccer star Pele (1976) and basketball superstars Julius Irving (1975), George McGinnis (1978), and "Magic" Earvin Johnson (1981; revised in 1988).

Exploring a Wide Range of Topics

tenet a principle generally accepted as true

Creole the speech of white people descended from early French or Spanish settlers of the Gulf states

Haskins' range of knowledge is tremendous. As editor of several series, he is able to explore other areas of expertise. The *Hippocrene Great Religions of the World* (1987–1992) differentiates the tenets and the history of various denominations. The *Hippocrene African Language Concise Dictionaries* (1997) includes Haitian Creole and Yoruba. The Black Star Biography Series (1998) underlines his commitment to record the contributions of African-Americans to history. Another series, *Black Eagles: African Americans in Aviation* (1995,

1997) tells about little-known pioneers such as Eugene Bullard, a hero of the French Foreign Legion during World War I, and Dr. Mae C. Jemison, the first female African American astronaut.

Awards and Honors

Haskins has received many honors for his writing, including the *Washington Post* Children's Book Guild Award for the body of his work. He has won several Coretta Scott King awards and honors for individual works, including *The Story of Stevie Wonder* (1976); *Lena Horne;* and *Black Dance in America: A History Through Its People.* He also earned the prestigious Carter G. Woodson award for the series *Black Music in America: A History Through Its People* (1987), as well as for single volumes such as *The March on Washington* and *The Harlem Renaissance* (1996). Other honors include the American Society of Composers, Authors, and Publishers—Deems Taylor Award for *Scott Joplin: The Man Who Made Ragtime Educational Philosophy* (1980).

In *Separate But Not Equal: The Dream and the Struggle* (1998) Haskins records the struggle of African Americans to obtain opportunities for education that are equal to citizens in the majority. Fully detailed and quietly dramatic, his account steadily builds toward the last page when he reminds us that although "separate but unequal schools have been unconstitutional for 43 years . . . in many areas of the nation, schools remain separate and unequal." His diagnosis about the adequacy of the American educational system reiterates the disappointment of his first book, *Diary of a Harlem School Teacher.* Haskins continues to use his writing to bring "undeservedly obscure" (National Council of Teachers of English lecture, 1997) heroes out of the shadows, fighting the kinds of ignorance which cause fear, apathy, and racism, and teaching through writing what has not yet been achieved in the classroom.

Selected Bibliography

WORKS BY JIM HASKINS

Diary of a Harlem Schoolteacher (1969; 1979)

Babe Ruth and Hank Aaron: The Home Run Kings (1974)

Yoruba an African language spoken in southwestern Nigeria and in parts of Benin and Togo

reiterate to repeat

apathy lack of emotion; indifference

If you enjoy biographies and other nonfiction books like Jim Haskins', you might also enjoy the work of Russell Freedman, Nat Hentoff, and Milton Meltzer.

Pele: A Biography (1976)

The Cotton Club (1977; 1984; 1994)

Who Are the Handicapped? (1978)

The New Americans: Vietnamese Boat People (1980)

Break Dancing (1985)

Diana Ross: Star Supreme (1985)

Black Music in America: A History Through Its People (1987)

Count Your Way Through the Arab World (1987)

Bill Cosby America's Most Famous Father (1988)

Mr. Bojangles: The Biography of Bill Robinson (1988)

Count Your Way Through Africa (1989)

Sports Great Magic Johnson (1989; 1992)

The Autobiography of Rosa Parks, with Rosa Parks (1990)

Black Dance in America: A History Through Its People (1990)

The Day Martin Luther King, Jr. Was Shot: A Photo History of the Civil Rights Movement (1992)

One More River to Cross: The Story of Twelve Black Americans (1992)

The March on Washington (1993)

Hippocrene Guide to Black New York (1994)

Black Eagles: African Americans in Aviation (1995)

Count Your Way Through Brazil, with Kathleen Benson (1996)

The Harlem Renaissance (1996)

Bayard Rustin: Behind the Scenes of the Civil Rights Movement (1997)

WORKS ABOUT JIM HASKINS

Brown, Jerry. *Clearing in the Thicket: An Alabama Humanities Reader.* Macon, Ga.: Mercer University Press, 1985.

Dear, Pamela S., ed. "James S. Haskins." *Contemporary Authors: New Revision Series.* Detroit: Gale Research, 1998, vol. 48, pp. 213–220.

Fader, Ellen, Review of *The March on Washington* In *Horn Book,* August 1993, pp. 477–478.

Gross, Ronald. Review of *Diary of a Harlem Schoolteacher.* In *New York Times Book Review,* 8 February 1970, pp. 6–7.

Sarkissian, Adele, ed. "James S. Haskins." In *Something About the Author Autobiography Series.* Detroit: Gale Research, 1987, vol. 4, pp. 197–209.

Senick, Gerald J., ed. "James S. Haskins." *Children's Literature Review.* Detroit: Gale Research, 1978, pp. 63–69.

How to Write to the Author

Jim Haskins
Professor of English
4326 Turlington Hall
University of Florida
Gainesville, FL 32601

Karen Hesse

(1952–)

by Lois T. Stover

With the 1991 publication of *Wish on a Unicorn*, Karen Hesse began to carve her niche in the world of books for young readers, and winning the Newbery Award for *Out of the Dust* (1997) in 1998 has cemented her position as an important voice in this field. Hesse is noted for the range of her work; she is as adept writing a picture book, such as the joyful *Rain* (1999) as she is in dealing with complex themes such as honesty and loyalty in titles for young adults such as *The Music of Dolphins* (1996). No matter what she is writing, Hesse's readers know they can trust her to tell the truth:

> I never consider telling anything less than the truth in the books I write. It is irresponsible and disrespectful to my readers to sugarcoat life, to leave out the pain. . . . Young readers are bright and perceptive, and they can spot a dishonest depiction or a half-truth a mile away. I wouldn't insult them or

Quotations from Karen Hesse that are not attributed to a published source are from a personal interview conducted by the author of this article on 22 November 1998 and are published here by permission of Karen Hesse.

niche place or position best suited to a person

theme central message about life in a literary work

waste their time with a less than honest portrayal of a time and place and people. True, there is tragedy in *Out of the Dust,* but there is also humor and life, tenderness, decency, kindness, and humanity. (*Out of the Dust,* interview)

Family Background and Early Life

solace comfort in grief or sorrow

Born in Baltimore, Maryland, on 29 August 1952, Hesse was skinny as a young girl, with an unruly mop of brown hair and big eyes. She had problems her friends did not experience and remembers that it was "hard to play with the same sense of abandon." Hesse found solace in several ways: through the unconditional love she felt from her grandparents; through the simple acts of kindness several teachers extended to her; and through entering into the world of books.

Dr. Seuss was the pen name of Theodor Seuss Geisel (1904–1991), an American illustrator and children's book writer. Some of his more famous works include *How the Grinch Stole Christmas* (1957) and *The Cat in the Hat* (1957).

Hesse credits Peggy Coughlin, a librarian at the Enoch Pratt Free Library in Baltimore, with helping her to survive her childhood and adolescence. In particular Hesse remembers the effect Dr. Seuss's *Horton Hatches the Egg* (1940) had on her. From that story of Horton the elephant, who takes charge of an egg abandoned by its mother, Hesse learned about honor, dedication, and loyalty. Horton became her model for what it means to be a humanitarian. Plus, she loved the inventive language of Dr. Seuss. Then, when she was about twelve years old, Hesse read John Hersey's *Hiroshima* (1946)—and that literary event marked the end of her childhood. In some ways, she regrets that she was exposed to the complexities of war and its horrors at such a young age, but she learned from the book that no matter how desperate people are, they can survive. She began to think about how it is always possible to transcend circumstances and become more than you are—an important theme throughout her work. She says, "Even if the only option is to retreat inside yourself, that is still an option." In her Newbery acceptance speech she states, "I love my characters too much to hurt them deliberately, even the prickly ones. It just so happens that in life, there's pain; sorrow lives in the shadow of joy, joy in the shadow of sorrow. The question is, do we let the pain reign triumphant, or do we find a way to grow, to transform, and ultimately transcend our pain?" (p. 423).

John Hersey (1914–) is an American novelist and journalist who won the 1945 Pulitzer Prize for fiction for *A Bell from Adano.* His best-known nonfiction work is *Hiroshima,* which portrays the destruction of that Japanese city by an atomic bomb during World War II.

transcend to rise above

integrity honesty

Responsibility, integrity, loyalty, commitment—these are the values that shaped Hesse's own early life and that now shape the experiences of her characters. As a child, Hesse became friends with a young boy named Joey. He wore a huge, ungainly hearing aid; although he was normal in all other respects, in the 1950s, his hearing impairment was enough to shut him off from daily life in the neighborhood. Because Joey was older and could cross streets, Hesse valued him because he could take her places she otherwise could not go. Although they did not engage in much conversation, they had a "silent friendship," as Ellen Huntington Bryant explained in "Honoring the Complexities of Our Lives: An Interview with Karen Hesse" (in *Voices from the Middle,* 1997). Now, in her novels, Hesse often features a character who is somehow set apart from others. In *Lester's Dog* (1993), Corey, like Joey, is hearing-impaired, while Muncie in *Phoenix Rising* (1994) is mocked for her short height, and Hannie in *Wish on a Unicorn* is mentally retarded.

The loyalty of her family and their unconditional love were also of utmost importance to Hesse as a child. In particular, she has drawn on her relationship with her grandparents, Orthodox Jews, and with her Aunt Bern in her writing. They gave her a gift that she tries to give her characters. Of her grandparents and aunt Hesse says,

> I could be weepy, I could be cranky, I could say nothing and they loved me. I felt their unconditional love whenever I was with them. I am sure that at times my aunt and my grandparents wanted to tear their hair out because I was not easy to be with, but I never felt it. I always felt that they loved me no matter what I did. (Bryant, p. 41)

Other important adults also gave the young Hesse a sense of her own potential. Hesse began to see herself as a writer when a fifth grade teacher put a check plus and a "very creative" on one of her papers. At that point, in response to that one small piece of praise in a life that otherwise did not receive much recognition, Hesse found an outlet and began writing. Her sixth grade teacher asked her to write the graduation speech. Once it was written, he asked her to read it. Hesse credits Mr. Ball with changing her relationship with her mother. She did read the speech and as a result, ". . . my mom saw me in a different way than she had ever seen me before. My mom had never really seen me before that day (Bryant, p. 42)."

Orthodox Jew a Jewish person who closely follows the authoritative law code of the Torah, as interpreted by rabbis, and applies it to daily living

Hesse dreamed of becoming many things after that experience. She began her college career at Towson University as a theater major, but after two semesters, she transferred to the University of Maryland, College Park, where she earned a B.A. in English with minors in psychology and anthropology. She notes she has earned a living as a waitress, librarian, nanny, agricultural worker, typesetter, mental health care provider, substitute teacher, and book reviewer. But, no matter what she was doing as her job, she still saw herself as a writer. She says, "I never gave up dreaming of publication. It took more than thirty years to see that fifth-grade dream come true. I don't know whether that makes me extremely patient or just plain stubborn" (*Out of the Dust,* interview).

At first, Hesse wrote mostly poetry. However, she talks clearly about how her changing family structure affected her writing. She lives in Vermont, with her husband of twenty-seven years, Randy. They have two nearly-grown daughters, and it was the birth of her children that changed the nature of her writing. Once she became a mother, Hesse found that part of her brain was always listening for her child. She found she could no longer bring to bear the concentration and focus that poetry demands.

For a time Hesse floundered. She knew she needed to write, but she no longer had a strong sense of what to write, or of what form it should take. One afternoon, she went to the library to find picture books for her daughter, Kate, and some novels for herself to read. She stumbled onto Katherine Paterson's *Of Nightingales That Weep* (1974) and fell in love with it. She remembers thinking to herself, "If this is children's literature, then I want to be a part of it!" Hesse became a devoted fan of Paterson's, reading every new title as quickly as it appeared, going to hear the author speak, and learning a new craft and way of being a writer from her. Thus, when Hesse's novel *Letters from Rifka* (1992) won an award that was to be presented at a conference of the International Reading Association, and Hesse found herself sitting side by side with Paterson, the keynote speaker, Hesse was delighted to be able to tell her "unwitting mentor" how much she had learned from the other's work.

The Newbery Book: *Out of the Dust*

After Hesse's daughters grew up and Hesse's brain allowed her to let go of her children for hours at a time, "poetry was al-

There is an article about Katherine Paterson in volume 2.

mentor a wise or trusted teacher

lowed to return." In 1993, Hesse took a trip to Colorado with a fellow writer, Liza Ketchum. As they entered Kansas, Hesse became infatuated with the landscape, with the sky that could turn as "green as a bruise," and with the wind that "caressed our faces," and the grass that moved "like a corps of dancers." Later, she read a series of articles in the 1934 *Boise City News* about an accident similar to the one that changes Billie Jo's life in *Out of the Dust.*

With the additional help of the Oklahoma Historical Society, Hesse

> lived through day after day, month after month, year after year of life in the heart of the Depression, in the heart of the dust bowl. I saturated myself with those dusty, dirty, desperate times, and what I discovered thrilled me. . . . I discovered there was still life going on, talent shows, dances, movies. Daily acts of generosity and kindness. ("Newbery Medal Acceptance Speech," pp. 424–425).

The frugality of life, and the grimness of the conditions, the way the dust was part of every bite of food and even covered the sheets of the bed, and the barrenness of the landscape all led to Hesse's conviction that Billie Jo's story should be told in free verse. The sparseness of the language echoes the sparseness of life in that time and place. As Susan Lemke notes in her review of the book in the 1 October 1997 *Booklist,* this approach allows for "distilling all the experience into brief, acutely observed phrases" (p. 330), and so the language of the story re-creates for the reader the intensity of Billie Jo's life. It also conveys the simple yet important underlying theme of the power of forgiveness among the people in the story, between the people and the land, and about every relationship—including the need for Billie to forgive herself.

An Ear for Language

Even though *Out of the Dust* was the first of Hesse's novels to be written as poetry, her ear for language and the physical nature of her writing have long been a hallmark of her work. In *Wish on a Unicorn* reviewers commented on Hesse's use of similes to depict the everyday environment of a family living in

Liza Ketchum writes for both young adults and younger readers. Her novels for young adults include the award-winning *West Against the Wind* (1987) and *Twelve Days in August* (1993) and its sequel, *Blue Coyote* (1997).

frugality the sparing use of resources

hallmark proof of excellence

simile a figure of speech that uses *like, as,* or *as if* to make a direct comparison between two essentially different ideas

palpable able to be touched or felt

a trailer: "the poverty is palpable" noted Hazel Rochman in her review of the book in the 15 March 1991 *Booklist.* In *Lester's Dog,* the reader feels a kitten as a "tiny fist of fur, knotted up" and in *Sable* (1994), we long to touch the silky inside of Sable's ear along with Tate, who finds and saves the dog. It is the colors of the quilt that Codie is making for her Aunt Alix that give such a softness and gentle quality to *Lavender* (1993). The strong, vigorous language of *Rain* compels the reader to experience the joy of the rain with the children who open their arms to the sky, and we, too, want to be part of the city in the storm: "Wet slicking our arms and legs, we splash up the block, squealing and whooping in the streaming rain. Jackie-Joyce, Liz, Rosemary and I, we grab the hands of our mammas. We twirl and sway them, tromping through puddles, romping and reeling in the moisty green air" (unpaginated galley proof).

In her novels for older readers, Hesse consciously adapts her language choices to the environment and themes she is attempting to convey. Therefore, in *Phoenix Rising,* about Nyle, 13, and her grandmother, who find themselves struggling through the aftermath of a nuclear power plant accident, the language echoes the grim, bleak setting in which Nyle comes to understand the importance of forgiveness and the way in which people move on with their lives through simple acts of kindness, rather than through large, dramatic, heroic deeds. Issues of the role of the government in individual lives, prejudice, loss, and death echo through its pages, as they do in *Out of the Dust.*

But it is in *The Music of Dolphins* that Hesse faced her most difficult challenge related to language. This novel had its inspiration in an interview Hesse heard on National Public Radio describing how Genie, a child who grew up in an abusive home without language, was handed over to the scientific community as a teenager. Speech pathologists tried to give Genie the power of speech, but their efforts ultimately proved to be in vain.

When Hesse's character Mila, a child raised by dolphins, is discovered by scientists, they do teach her to speak. Hesse uses short words typed in a large font to show her initial capabilities. Then the vocabulary and print style change to demonstrate her growth. Eventually Mila comes to realize that her true loyalties are to the dolphins. Through descriptions of Mila's encounters with both the scientists and Shay, another feral child, Hesse explores difficult and complex themes, such

feral not domesticated; wild

as what it means to be human, and how much choice individuals can and should have over how they live their lives.

Strong Female Role Models

Most of Hesse's titles have as main characters strong females who struggle to come into their own identities while they work to overcome adversity. *Letters from Rifka* and *Just Juice* (1998) are two quite different stories that share these characteristics with works already discussed. Rifka is based on Hesse's aunt, Lucy Avrutin, who escaped from Russia, traveled through Ukraine and Poland, and finally arrived in the United States. Rifka's family is Jewish, and to escape persecution from the Russian government, they flee their country. But Rifka is stopped at the Polish border because she has ringworm. While her family moves on to America, the Hebrew Immigrant Aid Society helps Rifka travel to Antwerp where she receives months of treatment at a Catholic convent, losing her hair in the process. Throughout her solitary journey, Rifka shows her appreciation for the small kindnesses that give her the strength to carry on by giving of herself to others in similar ways.

ringworm any of several contagious skin diseases caused by certain fungi

Antwerp is a city in Belgium.

Just Juice is not historical fiction, but place is once again an important element of the story. Hesse says the idea for the book came out of the combined poignancy of the town of Boone, North Carolina, and the delivery of her first child to college. Juice Faulstich lives with her family way out in the hills. She adores her father, and, like him, is good with her hands. But school is hard for Juice; she is repeating third grade because numbers and letters just do not make a lot of sense for her. However, Juice is able to help her family when the town says it will take away their home if Pa does not pay his back taxes. She becomes a hero, helping to save a baby's life and that of her mother, and she decides that it is enough to be "just Juice" (p. 138).

poignancy the quality of being deeply affecting or touching

In *Sable* Tate is angry. Tate has rescued a stray dog, Sable. But Sable will not stay where he belongs, and because Tate's mother has a long-standing distrust of dogs, after having been bitten by a dog as a child, Ma and Pa decide Sable has to live with Doc Winston, who lives in a different state. Determined to get her dog back, Tate builds a run for Sable out of leftover boards. She finds a ride to Doc Winston's house, during a terrible storm, only to learn Sable had run away weeks before. There is a happy ending, however.

Writing Process

Although Hesse has won numerous awards, from the Christopher Medal, and American Library Association Notable Book for Children, the American Library Association/Young Adult Library Services Association "Best Book" recognition, and the Newbery Award, she says "I will be learning my craft until I die." These days, she practices her craft in an attic room in Brattleboro, Vermont. She claims that she writes very fast, trying to make it through the first draft so that she knows what is going to happen. This draft is rather spare, more an outline of the basic events and the character. Then, after allowing herself to breathe and think about what is really central to the book, Hesse tackles another draft, taking "the time to really work the story up in a way that will satisfy the reader" (Bryant, p. 42). She plows through the story perhaps three pages at a time, going over the book seven to ten times, and then takes it to her writing group: Liza Ketchum, Eileen Christelow, and Bob McLean (an illustrator). She values these individuals because they keep her honest, helping her to be careful with both her craft and the emotions of her characters. She often shares a book with daughters Kate and Rachel, whom she says have a wonderful gift for critical analysis. The next step is to share the book with an editor; she tends to send it to the editor whom she feels will have the most affinity for that particular piece. Finally, when the book is almost done, she shares it with her husband. She advises young writers to do their best to view revision as "seeing again," and to take the comments of another reader in that spirit of another way to "see" the characters and their relationships.

Hesse encourages young adults to keep reading. "Reading," she says in her Newbery acceptance speech as reprinted in *Horn Book,* "gives us perspective. It gives us respite from the tempest of our present day lives. It gives us a safe place in which to grow, transform, transcend. It helps us understand that sometimes the questions are too hard, that sometimes there are no answers, that sometimes there is only forgiveness" (p. 427).

Hesse is committed to the reading/writing life, to a life spent in listening to the questions young people have about the world, and to helping them find their own answers so that her readers will, like her characters, be able to accept themselves, to find sustenance in the knowledge that someone be-

affinity feeling of preference or connection

sustenance that which supports or maintains something

lieves in them, and to find the courage to reach out to others through those small acts of humanity that have meant so much to Hesse herself.

Selected Bibliography

WORKS BY KAREN HESSE

Novels for Young Adults
Letters from Rifka (1992)
Phoenix Rising (1994)
A Time of Angels (1995)
The Music of Dolphins (1996)
Out of the Dust (1997)

Children's Books
Lester's Dog, illustrated by Nancy Carpenter (1993)
Poppy's Chair, illustrated by Kay Life (1993)
Rain, illustrated by Jon J. Muth (1999)

Chapter Books
Wish on a Unicorn (1991)
Lavender, illustrated by Andrew Glass (1993)
Sable, illustrated by Marcia Sewall (1994)
Just Juice, illustrated by Robert Andrew Parker (1998)

WORKS ABOUT KAREN HESSE

Bryant, Ellen Huntington. "Honoring the Complexities of Our Lives: An Interview with Karen Hesse." *Voices from the Middle,* April 1997, pp. 38–49.

Lempke, Susan, Review of *Out of the Dust.* In *Booklist,* 1 October 1997, p. 330.

"Newbery Medal Acceptance Speech." *Horn Book,* July/August 1998, pp. 422–427.

Out of the Dust Teacher's Edition. Includes unpaginated "About the Author" and "An Interview with Karen Hesse About *Out of the Dust*." New York: Scholastic, 1999.

Rochman, Hazel. Review of *Wish on a Unicorn.* In *Booklist,* 15 March 1991, p. 1493.

If you like the works of Karen Hesse, you will probably also appreciate the works of some of her favorite authors, including Virginia Euwer Wolff, Kyoko Mori, Paul Fleischman, and Katherine Paterson.

How to Write to the Author

Karen Hesse
c/o Liz Szabla, Editorial Director
Scholastic Press
555 Broadway
New York, NY 10012-3999

Lou Kassem

(1931–)

by Robert C. Small, Jr., and Donald J. Kenney

Lou Kassem: Seeing Life Through the Eyes of Young Adults

If you were about to enter middle school for the first day, what advice would you need to make survival possible? Well, Cindy has just been through her first year, so she's an expert. Here's her advice, which she explains as she goes along in Lou Kassem's *Middle School Blues* (1986):

> Rule No. *1: Don't laugh at funerals. Adults don't have a sense of humor like kids do.* (P. 9)
>
> Rule No. *2: Choose your enemies carefully. They might be more important than your friends.* (P. 37)
>
> Rule No. *3: Beware when parents say they know what's best for you. It's usually what's best for them!* (P. 45)

Quotations from Lou Kassem that are not attributed to a published source are from personal interviews conducted by the authors of this article between February and April 1999 and are published here by permission of Lou Kassem.

Rule No. *4: Be careful what you wish for—you might get it.* (P. 53)

Rule No. *5: Friends are like the weather—changeable.* (P. 67)

Rule No. *6: All people are valuable.* (P. 67)

Rule No. *7: Don't tell secrets in the restroom.* (P. 93)

Rule No. *8: Money is very important. There aren't many ways to earn it at our age. Babysit only as a last resort.* (P. 103)

Rule No. *9: Nothing is a sure thing. Don't count your honors before they're awarded.* (P. 121)

Rule No. *10: Never say* never (P. 181)

Lou Kassem seems to have been fated to write about life through the eyes of young people who, at least for the moment, are outsiders: Cindy in *Middle School Blues,* who has to cope with a new school, new friends, new enemies, new teachers; Penny Brown in *The Druid Curse* (1994), who is dyslexic and taunted by her classmates; Jayne in *A Haunting in Williamsburg* (1990), who has had a conflict at school and is visiting in Williamsburg, where she knows no one. Kassem's early years, described in *Something About the Author,* clearly prepared her to see life from this vantage point:

> By the time I finished high school I'd attended nine different schools. Perhaps as a result of my transient life, I became an avid reader. I couldn't take my friends along on each move but I could take my books. I loved school, climbing trees, reading, riding horses, telling stories, swimming, hiking, and roller-skating. My poor mother despaired of me ever becoming a 'proper' lady. And, being such an odd mixture of tomboy and bookworm, often I had trouble fitting in with the normal, stay-in-one-place crowd. (P. 91)

She has said of herself in "The Incredibly Shrinking World of Imagination," "Long before it was popular to be the New Kid on the Block, I was one. . . . We didn't always make these

---

dyslexic exhibiting a disturbance in the ability to read or use language

vantage point point of view

transient passing through places with only brief stays in each place

moves at the beginning of the school year either" (*ALAN Review*, winter 1992, pp. 2–3).

Kassem was born on 10 November 1931 in Elizabethton, Tennessee, to Edgar Roscoe and Dorothy Graham Morrell. She was the child of four generations of Southerners who had settled in the eastern mountains of that state, but her family moved to North Carolina and then to Virginia before returning to their home state. That experience, coupled with her love of reading and storytelling, started her early down the road to becoming a writer. "I thought writing was fun from the very start," she has admitted.

She wrote of one of her first days in a new school, a story that gives us a good idea of why she became a writer. "I'll always remember landing in Miss Bertie Summerland's class in the middle of the school year," she said with a faint smile.

> The in-class assignment on my first day was to write a few paragraphs on the Ages of Man's development— the Ice Age, Iron Age, Bronze Age, etc. I chewed off my eraser before I thought of something. Then I began writing furiously. I knew I was in trouble when several other students read their papers. Nevertheless, I stood up when called upon and read what I'd written. I had written a story about an Ice Age family being found frozen solid in a glacier. When the ice thawed the people came back to life! Needless to say, my classmates listened with open-mouthed wonder and quite a few giggles. Red-faced, I sat down . . . only to hear Miss Bertie *clapping*. 'That was an interesting story, Lou,' she said. 'You have a wonderful imagination. Now, class, what if Lou's story were true? How would these people be dressed? What language do you think they would speak? How would they be different from us?' The snickers stopped. Everyone began talking. I felt good about myself. ("Incredible Shrinking World," pp. 2–3)

Kassem attributes that experience and the school librarian, Mrs. Bachman, to opening the door for her to become a writer.

How She Became a Writer

Snuffy Smith was a character featured in the comic strip "Barney Google and Snuffy Smith." The character, a stereotypical Southern hillbilly, was also featured in the 1942 film *Private Snuffy Smith*. **The Beverly Hillbillies** was a television show that ran from 1962 to 1971. It featured a poor, down-to-earth family who strikes it rich and moves to Beverly Hills.

stereotypical conforming to a preconceived and often oversimplified notion about a person or a group

monologue extended thoughts of a character, especially those spoken aloud while the character is alone

Her recognition of the negative pictures of Southern mountain people came early, several years before attending East Tennessee State University. Snuffy Smith and the Beverly Hillbillies didn't sit well with her even as a young teenager. And she encountered that prejudice more than once herself. She remembers one experience that she thinks may have planted the seed to write about the people of Tennessee and the southern mountains in general. Filled with pride, she had traveled to Colorado as a part of the Tennessee team at the National Forensic Competition, only to be identified as being from Tennessee with the comment, "And wearing shoes!" "As if we all went barefoot."

Many years later, when she had moved to southwest Virginia with her husband, Shakeep Kassem, who was a student at Virginia Tech in the town of Blacksburg, she began to explore the stereotypical portrait of her people. She is quoted in *Something About the Author* as saying:

> . . . it wasn't until 1973, while working part-time as an assistant librarian in the Blacksburg Public Library, that the urge to become an author completely overwhelmed me. I was disenchanted with the typical view of mountain people. As a fourth generation daughter of the Appalachian mountains, I grew up listening to the stories of my early ancestors. I knew some of these independent mountain people. They were *not* shiftless, ignorant, and stupid as the movies, television, and books represented them. (P. 3)

But how did Kassem come to be a writer for young readers? Her love of storytelling, combined with her role as the mother of four children, seems to have guided her in that direction. "I spent twenty years being a mother. Later I wrote skits and plays for the church and for both the elementary and high school. I wrote monologues for my daughters to perform. And, of course, I told ghost stories at slumber parties," she said in her biography on the Avon Books website. She also said in *Something About the Author,* "In fact, long after my children were out of grade school I was still the 'Story Lady' at an elementary school. Sometimes I read the children books. Other times I made up my own stories. The children loved both. . . . It also was an outlet for the ham in me that Virginia will never cure" (p. 91).

Kassem is proud of being a writer whose works young adults flock to. "With no apologies," she said in *Something About the Author,* "I am a writer for young people. If I can hook one child on reading, all the rejection slips and endless waiting will have been worthwhile. Writers for children have the opportunity to make a real difference" (p. 92). Kassem is friendly and informal with her readers and likes them to call her "Lou." She often speaks to teachers, librarians, aspiring writers, and, of course, the students who read and praise her books. They have described her as "vibrant," "realistic," "funny," and "inspiring" and have said of her that she "just bubbles," "loves her craft," and is "someone who so obviously enjoys her work and is successful at it." These comments please her, but she admitted, "One of the best ways I know to get ready to write is to talk with young people." Visiting schools gives her the chance to walk up and down hallways, listening and eavesdropping on what students are talking about. She noted in *Contemporary Authors* that "visiting schools isn't a completely altruistic endeavor! Paper and pen are always at hand" (p. 243).

altruistic unselfishly regarding the welfare of others

Kassem spends a lot of time in schools: reading from her books, talking with students who have just finished reading them, and sharing ideas about writing. She said, "teachers are also asking authors into their schools to talk about writing and reading. In the past six years, I have visited 75 schools in five states. By doing this they not only encourage writing, they let students see that authors are ordinary people who could be living right next door, that all authors do not live in garrets or Ivory Towers in some far-away city" ("Incredibly Shrinking World," p. 3). Kassem's commitment to the integrity of her writing for young people is evidenced in her refusal to have *Middle School Blues* televised. She received a proposal to have the book made into a television special but turned it down when she found that the script was poorly written and did not capture the essence of the novel that so many youngsters found appealing.

garret attic

What Are Her Books About?

Kassem's novels deal with strong female characters of middle school age who, for one reason or another, are outsiders with few friends or are cut off from their friends and familiar places. In some cases, they are also living in a new, very different part of the country. But they cope. Lou Willett Stanek commented in *A Whole Language Approach for Teaching the Novels of Lou Kassem,* "Readers can't help but gain a stronger sense of self when they read about Cindy, a late bloomer; Peter, whose hearing is impaired; Margo, who's overweight; and Jeff, who can't live up to his father's expectations—kids who have problems and make mistakes just like the readers" (p. 1). Kassem suggested on the Avon Books Website that they are based on her daughters:

> You see a lot of my daughters in all of my books, because they taught me. My books have strong, independent characters. These are the people I care about, individuals who don't always fit into the mold of what is accepted. I want to tell kids it's all right to be totally different.

As these girls deal with the problems that face them, they each acquire at least one friend along the way, usually a boy, who helps them solve the problem. The problem may be dealing with other students who are unpleasant, coping with difficult teachers, or unraveling mysteries brought to them by ghosts who are unable to rest because of some unresolved problem in their past.

Looking at Some of Her Books

gamut variety or range

setting the general time and place in which the events of a literary work take place

plot the deliberate sequence of events in a literary work

Kassem's novels span the gamut of emotions, characters, and themes. Her books have received wide readership and praise from reviewers and teachers who recognize her unique use of these characters, settings, and plots to tell a story that appeals to young readers. Her works are consistently insightful on the growing-up problems of adolescents. Her characters are dynamic and engaging. Most important, she continues to use her craft to create new works that capture the essence of what adolescents are experiencing—whether they are in Ruffner Middle School, Colonial Williamsburg, or prehistoric Great Britain. Kassem's ability to weave setting, especially historic settings, with memorable characters into a whopping good tale keeps her devoted readers coming back to her books.

Kassem also uses the supernatural to look into the lives of young people, but not to terrify. Her ghosts are, with a few minor exceptions, young themselves, trapped in supernatural situations where they are innocent victims. As readers, we care about them and look to the living teenagers to rescue them from the situations that keep them caught between life and death.

Dance of Death

Kassem's first published book, *Dance of Death* (1984), was actually written after *Listen for Rachel* (1986), which suffered a number of rejections by publishers. Debra L. Maier commented in the August 1984 *Voice of Youth Advocates* about *Dance,* "There's enough tension and romance to please most readers" (p. 147). *Booklist* predicted that it would appeal to "teens who enjoy suspending logic and immersing themselves in the occult" (15 May 1984, p. 1339). The novel tells the story of Reagan Riley, whose parents are out of the country and whose dream of a career as a dancer is threatened by an injury to her knee. She feels isolated living with her Aunt Thelma and Uncle Malcolm in Ferncrest, an old mansion haunted by the Deuxville twins, who died there in the nineteenth century. Reagan dreams of the twins over and over again until she decides to solve their mystery. Unpopular with the other students at her school, she does make one friend, Jay, a star football player. Finally, they discover the buried secret about the mansion and its former owner.

Middle School Blues

Perhaps Kassem's best-known novel, *Middle School Blues* has been called "encouraging to readers approaching the middle school years" in the July/August 1986 *Bulletin of the Center for Children's Books* (p. 211). In her *ALAN Review* article, Kassem takes notice of a school to which *Middle School Blues* was especially important:

> A reading specialist in Torrington, Connecticut, noticed it took the new sixth graders in her school at least six weeks to feel at home in middle school. Reading *Middle School Blues* sparked an idea for a

get-acquainted day at Vogel-Wetmore School. First, she ordered classroom copies of the book. Skits, costumes, and competitions followed. The whole school went BLUE for a day: the teachers dressed in blue. 'Blue Suede Shoes' was played on the intercom, even the cafeteria served blue cake, and a conference call was held with the author in the middle of the day. (P. 3)

In the novel, Cindy tells the story of her first year at Ruffner Middle School. Going there is not something she looks forward to, but the experience of losing friends, making friends, and dealing with teachers, boys, and unpleasant girls gives her insights into herself, her parents, and life in general. One reviewer in the 1 April 1986 *Kirkus Reviews* said, "Cindy is a winning character," and went on to call the book a "fast-paced, believable novel about the trials of being 'the square person in a round family' " (p. 546). The Missouri Association of School Librarians and the Missouri Library Association awarded *Middle School Blues* with the Mark Twain Award in 1988–1989.

Listen for Rachel

Listen for Rachel is the story a of young girl, orphaned when a fire kills her parents, who moves in with her grandparents in the mountains of Appalachia. There she encounters a healer, Granny Sharp, who becomes her mentor in the art of using herbs and other plants to cure disease and injury. As the Civil War comes near, she uses her healing arts to care for both Northern and Southern soldiers. Then she meets Ben, a Yankee soldier, and while caring for his wounds, falls in love with him, as he does with her. Both Ben and Rachel struggle with the dilemma of staying in the mountains or going back to Pennsylvania, Ben's home. Would she fit in there? Would he find a place with the mountain people? Betsy Hearne in the January 1987 *Bulletin of the Center for Children's Books* review stated, "The setting is strong, the dialect handled naturally, and the romance between Rachel and the Yankee soldier she falls in love with innocently appealing" (p. 90). Kassem herself said in *Contemporary Authors* that "*Listen for Rachel* is the book of my heart, because it gives a true picture of the

dialect a regional form of a language

proud, independent people who settled the Appalachians" (p. 243). *Listen for Rachel* was named an ALA Notable Book in 1986, and was also selected for the Cultural Exchange Program with Russia in 1987.

Secret Wishes

Doris Fong said, in the April 1989 *School Library Journal,* of *Secret Wishes* (1989), a sequel to *Middle School Blues,* "A real sparkler that pulls no punches" (p. 126). A teacher once told Kassem a story about an unusual way in which *Secret Wishes* came to be on a list of books students were asked to read.

> A middle school counselor asked her English Department to put *Secret Wishes* on the required reading list. It was, she said, in self-defense. It seems every year after cheerleading tryouts, her office is filled with crying students and upset parents. She thought *Secret Wishes* might help explain what cheerleading was all about. ("Incredibly Shrinking World," p. 3)

The Druid Curse

Penny Brown struggles with the learning disability dyslexia, and many of the other students in her school tease her. But she loves the outdoors and has a talent for drawing the scenes she sees as she walks the trails near her home. On one of these walks, she meets a boy new to her town and hears his amazing story: Years ago a curse was cast, and girls who, like Penny, stumble on the Druid Oak disappear. He has come to complete the mission of his family to destroy the Oak. He and Penny set out to find the evil tree that threatens their lives and those of the people of the town.

A Haunting in Williamsburg

Jayne Curtis has had a difficult school year. When a classmate says an essay she wrote was really his, she remains silent, and the other students turn on her for stealing his paper. When school is over, she leaves to spend part of the summer with her aunt in Williamsburg, in a house that has been in her family for generations. For a while, the summer seems to drag.

Then Jayne meets Peter, handsome and deaf, and they begin to become friends. One night she wakes to see a figure in colonial costume at the foot of her bed; later, as she reads her family history, she meets that shadowy figure, Sally Custis, a ghost haunting the house where she lived in the late eighteenth century. Sally too remained silent two centuries earlier, when her brother died and was labeled a traitor. Jayne is drawn into Sally's efforts to clear her brother's name. She meets the ghost of Jeremiah and discovers who the traitor really was, survives an attack by the ghost of the traitor, and carries the messages between Sally and Jeremiah that end their hauntings. In 1990, *A Haunting in Williamsburg* received the Virginia State Reading Association Award.

Her Latest Novel—*The Quest*

In March 1999, Kassem told us with great excitement that she had just mailed off her most recent writing project, a novel titled *The Quest*. Of course we asked her what it was about, and she told us that it started in "the dog days of summer—hazy, hot, humid, and boring." Then she explained, "The boredom is broken for the eight Colonial Heights kids when they begin LARPing [Live Action Role-Play]. Everything is fun until one girl simply vanishes. A game played by teens throughout the city of Templeton—it's a battle between Good and Evil set in Tolkien's Middle Earth." When we asked for more, she said, "You'll just have to read it." And so we will!

Advice to Young Writers

Kassem often conducts workshops for the readers for whom she writes, inspiring them to try their hands at authorship. She said in her biography on the Avon Books Website, "I think writing can be taught. And, I think anybody can learn to write. What I can't teach is the absolute desire to write, to have a story to tell. I can motivate kids to read, but not all readers are writers. But let me tell you, that all writers are readers. I think motivating kids to read is primary." She has called books "the best imagination stretchers in the world."

"My first advice for aspiring writers is: Read, read, read," she noted in *Contemporary Authors*. "Read the good, the bad, and the ugly" (p. 243). She suggested that aspiring authors read the five latest books published to understand pacing, vocabulary, and how the books begin and end. "Read for fun and read critically. See how other authors do things. Would you have handled the situation differently? How? Why? Books are excellent teachers" (pp. 243–244). Most important, the author has to have a whopping good tale to capture a reader.

"My second and best advice is: Just do it! No book was ever written by simply thinking about it. As H. L. Mencken said, 'Apply butt to chair' " (p. 244).

Selected Bibliography

WORKS BY LOU KASSEM

Novels for Young Adults

Dance of Death (1984)

Listen for Rachel (1986)

Middle School Blues (1986)

Secret Wishes (1989)

A Summer for Secrets (1989)

A Haunting in Williamsburg (1990)

The Treasures of Witch Hat Mountain (1992)

Odd One Out (1993)

The Druid Curse (1994)

The Innkeeper's Daughter (1996)

Sneeze on Monday (1997)

Short Stories

"A Game of Love," *Chicken Soup for the Kid's Soul: 101 Stories of Courage, Hope, and Laughter.* Edited by Jack Canfield. Deerfield Beach, Fl.: Health Communications, 1998.

Articles

"The Incredibly Shrinking World of Imagination." *The ALAN Review,* winter 1992, pp. 2-3.

Audiovisual Materials

An Evening with Lou Kassem. 60 min. Radford, Va.: Radford University Telecommunications Bureau, 28 June 1994. [Kassem reads from her novel *The Druid Curse* and discusses the research she did on the Druids to prepare for the writing of the novel.]

H. L. Mencken (1880–1956) was an American journalist, critic, and editor. He was one of the most important literary figures of his time and was known for his savage wit.

If you like the works of Lou Kassem, you might also like the works of Judy Blume, Anne C. LeMieux, Norma Fox Mazer, and Stephanie Tolan.

Lanier, Parks, host. *A Conversation with Lou Kassem.* 30 min. Radford, Va.: Radford University Telecommunications Bureau, 28 June 1994. [Kassem discusses writing and her creative process.]

WORKS ABOUT LOU KASSEM

Avon website author biography. *www.avonbooks.com*

Commire, Anne, ed. *Something About the Author.* Detroit: Gale Research, 1990, vol. 62, pp. 90–92.

Jones, Daniel, and John D. Jorgenson, eds. *Contemporary Authors.* Detroit: Gale Research, 1998, vol. 62, pp. 243–244.

Stanek, Lou Willett. *Using Literature in the Classroom: Whole Language Approach for Teaching the Novels of Lou Kassem.* New York: Avon, 1991.

How to Write to the Author

Lou Kassem
715 Burruss Drive, NW
Blacksburg, VA 24060

Stephen King

(1947–)

by Patricia L. Daniel

Early Years

Stephen King was born in Portland, Maine, on 21 September 1947. His father, Donald, abandoned the family when King was only three years old, so King and his older brother, David, were raised by their mother, Nellie Ruth Pillsbury King. He and his brother, "who held [his] hand crossing West Broad Street," had a very close relationship—King even dedicated *Cujo* (1981) to David. Today King lives in Bangor, Maine, with his wife, Tabitha, and their three children—Naomi, Joe, and Owen.

King graduated from the University of Maine in 1970 with a degree in English and qualified to teach at the high school level. King and his wife were living in a trailer with their infant daughter at the time. He had finished his third book and was working in a laundromat for $60 a week, unable to find a teaching position. He admits that he was not sure that he wanted to teach; he was afraid that teaching would mean giving up writing, which he loved. However, his third book was rejected for publication as the previous ones had been, and now the King family had grown to include their first son. King finally began teaching high school English, and his writing time was cut to an hour or an hour and a half a day.

He was drinking a lot, and his $6,400 a year teaching salary was not enough to pay the bills. He was in a dry spell with his writing and felt like everything was spinning out of control. During this time, he sold a few short stories to *Cavalier* magazine, and he was working on a story titled "Carrie." Up to this point (fall of 1972), King had not considered writing a horror novel. He acknowledges that he had only written and sold horror short stories, but three of his rejected works had been suspense novels and one had been a science fiction novel.

King remembers that *Carrie* (1974) was very difficult to write. He did not have firsthand knowledge about what he was writing: the opening scene is that of a girls' shower room, and Carrie has her first (and late) menstrual period. King had never experienced a menstrual cramp, did not know how much sanitary napkins cost, or even if they were supplied to students much like toilet paper. Recognizing that he was out of his league, he threw the two pages of manuscript in the trash can. His wife, Tabby, found them, read them, and urged him to continue. By the time King was through writing the shower scene, he realized that the story would be too long to be submitted to *Cavalier* as a short story.

In February 1973, having rewritten the last fourth of the story according to his editor's suggestions, King borrowed $75 from Tabby's grandmother so that he could travel to New York City and meet with his editor. A month later, King received a telegram saying that Doubleday would publish *Carrie* and offering an advance payment of $2,500. King relates his excitement at being a first-time published novelist, his caution to Tabby to not expect another penny from this book, and his suggestion that they use the advance to pay cash for a compact car. Still, he ventured to hope that they would make a paperback deal and clear as much as $30,000; if that dream came true, King proposed to quit teaching for two to three years and write full-time. Instead, King was offered $400,000 on Mother's Day 1973.

keenly intensely

King has enjoyed huge success as a writer ever since, but he keenly remembers what it is like to struggle, to be afraid to hope for something that he really wants but may not get. In fact, in *Fear Itself: The Early Works of Stephen King* (1982),

King recalls how he felt during the three or four months it took him to write the first draft of *The Shining* (1977):

The Shining was made into a film starring Jack Nicholson in 1980.

> I seemed to be back in that trailer in Hermon, Maine, with no company but the buzzing sound of the snowmobiles and my own fears—fears that my chance to be a writer had come and gone, fears that I had gotten into a teaching job that was completely wrong for me, fears most of all that my marriage was edging onto marshy ground and that there might be quicksand anyplace ahead. (P. 36)

King sees *The Shining* to be "about a miserable, damned man who is very slowly losing his grip on his life, a man who is being driven to destroy all the things he loves" (*Fear Itself,* p. 36).

Writing Habits

King writes 361 days of the year, taking time off for his birthday, Christmas, Easter, and the Fourth of July. He considers the deadline to be his boss. His job is to write. In *Reading Stephen King: Issues of Censorship, Student Choice and Popular Literature* (1997), King says "I write . . . because my heart demands it and would break without it" (p. 17).

King writes each book twice. In the first writing, he is consumed by the emotion he is relating. Again as related in *Reading Stephen King,*

> What I want is to reach through the page and grab the reader. I don't want to just mess with your head; I want to mess with your *life*. I want you to miss appointments, burn dinner, skip your homework. . . . With me, that first time through, it's personal, and it's really more about you than it is about me. I want you sweating bullets and looking behind doors. (P. 15)

"I don't want to just mess with your head; I want to mess with your life. I want you to miss appointments, burn dinner, skip your homework. . . . I want you sweating bullets and looking behind doors."

Characters We Know

King exposes the vulnerability of his characters so that we recognize them as people they know, or even as ourselves. The characters are often ordinary people (sometimes they have a special gift, but they do not have directions for using this gift) presented with an extraordinary situation. They are afraid. They are unsure. They do not know what to do, but they try. They do their best. They work through their fear. They confront their terror. As readers, we continue to turn the pages to get them to safety, preparing ourselves for the certain battle ahead.

We see ourselves in King's characters. They have problems such as ours. For those of us who have been outcasts when we desperately wanted to belong, we identify with Carrie White in *Carrie*. For those of us who have stepped on the bathroom scale and vowed to eat less chocolate and to exercise more, we understand Billy Halleck's preoccupation with weight in *Thinner* (1984). For those of us who have longed to have another day with a loved one who has died, we sympathize with Louis Creed's willingness to do anything to bring his son back to life in *Pet Sematary* (1983). King shows us that getting what we want may be more than we can handle, a point he makes very clear in *Needful Things* (1991).

Children and adolescents in King's stories are treated with dignity; they are acknowledged as real people. It is not surprising that middle school and high school students avidly read King's books; they find themselves in his stories, and they are treated with respect; they are taken seriously. Young people quite naturally and honestly size up others as they are forming their own identities and trying on different roles. They know to look beyond the obvious to a person's core being. It is through young people that King explores a wider range of possibilities than he could realistically do through adults, who pride themselves, albeit limiting themselves and their possibilities, on their rational abilities. Children and adolescents are more open to supernatural powers and do not question how they know what they know, as in *It* (1986), "The Body," (in *Different Seasons*, [1982]), and *Salem's Lot* (1975).

King also allows alcoholics and those who are mentally challenged to be perceptive when their rational mind does not filter everything. It is the alcoholic in *Carrie* who first realizes who is responsible for the town's eradication, and Jim Gardener in *The Tommyknockers* (1987) whose consumption of Scotch seems to help him understand the bizarre tale he is witnessing and who also has a plate in his skull to protect his thoughts from being communicated. It is through Tom Cullen in *The Stand* (1978) that the dead are able to provide guidance

---

Thinner was made into a movie in 1996, *Pet Semetary* in 1989, and *Needful Things* in 1993. A sequel to Pet Semetary was released in 1992.

avidly very eagerly

albeit even though

It was filmed for television in 1990. **"The Body"** became the film *Stand by Me* (1986). *Salem's Lot* was filmed for cable television in 1979. A sequel called *A Return to Salem's Lot* followed in 1987.

eradication total elimination

for the living, and Dolores Claiborne in *Dolores Claiborne* (1992) who is able to achieve justice for those who have been wronged.

King writes of the world we know. He opens what we thought we had concealed. He brings to light what we thought we left in the dark. He makes public what we thought was ours in private. In *The Stand* a character blows his nose and then opens the handkerchief to see what came out, and Harold Lauder enjoys sniffing his own bed farts.

Our Fears Exposed

King confronts all our fears; he exposes some we may not have even considered, but when we do consider them, we are frightened and own them as our own. However, King does not allow us to be consumed by fear because he provides ordinary good people who will risk their lives for another. He describes in graphic detail and up close what we live through and see in everyday life, but he also presents a recurring theme that most people are good and will do the right thing in a tough situation. We are comforted by the hope that we discover in ourselves and in each other when we stick together to face our most horrifying fears. Although King has been called a "horror fiction" writer, much of the horror he relates is shown on television's evening news and written in every city newspaper.

King's overarching and recurring theme is the battle between good and evil forces. Sometimes that battle includes supernatural forces, as in *Carrie, Salem's Lot, Firestarter* (1980), *The Shining, Pet Sematary, Thinner,* and *Bag of Bones* (1998). Sometimes, however, the battle is just between good and evil people, as in *The Dead Zone* (1979), *Misery* (1987), *Rage, Dolores Claiborne, Rose Madder* (1995), and *The Green Mile: A Novel in Six Parts* (1996). King explores the good and evil forces from a technological vantage point in *The Tommyknockers* and *The Stand.* He tests the good and evil forces from an American western setting in the Dark Tower series.

In *The Stand,* 99 percent of the population is annihilated by a flu virus that is accidentally released by the U.S. armed forces. This fear probably has occurred to most of us, but we choose not to dwell on the idea. King buys the deed to the idea and begins building on it; first, he clears out most of the people, and then he sets the stage for the ultimate battle between good and evil.

The made-for-television movie version of *The Tommyknockers* was released in 1993. *The Stand* was filmed as a television miniseries and released in 1994. *Dolores Claiborne* was filmed in 1994.

theme central message about life in a literary work

Firestarter, starring Drew Barrymore, was released as a film in 1984. The 1983 movie *The Dead Zone* featured Christopher Walken as Johnny Smith. Kathy Bates won both the Oscar and Golden Globe awards for best actress in the 1990 movie *Misery.* She also starred in *Dolores Claiborne* (1994). *The Green Mile* was released as a film in 1999.

vantage point point of view

annihilated caused to cease to exist; killed

The forces for good and evil are gathered. Those who choose the force for good with Mother Abagail are free to leave, as Harold Lauder does, and join the evil side. However, those who are on the side of evil and Randall Flagg are not given choices; they are made to stay evil. They are confined within evil; they are enslaved to their greed and vices. For "the stand" to be made, the people representing the good force had to venture to the evil side; Flagg could not trust his people outside of his control. Another story is just beginning even as the good force wins. Stu Redman and Fran Goldsmith take their baby and choose to leave the community, which was fashioned after the democratic ideal, and begin anew. Alas as Redman returns to the Free Zone, the police are carrying weapons. Is the cycle continuing? Will there be other societies who will fight the Free Zone? King leaves readers with hope without providing all the answers. As long as there are individuals who are willing to pioneer, to choose the path less traveled, there is hope. The responsibility for good always rests with the individual. That is each of us.

King's characters expose our fears by asking the questions that we, his readers, ask. As frightening as our fears are, they are less frightening in the open than they are when we try to hide them. King's characters question authority and those in power, as in *The Long Walk* (1979). Why do we have the rules/laws that we have? What is their purpose? Are they working? Also, as in *The Tommyknockers* and *The Stand,* can we learn to live within some limitations, or must we continue to explore and exploit our technological advances? King's readers know evil is real. Bad things happen to good people. There are more random acts of violence than random acts of kindness. It does not make sense. What can be done? It depends. How strong are you? What are you willing to do?

Bag of Bones

In *Bag of Bones,* King reached out and grabbed this reader and had her crying with the protagonist, Mike Noonan, on page 2. How does an author get a reader to care enough to cry by the second page? He strips away any pretense. Noonan is simply reporting the facts of his wife's death, including what she had bought in the drugstore, which happens to have included an impulsive purchase of a piece of chocolate-covered marshmallow. Noonan is sitting at their kitchen table when he

protagonist the main character of a literary work

finds it in her purse; he unwraps it and partakes of it; "and it was like taking Communion" (p. 2).

Noonan is a writer, and as he grieves over his wife's death, he also succumbs to writer's block, about four years' worth when the reader joins the story. He is unmotivated to write; he is consumed and haunted by the mystery surrounding the last year of Jo's life. He has to doubt their sacred love and confront the forces that seem to be accusing her of having had an affair. He has to go to their secluded summer home to find the truth. As in *The Stand,* the force of good has to venture into evil in order to do battle.

While there, Noonan meets a young widow, Mattie, and her daughter, Kyra. Mattie and Noonan begin to fall in love, even though Noonan tries hard rationally not to do so. The scene is set for a major battle between the spirits in the spirit world and Noonan, Mattie, and Kyra. But the battle is not of the spirit world; the townspeople have their own secrets to protect and fight to the death. From the spirit world, Jo continues to beckon Noonan to fight the good fight. Evil is so strong, but everyone must not die in vain. Mike Noonan must champion "the little guys" for all of us.

Conclusion

I was introduced to Stephen King by a member of my bowling team. I was a first-year teacher and was trying to get involved in the community. Jennifer, my teammate, began telling me about a book she was reading. It was *The Shining.* I could hardly wait until the next Wednesday night, when I would get the next installment. At the time, I was enthralled with Jennifer's storytelling ability. I later realized she was just retelling the story; King was the master storyteller. I enjoyed the same sense of "installment" anticipation when reading *The Green Mile.*

enthralled captivated

Ever since that retelling, I have bought every book Stephen King has written. My partner gets the latest as a Christmas gift. King has only disappointed us once in not having a new one for the holidays. I wouldn't say that I am his "Number One" fan because Annie Wilkes in *Misery* terrorized Paul Sheldon with her fanaticism. I will say that this university professor has been one of his fans for more than twenty years, and I continue to look forward to reading a Stephen King book because he is such a wonderful storyteller.

However, Stephen King is more than a good storyteller. Stephen King is a truth teller. King says that everyone knows he has the heart of a young boy; he keeps it in a jar on his desk. I agree. Any of us who eagerly read his newest book know he has the heart of a young boy who emotionally risks it all every time he writes a story. The jar routine is just for effect. When I finish reading one of his books, I feel like we went through the conflict together. I feel like I know him as a person, and I like the person he is because he writes the truth, when it is ugly and painful and when it is beautiful and comforting.

If you like the works of Stephen King, you might also enjoy the works of Robert Cormier and Lois Duncan.

Selected Bibliography

WORKS BY STEPHEN KING

Novels Written as Stephen King

Carrie (1974)

Salem's Lot (1975)

The Shining (1977)

The Stand (1978)

The Dead Zone (1979)

Firestarter (1980)

Cujo (1981)

The Dark Tower I: The Gunslinger (1982)

Christine (1983)

Cycle of the Werewolf (1983)

Pet Sematary (1983)

The Eyes of the Dragon (1984)

The Talisman, with Peter Straub (1984)

It (1986)

The Dark Tower II: The Drawing of the Three (1987)

Misery (1987)

The Tommyknockers (1987)

The Dark Half (1989)

The Stand (1990) [Uncut version.]

The Dark Tower III: The Waste Lands (1991)

Needful Things (1991)

Dolores Claiborne (1992)

Gerald's Game (1992)

Insomnia (1994)

Rose Madder (1995)

Desperation (1996)

The Green Mile: The Bad Death of Eduard Delacroix (1996; Part 4)

The Green Mile: Coffee on the Mile (1996; Part 6)

The Green Mile: Coffey's Hands (1996; Part 3)

The Green Mile: The Mouse on the Mile (1996; Part 2)

The Green Mile: Night Journey (1996; Part 5)

The Green Mile: The Two Dead Girls (1996; Part 1)

The Dark Tower IV: Wizard and Glass (1997)

Bag of Bones (1998)

The Girl Who Loved Tom Gordon (1999)

Novels Written Under the Pseudonym Richard Bachman

Rage (1977)

The Long Walk (1979)

Roadwork (1981)

The Running Man (1982)

Thinner (1984)

The Regulators (1996)

Short Stories

Night Shift (1978)

Creepshow (1982)

Different Seasons (1982)

Skeleton Crew (1985)

Four Past Midnight (1990)

Nightmares and Dreamscapes (1993)

Screenplays

Creepshow (1982)

Cat's Eye (1985)

Silver Bullet (1985)

Maximum Overdrive (1986)

Storm of the Century (1999)

How to Write to the Author

Stephen King
c/o Simon and Schuster
Publicity Department
1230 Avenue of the Americas
New York, NY 10020

You can also e-mail Stephen King through his website at
www.stephenking.com

Nonfiction

Danse Macabre (1981)

Nightmares in the Sky: Gargoyles and Grotesques (1988)

WORKS ABOUT STEPHEN KING

Power, Brenda Miller, Jeffrey D. Wilhelm, and Kelly Chandler, eds. *Reading Stephen King: Issues of Censorship, Student Choice and Popular Literature,* Urbana, Ill.: National Council of Teachers of English, 1997.

Underwood, Tim, and Chuck Miller, eds. *Fear Itself: The Early Works of Stephen King.* Lancaster, Pa.: Underwood-Miller, 1982.

David Klass

(1960–)

by Elaine C. Stephens

Talented author David Klass writes in two very different genres: novels for young adults, usually involving high school sports, that explore difficult social issues and complex relationships with empathy and sensitivity; and screenplays for hard action and thriller Hollywood movies. He describes the differences between the two genres:

> Screenplays are about dramatic conflict, so in a weird way, a screenplay can be summed up in a sentence where you describe the main conflict. A book to me is really about character, and if you find an interesting enough character who has a distinctive enough voice, you can follow him or her truthfully through a story. With a story you can achieve some kind of truth and that is very different from what a screenplay is. Part of why I love writing books and part of what I hope to achieve is catching the voice of a character I like or find interesting.

Quotations from David Klass that are not attributed to a published source are from personal interviews conducted by the author of this article between December 1998 and January 1999 and are published here by permission of David Klass.

genre type of literature, such as science fiction or romance

empathy sincere concern and understanding

125

0709

Characters with Distinctive Voices

protagonist the main
character of a literary
work

The protagonists in David Klass's young adult novels have distinctive voices. The clarity of their voices and commitment to their beliefs are hallmarks of his work. His characters confront difficult issues that are genuine, contemporary, and gripping. Klass's books provide perceptive insights into how young adults struggle to make sense out of their worlds and their significant relationships.

hallmark proof of excellence

In *A Different Season* (1988), star pitcher Jim Roark opposes any girl joining the school baseball team. His position is complicated by his attraction to Jenny, the star second base player of the girls' softball team. When she is allowed to join the boys' team, their personal feelings are put on hold while they struggle with their different philosophies. Although they eventually come to an accommodation, each remains true to his or her beliefs. The need to take a stand and to act in accordance with one's beliefs is explored in *Wrestling with Honor* (1989). Ron Woods, captain of the wrestling team, honor student, and the world's straightest teenager, refuses to retake a mandatory drug test because he believes it is a violation of an individual's constitutional rights. This refusal means that he will not be allowed to wrestle during his senior year. Ron struggles with his personal code of honor and with his deep-seated anger toward his dead father, who he believes violated that code. For John Rodgers in *California Blue* (1994), there is the struggle of being an outsider. He is a serious student and long distance runner in a family of former football stars who view school as little more than a forum for football. His outsider status is complicated even more when his discovery of a rare species of butterfly places him in an environmental battle with his father, his friends, and the logging community where they live. All of these novels reflect Klass's understanding of how challenges enable young people to learn about themselves and grow.

forum a public meeting place

Home, School, and Sports

David Klass was born in Vermont on 8 March 1960, but grew up in Leonia, New Jersey, a small suburban town, where he attended public schools from third grade through high school. He describes those years in this manner:

I was the only one in my family interested in sports and for years growing up all I did was play baseball and soccer. I come from a family where writing and reading and literature were prized above almost everything else. I was rebellious—I didn't read the way the rest of my family did and didn't spend that much time writing the way they did. I come from the most delightful, slightly eccentric, academic family and in some ways my rebellion took the form of being an average, more conservative "normal" kid.

> **eccentric** odd and quirky

Klass's parents are both college professors and his mother is an accomplished writer of novels for both adults and young adults. His older sister is a doctor and author and his younger sister is a playwright. Klass humorously states, "I am the middle child between these superwomen. I guess I always felt myself to be, and am by far, the least intellectual member of my family. I come from this family of writers, and I sometimes think I was the least likely person in the world to become one myself."

Although Klass didn't consider himself a writer, his first published piece appeared when he was a senior in high school. His older sister had entered and won several times a short story contest in *Seventeen* magazine. According to Klass, he doesn't know how many boys had ever entered the contest, but he did, out of "pure sibling rivalry," and won it.

Klass's school experiences influenced significantly his attitudes toward life and provided him with material for his young adult novels. He states that many aspects of his young adult novels—the descriptions of small-town life, the public schools, the students, the teachers, and the sports teams—come from those years in Leonia. Klass states:

A lot of my attitudes toward life and winning and getting along with people are things I learned on the playing fields. I believe that sports are a real proving ground and testing ground for character. The positive and negative things you encounter in sports in junior high and high school and college—the tough coaches, the fights with teammates, the people from different backgrounds or who have very different approaches to life—all of those challenges are very different from the challenges of school work. They go a very long way in determining your character and giving you an opportunity to grow and test yourself in ways that you would not if you just competed scholastically.

Klass's experiences and beliefs are visible in the characters he creates—Ron Woods in *Wrestling with Honor,* Jimmy Doyle in *Danger Zone* (1995), Jim Roark and Jennifer Douglas in *A Different Season,* and Tony in *Breakaway Run* (1986)—all top athletes who face serious tests both on and off the playing field.

Japan and Hollywood

Klass graduated from Yale with a degree in history in 1982 and thought about going to law school like many of his friends. He worked for a year in Washington, D.C., as a clerk in an entertainment law firm and hated it. Then he decided that although he did not want to become a lawyer, he did want to have an adventure. The Japanese Ministry of Education hired Klass to teach conversational English to middle and high school students, and after a week of training in Tokyo, he was sent to Atami, one of the oldest and most beautiful hot springs resort cities in Japan. He recalls, "Literally the first day there I remember digging my typewriter out and putting it on the desk, and starting, with no previous forethought, *The Atami Dragons* [1984]. Much to my surprise, it was published."

option here, to obtain a contract giving the right to make a movie from a literary work

While in Japan, a Hollywood producer informed Klass that his studio had optioned the screen rights of *The Atami Dragons* and encouraged him to go to Hollywood. Klass reflects back upon this experience:

I thought to myself that I had taken a step into the unknown when I went to Japan and that worked very well, so why not take another step into the unknown and go to Hollywood? So I did. *The Atami Dragons* project fell through as so many of them do and I found myself one of 50,000 young, aspiring screenwriters with no family connections, very few friends, and in a city I didn't know at all.

Although Klass's years in Los Angeles trying to break into the film industry were difficult ones, they did result in many of his strongest young adult novels. Klass describes this period of his life:

> I spent eight or nine years of my life in L.A. trying desperately to break in and struggling and feeling very lonely and out of place. During this time I can honestly say that my young adult writing kept me sane and solvent through some very, very difficult years. A lot of the difficulty and loneliness that I was experiencing found its way into my novels. For example, during one of the most difficult years of my life, I wrote *Wrestling with Honor.* And I think some of these sadness and isolation in parts of that book was really a reflection of what I was feeling. I also wrote *A Different Season, California Blue,* and *Danger Zone* during those years and finished *Breakaway Run,* which I had started in Japan.

While living in Los Angeles, Klass earned a master's degree in production from the School of Cinema and Television at the University of Southern California in 1989. Discouraged in his mid-thirties by his lack of success in the entertainment business, Klass contemplated giving up and even thought about going to medical school, when suddenly the door opened for him in Hollywood. He wrote the screenplays for *Kiss the Girls* and *Desperate Measures,* an action/thriller based on his original idea.

Personal Experiences and Writing Philosophy

Writers frequently draw upon their personal experiences, conflicts, and emotions in creating fiction. While Klass's young adult novels are not autobiographical, they do reflect some of his own significant experiences: his intense love of sports, his two years in Japan, his struggles to succeed in Hollywood. There is one notable exception, however. Klass notes:

> For some reason that I cannot explain, virtually all of my books, no matter what I set out to write, seem

solvent able to pay all debts

Kiss the Girls (1997) stars Morgan Freeman as a forensic psychologist trying to identify a person that has been kidnapping young women. Ashley Judd plays a kick-boxing doctor who has been the only one to escape the kidnaper alive.

Desperate Measures (1998) features Andy Garcia as a San Francisco cop whose child has leukemia. The only potential bone marrow donor is Michael Keaton, who plays a convicted killer who continually escapes capture.

autobiographical related to the author's own life

to boil down to father-son relationships. I cannot explain why, and why the fathers are dead or mean or have deep-seated problems. I have the most wonderful father in the world, and we have an extremely close relationship. If I could ever be one-tenth the father to my kids that he's been to me, then I could consider myself successful. I don't know where it comes from, but it does seem to find its way into my books.

Creating the intense father-son conflict in *California Blue* enabled Klass to tell a story that he struggled with for several years. Klass calls *California Blue* his favorite book and describes how he came to write it:

California Blue is a story I tried to tell for two or three years as a screenplay, as a stage play, and also as an adult novel. I was fascinated by what was happening in the Northwest. What I saw was a real American tragedy played out on a town by town level. I was interested by it because I didn't know who was right or if anyone was right. I heard these stories of people put out of work, but there are endangered species that I thought had a right to survive. I could see both sides and I tried to tell it for so long, but I could not tell the story and that doesn't happen to me that often and I found it infuriating. All I had was a story of a boy who happens to find a butterfly in a company forest and is set against his town. Finally I put it aside and after awhile, a year or two later, I came up with the idea of a father and the fact that while the boy was the one who found the butterfly, the father had worked at the mill and represented everything the boy was putting in jeopardy. As soon as I had the character of the father, the story came alive, and I was able to write it fairly quickly.

David Klass believes that one of the greatest services authors can provide for young adults is to write books that they will want to read. He believes that his novels must reflect what young people are thinking about and the kinds of situations they get into, not done sensationally, but truthfully. He explains the teacher-student relationship in *California Blue:*

> I felt very strongly that the relationship was true, and there was nothing wrong with it. Boys and girls do have crushes on their teachers and young teachers can like their students. I was both a teacher and a student, and I know from both sides that it can happen and that people can act honorably and nobly. This situation grew naturally out of the character—a boy who wasn't that close to any of his peers and was very isolated from his family and the other people in the town. He was interested in science and the idea that he had formed a crush on his science teacher made sense to me in many ways.

This philosophy is also apparent in Klass's other books. He describes an aspect of it in *Wrestling with Honor:*

> I was trying to paint a picture of a young man who was such a straight arrow that everyone who knew him really well knew he could not have taken drugs. One aspect of this was his relationship with girls. The "make-out" scene grew out of my desire to paint him as someone who lived by his own very narrow, and in some cases, too narrow, prescriptive world. It was a strange book to receive some very angry letters about, because to me it was about a character exploring honor—issues of honor that went back two generations—and trying to be a moral person in a very difficult world.

Another aspect of this philosophy is apparent in *Danger Zone,* where Klass creates two complex characters, one white and the other African American. Jimmy Doyle and Augustus LeMay, while on the same champion basketball team, come from very different worlds and these worlds collide. Klass explains:

> I lived in Los Angeles during the riots, and I never thought I would live in an American city that seemed

sensationally in a way that is shocking, intense, and disturbing (such emotional responses are often achieved by using gruesome details)

prescriptive characterized by having laws and rules

In April 1992 an all-white jury acquitted three white police officers of all charges in the Rodney King beating trial. A fourth white officer was acquitted of all but one charge. This shocking verdict led to an outbreak of rioting, looting, and arson, mainly in black areas of South-Central Los Angeles. The riots resulted in 2,100 injuries, 51 deaths, and over $1 billion in property damage.

adversity the condition of hardship

to be at war with itself. I played a lot of basketball all over L.A. and saw some of the tension and anger, as it was ripping up the city, reflected on the basketball courts. I wanted to try to catch some of what I saw— some of the tension and feelings that black people and white people couldn't even talk to each other and this huge gulf that seemed to separate them. I wanted to try to catch that within the context of a young adult story.

Klass's characters are multidimensional young people confronting contemporary issues, including morality, racism, and environmental concerns. They face difficult personal conflicts, including betrayal, divorce, and death. Yet Klass's novels are not grim, hopeless portrayals of reality. The young people in his novels laugh and play and enjoy the successes and failures of athletic challenges. They experience the highs and lows of dating, friendships, and family life. They grow and change because of their experiences and ultimately, demonstrate a greater strength of character and understanding of themselves and others, learned through adversity and tough times.

The Author Now

David Klass lives in New York City where he writes full time. He is under contract to Universal Studios to write more screenplays and is broadening his scope from action/thriller movies to other types of movies. He also continues to write young adult novels, looking for ways to stretch himself as an author and tell a good story that young people will want to read. One of Klass's dreams is that one day the two areas of his writing will meet and he'll write a young adult novel adapted into a movie. His love of sports and his belief in their importance continues, with Klass playing several sports and organizing a men's soccer team in the city.

If you like David Klass, you might also like Chris Crutcher and Will Weaver.

Selected Bibliography

WORKS BY DAVID KLASS

Novels for Young Adults
The Atami Dragons (1984)

Breakaway Run (1986)

A Different Season (1988)

Wrestling with Honor (1989)

California Blue (1994)

Danger Zone (1995)

Screen Test (1997)

Adult Novels

Night of the Tyger (1990)

Samurai, Inc. (1992)

Short Stories for Young Adults

Baseball Camp (1999)

Screenplays

Kiss the Girls (1997)

Desperate Measures (1997)

How to Write to the Author

David Klass
c/o Scholastic, Inc.
555 Broadway
New York, NY 10012-3999

Annette Curtis Klause

(1953–)

by Alleen Pace Nilsen

Annette Curtis Klause was born on 20 June 1953 in Bristol, England, where one of her early adventures was exploring the bombed ruins of buildings left over from World War II. Annette was seven years old in 1960 when her family moved north from Bristol to Newcastle-upon-Tyne, and she changed the setting of her explorations from spooky, old houses on cobblestone streets to imaginary explorations through the books she found in the public library. She began writing poems, then writing and illustrating her own books. Several of these are about cats, which she still loves and puts into her stories. During our telephone interview in January 1999, she was teaching a new kitten to fetch by tossing it a play mouse.

When Annette was fifteen, her father, a radiologist, was invited to Washington, D.C., for a one-year assignment. This assignment turned into a permanent job, and so the Curtis family (father Graham Trevor, mother Mary Frances, Annette, her two sisters, and one brother) settled in the Washington,

Quotations from Annette Curtis Klause that are not attributed to a published source are from a personal interview conducted by the author of this article on 29 January 1999 and are published here by permission of Annette Curtis Klause.

radiologist a doctor who specializes in the use of radiant energy to diagnose and treat diseases

135

D.C., area, where Annette still lives and works as a librarian. She graduated from the University of Maryland in 1976 and earned a master's degree in library science in 1978. The next year she married Mark Jeffrey Klause, and the two settled into a home in Hyattsville, Maryland, with a few cats and many books—mostly science fiction, fantasy, and horror. For fun they collect first and limited editions of such books and take trips to science fiction conventions.

A Love of Science Fiction

In an article that Klause wrote for the *School Library Journal* in September 1988, she said that she agrees with editor David Hartwell who declared that "the golden age of science fiction is 12." She was about this age when she discovered some old boxes filled with her father's science fiction books and magazines. Her mother referred to them as "that rubbish," but Annette was sucked in by the magazines with their surreal covers and such names as *Analog, Galaxy, Amazing Stories,* and *If.* "At first," she says, "I just looked and dreamed. I took them all out of the boxes and sorted them. Even the smell of the yellowing pages was wonderful. I flipped through them, a little afraid of the unknown words." But then she discovered that the small classroom library at her school had Robert Heinlein's books. Looking back, she now wishes they had also had Andre Norton's, but her successful reading of Heinlein's *Tunnel in the Sky* (1955) and *Farmer in the Sky* (1950) gave her the courage to return to her father's collection where she began fighting her "way through jargon as unrelentingly as spacemen fight through alien jungles."

As she became "hooked," her vocabulary changed and so did her way of thinking. Her father "attained even greater status" in her eyes because she "knew his secret—he wasn't a grown-up." But at the same time, he had a successful career as a respected radiologist and so she "concluded that intelligent, successful people read science fiction."

While she confesses to occasionally being "seduced by the dark side of the force—horror fiction," Klause always comes back to her first love of science fiction. She notes it "can include horror, mystery and romance; it can be funny or awe inspiring; it can be grittily real, or ethereal," and sometimes "it can be just plain bad."

surreal characterized by fantastic imagery

Robert Heinlein (1907–1988) was a controversial American science fiction writer. *Tunnel in the Sky* is the story of a group of children accidentally stranded on an alien world. *Farmer in the Sky* is about a family trying to farm on one of Jupiter's moons, despite many setbacks.

Andre Norton (1912–) is an American science fiction author. She changed her name from Mary Alice to Andre when she feared her first novel might be rejected if publishers knew a woman had written it.

jargon specialized vocabulary of a particular genre

ethereal relating to regions beyond the earth; unworldly, spiritual

A Soft Spot for the Alien Among Us

Klause says that when she was young, her red hair, her literary bent, and her tendency to stare dreamily out of the window, oblivious to the realities of school and daily life, made her feel like an outsider. Her favorite picture books were about an independent orange tomcat named Orlando, and she fondly remembers reading C. S. Lewis' Chronicles of Narnia (1950–1956) again and again. When she found her father's science fiction collection, she had already written her first horror story, "The Blood Ridden Pool of Solen Goom," and had become entranced with "different" worlds and "different" peoples. While her mother had read and sung the childhood "classics," her father had entertained her by telling her plots of popular horror stories and gangster and monster movies. At the library he would hand her Edgar Rice Burroughs' books and say "This is a fairy tale for grown-ups," or he would bring home stacks of old comic books that he had found in used bookstores.

The first book that Klause read about vampires was *The Shiny Narrow Grin* (1964), by Jane Gaskell. Gaskell's book inspired Klause to begin writing poems and short pieces about ghouls, the supernatural, and the macabre. She called her collection "The Saga of the Vampire." When Klause moved to America, she still felt like an outsider, but she found that being "different" wasn't all bad. She sensed a new kind of acceptance from American teenagers who viewed her British accent and her literary interests as exotic. In a renewed frame of mind, she turned from writing about vampires and ghouls to writing "soppy love poems."

As an adult, she laughs about how pretentious and overwritten the pieces now sound. Nevertheless, she keeps going back to her high school writing notebooks for inspiration, because even if they aren't smooth, they were inspired by genuine teenage concerns, fears, and interests.

During college, her busy schedule slowed down her writing, but she attended poetry workshops and remembers switching from romance to shock and irreverence. When she completed her library training, she began working in various libraries throughout Maryland, most often serving young readers. She began submitting poetry and short stories for publication. Although she admits to receiving her share of rejection notices, she had poems accepted by *Takoma Park Writers 1981, Cat's Magazine, Visions,* and *Aurora.*

There is an article about C. S. Lewis in volume 2.

Edgar Rice Burroughs (1875–1950) was an American science fiction author who created the character of Tarzan in 1912. He is also known for a series of books that are set on the planet of Mars.

Jane Gaskell (1941–) is the pen name of Jane Gaskell Lynch, a science fiction author who wrote several novels during the late 1950s and 1960s.

macabre dealing with the gruesome

irreverence lack of proper respect

Turning Professional

In the mid-1980s, Klause enrolled in a writing workshop with Larry Callen. He encouraged her to become a professional writer and introduced her to a group in which she still participates with approximately a dozen authors. They meet twice a month to listen to each other's work, to ask questions, and to make suggestions. When we talked early in 1999, she had just read to the group the beginning of her new book, and she could tell by their questions that they understood the protagonist she was envisioning. She didn't want to talk about the new book except to say that it is "another weird romance" and that this time she is telling it from the boy's perspective.

When I asked her if, and how, her books tie into today's world, she laughingly said that "No one has been impeached, but there has been some furtive sex." Being a librarian, she is well acquainted with censorship problems and has been somewhat surprised that her books have not become primary targets. Referring to the sensuality in *The Silver Kiss* (1990) and *Blood and Chocolate* (1997), she says, "But that's okay. I would just as soon have it be a secret between me and my readers." She was amused when she recently spoke at a meeting of middle school media specialists, and many of the librarians came up to have newly purchased copies of *Blood and Chocolate* autographed to themselves rather than to their libraries. They explained that while they could not buy the book for their junior high libraries, they nevertheless wanted to read it.

Along another line, she agreed with my conjecture that her stories go beyond entertainment to illustrate the desirability of people with genuine differences learning to live together. She models possibilities by showing how creatures with no power and no authority manage to negotiate their differences.

However, Klause disagreed somewhat with my conclusion that in her kind of writing, novels work better than short stories because authors need more space to develop unusual or alien characters. While acknowledging that it is hard to develop characters in a short space, she said the requirement is almost the same for novels as for short stories because readers have to be drawn to the characters within the first few paragraphs, or they won't stick with the book.

---

protagonist the main character of a literary work

censorship the suppression of something that one finds objectionable

conjecture conclusions reached by guesswork

Klause's Books

The main characters in each of Klause's three novels are decidedly different. They use their unique strengths to overcome their problems. Klause's first young adult novel was published in 1990. *The Silver Kiss* is the story of Zoë, a shy seventeen-year-old girl who spends most of her time alone. She is an only child, her mother is dying of cancer, and her best (and pretty much only) friend is moving away. Zoë used to be close to both of her parents, but now that her mother is hospitalized and her father is either working or visiting his wife, Zoë broods about death and how she will cope with her own life after her mother is gone.

Zoë likes to walk in the neighborhood park and sit in front of the old-fashioned gazebo, where one night "a shadow crept inside, independent of natural shades." Then she saw his face:

> **He was young, more boy than man, slight and pale, made elfin by the moon. He noticed her and froze like a deer before the gun. They were trapped in each other's gaze. His eyes were dark, full of wilderness and stars. But his face was ashen. Almost as pale as his silver hair. (P. 12)**

With a sudden ache, Zoë recognizes his beauty and as the tears she has been holding back spill from her eyes, he flees while she sits weeping for all the things that are lost.

The boy she has seen is Simon, a three hundred-year-old vampire who has followed his brother Christopher across the ocean in an attempt to control him. Three hundred years earlier, Christopher had killed the boys' beloved mother and turned Simon into a vampire. Christopher is now responsible for an outbreak of gruesome murders in Zoë's contemporary suburban town.

In spite of being a vampire, Simon is not at all like his brother. As Simon and Zoë continue to meet, Zoë reluctantly allows him, the shocking outsider, into her mind and heart where he helps her see how strong and capable she can be. He convinces her to let go of her mother willingly so that they can both rest in peace. Zoë, in turn, helps Simon in his final struggle against Christopher.

The story is so unusual and is told with such tenderness that the book was chosen a favorite in contests sponsored by state library groups in South Carolina, Oklahoma, California, Maryland, and Michigan. Editors of *School Library Journal* and *Booklist* both chose it as one of the "Best Books" of 1990, as did the American Library Association. In her review of the book in the December 1990 *Wilson Library Bulletin,* critic Cathi MacRae described the scene where Zoë accepts Simon's "sharp, sleek kiss, the silver kiss, so swift and true. . . ." as "perhaps the most thrillingly sensual scene in YA literature." William Sleator called the book a "marvelously grisly thriller. . . . full of compassion," while Robert Cormier said that it unforgettably "blazes a bloody trail in YA literature."

Klause's second book, *Alien Secrets,* was published in 1993 for slightly younger readers. In 1993, she wrote in *Speaking for Ourselves, Too:*

> It was natural that I should attempt a science fiction book next, but writing science fiction is much harder than reading it. *The Silver Kiss* was such a visceral story that it just seemed to roll out of me; *Alien Secrets,* however, entailed extensive outlining in order to create a future world that was believable, give the characters background, and make the mystery element in the plot work logically. And then most of the details don't even show up in the book! (P. 110)

The heroine is thirteen-year-old Puck, a girl with no interest in romantic relations or the macabre. She is more intrigued by her own predicament of having to travel on a cargo spaceship to join her parents on the planet of Shoon after being expelled from boarding school for getting bad grades. Puck is actually named Robin Goodfellow after the mischievous little elf in Shakespeare's *A Midsummer Night's Dream,* which provides for some interesting allusions. The captain of the spaceship asks Puck to befriend a sad and lonely alien nicknamed Hush, who is also traveling through outer space to the planet of Shoon, his native land. As Hush comes to trust Puck, he shares his story. He too is "in disgrace" because he was to return a prized symbol of his people's freedom home to Shoon. But the symbol, in the form of a statue, has been stolen from Hush and is hidden somewhere on the spaceship. Puck turns into a super-sleuth, Nancy Drew-type heroine, and together she and Hush manage to return home as heroes.

visceral dealing with basic emotions

There is an article about William Shakespeare in volume 3.

The **Nancy Drew** series was created by Edward Stratemeyer. There is an article about him in volume 3.

Roger Sutton in the September 1993 *Bulletin of the Center for Children's Books* described *Alien Secrets* as "murder on the Orient Express, space style," while Donna Scanlon in the August 1993 *VOYA* praised Klause for the way she shows that Hush's "imperfect" command of English has its own communication strength. For example, when Puck asks why Hush didn't continue telling a skeptical police officer about the treasure, Hush says, "Do you think he would have unfolded his ears?"

While advanced science fiction fans have quibbled with some of the technical references to hyperspace, others have praised the book for avoiding the kind of jargon that intimidated Klause at age twelve when she first met science fiction. They have also praised the way she brought a "human" touch to the spaceship with such nonhuman creatures as ghosts, cats, and a likable alien. The American Library Association put the book on its "Notable" list for 1993, as did the New York Public Library, *Booklist,* and *School Library Journal.*

Klause says that most of the letters she gets from boy readers are about *Alien Secrets.* However, she recently noticed a boy sitting outside the Aspen Hills Community Library hunched over something in a suspicious way. It was during school hours, so she knew he was ditching. When she approached him, he grinned and held up *Blood and Chocolate* with the explanation, "I'm reading your book!" How could she ask such a discerning reader why he wasn't in school?

Blood and Chocolate returns to the paranormal as readers are flung into the mind of a sixteen-year-old female werewolf named Vivian. The book made its way to the same kinds of "Best" lists as did *The Silver Kiss.* The title comes from a sentence in Hermann Hesse's *Steppenwolf* (1927), "In fear I hurried this way and that. I had the taste of blood and chocolate in my mouth, the one as hateful as the other." A second quote on the preface page is from Rudyard Kipling's poem "The Law of the Jungle" (1894): "Ye may kill for yourselves, and your mates, and your cubs as they need, and ye can; / But kill not for pleasure of killing, and *seven times never kill Man!*"

Readers see the inner workings of Vivian's wolf clan family along with their relation to humans as the wolves form their own subculture within "normal" society. In many respects, Vivian is an average high school student interested in having fun and exploring new relationships. She struggles to fit in with her peers and finally feels accepted when she becomes Aiden's girlfriend. He is a human schoolmate who shows a

Hermann Hesse (1877–1962) was a German novelist and poet who won the 1946 Nobel Prize for literature.

discerning having clear insight and understanding

Rudyard Kipling (1865–1936) was a British poet, short-story writer, and novelist. He received the Nobel Prize for literature in 1907. **"The Law of the Jungle"** is from *The Jungle Book,* a famous children's story.

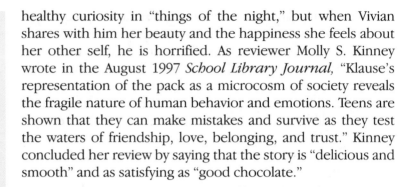

microcosm the universe in miniature

healthy curiosity in "things of the night," but when Vivian shares with him her beauty and the happiness she feels about her other self, he is horrified. As reviewer Molly S. Kinney wrote in the August 1997 *School Library Journal,* "Klause's representation of the pack as a microcosm of society reveals the fragile nature of human behavior and emotions. Teens are shown that they can make mistakes and survive as they test the waters of friendship, love, belonging, and trust." Kinney concluded her review by saying that the story is "delicious and smooth" and as satisfying as "good chocolate."

If you enjoy Annette Curtis Klause, you might also enjoy Peter Dickinson, Margaret Mahy, and William Sleator.

Selected Bibliography

WORKS BY ANNETTE CURTIS KLAUSE

Novels for Young Adults
The Silver Kiss (1990)
Alien Secrets (1993)
Blood and Chocolate (1997)

Short Stories
"The Bogeyman." In *Night Terrors: Stories of Shadow and Substance.* Edited by Lois Duncan. New York: Simon & Schuster, 1996.

"The Hoppins." In *Short Circuits: Thirteen Shocking Stories by Outstanding Writers for Young Adults.* Edited by Donald R. Gallo. New York: Delacorte, 1992.

"Librarians from Space." In *The U*n*a*b*a*s*h*e*d Librarian,* vol. 51, 1984.

Essays
"Annette Curtis Klause." *Speaking for Ourselves, Too: More Autobiographical Sketches by Notable Authors of Books for Young Adults.* Compiled and edited by Donald R. Gallo. Urbana, Ill.: National Council of Teachers of English, 1993, pp. 109–110.

"A Hitchhiker's Guide to Science Fiction." *School Library Journal,* September 1988, pp. 120–123.

WORKS ABOUT ANNETTE CURTIS KLAUSE

Jones, J. Sydney. "Annette Curtis Klause." In *Contemporary Authors.* Edited by Kathleen J. Edgar. Detroit: Gale Research, 1995, vol. 147, pp. 254–257.

Jones, J. Sydney. "Annette Curtis Klause." In *Something About the Author.* Edited by Kevin S. Hile. Detroit: Gale Research, 1995, vol. 79, pp. 115–118.

MacRae, Cathi. "Young Adult Perplex." In *Wilson Library Bulletin,* December 1990, pp. 599–600.

Vandergrift, Kay E. "Annette Curtis Klause." In *Twentieth-Century Young Adult Writers.* Edited by Tom Pendergast and Sara Pendergast. Detroit: St. James, 1999, pp. 458–459.

How to Write to the Author

Annette Curtis Klause
c/o Delacorte Press
1540 Broadway
New York, NY 10036

Ronald Koertge

by Patricia P. Kelly

A college professor, a poet, and a novelist, Ronald Koertge (pronounced *Kur*-chee) has even written a poem, "Pronouncing My Name," about the difficulty that people have with his name: "When someone leans in and says, 'Koochurch? Curcheese? Curgoo?' I just nod. Believe me, it's easier" (*Life on the Edge of the Continent: Selected Poems of Ronald Koertge,* 1982, p. 42). As someone who writes every day, Koertge says that, when he gets an idea, he's "like an ostrich with an egg," staying with it until something happens.

The settings for Koertge's novels mirror his own experiences. He was born in Illinois on 22 April 1940, the only child of Bulis Olive and William Henry, an owner of an ice cream store and school janitor. The family lived in a town twenty miles from the Mississippi River. He sets both *Where the Kissing Never Stops* (1986) and *The Boy in the Moon* (1990) in a fictional, small Midwestern town called Bradleyville, Missouri; and both Billy in *The Arizona Kid* (1988) and Gabriel in *The Harmony Arms* (1992) live there, but each spends a summer in Arizona and California, respectively. Koertge received his

Quotations from Ronald Koertge that are not attributed to a published source are from a personal telephone interview conducted by the author of this article on 26 January 1999 and are published here by permission of Ronald Koertge.

undergraduate degree from the University of Illinois and later received his master's degree from the University of Arizona. He teaches English at Pasadena City College in California. Therefore, his subsequent novels have had a range of California settings, from the beach to the desert, to the suburbs, to the inner city. Another element of setting that stems from Koertge's experiences is horses and horse racing, both central to *The Arizona Kid* and *Mariposa Blues* (1991). He says that Bradleyville was the name of a horse that made him "a lot of money because he would put his ears back and run," and thus the name for Koertge's small fictional town was chosen. He does not currently own a horse but still visits race tracks and talks to trainers.

Having written novels for adults previously, Koertge's switch to writing young adult novels brought quick recognition. *Where the Kissing Never Stops* and *The Arizona Kid* were chosen as American Library Association Best Books, and *The Arizona Kid* was selected for the prestigious 100 Best of the Best ALA List, representing the best from twenty-five years of young adult literature. These awards and others that his later novels have received recognize Koertge's affinity for describing the uncertain journey through adolescence, for depicting a range of family relationships, for raising awareness of selected social issues, and for writing that is both poetic and humorous.

affinity feeling of preference or connection

Adolescent Angst as a Theme

Koertge, by remembering his own youth, captures through humor and sensitivity the angst, the anxiety, the insecurity of adolescence. He states this theme explicitly in his first book, *Where the Kissing Never Stops,* when Walker realizes that "all over town kids lay awake and wondered: am I smart enough, pretty enough, strong enough, tall enough. If our fears had been smoke, the town would be covered night and day by an inky pall" (p. 112). Earlier in the novel Walker stands in front of a mirror naked and hates his body: "I feel like I'm the only resident of this big, ugly hotel, and I didn't choose it, somebody checked me in while I was unconscious and now I can't get out" (p. 90). To make matters worse, he eats when anxiety sets in. He thinks about kissing a lot and what kissing can lead to. And he is miserable when he breaks up with Rachel: "School was just another trip to the Planet Misery. . . . Everywhere out

angst anxiety or anguish

pall a dark, gloomy covering

there reminded me of Rachel—where we had eaten lunch or made love or taken a nap or talked about what we would do" (p. 197). However, ultimately, though nothing is the way he has imagined, Walker is happier than he has ever been in his life because he has gained some understanding of himself and others.

Billy in *The Arizona Kid* also suffers from insecurity, describing himself as "a shrimp" and "a virgin" (p. 7). He has come to spend the summer with his Uncle Wes, who has gotten him a job at a race track. There he has to stand his ground with other more experienced hands; he has to change his sneakers for cowboy boots, his straw hat for a cowboy hat, and his sunscreen for a tan. His new macho demeanor does not prepare him for the hurt of parting from Cara, his first love. Uncle Wes teaches him that it is all right to cry, and Cara's father wisely tells her that she will "be in love a thousand times before you're done" (p. 223). Though Billy thinks he is going to die when telling Cara goodbye, he leaves Arizona with a better self-image: "I'm as tall as I am. It's okay" (p. 225).

Mr. Evars in *The Boy in the Moon* gives his English class the task of writing a thoughtful, extraordinary paper titled "Who Am I?" because he knows it is a question that each must answer or at least struggle with. Nick thinks of himself as the son of a poet and a police chief and as a friend of Kevin and Frieda, but he also describes his acne-scarred face as "the face of the moon . . . lunar, bare, and ruined" (p. 8). Nick's journey to understanding the title question leads him to understanding others as well. He knows that Kevin, though deserted by his preacher father, will be happier with his mother in California; he learns about love with Frieda, who soon will leave for college; and he realizes that the three of them will never be the same again. Yet Nick is content with who he is at this moment in time because he has made the journey from the moon, where he has placed an emphasis on his outward appearance, to the earth, where people and friendships are most important.

Graham in *Mariposa Blues* describes his adolescent angst as "one of those rides at Magic Mountain that turn you every way but loose . . . [with] no safety bar" and you don't know where you are when you stagger off (p. 7). He wants to spend his days surfing, grow taller than his father, and make his own decisions. He disappoints his father by going to work for another horse trainer because he and his father seem to argue all

demeanor outward manner

Cara's father wisely tells her that she will "be in love a thousand times before you're done."

the time. He likes Leslie and is hurt and confused by her talk of Todd, her boyfriend, and the questions she asks Graham about boys' feelings and reactions. At fourteen both are trying to learn to cope with their changing bodies and feelings.

Having moved four times in four years, Tony in *Confess-O-Rama* (1996) is again in a new school and without friends. Because his mother has not coped well with her fourth husband's death, Tony takes care of her as well as himself. Fortunately, cooking is his passion. He pours out his anxieties to Confess-O-Rama, a taped message service for people with problems, only to discover later that the tapings are for an art project that his girlfriend, Jordan, is doing. When his mother talks about moving again, Tony despairs as he thinks of Jordan: "I want everything—I want to be friends, I want to kiss you, I want to stay in West Paradise, I want to know what to do with my life" (p. 106). Such is the angst of adolescents: the need for friends, an uncertainty about their emerging sexuality, a desire for stability, a dislike of who they are, and fear of what their lives will become.

Although Gabriel worries about being skinny and is embarrassed by his father's hand puppetry, the person in *The Harmony Arms* who best voices the meaning of adolescent angst is Sumner, Gabriel's father. Describing his own youthful anxiety, he says: "I was too shy and afraid. . . . I had friends who were girls, but no girlfriends. . . . I was never one of the guys. I was happier planning things or getting there early and decorating or cleaning up afterward" (p. 132). Ironically, Sumner marries an energetic, restless, hard-to-please woman, but he as well as his son, Gabriel, come to understand that their divorce is not a reflection of failure but of insurmountable differences. As a product of these two divergent people, Gabriel has a bright future because in him the two parents have come to harmony; he is a combination of the best of both. As a result of the California summer with his father, Gabriel has gained an appreciation for both of his parents and their individuality.

insurmountable unable to be overcome

Family Relationships as a Theme

Characters' sense of otherness, of being different, which is central to Koertge's novels, extends into the family relationships he develops for his characters. The most volatile father-son relationship appears in *Mariposa Blues,* which Koertge says is based on a trainer he knew "who was having trouble

volatile explosive

with his son." After a disagreement over the readiness of a horse to race, Graham openly breaks with his father when he takes a job with another trainer. Asserting his independence, he tells his mother, who is the bookkeeper for the family's training business, that "at least I'm gonna get paid, and I'm not gonna run around after Dad like you do" (p. 116). His mother tries to make him understand that the business and marriage are partnerships and that she is her "own person" (p. 117), but Graham believes his father just wants him to agree with him about everything. When they reconcile after the last race of the season, Graham's father admits, "I hear myself . . . arguing with you or telling you to do something you don't want to do, and it's almost me and my dad all over again" (pp. 170–171). When Graham concedes he is glad he is like his father, he notices his father's hand on his shoulder, guiding him "so lightly I barely knew it was there" (p. 171).

reconcile to restore to harmony

Koertge's depiction of mother-son relationships, though based on caring, is nonetheless unconventional. In *Where the Kissing Never Stops* Walker is ashamed that his mother has become an exotic dancer after his father's death. His father had not been a warm, touching person, but his mother's revelations about their relationship confuse Walker, who realizes he did not really know his dad and makes him wonder "Who had I loved?" (p. 55). After getting into one of his mother's shows, which he sees as rather sedate and even artistic, Walker feels an exhilarating resurgence of love for her. Other facets of his life are still unsettled, but he has a new appreciation of his mother. Tony in *Confess-O-Rama* has assumed most of the responsibility for cooking and cleaning because his mother is suffering from depression. She admits that she has had Tony "to lean on" (p. 75) but conversely is overprotective, fearful to let him drive. Gradually she emerges from her depression. She dresses, begins visiting, and eventually takes a job with Sheila's Coffin Corral, because after all she has had some experience, having had four dead husbands. She knows that one way she can repay Tony for all he has done for her is to stay in West Paradise until he graduates with his friends. For Tony, it is good to hear his mother laugh again.

sedate calm; unhurried

resurgence the recurrence of a feeling or activity

facet aspect

conversely in an opposite manner

Nick's relationship with his parents in *The Boy in the Moon* is uncertain. He respects his father, a police chief, but feels distant from him. He loves his mother and likes "helping her choose poems to mail to grant committees because she actually listened to me" (p. 147) and attends her poetry read-

narrative a story told in fiction, nonfiction, poetry, or drama

plot the deliberate sequence of events in a literary work

ings. Yet he is puzzled by his parents' relationship because they sleep in separate bedrooms and have different interests. When Nick is sad because his girlfriend, Frieda, will soon leave for college, his mother talks to him about love and consideration, the foundation for the shape of his parents' lives. She is writing a poem called "The Burden of Narrative" about a person who lives out "the standard plot," living in such a way that there are no "alternative endings" (p. 151). Nick begins to understand that loving means giving a loved one space to grow and in doing so gaining more possibilities for oneself.

Social Commentary as a Theme

Koertge says that he is "not an issue writer," yet there are elements of social commentary in his novels. He recalls that "the idea for *The Heart of the City* [1998] came from reading about a homeless guy in Detroit, who decorated a house and saved a neighborhood." When Gregory Fontaine, an artist, moves his family into a remodeled home in an inner-city neighborhood, the family's friends refuse even to visit. But Gregory believes his art needs the rawness and reality of Ibarra Street. Dimitrios, the homeless man, with his customized grocery carts, is a fixture of the neighborhood. However, he represents just one of the many lifestyles and colors of the rainbow community. When Joy and Neesha decide to thwart the efforts of drug dealers to use a vacant house by painting and decorating it unconventionally in order to draw attention to it, it is Dimitrios who furnishes the mirrors that provide the final touch. Their plan works and the community is united, but it is evident that keeping the drug dealers out will require a sustained, ongoing effort.

In *The Arizona Kid* Koertge deals with the topic of homosexuality through Billy's Uncle Wes, with whom he is spending the summer. Wes is not a stereotype, though he is decidedly gay. Billy knows that his father worries about Wes and especially about AIDS. However, Wes openly discusses the issues with Billy. Wes's friend dies of AIDS, and in another scene Wes is harassed for being gay. Although Billy does not understand completely, he constantly corrects references to his uncle as queer, by responding with "Gay . . . not queer." "Yeah, whatever," someone may reply, but at least Billy understands the importance of language in shaping ideas (p. 41).

Aging is the major theme of *Tiger, Tiger, Burning Bright* (1994). Pappy, Jesse's grandfather who taught Jesse how to

stereotype universal type; character that conforms to a preconceived and often oversimplified notion about a person or group

ride and survive in the desert, is becoming forgetful in dangerous ways. Jesse's mother wants to send him to a nursing
home, and Jesse fears that Pappy's insistence that he has seen
tiger tracks in the desert will prove his failing competence.
Just as Pappy cared for Jesse as a child, Jesse now lives with
and cares for Pappy. Ironically, Jesse serves the caretaker role
rather than Jesse's mother, who lives in an apartment behind
the house. Pappy is proven correct about the tiger tracks,
made by tigers illegally brought to a ranch for a hunt. The
desert town unites to support Jesse as he watches out for
Pappy, and his mother relents. After all, she loves her father,
too, but is saddened by his decline.

Stylistic Characteristics

Judy Sasges in her review of *Tiger, Tiger, Burning Bright* refers
to "the trademark Koertge dialogue" (*Voice of Youth Advocates,* June 1994, p. 86). And that is true for all his novels. The
dialogue is natural, oftentimes funny and offbeat, and he is the
master of the one-liner, the quick verbal comeback. Koertge
says that he has a "poet's ear" for language and that he "writes
dialogue easier and faster than narrative." In *The Arizona Kid*
Billy asks about what the trainers are telling the jockeys before
the race, and Lew responds, "To go to the front, and improve
their position" (p. 52). When Sully tries to get Walker interested in a new girl in town, they banter back and forth, and finally Sully says, "She needs you. Two lonely souls. She hasn't
got a mother." To which Walker quips, "Shouldn't we call the
Pope? Isn't that a miracle?" (*Where the Kissing Never Stops,*
p. 20). On a trip to Venice Beach in *The Harmony Arms,* Tess
wryly comments on the way the day has gone: " 'What'd you
guys do at the beach, make out and pig on junk food?' 'Nah,
we almost got in a fight. Then we put on Sun Block 9000 and
talked about who was dead' " (p. 147). From quips to under-
stated humor to outright laughs, Koertge's characters move
the plots along with their dialogue.

Another feature of Koertge's style is his ability to develop
believable, though diverse, characters. Every novel contains
the unusual, the offbeat, or quirky character, especially *The
Harmony Arms* and *Tiger, Tiger, Burning Bright.* Alice Casey
Smith, in her review of *The Harmony Arms* in the *School Library Journal* of August 1992, describes the characters as a
strength of the novel: "Bizarre at first glance, Koertge's adult

dialogue conversation between characters

banter to speak in a witty or teasing manner

quip to make a funny or witty observation, usually on the spur of the moment

quirky full of peculiar actions, thoughts, and behaviors

characters, for all their imperfections and oddities, grow on readers. Their love, wisdom, and solid, if seemingly unconventional, values remind all of us that the only truly perfect people are the ones created for television, not by life." Until Gabriel meets the tenants of the Harmony Arms apartment complex, his father has been the oddest person he has known. There Gabriel meets and learns to care for an elderly nudist, a sometimes right–sometimes wrong psychic, an unsuccessful actress who makes commercials, and a teenage girl who carries a camcorder because she is filming her life. Similarly, offbeat characters bring life to a California desert town in *Tiger, Tiger, Burning Bright*—for example, Bobby, who introduces ostrich racing to the town, and Jesse's mother, a chiropractor who takes cheese and garden vegetables in exchange for services. And it is not only the adults who make readers laugh in this novel. For instance, when Jesse's study group meets, they are challenged to hold a dime-sized frog in their mouths to prove they are men. Jesse describes the frog as hopping around, ricocheting off his teeth. But Walter, the skinny kid, who "coughed, grimaced, squirmed" (p. 47), then declares proudly that he has swallowed his frog.

Other offbeat but believable characters interact with the more conventional characters in every novel. On Ibarra Street, Dimitrios—dressed in his "red pants, sandals with tire soles, yellow shirt. . . . Dreadlocks," hanging over his face, pushing his train of grocery carts that hold all his belongings—soon becomes a familiar sight to ten-year-old Joy in *The Heart of the City* (p. 67). Sixteen-year-old Jordan, an artist in *Confess-O-Rama* and one who Koertge confesses is "a favorite character of mine," dresses in black to express her artistic nature but is suspended from school for wearing chains and wild bras to protest sexism in a type of performance art. Another female character who expresses herself through clothes is Peggy in *Where the Kissing Never Stops*. Peggy, a cosmetologist, is not exactly the type of girl that Sully, headed for a career as a lawyer, should like, but he does. Clothes are costumes for Peggy. When she visits Walker's farm, she wears "green pedal pushers, a man's green shirt tied at the waist, and a green hat with a veil, [looking] like every stringbean's idea of Beauty" (p. 107).

Another characteristic of Koertge's style, drawn from his poetry writing, is the vivid language and sharpness of images he uses to describe people, places, and events. Laurel Graeber

dreadlocks a hairstyle consisting of ropelike strands of hair that are braided or matted

pedal pushers women's pants that end at the calf

in the 21 August 1988 *New York Times Book Review* praises Koertge's "writing, which offers lively metaphors on virtually every page." In *Tiger, Tiger, Burning Bright* a run-down house "sagged on one side, like a mail carrier," (p. 36); "the big room began to develop like a photograph" (p. 162); and Jesse "felt like something in a petri dish" (p. 108). When Gabriel and Tess in *The Harmony Arms* try to re-create their passionate kissing scene for Tess's film biography, they have difficulty, but a "little of yesterday came back then, like an accident victim regaining consciousness" (p. 125). In *The Boy in the Moon* Nick sees the countryside as "coloring book weather: blue sky, white clouds, red barns" (p. 63). Later Kevin, Nick's friend who has discovered that his newly acquired California persona does not work with his friends in a small Midwestern town, describes himself: "Sometimes I feel like day-old cake with a lot of fresh icing" (p. 118). In *Where the Kissing Never Stops* Koertge describes dark birds high above: "not a quarter mile away the sky was full of punctuation" (p. 99). At another point, when Walker leaves with Rachel for a date, her father tells her to be careful: "a comment that had as many layers as a wedding cake" (p. 115). Koertge also uses unique comparisons in every novel to help readers imagine settings; the sky over Ibarra Street in *The Heart of the City* "looked like good silverware that'd been kept in a bottom drawer too long. That tarnished color" (p. 66). In the same novel he cleverly compares a row of soda bottles to the multicultural neighborhood: "the colas, the orange, the strawberry, the 7UP. All standing together" (p. 71).

Although certain stylistic characteristics and themes cut across all of Koertge's novels, each is a distinct, unique story told through unforgettable characters and snappy dialogue. Through his main characters, usually high school age males with varying problems and relationships, Koertge tells his coming-of-age stories with honesty and humor.

Selected Bibliography

WORKS BY RONALD KOERTGE

Where the Kissing Never Stops (1986)

The Arizona Kid (1988)

The Boy in the Moon (1990)

Mariposa Blues (1991)

metaphor a figure of speech in which one thing is referred to as something else; for example, "My love is a rose"

persona the personality someone displays in public

If you like the male characterizations in Ronald Koertge's novels, you might like *Rats Saw God* by Rob Thomas and novels by Alden Carter, Chris Crutcher, and Walter Dean Myers. If you like Koertge's quirky, offbeat characters, you might like the Weetzie Bat books by Francesca Lia Block.

The Harmony Arms (1992)

Tiger, Tiger Burning Bright (1994)

Confess-O-Rama (1996)x

The Heart of the City (1998)

How to Write to the Author

Ronald Koertge
1570 East Colorado Boulevard
Pasadena, CA 91106

WORKS ABOUT RONALD KOERTGE

Hal, May, and Deborah A. Straub, eds. *Contemporary Authors: New Revision Series,* Detroit: Gale Research, 1989, vol. 25, p. 253.

Hedblad, Alan, ed. *Something About the Author.* Detroit: Gale Research, 1997, vol. 92, pp. 109–112.

Trudy Krisher

(1946–)

by Connie S. Zitlow

Trudy Krisher became known as a writer for young adults when *Spite Fences* (1994) was published, but her story began many years earlier. It goes back to an annual school-shopping trip when seven-year-old Trudy and her mother, Lois, took the bus downtown to buy new shoes. Thirsty and attracted by the word "colored" over the water fountain, Trudy headed toward it to get a drink. She wondered if the water would be blue or maybe even pink; certainly it would be more interesting than the usual clear stuff, she recalls in the summer 1997 issue of the *Ohio Journal of the English Language Arts (OJELA).* Although her mother gently pointed her in the direction of the place where she should get her drink—at the fountain marked "white"—the sense of injustice stayed with Trudy. This feeling and her memory of living in the "Jim Crow South" led eventually to her writing a realistic story set in 1960 in the fictional town of Kinship, Georgia. This award-winning novel, *Spite Fences* was published in 1994 and was followed in 1997 by *Kinship,* Krisher's second book for young adults.

The "**Jim Crow South**" refers to the southern United States during the existence of Jim Crow laws. These laws provided for the legal enforcement, from 1890 to the 1960s, of racial segregation and social exclusion of African Americans.

Difference and Discrimination

Like thirteen-year-old Maggie Pugh who tells the story of *Spite Fences,* Trudy Krisher grew up in the South. Born on 22 December 1946 in Macon, Georgia, and raised in southern Florida along with her sisters Gayle and Lella, she found it confusing to live in places where the reality of injustice and discrimination was very different from the equality people talked about. Many years later in another setting, she again witnessed a painful kind of discrimination when Kathy, the second of her three children, was diagnosed with bone cancer, something that made her different from those around her. Following Kathy's successful battle with Ewing's sarcoma, Krisher wrote *Kathy's Hats: A Story of Hope* (1992), a picture book illustrated by Nadine Bernard Wescott. In it she explores the feelings of a child who loses her hair and faces many challenges with courage and creativity.

Krisher first wrote *Kathy's Hats* as a project for a class in children's literature. It was at a time when she and her children had faced so many struggles that she didn't think she would ever write again. But she now feels the book, which she first self-published, and the response to it, gave her back her life. She even did a book-signing with children from the hospital, an event held at a local bookstore, complete with hats for the young cancer patients. After someone sent the book to a "real" publisher who asked what else she had written, Krisher pulled out the writing that became *Spite Fences.* For it she received an International Reading Association Children's Book Award and the Jefferson Cup, an award given by the Virginia Library Association to a work of historical fiction. *Spite Fences* was named a *Parents' Choice* Honor Book and an American Library Association Best Book for Young Adults, an honor also received by *Kinship.*

For many years before her books were published, Krisher, who was divorced when her children were very young, struggled to survive what she calls emotional and financial "fences." She worked at several part-time teaching and freelance writing jobs, including reviewing one book a week for ten years for the *Dayton Journal-Herald,* work she says was a wonderful education in fiction. Her admiration of the photos of the authors of the books, many done by Jill Krementz, led to Krisher's opportunity to write the introduction for *The Writer's Image: Literary Portraits* (1980), a collection of Krementz's works.

Krisher majored in English at the College of William and Mary and earned a master's degree in education from Trenton

freelance work done independently, not for an individual employer

State College. She now lives in Ohio with her children and pets and teaches writing at the University of Dayton, where she also directs the writing center. In a composition textbook called *Writing for a Reader: Peers, Process, and Progress in the Writing Classroom* (1995), she tells about ways she helps developing writers improve by imagining what readers need to understand a written work.

Fences

Krisher has said that her father, Whitley, shared his love of history by telling her interesting tidbits and specific details about historical figures. Her mother taught her compassion. In her writing, Krisher looks at sensitive issues by confronting social injustice and exploring links that can break down the fences—the racial and economic walls—that people build against each other. In *Spite Fences* Maggie, who is white, tells the story of the fences that surround her and the members of her town, particularly her black friends Zeke Freeman and George Hardy. Zeke and George help her find the courage to confront the tensions in her family and community. Zeke's gift of a camera helps her to define these tensions. Maggie lives in the town of Kinship with her gentle, withdrawn father, abusive mother, and pretty little sister Gardenia. Although her poor family needs the money she earns cleaning the house of Zeke's friend, she knows she cannot tell them that her secret employer is a black man.

There are other secrets, one particularly horrible memory she is not able to face. Because she cannot bring herself to talk about the terrible things Virgil Boggs and the other cruel, bigoted men did to Zeke, the images remain hidden: "My camera eye snapped shut. Inside my mind something had gone black, . . . I knew that there were other memories inside the camera that was me, other undeveloped snapshots" (p. 70).

bigoted prejudiced against others

In Maggie's town, blacks cannot check out a library book; they can only sit in the balcony at the movie theater; and they must stand, not sit down, at the lunch counter at Byer's Drugs where Maggie's friend Pert Wilson works. Krisher says,

> *Spite Fences* **is about many things: a young girl's developing social consciousness; the early days of the civil rights movement; deep and abiding friendships; the liberation that comes from art; the prejudices**

abiding enduring; lasting

The **civil rights movement** of the 1950s, 1960s, and 1970s was a political campaign to gain civil rights for all people, particularly African Americans, regardless of sex, ethnicity, or color. Civil rights are the freedoms and rights that a person may have as a member of a community, state, or country, including the right to receive fair and equal treatment under the law, and the freedoms of speech, religion, and the press.

that gnaw at the social fabric where Baptists hate Roman Catholics, where white is pitted against black, and where even family members can behave like enemies. (*OJELA,* Pp. 8–9)

It is not just the fence her mother insists must be built around their house that traps Maggie. She also feels she must find a way out of the fence that is Kinship. By climbing her favorite pecan tree or going on a "sneak" with her spunky friend Pert, Maggie can temporarily escape her mother's harsh words and vicious slaps and get away from Virgil Boggs's torture. She is afraid that she will catch her mother's meanness if she stays home.

Colors and the "Colored"

Krisher, influenced by the way her seventh grade English teacher helped students notice smells and colors in literature, paints vivid colorful images with her words. Maggie's story is full of color. Her mama serves lots of jelly, collects the colorful glasses, and lines them up where light can shine through because somehow she feels her display rescues the family "from the ranks of the no-account." Maggie recalls using her daddy's red paint so she and Pert could put their handprints all over Kinship. "When Mama found out, her own handprint rose up red on my own bottom" (p. 3). Later Maggie is forced to use the red paint to cover the fence that is built to wall out the awful Boggs family who lives next door.

Maggie and her mama have different ways of focusing on color and on what is "colored." Mama cannot understand why Maggie refers to "colored" people as "black," but the color red is more vivid than black and white in *Spite Fences*—the red of paint, of clay soil, of the bricks in the black people's church, and the red of blood. In the climactic scene of *Spite Fences,* members of the black neighborhood sit down at the lunch counter at Byer's Drugs and a terrible fight takes place. Maggie sees many colors through the shutter of her camera. She tells herself what must be done:

Remember your big strong hands. Cock the shutter. . . . You know what you're seeing here. You've got to get it down.

Everything was out of control. The colors melted together like a watercolor gone wild: Missy's purple scarf, Bigger's yellow vest, Virgil's black pants, Cecil's blue neckerchief. I saw that it didn't matter what side you were on. When it came to this, it was wrong, wrong. . . .

I held the camera to my eyes, steadying it against my shaking fingers. The image before me swam red, filling up the lens. *Trip the shutter, Maggie Pugh.* What filled my lens was more than the blood gushing from my sweet friend. It was the red color of the fence, the red color of the earth on which I stood. It was red, the color of my life this summer. *Cock. Trip.* Red: it was the color of Kinship. (Pp. 271–272)

Maggie knew she must tell the world about the awful things that were happening and about what these men had done to Zeke Freeman.

The Power of Language

Krisher believes words can be the bridge that helps us vault fences and link us to each other as we connect what we observe inside to the world outside. "Without language, we could never begin to say what we see, to explore what we think, to connect with the teeming world. It is no accident that I portrayed my heroine, Maggie Pugh, at the end of *Spite Fences,* finally vaulting a fence. . . . We cannot feel separated from our own experience . . . when we possess the power of language" (*OJELA,* p. 9).

teeming overflowing

Words are important in Maggie's story. In an interesting twist, it is Zeke's gift of a camera that helps Maggie gradually find the words to tell what is inside her. Maggie shows her gratitude to Zeke by helping him learn to read the words in the Bible he knows by heart. Words change Maggie's image of herself after she reads a note from George Hardy, her secret employer, who thanks her for her "splendid work," a vivid contrast to the demeaning language her mama uses when talking to her. Maggie becomes "Magnolia April Pugh, Housekeeper."

demeaning putting down; belittling

Kinship

monologue extended thoughts of a character, especially those spoken aloud while the character is alone

Like *Spite Fences,* the story called *Kinship,* which is about fifteen-year-old Pert Wilson, is full of color: Alice Potter's bottle tree; Rae Jean Wilson's pale blue eyes and colorful paintings; gray trailers transformed to yellow, pink, blue, and green to show they are permanent homes; and the colors Miss Claggett thinks must be served on a plate of food. Pert lives with her mother Rae Jean, and brother Jimmy, but she misses her daddy "like the devil." As Pert tells the story, her chapters alternate with short monologues narrated by ten offbeat characters who are her neighbors in the trailer park called "Happy Trails." The authentic sounds spoken by the different people in *Kinship* show the result of Krisher's careful research in southern regional speech and dialect.

dialect a regional form of a language

kin one's relatives

Readers familiar with *Spite Fences* will not be surprised that Pert was fired for serving "coloreds" at the drug store. Pert talks about Maggie Pugh and her dad, and also her friend, Zeke Freeman. In *Kinship,* Krisher explores issues of home, community, and the difference between family and "kin." She uses the image of wheels to convey Pert's feelings of being "pressed down and driven over" and her desire to find a way out of Kinship. Yet Pert is fond of her family and friends in the trailer park where the residents do not think of their homes as mobile. The image of wheels is a part of Krisher's use of the trailer park as a metaphor for commitment and people's decisions to stay and care for each other.

metaphor a figure of speech in which one thing is referred to as something else; for example, "My love is a rose"

There are times when Pert feels ashamed because her family is so poor; other girls have daddies who live with them and bring a paycheck home. At the same time she admires how hard her mother works to keep the family together. Pert also sees her mother's quiet strength when Miss Nympha Claggett, the home economics teacher, comes to check on what she assumes is the bad home condition and the reason for Pert's failing grade.

Images of Self

resilient able to easily recover from change or misfortune

Maggie and Pert are examples of young people who struggle with images of who they are, but they do more than survive their difficult experiences. They are resilient, and they become aware of their own identity as they look at themselves in connection to others. Maggie contrasts the kindness and courage of her friends Zeke and George with the madness of her Mama who seems as fragile as the jelly glasses she hurls at Maggie while saying "No daughter of mine's friend to no colored man." Realizing how tired she is of all the fighting, Maggie notices that her wide and strong bones are different from her mama's. Maggie knows it takes will and money to make things different: "From Mama I had been given the will. From *Life* magazine I had been given the money. They allowed me to go to Atlanta" (p. 279).

Pert also understands more about herself when she looks at others and is honest with herself about her family. She sees her mother and brother as mild and meek souls, different from her daddy and her.

> **I was tired to death of all the things I had carried over the years. The rent checks. The TV dinners. The wagging tongues of folks like Nympha Claggett. I was tired of trying to make things come out right. Trying to defend my family. Trying to pretend that everything was just fine. Trying to say that we wasn't suffering when, fact was, we was suffering every single day of the year. (P. 250)**

Pert sometimes wonders if she can handle any more trouble. Her smooth-talking father comes back for awhile, but his deception puts the future of her home and the whole trailer park in jeopardy. Pert must also decide how to respond when Jimmy's fiancée wants help in getting an abortion.

Even though she wonders if her family is falling apart, Pert is resilient. Her response to life is portrayed by the color Alice Potter chooses for the bottle tree: "Red's the right color for Pert. . . . Red's the color of fire. The granny woman says *Fire in the eye, Heart won't lie. . . . Fire in the heart, Feels love's dart.* It don't much matter in Pert's case. She's got fire both places" (p. 266). Pert learns that she does have a family, not the perfect family she had imagined, but the kind of folks that stay, and they are not all her kin.

Other Works

Although *Spite Fences* won an award given to a work of historical fiction, Krisher had not thought of it as history, because she lived during that time. With her newer works, also set in earlier times, she continues to explore social issues and to deepen her appreciation of other people. For Donald R. Gallo's collection of short stories about the twentieth century, she wrote a story called "We Loved Lucy." In early 1999, Krisher was working on a novel set in the 1840s. The story, with a working title of *A Stubborn Faith*, stemmed from Krisher's interest in biographies about women who did important work for society during times of social reform when lots of changes were occurring. She wondered what made these unsung heroines do what they did.

A Stubborn Faith is about a young girl coming of age at the same time her mother is gaining the strength to see new possibilities for women. The young girl, like Maggie and Pert, must decide how she wants to be like her mother, and in what ways she will be different. According to Krisher, writing this book is hard work, requiring extensive research to be sure the details are accurate. It is sure to be another good story filled with intriguing and courageous characters and gripping narrative, told with Trudy Krisher's lyrical blend of sensitivity, insight, honesty, and humor.

unsung not celebrated or praised

narrative a story told in fiction, nonfiction, poetry, or drama

If you enjoyed *Spite Fences* and *Kinship*, you might also enjoy Bette Greene's *Summer of My German Soldier*, Carolyn Meyer's *White Lilacs*, Gary Paulsen's *Night John*, and Harper Lee's *To Kill a Mockingbird*.

Selected Bibliography

WORKS BY TRUDY KRISHER

Novels and Stories

Kathy's Hats: A Story of Hope, illustrated by Nadine Bernard Wescott (1992)

Spite Fences (1994)

Kinship (1997)

"We Loved Lucy." In *Time Capsule: Short Stories About Teenagers Throughout the Twentieth Century.* Edited by Donald R. Gallo. New York: Bantam Doubleday Dell, 1999.

Other Works

Writing for a Reader: Peers, Process, and Progress in the Writing Classroom (1995)

"Affirming with Language: Building Bridges, Dismantling Fences." *Ohio Journal of the English Language Arts,* summer 1997, pp. 6–9.

WORKS ABOUT TRUDY KRISHER

Carpenter, Emily. "The Writing Instinct." *The Dayton Voice,* 2–8 July 1998, pp. 8–9.

DeBrosse, Jim. "Keen with Teens." *Dayton Daily News,* 15 February 1998, pp. 1C, 4C.

Hile, Kevin, ed. "Trudy Krisher." In *Something About the Author.* Detroit: Gale Research, 1996, vol. 86, pp. 132–134.

Rizvi, Teri. "Novelist Earns Acclaim." *Campus Report,* 26 September 1997, pp. 4–5.

How to Write to the Author

Trudy Krisher
c/o Delacorte Books
for Young Readers
Random House Publishers
1540 Broadway
New York, NY 10036

You can also e-mail
Trudy Krisher at
Krisher@worf.udayton.edu

Anne C. LeMieux

(1954–)

by Pamela Sissi Carroll

> In life, there is something for you, uniquely, to do. Life is for figuring out what and how. There is grievous loss built into the human condition, but there's redemptive power in love, which is a verb, a word of action, and while we're here on earth, we are at our best, each other's salvation.
>
> —Anne C. LeMieux, 10 February 1999,
> personal correspondence

Books for Young Adults and Adolescents

Anne C. LeMieux, who has also published under the name A. C. LeMieux, is not a writer who fits neatly into a single category. In fact, she likes to "shift writing gears" often. How does she shift gears? Here are three ways: she alternates between writing for young adults—readers who are in high school—and writing for younger adolescents who are in the middle

Quotations from Anne C. LeMieux that are not attributed to a published source are from personal correspondence to the author of this article between January and February 1999 and are published here by permission of Anne C. LeMieux.

first person the position or perspective of someone inside the story, using the pronoun "I"

third person the position or perspective of someone outside the story

grades; she uses first-person and third-person points of view, writing from the perspective of a 16-year-old male in one book and of an 11-year-old female in another; besides writing novels, short stories, and poetry for young people, she is completing a screenplay for adults. These examples of LeMieux's versatility contribute to an impressive list, especially for a writer who gave up creative writing for a few years after her graduation from Simmons College in 1976 because she worried that she would have "nothing original to say." LeMieux avoided writing fiction for many years because she did not want to become merely "a mediocre imitator" of other authors. Few would suspect that this popular fiction writer first had to write news articles on European folk music for an alternative paper, articles on sailing, and an unpublished children's novel before she would find a comfortable home as a writer for young people.

LeMieux first became popular among teens and their teachers, parents, and media specialists as the author of *The TV Guidance Counselor* (1993), a novel that began as a short story, then became a screenplay before it was published in 1993 and named an ALA Best Book for Young Adults. This book is a tender story of Michael's descent into depression when his family falls apart. He uses a camera to try to better understand his world and the people who are important to him, including his sometimes-girlfriend, the generous yet

melancholy depressed in spirits

melancholy store owner who gives him not only a job but a focus, and the troubled woman who regularly inspects copies of *TV Guide* at the grocery store where he works. How is LeMieux able to write convincingly from a teen male's perspective? She is the only sister of six brothers.

LeMieux's second book for older adolescents, *Do Angels Sing the Blues?* (1995), was awarded the Parents' Choice Silver Medal following its publication. This novel reveals the depths of friendship, happiness, and despair that a small, close group of high school students experiences. The founding members of a successful blues band, "Boog," a quiet misfit, and Theo, the

gregarious sociable

gregarious leader, become inseparable—at least until Theo is smitten with moody and troubled Carey Harrigan, who insists on being an outsider, and until Boog and Carey are pierced by

prequel a dramatic work in which the story takes place before that of an earlier work

the brutal pain of the freak accident that claims Theo's life. Readers were so eager to know more about these characters, and so disturbed by Theo's death, that LeMieux wrote a short story that reads as a prequel to the novel. Theo and the others are presented in a humorous, lighter tone in "Just Say . . . ," a short story in the collection *New Year, New Love* (1996).

Anne C. LeMieux has also published novels that feature characters who are in the middle grades: *Fruit Flies, Fish & Fortune Cookies* was the first, published in 1994; it was followed by *Dare to Be, M.E.!* in 1997. In *Fruit Flies,* readers become acquainted with 11-year-old humorous and assertive Mary Ellen Bobowick, who gathers data about the fish in her aquarium as eagerly as she examines her own figure for evidence that her breasts are growing. We also meet her best friend, Justine, who disrupts the girls' routines when she moves to Paris for most of their sixth-grade year. The same main characters appear again, during the summer before they begin seventh grade, in *Dare to Be, M.E.!* Like the protagonists themselves, the second novel is a bit more sophisticated than the first; even its appearance—smaller print and approximately thirty additional pages—indicates that readers must grow up with Mary Ellen and Justine in order to keep up with their story. In *Dare to be, M.E.!,* Justine has returned from Paris, bringing with her a new hairstyle, a transformed wardrobe, and two difficult secrets: her father has left her mother, and she has developed an eating disorder, bulimia nervosa. One of Mary Ellen's challenges is to help Justine overcome feelings of self-hatred that make her hide, during PE class, under a heavy sweat suit, even on hot days. Other problems she must deal with include her feelings about Ben, who is moving to another city only days after he kisses her for the first time, and her campaign for election to the Student Council. In an episode that is both funny and serious, Mary Ellen presents her project for the DTBD ("Dare to Be Different— Dare to Be Yourself") class. For the class project, she creates two cardboard, life-size teenage females; one has average proportions and one reflects the proportions of a Barbie doll. Readers will quickly recognize the lesson that Mary Ellen is trying to relay to her classmates about body image and reality, but they are given some imaginative assistance through pencil-sketch drawings that illustrate select scenes in both books.

Two other young adolescent females team up in the Fairy Lair trilogy. In the first novel of the trilogy, *A Special Place,* published in 1997, fifth grader Sylvia Widden befriends misunderstood, unusual Dana Brennen. Dana is at first reluctant, then eager to reveal that she knows many secrets of the fairy world and that together, she and Sylvia can learn even more

protagonist the main character of a literary work

bulimia nervosa an eating disorder characterized by extreme overeating followed by purging, usually by means of forced vomiting or laxatives

from their neighbor, Mr. MacCooney. Dana teaches Sylvia how to communicate with the good fairies that circle around and how to avoid the mean-spirited ones. At the same time, Sylvia teaches Dana simple yet powerful lessons about friendship and loyalty among human beings, lessons that Dana finds difficult because of her experiences as a school outcast. Their adventures in the fairy world continue in *A Hidden Place* and *A Magic Place,* both published in 1998. Although this fairy world is significant in each of the books of the Fairy Lair series, so are less magical notions, such as the tenuous ecology of the planet and the value of friendship.

tenuous delicate or weak

Three Defining Characteristics: LeMieux's Respect for Her Readers

Despite the fact that her books appeal to readers of varying ages and interests, adolescent readers can always count on LeMieux to treat them with respect for their intellects and feelings. She achieves this respect in at least three ways. First, she engages in careful research before writing her books, so that when readers enter the world of the books, they are provided with full descriptions of the hobbies and interests of the characters. She claims to have always been an "obsessive researcher purely to satisfy the cravings of [her] own curiosity." She provides a powerful example from her own life when she explains that, in college, she "went on a King Arthur binge, initially sparked by the impact of reading T. H. White's *The Once and Future King.*" The "binge" led to her research of the "historicity of King Arthur" and finally resulted in her completing an independent study project in England so that she could become acquainted with "some of the geographical sites associated with the legends."

binge unrestrained and often excessive indulgence

T. H. White (1906–1964) was an English novelist and historian most noted for his adaptation of Sir Thomas Malory's fifteenth-century romance *Morte D'Arthur* into a quartet of novels called ***The Once and Future King*** (1958). This quartet was later adapted as the musical play and movie *Camelot.*

The Arthurian legend is working its way into a book for young adults that she is writing, tentatively called *Jester's Quest.* This book, to which LeMieux refers as "really an experiment," has an unusual and challenging structure: in it she "weaves several story lines together, through e-mail correspondence, on-line fantasy free-form gaming story boards," and uses a setting that is "half in cyberspace and half in the real world." Despite the unusual structure of this newest project, though, LeMieux states that the tone of the book is primarily comic and that the topics are ones that are characteristic of many contemporary young adult books: identity, masks, divorce, and stepfamily.

Readers of each of her books reap the benefits of LeMieux's hungry curiosity. For example, information on jazz theory, flowering plants, and acoustic finger guitar are woven into *Do Angels Sing the Blues?* In the Fairy Lair trilogy, Dana translates poems from ancient runes, or alphabets, to better understand the problems that are plaguing both the hidden fairy world and the easily observable "real" world. LeMieux encourages young readers and writers to do research because, as she asserts, "It's not just the possession of knowledge that matters, but the experience of acquiring it, the learning, which . . . is one of our most important tasks as human beings, the reason why we're here—to learn."

The second means by which LeMieux shows respect for her readers is through the way she presents female characters. When asked if she makes a conscious effort to portray females as strong and independent, she replies that the decision is a conscious one, yet one that is born "out of an awareness of the complexity of women's lives today." LeMieux further explains that, as a graduate of an all-girls' high school and of Simmons College, a women's college, she grew up in environments "where traditional or common gender roles weren't reinforced." Readers find in LeMieux's books a refusal to assign stereotypical roles to females. Mary Ellen's fondness for engaging in scientific inquiry and her mother's occupation as a biology professor are examples from the Fruit Flies series. Readers who assume that "Dr. Bobowick" is Mary Ellen's father, instead of her mother, are gently reminded to check their own assumptions about male and female roles in today's society.

LeMieux acknowledges a fact that writers who deal in stereotype are unable to recognize that females are often interested in mathematics and science as well as in the humanities. Her personal circle of friends includes women who have deep and varied interests, women with whom she is able to "discuss things like the brokering of political power in the third world, or theology, along with trading recipes." In reflecting on her own education, in fact, LeMieux finds that the two aptitudes—one for science and mathematics, the other for the humanities—have complemented each other. For example, she states that the best part of biology for her was doing the required drawings in her lab notebook, and that

stereotypical conforming to a preconceived and often over-simplified notion about a person or group

aesthetic relating to ideas about art or beauty

multifaceted having several aspects

when she studied music, she "delved into the physics and acoustics and the mathematical relationships between musical notes." Her personal friendships and educational experiences convinced LeMieux that "the scientific/mathematical view and the aesthetic view show flip sides of the same coin." This combination of scientific and aesthetic interests does not appear frequently in other writers' depictions of young females in contemporary young adult or adolescent fiction. Her development of multifaceted adolescent female characters may be one of LeMieux's major contributions to the genre.

The third way in which LeMieux shows readers respect is by providing them with a sense of hope through her fiction and poetry. She feels particularly obligated to show younger readers the positive aspects of life, while recognizing that life is not always bright, even for adolescents:

> **When differentiating between middle-grade books and young adult books, for me the primary difference is that older kids inhabit a perceptually larger world, and this broader scope of vision can often include first confrontations with the bleak or the dark side of human existence, with human failures, irrevocable loss, moral lapses, as well as a growing awareness of our part and responsibility to ourselves, to others, to the world, our place in the scheme of things. These are weighty issues to struggle with, especially for many adolescents, who haven't lived long enough to have the scope to see the cyclical nature of life and growth, which includes healing. I try to demonstrate that we have tools, the capacity for empathy, for humor, for perseverance, for co-creation of our world, and most important, for love, which I believe is the primary redemptive agent.**

LeMieux, through her careful research, her attention to the potential within female characters, and her goal of providing a glimpse of hope, through the power of love, to adolescent readers of all ages, will continue to be able to speak to middle and high school readers because those readers recognize in her a voice that they can trust, the voice of one who strives to understand their world from their perspectives.

Other Works

Anticipating the spring 2000 release of *All the Answers,* the third book about Mary Ellen and Justine, LeMieux expressed eagerness for readers to respond to the book because, unlike the other two in the Fruit Flies series, it is written in the first person, from the perspective of Jason Hodges, one of the boys whom Mary Ellen and Justine have tried to avoid in the earlier books. LeMieux said that because the characters have moved into eighth grade in this novel, "it's not exactly middle grade" but is more likely to be read as "a bridge between middle grade and young adult" fiction. The book focuses, according to LeMieux, on "mathophobia, the first round of the father-son separation dance, and . . . value formation and integrity."

In addition to *Jester's Quest,* described earlier, LeMieux was also working on another young adult book in the late 1990s, *Lovespeed.* In writing it, she explained, she was "experimenting with a structure of linked short stories, alternating first-person narratives of two main characters." This book was influenced by LeMieux's visit to an exhibit of the twentieth-century visual artist, Ross Bleckner, and as she explained, the story "revolves around art and physics, as well as emotional abuse, intergenerational family pathologies, and breaking those cycles." Does LeMieux worry that the topics she has selected for this book might be too deep for high school readers—that psychological problems and quantum physics, for example, might be too much for readers to handle? Yes; yet, because she trusts in the intellectual capabilities of young readers, she accepts the challenge of simplifying the "rarified intellectual domain" that one of the main characters lives in, so that adolescent readers can enter and make sense of his world.

> **narrative** a story told in fiction, nonfiction, poetry, or drama

LeMieux again shifted gears in *Jester's Quest* and *Lovespeed;* readers will be eager to test the results. She did not stay in that gear long, either. LeMieux wrote a collection of poetry; one of her poems, "Gulls and Buoys," appeared in Lee Bennett Hopkins' *These Great United States* (2000), which is the companion to Hopkins' *Hand in Hand: An American History Through Poetry* (1994). She was also working on several short stories, with a goal of publishing her own collection of stories, and on an adult screenplay, which she described as "an ensemble comedy-drama."

It appears as if there is no stopping this creative, optimistic, literary advocate for adolescents. We can eagerly look forward to many more works of art from this fine writer of literature for young people in the years to come—and we hope that her family, including a daughter in college and a son and husband with whom she shares a home in Southport, Connecticut, will continue to be tolerant when she feels the need to delay domestic duties or to run from the dinner table to "jot down a story note before it flees."

If you like Anne C. LeMieux, you might also like Francesca Lia Block, Sue Ellen Bridgers, Norma Fox Mazer, Katherine Paterson, Cynthia Voigt, and Virginia Euwer Wolff.

Selected Bibliography

WORKS BY ANNE C. LEMIEUX

Novels

The TV Guidance Counselor (1993)

The Case of the Missing Marble (1994)

The Case of the Stolen Snowman (1994)

The Case of the Yogurt Poker (1994)

Fruit Flies, Fish & Fortune Cookies (1994)

Super Snoop Sam Snout (1994)

Do Angels Sing the Blues? (1995)

Dare to Be, M. E.! (1997)

Fairy Lair: A Special Place (1997)

Fairy Lair: A Hidden Place (1998)

Fairy Lair: A Magic Place (1998)

All the Answers! (2000)

Short Stories and Poetry

"Roast Beast Battle." In *Food Fight: Poets Join the Fight Against Hunger with Poems About Their Favorite Foods.* Edited by Michael J. Rosen. San Diego: Harcourt Brace/ Share Our Strength, 1996.

"Just Say . . ." In *New Year, New Love.* Edited by Cameron Dokey. New York: Avon Flare, 1996.

"Gulls and Buoys." In *These Great United States.* Edited by Lee Bennett Hopkins. New York: Simon & Schuster, 2000.

Nonfiction

"The Problem Novel in a Conservative Age." *ALAN Review,* spring 1998, pp. 4–6. (Transcript of speech given at NCTE Conference, Chicago, November 1996.)

"Using *The TV Guidance Counselor* to Study Suicide and Its Effects on Families." With Jenifer Nields, M.D. In *Using Literature to Help Teenagers at Risk Coping with Family Issues.* Edited by Joan Kaywell. Westport, Conn.: Greenwood Press, 1999.

WORKS ABOUT ANNE C. LEMIEUX

Carroll, P. S.; M. Z. Cleveland; and E. M. Myers. "Eating Disorders in Young Adults' Worlds and Their Literature: Starving and Stuffing Families." In *Using Literature to Help Troubled Teens Cope with Their Family Issues.* Edited by Joan Kaywell. Westport, Conn.: Greenwood Press, 1999, pp. 165–191.

Hedblad, Alan, ed. *Something About the Author.* Detroit: Gale Research, 1997, vol. 90, pp. 142–145.

Rooney, Terrie M., ed. *Contemporary Authors.* Detroit: Gale Research, 1997, vol. 155, pp. 294–296.

How to Write to the Author

Anne C. LeMieux
490 Pequot Court
Southport, CT 06490

You can also e-mail Anne C. LeMieux at Swan522@aol.com

Carolyn Meyer

(1935–)

by Betty Carter

Jim Koonuk lives with his family near the Bering Sea, in northern Alaska, where the family straddles two cultural worlds. The *gussak* influences from the contiguous United States have so eroded the Koonuks' traditional way of life that they cannot survive through their time-honored methods of hunting, fishing, and bartering. On the other hand, as members of a particular culture bound by both tradition and geography, Jim and his family cannot fully accept or participate in the values and lifestyles of those in the lower forty-eight states either. Jim is a composite character Carolyn Meyer created for one of her earlier books, *Eskimos: Growing Up in a Changing Culture* (1977).

To prepare for college, a *gussak* ideal, Jim attends boarding school. But Jim sees school as boring; the joy in his life comes when he returns to his village for the annual seal hunts, an important milestone in his Yup'ik culture. Like many such villages, the Koonuks' community has no running water, and Jim's younger brother must fetch water from a distant well. To

Quotations from Carolyn Meyer that are not attributed to a published source are from personal interviews conducted by the author of this article in November 1998 and February 1999 and are published here by permission of Carolyn Meyer.

gussak the Yup'ik word for white people

contiguous touching along boundaries

composite consisting of distinct parts

do this, he drives his father's snow machine, a symbol of economic prosperity. Jim's father, Charlie, works as a maintenance man at the local school. Once honored as a fine hunter, his respect now comes because he has a job.

The old men in the village point out that "the white man cannot take anything away that the Eskimos do not choose to give" (p. 19). Jim must decide what of himself to give to the *gussak* and what to keep of his traditional ways. In doing so, Jim acknowledges that he will never be accepted completely by either world. Jim is much like the protagonists who populate Carolyn Meyer's novels and the other individuals who unify her nonfiction: outsiders seeking to find their places within their families, their communities, and their cultures.

protagonist the main character of a literary work

There's Teddie from *The Summer I Learned About Life* (1983), a character torn between her 1928 middle-class family's expectations that she become a good wife and mother and her own dreams of becoming an aviatrix. Texas McCoy/ (*The Luck of Texas McCoy,* 1984) also precipitates a rift in her family: Texas and her grandfather, Ben, side against "the girls"—her grandmother, mother, and sister. Ben and Texas have dreams for the family ranch; "the girls" want to abandon the harsh surroundings and live in town. Before he dies, Ben tells Texas the ranch will be hers:

aviatrix a woman who operates or pilots an aircraft

> "I know, see, if I leave it to the other ones, they'll sell it, slick as a whistle, and you'll find yourself living in town in a tract house with a little barbecue thingamajig on the patio and a couple of junipers stuck in twelve square feet of brown grass."
>
> [Texas replies,] "Might as well be dead as live like that." (P. 8)

Teddie decides to fly; Texas, to make a go of raising horses. Only by choosing to live outside their families' conventions can they find contentment.

tenet a principle generally accepted as true

An outsider because he struggles with the tenets of his family's religious beliefs, Samuel Beiler, a seventeen-year-old Amish boy (*Amish People: Plain Living in a Complex World* [1976]), wants a car, even though the *Ordnung,* the set of church rules that dictate every part of his life, forbids it. But unlike Gideon Stoltzfus, the main character in *Gideon's People* (1996), Samuel does not consider leaving his close-knit Amish community. Gideon does. The year is 1911; the setting, near Lancaster, Pennsylvania. Gideon worries about his upcoming baptism, which means "promising to accept the *Ordnung* and never to depart from it; never to sit down and read *Treasure Island,* if he wished; never to play a tune on the mouth organ if he felt like it, that was the problem" (p. 62). Gideon's disharmony, his sense of being an outsider, comes from his father, an uncompromising man who finds fault with everything Gideon does. When his sister, Annie, asks why he wants to leave and thus face *Meidung,* or shunning, Gideon replies:

> **Because of Datt, mostly. . . . If Levi does something, it's fine; if I do it, it's all wrong. If Amos says something, that's all right; if I say it, I've got the devil in me. And not just that, it's his temper, too. I'm the only son without red hair, and that makes me different. *Dopplig,* that's his favorite word for me. . . . (Pp. 98–99)**

When he runs away to another Amish settlement, Gideon chooses to live apart from his family but not outside his religion.

Cynthia Ann Parker, the historical figure who takes center stage in *Where the Broken Heart Still Beats* (1992), never resolves her sense of being an outsider. Kidnapped by the Comanches as a child, she lives her early life as a slave to the People. Her situation changes dramatically when Speckled Eagle's family adopts her and gives her the name Naduah: She Who Carries Herself With Dignity And Grace. Naduah learns the family's language, customs, and skills. No longer an outsider, she marries a Comanche chief, Peta Nocona; has three children; and considers herself a respected insider among the People. In 1861 a band of Texas Rangers captures Naduah and returns her to family members, forcing Cynthia Ann to be an outsider once again, misunderstood by the community in which she lives. Unable to return to the Comanche and unable to live with her white family, Cynthia Ann spends her last years alone, separated from both cultures.

In Carolyn Meyer's works, some outsiders inhabit less exotic and more contemporary settings. Win Kelly, living in present-day Santa Fe in *Elliott & Win* (1986), is different from his immediate circle of friends. His best friend, Paul, believes that

---

The **Amish** are Mennonite Christians who first settled in America in the seventeenth century. They are known for a simple way of life that rejects modern technology.

setting the general time and place in which the events of a literary work take place

Treasure Island was written by Robert Louis Stevenson. There is an article about Stevenson in volume 3.

Here, the **People** are the Comanche. According to Meyer, all native groups call themselves "the People" in their own languages.

ascot a broad scarf that is worn around the neck and looped under the chin

Elliott, the older man who has befriended Win through the local Amigos ("friends") program, is gay because he lives alone, wears an ascot, and attends the opera. Paul taunts Win, "You hang around with a faggot, people are going to start thinking you're a faggot too" (p. 27). Win, on the other hand, thinks Elliott's ambition, his inquisitiveness, and his satisfying bachelor life make him an individual worth knowing. Paul also ridicules Heather Key because her breasts are large; he calls her a cow and a whore. After all, Paul and his friends reason, "anybody with boobs like that has got to be a tramp" (p. 81). To Win, Heather is an honest, down-to-earth, sympathetic friend. Win eventually rejects Paul, his friends, and their cruel and unfounded assessments of the world around them. He realizes he wants to be an outsider to that group, and like Teddie and Texas, he finds contentment in making his own way.

Carolyn Meyer writes, "My pleasure in making up stories goes back to when my daddy used to tell me bedtime stories but often fell asleep in the middle and I'd finish them for him" ("Reality Check," *ALAN Review,* spring 1993, p. 8). She began making up those stories in the small town of Lewistown, Pennslyvania, where she was born on 8 June 1935 to Sara and H. Victor Meyer. All through high school, she dreamed of becoming a writer. Meyer adds, "Still cherishing that dream, I majored in English at Bucknell University. But, unable to think how that dream might become a reality, I took secretarial courses and at one time worked as a secretary in New York City." Both backgrounds served her well; the first short story Meyer had accepted for publication was published in shorthand.

Carolyn Meyer's first books for teenagers were how-to books, written in the late 1960s and early 1970s and covering such diverse topics as sewing, baking bread, and woodworking. She comments: "How-to books were a new thing back then, and I found I was good at explaining."

Meyer expanded her nonfiction in 1975 with *People Who Make Things: How American Craftsmen Live and Work,* combining a history of occupations such as silversmithing, quilting, woodworking, and bookbinding with discussions of contemporary artisans who preserve these crafts. This combination of historical narrative anchored by modern individuals also shapes *Amish People: Plain Living in a Complex World,* in which she has created a community that illustrates how many Amish live today and how their history influences their

narrative a story told in fiction, nonfiction, poetry, or drama

present beliefs. When asked about the changed focus in her writing, Meyer explained: "This is when I got more interested in people than things."

Meyer's childhood ties to Pennsylvania led her to set three books there: *Killing the Kudu* (1990), *Gideon's People,* and *Amish People.* Still, the character of Alex, the protagonist in *Killing the Kudu,* is based on a paraplegic boy she met in South Africa, thousands of miles away from her comfortable roots. Also, Meyer had no early contact with the Amish, who are central to both *Gideon's People* and *Amish People.* The impetus for writing about them came in her adult life. She returned to Lewistown for a visit. One day, as she was walking through town, she saw an Amish couple. "On impulse—I had never done it before—I waved. The young man raised his hand; his wife smiled. . . . And I knew that I wanted to learn about the Amish" (*Amish People,* p. 134).

paraplegic one who is paralyzed from the waist down

Meyer, now firmly "more interested in people than things," realized she wanted to learn about the Eskimos when she was teaching a writing course by correspondence. One of her students, Bernadine Larsen, lived in Chefornak, Alaska. The two "developed both a professional and a personal relationship. Out of it evolved the idea of writing this book" (*Eskimos,* p. 214). Meyer did some research and then traveled to Chefornak, lived with the Larsens, talked with the people of the village, and listened to their stories.

impetus the driving force, or stimulus

Over the years, Meyer wondered about the community: how the people were getting along and what changes had occurred there. In 1994, eighteen years after she had first visited Alaska, Meyer returned to Chefornak. Again she talked with the people and listened to their stories. Again she wrote a book, and again she created composite characters, this time looking at the changes the years had brought to the community. Jim Koonuk is married; his children tell their story, *In A Different Light: Growing Up in a Yup'ik Eskimo Village in Alaska* (1996), in much the same way Jim did in the earlier work.

The ability to find information and then explain it, honed so carefully in her nonfiction works, serves Meyer well in her fiction. In *Rio Grande Stories* (1994), she describes in great detail the step-by-step process of making a pueblo pot. Elliott, a skilled amateur photographer, instructs Win in the art of photography as surely and clearly as a professional sharing his expertise with an eager protégé. In *Where the Broken Heart*

honed sharpened

protégé one who is trained by an experienced or prominent person

Still Beats, Meyer works Cynthia Ann Parker's descriptions of a cradleboard, her buffalo robe, and the process of tanning naturally into her novel, thus giving readers an authentic background to frame Cynthia Ann's story.

In 1978 Meyer went to New Mexico to work at a writers' colony. After living there for two months, she "decided then and there that New Mexico would be my home" (*Rio Grande Stories,* p. viii). She married and stayed for twelve years. Her strong attachment to the region shows in the novels she has set there: *The Luck of Texas McCoy, Elliott and Win, Wild Rover* (1989), and *Rio Grande Stories.* Even so, these books are not autobiographical, although some characters are based on people she has met. *Wild Rover* grew out of a conversation Meyer had with a man who was remodeling her house. By chance, she found out he had been in prison—for murder. They talked. When he left, she had the beginnings of a novel.

In 1990 Meyer and her husband moved to Texas, and her subsequent novels are set in the Lone Star State.

> I was working on that book, *Where the Broken Heart Still Beats,* when I took a break one blustery February afternoon to attend the dedication of a historic plaque in our town park. The plaque commemorated the one-time existence of an African American community that had occupied that site from after the Civil War until the early 1920s, when the white people decided to take it over to make way for their park. . . . The idea for *White Lilacs* [1993] was sparked. ("The Toad's Precious Jewel: The True Story Behind *Drummers of Jericho,* 1998," p. 8)

Books often begin in this way for Carolyn Meyer. She will have a chance encounter with a person, a situation, or a piece of history and ask, "What must it have been like? What must it have been like to be kidnapped as a child? To live in a close-knit community and know you have to move?" Carolyn Meyer, the outsider, looked at Texas history with fresh eyes, found two of its stories, and shared them with others.

Her next novel, *Drummers of Jericho* (1995), was much more personal. In 1991, Meyer's husband's daughter, Vered, came to Texas. Vered is Jewish and had been living in Israel. When relations between Israel and Iraq worsened, Vered left.

autobiographical related to the author's own life

subsequent following

Vered, a flute player, joined the high school marching band. On the first day of practice, she was given an arrangement of Christian hymns, the music the band would perform at halftime on the opening night of football season. Playing the hymns didn't bother Vered; the music was fine and she didn't know the words. But the band members were to march in the shape of a cross, and that did bother her. She did not want to be a part of a symbol that represented a religion in which she did not believe. She asked the band director to compromise. He refused.

Meyer and her husband believed the band director was violating the First Amendment to the U.S. Constitution, which guarantees separation between church (the hymns and the cross) and state (the public school system). A lawyer agreed that this practice was unconstitutional and obtained a court order to stop the planned halftime program. Band members turned their anger on Vered, the outsider.

> **Kids at school quickly figured out who was behind the legal action: that Jewish girl. They had treated her as a misfit from the first. She looked different (it was the long dark hair; the harem pants didn't help; probably the toe ring was the last straw). They knew that she had lived in a foreign country and could speak a foreign language. They had been calling her "the foreign girl." Now they knew that she was a troublemaker. ("The Toad's Precious Jewel," p. 9)**

harem pants loose pants that fit closely at the ankle, usually worn by women

Soon band parents and members of the community took up the cause. Many believed that this outsider wanted to keep them from practicing their religion, and seniors from enjoying their last year at the high school. The mass media reported the incident in national newspapers, on television, and through radio talk shows—and Carolyn Meyer wrote *Drummers of Jericho*.

This novel introduces Pazit, a Jewish girl who moves to a town called Jericho, plays in the band, and protests both the Christian selections and the marching formation of a cross. Fact or fiction? Meyer says, "It's a fictionalized story told against a background of fact." Although the events that sparked *Drummers of Jericho* occurred in a small town in Texas, the novel has no specific setting. Meyer explains why:

This is *not* intended to be Texas, but Anywhere, U.S.A.

There's a reason for that. I'm convinced that this kind of disregard of First Amendment rights—whether the casual infringement or the vicious attack—is a *national* problem. Events such as those we experience are repeated, with variations, in town after town, state after state, all across the country. A Jewish boy in an Ohio community is tormented when he refuses the gift of a New Testament being given out by the Gideon Society; a girl in a high school chorus in Salt Lake City is harassed for not wanting to sing Christmas carols in the annual concert. ("The Toad's Precious Jewel," p. 10)

Is Carolyn Meyer an outsider? "Yes," she admits. "It's a more interesting place to be," and interesting are the places she takes her readers and the characters she introduces in her books. Whether writing fact, fiction, or fiction based on fact, Carolyn Meyer delivers powerful narratives. In 1990 the Pennsylvania School Librarians Association named her Author of the Year. The American Library Association honored seven of her books by designating them Best Books for Young Adults. Carolyn Meyer is no outsider to critical praise and devoted readers.

infringement the gradual or stealthy violation of the rights of another

The **Gideon Society,** or Gideons International, is an association of Christian business and professional men formed in 1899. Their mission is to promote the Christian gospel and the acceptance of Jesus Christ. Since 1908, they have been placing bibles in hotel rooms as well as distributing them to hospitals, prisons, students, public nurses, and military personnel.

If you like the works of Carolyn Meyer, you might also like the works of Sue Ellen Bridgers, Richard Peck, and Colby Rodowsky.

Selected Bibliography
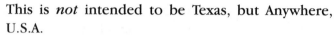

WORKS BY CAROLYN MEYER

Novels for Young Adults

The Summer I Learned About Life (1983)

The Luck of Texas McCoy (1984)

Elliot & Win (1986)

Wild Rover (1989)

Killing the Kudu (1990)

Where the Broken Heart Still Beats: The Story of Cynthia Ann Parker (1992)

White Lilacs (1993)

Rio Grande Stories (1994)

Drummers of Jericho (1995)

Gideon's People (1996)

Nonfiction

People Who Make Things (1975)

Amish People: Plain Living in a Complex World (1976)

Eskimos: Growing Up in a Changing Culture (1977)

In A Different Light: Growing Up in a Yup'ik Eskimo Village in Alaska (1996)

Articles

"The Toad's Precious Jewel: The True Story Behind *Drummers of Jericho,*" *SIGNAL,* summer/fall 1998, pp. 8–10.

"Reality Check." *ALAN Review,* spring 1993, pp. 8–10.

WORKS ABOUT CAROLYN MEYER

Commire, Anne, ed. *Something About the Author.* Detroit: Gale Research, 1976, vol. 9, pp. 140–142.

Commire, Anne, ed. *Something About the Author.* Detroit: Gale Research, 1993, vol. 70, pp. 160–163.

How to Write to the Author

Carolyn Meyer
c/o Writers House
21 West 26th Street
New York, NY 10010

Arthur Miller

(1915–)

by Leila Christenbury

"I write out of life as I know it," Arthur Miller once observed in a letter, and what a life it has been.

Born into a wealthy family, Arthur was poor during his teen years when his father, like so many in the United States, went bankrupt during the Depression. A weak student in high school, only allowed into college on probation, he later became a prize-winning academic star. Tall, shy, not conventionally handsome, Arthur won the heart of a famous, sexy movie actress who is still considered one of the world's most beautiful women. Accused of being a communist by a Congressional committee, investigated, convicted, and fined, Miller refused to betray his beliefs or his friends and later was exonerated by the U.S. Supreme Court. As a young playwright, Miller's first Broadway production closed after only four performances; today, his many plays, in particular the Pulitzer-Prize winning *Death of Salesman* (1949), are performed all over the world.

Now in his eighties, Arthur Miller must surely look back and marvel at his rich and eventful life, a life which has been full of twists and turns and surprises.

Early Life (1915–1932)

When Arthur Asher Miller was a young boy, he probably felt lucky and secure. Born 17 October 1915, on East 112th Street in New York City, he and his family lived in a luxurious apartment in fashionable Harlem. His father's business, the Miltex Coat and Suit Company, employed almost 1,000 people. The Miller family was well-off: they owned a small vacation house in the country, and they had a limousine and a driver. Young Arthur, the second son of Isidore and Augusta Miller, argued frequently with his older brother Kermit—they were competitive as kids—but life in general was good. Even though he could barely read and write, Arthur's father, Isidore, was successful and wealthy, the embodiment of the American dream. An immigrant from Poland, Isidore Miller had come to the United States as a penniless child and was proof that a poor Jewish boy could make a good life in America if he was hardworking and talented.

Then, in 1929, Arthur's world as he knew it came to an end. There was a worldwide economic crisis, the Depression, and with the changes in the economy came the loss of Isidore Miller's business and hard times for the family. It was so hard, in fact, that three men in Arthur's neighborhood, faced with similar circumstances, committed suicide rather than endure bankruptcy.

What did this mean for young Arthur? It meant that he and his family moved from their beautiful apartment to a much smaller one in Brooklyn. It meant that the prestigious high school Arthur was supposed to attend was replaced by Abraham Lincoln High School, where Arthur did little of note but play football. After his high school graduation in 1932, it also meant that there would be no college education for Arthur—who had once dreamed of going to West Point—as there was absolutely no money.

Making It (1933–1938)

But young Arthur Miller, like his father before him, believed that hard work could change things. Arthur got a job driving

---

The Great **Depression** was a severe recession that began when the stock market crashed in 1929. It lasted almost ten years. By the winter of 1932 to 1933, between 14 and 16 million Americans were unemployed. Many died from a lack of food and inadequate living conditions.

prestigious honored or well-known

West Point is the U.S. military academy that prepares men and women to serve in the U.S. Army. It is located in West Point, New York.

trucks and then worked in an auto parts warehouse. Getting the job was difficult—most likely because he was Jewish, and Jews were discriminated against at the time in employment—but Arthur persevered. And he never lost sight of his goal of going to college. Although initially rejected by Cornell University, Arthur entered the University of Michigan on academic probation in 1934. He had worked and saved for two years to pay his tuition.

Once there, young Arthur caught fire. He studied playwriting and journalism, and he was in a great place to do both. The University of Michigan was also known as politically radical, and Arthur became interested in communism. At the time, many felt the American system was not fair to poor people, racial minorities, or factory workers. Accordingly, a number of Americans not only joined the Communist Party but also worked for issues that communism advocated. For young Arthur, the theater became a way he could talk about equality, politics, and social justice. Thus two themes emerged that would weave through Arthur's writing the rest of his life: economic inequity, as exemplified by what happened to many Americans in the Depression, and discrimination against Jews, which would take a horrifying turn in the coming Holocaust during World War II.

In college Arthur entered theater competitions for two of his plays, *Honors at Dawn* (1936) and *They Too Arise* (1937)—first titled *No Villain* and then, after revision, *The Grass Still Grows.* He won the competitions, and when he graduated from the University of Michigan in 1938, he returned to New York City with confidence.

Hard Work and Success (1939–1947)

Once in New York, Miller wrote plays for the Federal Theatre Project and then scripts for CBS and NBC radio. In 1940 he married his college sweetheart, Mary Grace Slattery. (They later had two children: Jane, born in 1944, and Robert, born in 1947.) Because of a football injury, Miller could not enlist in the armed services during World War II and worked instead in the Brooklyn Navy Yard. Miller did not, however, give up writing plays. He finished *The Man Who Had All the Luck* (1944), an ironically titled play as its 1944 Broadway run lasted all of four days. But *Luck,* though not popular, won the Theatre Guild National Prize. Miller was encouraged. He published a

The **Communist Party** is a political organization that supports communism. Communism is a political and economic system based on the ideas of Karl Marx, who believed that workers would eventually rise up against management and create a classless society.

theme central message about life in a literary work

The **Holocaust** was the mass murder of at least 11 million people, especially Jews, by the Nazis during World War II. The word "holocaust" means "thorough destruction by fire."

novel, *Focus,* in 1945 and kept working. As it turned out, real success was just around the corner.

When *All My Sons* opened in 1947, it was a triumph and won the New York Drama Critics' Circle Award. The play is based on a real incident when a man during World War II knowingly manufactured and sold faulty airplane parts and thus caused the unnecessary death of almost two dozen pilots. *All My Sons* reflected Miller's interest in politics and morality. In fact, although Miller had worked hard for his success, he was overwhelmed by the acclaim for *All My Sons.* He feared becoming some sort of fancy, high-paid playwright. He was so upset that he got a job working in a factory for 40 cents an hour, stuffing wooden dividers into shipping boxes for beer bottles. While Miller stayed at that job for only a week, the gesture was characteristic: identifying with the working class, young Miller wanted to go back to his roots.

Death of a Salesman (1948–1949)

But the stage continued to beckon. In 1949, Arthur Miller's masterpiece, *Death of a Salesman,* premiered on Broadway. It won the New York Drama Critics' Circle Award, the Antoinette Perry Award, the Theater Club Award, the Donaldson Award and most importantly, the Pulitzer Prize, one of the highest honors in American literature. Written in realistic dialogue about ordinary people, *Death of a Salesman* was based in large part on Miller's family's experiences during the Depression and his passionate belief in the honor of work and the difficulties of living the American dream. *Death of a Salesman,* Miller's best known and likely most important contribution to American theater, ran for 742 performances on Broadway and toured the country to enthusiastic audiences.

The Crucible and Political Trials (1950–1957)

What happened after *Death of a Salesman* was a roller coaster ride. Miller was a prolific writer, and his adaptation of Henrik Ibsen's play *An Enemy of the People* followed in 1950. He then wrote the *The Crucible* in 1953, a play second only to *Death of a Salesman* in popularity and importance. Winner of the Antoinette Perry Award, *The Crucible* solidified Miller's reputa-

dialogue conversation between characters

prolific marked by producing many works

Henrik Ibsen (1828–1906) was a Norwegian playwright known as the father of modern drama. His complex characters and realistic dialogue were considered an innovation in his time. *An Enemy of the People* (1883) and *A Doll's House* (1879) are some of his more famous works.

tion. Its subject, the Salem witch trials of the seventeenth century, was not only all-American but also Miller's barely disguised commentary on what was happening politically at that time in the United States.

In the mid-1950s in the United States many people, concerned about the worldwide rise of communism, called for investigations of selected American citizens suspected of having communist ties. Although in the 1930s many had seen the Communist Party as a voice for justice, now a number of influential people deeply feared communism and its possible threat to the United States. Miller who had been involved for years in liberal causes, became a prime target for investigation. Refused the renewal of his passport by the U.S. State Department to attend the Brussels opening of *The Crucible*, Miller was summoned to appear before the now infamous House Un-American Activities Committee (HUAC). HUAC, led by the ferocious Senator Joe McCarthy, was interrogating citizens—in particular artists—and in some cases punishing them with prison sentences and fines for suspected communist sympathies. It was, for many, a terrifying time as not only were individuals asked to testify about themselves, but they were also put under tremendous pressure to give HUAC names of their friends who might have—or might have had—communist leanings. Some, after their mandatory testimony, were blacklisted and never worked again.

When Miller was called in June 1956 to testify before the HUAC, he was calm and brave, refusing to name friends who might be suspected communists. In 1957, was convicted of contempt of Congress, fined, and given a 30-day suspended sentence. But his case was not as terrible as others: Miller lost some contracts from organizations after his leftist activities were condemned in a New York newspaper, but when he appealed the committee's decision, the U.S. Supreme Court reversed his conviction in 1958.

The **House Un-American Activities Committee (HUAC)** was established by the U.S. House of Representatives in 1938. Its primary goal was to seek out communists inside and outside government. **Joseph McCarthy** (1908–1957) was a Republican senator from Wisconsin who charged that communists had infiltrated the U.S. government. Many of his claims were unfounded. People accused by HUAC of associating with communists were often **blacklisted**, or denied employment.

Marilyn Monroe and "The Misfits" (1957–1963)

In Miller's personal life, events were also dramatic. Although his work continued—in 1955 Arthur had written two one-act plays, *A Memory of Two Mondays* and *A View from the Bridge*—he and Mary Slattery divorced in June 1957. The reason became

Marilyn Monroe (1926–1962) was an American movie actress. She starred in *Some Like It Hot* (1959) and *Gentlemen Prefer Blondes* (1953), among many other films. *The Misfits* was the last movie she made before she died from an overdose of sleeping pills at the age of 36.

clear just days after the divorce when Miller married the famous starlet Marilyn Monroe. While the two did not make a happy couple for long, Miller loved Marilyn's vulnerability and beauty. Some of the incidents from their marriage found their way into his later play, *After the Fall* (1964), and as a tribute to Marilyn, Miller turned his short story, "The Misfits," into a film script for a movie starring his wife. Sadly, however, Miller and Marilyn were divorced by the time the movie was released in 1961. Miller married Austrian photographer Ingeborg Morath in 1962, the same year the troubled Marilyn died of a drug overdose. Marilyn's death was difficult for Miller, but he was happy with Inge: the two had a daughter, Rebecca, in 1963, and they remained married.

Prolific Years (1964–on)

In the decades that followed, Miller continued to write. Short stories, travel accounts (illustrated by Inge's photographs), critical essays on the theater, and many more plays, some full-length, some one-act, were part of his production. The list includes: *After the Fall* and *Incident at Vichy* in 1964; *The Price* in 1968; *The Creation of the World and Other Business* in 1972; *The Archbishop's Ceiling* in 1977; *The American Clock* in 1980; *Some Kind of Love Story* and *Elegy for a Lady* in 1982. Miller also had great success with the dramatization of the story of concentration camp survivor Fania Fenelon in the television drama, "Playing for Time" (1980), and he wrote a stage version in 1985.

There are several filmed versions of ***Death of a Salesman.*** One version, made for television in 1985, starred Dustin Hoffman as Willy Loman.

As the years went on, Miller's acclaim mounted. His autobiography, *Timebends: A Life,* appeared in 1987 to much praise; *Death of a Salesman* was revived and then also filmed; and *The Crucible* was made into a major motion picture. His 1992 novel, *Homely Girl: A Life,* was printed in Britain in 1995 as *Plain Girl: A Life.* Some of Miller's other works at the time include: *Danger! Memory,* performed in 1987; *The Ride Down Mount Morgan,* performed in 1991; *The Last Yankee,* performed in 1992; and *Broken Glass,* performed in 1994. International audiences loved Miller's plays, and British critics in particular gave him much praise. In fact, in 1989 The University of East Anglia in the United Kingdom opened the Arthur Miller Centre for American Studies. Deeply concerned about political affairs, as president of PEN, the international writers society for poets, essayists, and novelists, Miller had worked tirelessly in the mid-1960s for imprisoned writers around the world and continued that work well into the late 1990s.

A Brief Look at *Death of a Salesman* and *The Crucible*

While many of Arthur Miller's plays are considered brilliant—in particular *All My Sons, A View from the Bridge,* and *After the Fall*—it is both *Death of a Salesman* and *The Crucible* that are the best known and the most widely read in schools. These two plays are still performed all over the world.

Death of a Salesman is the story of Willy Loman, an older traveling salesman whose career has ended in failure. The story is told in realistic, natural language and uses a technique of intercutting standard chronological presentation with dreamlike sequences and flashbacks to the past. Willy Loman has been recently fired, and he and his wife Linda are struggling to pay the bills. Willy's two sons, Biff and Hap, are not helpful either. As the play goes on, it is revealed that Hap is a self-deluded, womanizing young man and Biff, home for a visit after a long absence, is an habitual thief who appears headed for a lifetime of failure. Willy, who had so hoped for success for himself and his sons, feels that his best option is to commit suicide, thus giving both his wife and his sons some insurance money with which to improve their lives.

How this plays out in *Death of a Salesman* is beautifully, tragically presented. We see both the past and present of the Loman family, their dreams and delusions. In a series of scenes, it is revealed that not just Willy but all of the Lomans have worked hard for years to avoid the truth. Willy is equally noble and pathetic, and his sons are only too happy to both praise and condemn their flawed, often bombastic, often in-spirational father. At the end, when Willy does indeed commit suicide, there is deep sadness, and the last scene at the gravesite is somber and pitiful.

In *Death of a Salesman* are some of the most important, memorable lines in American theater. A few include: "A salesman is got to dream, boy. It comes with the territory"; "A small man can be just as exhausted as a great man"; and the most famous, "Attention, attention must be finally paid to such a person."

The Crucible, set in America in 1692 during the Salem, Massachusetts, witch trials, is the story of Puritan John Proctor. John Proctor's community is tense, and neighbor is turned

The movie version of ***The Crucible*** was released in 1996, starring Daniel Day-Lewis and Winona Ryder.

self-deluded deceived by oneself

bombastic using pretentious language

against neighbor: it was believed at the time that individuals could make pacts with the Devil and thus have supernatural powers to enchant or harm others. A person suspected of witchcraft could be accused on very little evidence, tried, and if found guilty (as most were), put to death.

John Proctor is a flawed man—he has had an adulterous affair with Abigail, a teenage girl in the community—and she is clamoring for the relationship to continue. But John's conscience will not allow him to continue the affair, even when Abigail threatens to falsely accuse John's wife, Elizabeth, of witchcraft. To forestall Abigail's deadly plan, John admits to the community his adultery with Abigail and because he refuses to testify falsely, he is condemned to death. The combination of sexual hysteria, greed, and envy are central to *The Crucible,* and John Proctor's refusal to lie to save his life is considered a great moment in American theater. In a climactic scene, John Proctor explains why he will not sign a false confession: "Because it is my name! Because I cannot have another in my life! . . . How may I live without my name? I have given you my soul; leave me my name!"

clamoring repeatedly demanding

Conclusion

Arthur Miller's concern for social justice, his work in all forms of writing—plays, scripts, novels, short stories, travel accounts, essays—make him one of America's most important literary figures. In the late 1990s, Miller was still active and still working for the betterment of society. To this great playwright, as well as his unforgettable character Willy Loman, "attention, attention must be paid."

If you like the work of Arthur Miller, you might also like the work of Thornton Wilder.

Selected Bibliography

WORKS BY ARTHUR MILLER

Plays

The Man Who Had All the Luck. In *Cross-Section: A Collection of New American Writing.* Edited by Edwin Seaver (1944)

All My Sons (1947)

Death of a Salesman (1949)

An Enemy of the People (1950)

The Crucible (1953)

A Memory of Two Mondays and *A View from the Bridge* (1955), published as two one-act plays

A View from the Bridge (1957), two-act version

After the Fall (1964)

Incident at Vichy (1964)

The Price (1968)

The Creation of the World and Other Business (1972)

The Archbishop's Ceiling (1977)

The American Clock (1980)

Two-way Mirror: Some Kind of Love Story and *Elegy for a Lady* (1984)

Danger: Memory! Two plays: *I Can't Remember Anything* and *Clara* (1987)

The Ride Down Mount Morgan (1992)

The Last Yankee (1993)

Broken Glass (1994)

Prose Fiction

Focus (1945)

The Misfits (1961)

I Don't Need You Any More (1967)

Homely Girl: A Life (1992), retitled *Plain Girl: A Life* (1995)

Nonfiction

Situation Normal (1944)

"Salesman" in Beijing (1984)

Autobiography

Timebends: A Life (1987)

Critical Essays

The Theater Essays of Arthur Miller, edited by Robert A. Martin (1978)

The Theater Essays of Arthur Miller, edited by Robert A. Martin and Steven R. Centola (1996)

Travel Accounts

In Russia (1969)

In the Country (1977)

Chinese Encounters (1979)

Screenplays
Playing for Time (1980)

Everybody Wins (1990)

Collected Works
Collected Plays (1957)

The Portable Arthur Miller, edited by Harold Clurman (1971)

Collected Plays: Volume Two (1981)

WORKS ABOUT ARTHUR MILLER

Biographical and Critical Studies

Bigsby, Christopher, ed. *The Cambridge Companion to Arthur Miller.* Cambridge: Cambridge University Press, 1997.

Bigsby, Christopher, ed. *Arthur Miller and Company: Arthur Miller Talks About His Work in the Company of Actors, Designers, Directors, Reviewers and Writers.* London: The Arthur Miller Centre for American Studies, 1990.

Evans, Richard I. *Psychology and Arthur Miller.* New York: Praeger, 1981.

Griffin, Alice. *Understanding Arthur Miller.* Columbia: University of South Carolina Press, 1996.

Kazan, Elia. *A Life.* New York: Knopf, 1988.

Kolin, Philip C., ed. *American Playwrights Since 1945: A Guide to Scholarship Criticism, and Performance.* Westport, Conn.: Greenwood Press, 1989.

Lahr, Jon. "Making Willy Loman." *The New Yorker,* 25 January 1999, pp. 42–49.

Martin, Robert A., ed. *Arthur Miller: New Perspectives.* Englewood Cliffs, N.J.: Prentice-Hall, 1982.

Martine, James J. *Critical Essays on Arthur Miller.* Boston: G. K. Hall & Company, 1979.

Murphy, Brenda. *Miller: Death of a Salesman.* Cambridge: Cambridge University Press, 1995.

Roudane, Matthew C., ed. *Conversations with Arthur Miller.* Jackson and London: University Press of Mississippi, 1987.

Schlueter, June, ed. *Feminist Rereadings of Modern American Drama.* Rutherford, N.J.: Fairleigh Dickinson University, 1989.

Schlueter, June, and James K. Flanagan, eds. *Arthur Miller.* New York: Frederick Ungar, 1987.

Weales, Gerald, ed. *The Crucible: Text and Criticism.* New York: Viking, 1971.

Welland, Dennis. *Miller: The Playwright.* London and New York: Methuen, 1979.

Zeineddine, Nada. *Because It Is My Name: Problems of Identity Experienced by Women, Artists, and Breadwinners in the Plays of Henrik Ibsen, Tennessee Williams, and Arthur Miller.* Devon, England: Merlin, 1991.

Bibliographies

Ferres, John H. *Arthur Miller: A Reference Guide.* Boston: G. K. Hall, 1979.

Hayashi, Tetsumaro. *An Index to Arthur Miller Criticism.* 2d ed. Metuchen, N.J.: Scarecrow Press, 1976.

How to Write to the Author

Arthur Miller
c/o Viking
375 Hudson Street
New York, NY 10014

Margaret Mitchell

(1900–1949)

by James M. Brewbaker

Imagine Atlanta in March 1921, less than sixty years since the city lay in ruins following the Battle of Atlanta in 1864. There is a population of fewer than 100,000 souls, no comparison to the three million Atlantans who in 1996, would host the summer Olympics. But for all of March's dogwood and azaleas, Atlanta in 1921 is no picturesque Southern town in the aftermath of Reconstruction. No, this Atlanta is a profitable railroad and commercial center. This Atlanta, the progressive center of the New South, looks to the future, not the past.

This Atlanta in 1921 has a growing African American middle class. The city's first African American millionaire, Alonzo Herndon, lives in a mansion west of downtown, and in the Sweet Auburn district, the Ebenezer Baptist Church, where Martin Luther King Jr. will one day be pastor, is under construction.

A debutante ball is under way at the Georgian Terrace, a glitzy residential hotel. Sponsored by the Daughters of the American Revolution (DAR), an organization of women who trace their ancestors to colonial times, the event draws the

The Civil War **Battle of Atlanta** lasted from May to September 1864. Union forces besieged the city and cut off supply lines until the Confederate forces evacuated the city. Union forces then burned parts of Atlanta.

The National Society of the **Daughters of the American Revolution (DAR)** was founded in 1890 and was chartered by Congress in 1896. There are more than 212,000 members of the DAR.

197

cream of Atlanta society. As the orchestra takes a break, twenty-year-old Peggy Mitchell and her partner, a Georgia Tech student, perform the sensuous Apache dance. They dip, they swivel their hips, they clutch at each other almost as if making love. The dance ends with a passionate kiss.

The ladies of the DAR, some of them, at any rate, are not amused. They had expected an Indian dance, not a steamy French spectacle. To them, it is obscene. As a result, young Peggy Mitchell—who fifteen years later would pen *Gone with the Wind* (1936), the most widely read American novel of the twentieth century—is dropped from the list of young women invited to membership in the Junior League. Resenting the snub, she will return the favor in 1939, when *Gone with the Wind* premieres at the Loew's Grand Theater. Invited as guest of honor to a Junior League party, Peggy Mitchell, whom the world remembers as Margaret Mitchell, will ignore the event.

Who was Margaret Mitchell? What sort of life did she lead as a child and teenager? What events shaped her as a young woman in the years between World War I (1914–1919) and the Great Depression of the 1930s? How did she learn to write, and how did she come to create the characters most adult Americans recognize by their first names alone: Scarlett, Rhett, Ashley, and Melanie? Why has *Gone with the Wind,* whose famous author died on 16 August 1949, after being struck by a car as she crossed Peachtree Street several days earlier, had such a lasting appeal? Why, decades later, does the book stir controversy?

The **Junior League,** founded in 1921, is a community service organization for women from age 18 through 45.

The **Great Depression** was a severe recession that began when the stock market crashed in 1929 and lasted almost ten years. By the winter of 1932 to 1933, between fourteen and sixteen million Americans were unemployed. Many died from a lack of food and inadequate living conditions.

Early Years: A Granddaughter of Plantation Georgia

Born on 8 November 1900, Margaret Munnerlyn Mitchell was part of the fifth generation of her family to live in and around Atlanta. In a 1936 letter printed in *Margaret Mitchell and John Marsh: The Love Story Behind* Gone with the Wind (1993), she wrote, "I spent the Sunday afternoons of my childhood sitting on the bony knees of Confederate Veterans and the fat slick laps of old ladies who survived the war and reconstruction." (Walker, p. 17). The girl's connections to the older generation affected both her values and her view of American history.

The bony-kneed veterans and slick-lapped ladies had survived the most traumatic era in American history. They wanted the younger generation to know the realities of Southern history as they understood it. *Gone with the Wind* acknowledges their view of Southern history to some extent—its beautiful women in pastel gowns attracting beaux, its young men arguing about war—but in the novel, Margaret Mitchell also describes an antebellum (prewar) South that is more the world of rough-and-ready self-made men than it is of aristocratic blue bloods.

The Sundays Mitchell referred to were spent just south of Atlanta at the site that inspired Tara, Scarlett's home in *Gone with the Wind.* Along Jonesboro Road, the girl's mother pointed out stark chimneys of homes destroyed as Sherman's armies advanced from Atlanta toward Savannah. Maybelle Mitchell taught Peggy that life is unpredictable, that land and money may be lost, and that women need education in order to make their own way regardless of what happens to the men in their lives. From her mother, Mitchell acquired the tough-minded ideals of a strong-willed survivor—not unlike Scarlett O'Hara, who during the late 1860s, builds a profitable lumber business despite her wishy-washy husband, Frank. Mitchell also regarded Maybelle as the embodiment of womanly virtue and refinement, similar to the saintly Ellen O'Hara of *Gone with the Wind,* who died after contracting typhoid fever while nursing the poor-white Emmie Slattery.

Margaret Mitchell spent her childhood with her older brother, Stephens, in a spacious house in the Virginia Highlands area of Atlanta. Here she played, read the latest books, learned to ride horses, and wrote adventurous stories. She was a tomboy, wore her hair short, and often preferred pants to dresses and skirts, thought to be more suitable for young girls. In 1917, much of the neighborhood was destroyed by fire. Five years earlier, however, the Mitchells had moved to fashionable Peachtree Street and into a grand home that Margaret's father, Eugene, had built for his wife. This home was demolished in 1952.

As a teenager, Mitchell experienced typical adolescent feelings. In her journal, she wrote at age fourteen, "I don't suppose there's anything about me to be proud of. I'm not pretty, that's certain. I'm lazy. I can't study. I can't do mathematics. I guess my morals are mighty low and I don't give a damn for anything that happens." In the same entry, she reveals an ambitious side. "I want to be famous in some way—a speaker, artist, writer, soldier, fighter, stateswoman, or anything nearly. If I were a boy,

beaux sweethearts for girls or women

blue blood a member of a noble or socially prominent family

General William Tecumseh **Sherman** (1820–1891) fought for the Union during the Civil War. He led the attack on Atlanta in 1864.

typhoid fever a communicable disease caused by a bacterium and marked by fever, diarrhea, headache, and intestinal inflammation

West Point is the U.S. Military Academy, which prepares men and women to serve in the U.S. Army. It is located in West Point, New York

Courtenay Ross was also the name of Margaret Mitchell's best friend.

I'd try for West Point, if I could make it, or well I'd be a prize fighter—anything for the thrills" ("Writings of a Teenage Mitchell Found," 1998).

At age sixteen, Mitchell, who "wanted to be famous in some way," wrote her first novel, a historical romance. Discovered by accident and published in 1996, *Lost Laysen* is set in the South Pacific. Its heroine, Courtenay Ross, must choose between loyalty to one man and the excitement of a new lover. Written in about a month, *Lost Laysen* introduced themes Mitchell developed more fully in *Gone with the Wind*.

Education, Marriage, and a Career in Journalism

Peggy Mitchell attended Washington Seminary, a private school within walking distance of home. Shorter than most girls her age, she gained the nickname "Piano Legs" from her not-so-kind classmates. Her grades were mediocre in subjects such as geometry but better in subjects she liked such as history.

By 1918, Mitchell was ready for college. Her parents sent her to Smith, a college for women in Massachusetts. Back at home, however, tragedy struck. Maybelle Mitchell fell victim to the swine flu epidemic that killed hundreds of thousands of Americans in 1918 and 1919. She died while Peggy was on her way home. Though Peggy returned to Smith to finish her freshman year, she knew she was needed at home. Thus ended her formal education.

Back in Atlanta, Mitchell become the lady of her father's mansion, managing servants, planning social events, and paying the bills. This was no small task for a teenager. Soon she became involved in the swirl of Atlanta society. She moved with a set of young intellectuals who visited illegal night spots serving bootleg gin, where they discussed events of the day such as the rise of communism in Europe.

bootleg alcohol that is produced and distributed illegally, such as during Prohibition—the period between 1920 and 1933 when the manufacture, sale, and transportation of alcoholic beverages were forbidden by an amendment to the U.S. Constitution

Among her male friends were Red Upshaw, an attractive ne'er-do-well living off a dwindling family fortune, and his roommate, John Marsh, a journalist several years older than she. Upshaw attracted women easily; Marsh was shy and just barely making ends meet on a reporter's salary. Both loved Mitchell's energy, intelligence, and good looks. The nickname "Piano Legs" forgotten, she became engaged to Upshaw. Marsh was a reluctant best man at their wedding in September 1922.

The marriage soured quickly, however Red Upshaw showed little ambition, became involved in bootlegging, and physically abused his wife. A Catholic, Mitchell could not divorce and remain in the church, but her situation was desperate. Fourteen months after they married, in November 1923, Red and Peggy were divorced. Family members were scandalized. To them, divorce was a sin.

Marsh and Mitchell had been friends throughout her marriage to Upshaw, and their relationship developed into romance soon after the divorce. Mitchell found in John Marsh all the good qualities that Red Upshaw lacked. Clearly, she had married the wrong roommate. After several delays, they were married on 4 July 1925.

During her difficult first marriage, lacking any steady income, Mitchell had taken a job as a writer for the *Atlanta Journal*'s *Sunday Magazine.* Her first story appeared late in 1922, and she kept the job until May 1926. Mitchell was the first female in her family to be employed.

Writing *Gone with the Wind,* 1926–1935

The Marshes, John and Peggy, were immediately as happy as she and Red had been miserable. Rarely content when apart, they remained devoted to each other until her death in 1949. They moved into a modest apartment they lovingly referred to as "the Dump," today the site of the Margaret Mitchell Museum. It was there, beginning in 1926, that Mitchell penned the greatest part of *Gone with the Wind.* A slow-to-heal broken ankle forced her to resign from the *Atlanta Journal.* With time on her hands, she began to write—relentlessly.

Mitchell was very secretive as a writer. Her acquaintances had no idea what she was writing although—as she visited the library to research portions of the book—they teased her about writing "the great American novel." Little did they know. Peggy claimed that no one, not even John, had read the manuscript in its entirety before she sold it to the publishing company Macmillan. He, in fact, a seasoned journalist, had worked closely with Peggy during her reporter days. He also later played a major part in editing Peggy's massive manuscript, which in rough form was stuffed into manila envelopes around the apartment. Still, Mitchell's claim that John hadn't read the novel "cover to cover" was justified because she wrote its last chapter first. She had a clear plan in mind for

seasoned experienced

Gone with the Wind, and its somber climax—with Melanie dead, Rhett packing his bags and no longer "giv[ing] a damn," and Scarlett facing an uncertain future—provided a focus for all the rest she would write.

By 1930, much of the creative work of writing was done. What remained was the drudgery of rewriting, editing, and checking for historic accuracy. Mitchell insisted on including only those details that historians and old-timers would recognize as accurate.

The Marshes continued editing into the summer of 1935, when Peggy sold the still-untitled manuscript to Macmillan. In fact, she wrote and rewrote for months thereafter. Once and for all, she finished the first chapter, then rearranged chapters two through six. She settled on a title, rejecting *Tomorrow Is Another Day* in favor of *Gone with the Wind,* and even changed the name of her heroine from Pansy to Katie Scarlett. She responded to critiques from well-known historians.

Published in June 1936, the novel sparked mixed reviews at first, then lavish praise from both critics and historians. Sales were phenomenal—1,700,000 copies during the first year, with foreign language editions selling by the tens of thousands in Europe. The next year, 1937, Mitchell's 1,037-page epic won the Pulitzer Prize, America's most noted award for fiction.

drudgery dull, bothersome work

epic unusual in size or scope

The film version of *Gone with the Wind* earned eight Oscars, including Best Picture, Best Actress (Vivian Leigh as Scarlett), Best Supporting Actress (Hattie McDaniel as Mammie), and Best Director (Victor Fleming).

plot the deliberate sequence of events in a literary work

Gone with the Wind as Novel and Film: Some Basic Differences

Readers and movie fans need to bear in mind that novels and films are very different forms and that adapting one to the other inevitably causes significant change. In the case of *Gone with the Wind,* the differences involve more than plot details.

The 1939 film opens with words that never appear in the novel:

> There was a land of Cavaliers and Cotton Fields called the Old South. Here in this pretty world, Gallantry took its last bow. Here was the last ever to be seen of Knights and their Ladies Fair, of Master and of Slave. Look for it only in books, for it is no more than a dream remembered, a Civilization gone with the wind.

This is *not* the world Mitchell describes in the novel, however. Rather than supporting the myth of the South as a "pretty world," she comes closer to portraying it as an accident waiting to happen. Through the complacency of aristocrats such as Ashley Wilkes, the Old South will collapse. It is the industrious survivors and opportunists, people such as Scarlett and Rhett, who are the wave of the future.

In the film, there are three classes of people: planters, shiftless poor whites, and slaves, the last group comfortable with their lives serving whites. The novel, though, includes another group: the rough, self-made small farmers around Tara who grew rich off cotton but were no aristocrats. One of them, Will Benteen, marries Scarlett's sister Suellen and through hard work does as much to save Tara as the money Scarlett borrows from Rhett Butler.

A key African American character, Dilcey, is also left out the film. The mother of Prissy, Dilcey conveys an intelligent nobility other slaves in the narrative lack. Her absence makes other African American characters confirm more strongly the stereotypes of the day.

Tara, readers know, is a rambling, less elegant place in the novel than it is in the film. Despite Mitchell's attempts to show the producers what real plantation houses were like, they created a film Tara more to their liking.

Among other differences between the novel and film are the fact that in the novel Scarlett has three children, not one. The ending differs slightly but significantly as well. In the final chapter, Rhett is upstairs packing; in the film, he walks away after muttering Hollywood's most famous closing line, "Frankly, my dear, I don't give a damn."

Gone with the Wind as Social History: Gender, Class, and Race

Peggy Mitchell wanted her novel to be historically accurate. Her care in chasing down the details of battles and planter lifestyles is well documented. She was not as well informed about the social history of that era, especially as it concerned African Americans.

Most popular American writers from the 1870s on supported a view of the Confederacy as a virtuous culture where kindly planters grew rich from the toil of ignorant slaves who needed protection. This world, the story goes, fell victim to

---

complacency calmness and self-satisfaction accompanied by an unawareness of dangers or deficiencies

opportunist a person who takes advantage of opportunities or situations without regard for possible consequences

stereotype universal type; character that conforms to a preconceived and often oversimplified notion about a person or group

In the novel, before Rhett goes upstairs to pack, he delivers this final line: "My dear, I don't give a damn."

prevailing currently in fashion

old guard a well-known, established group with great influence

W. E. B. Du Bois (1868–1963) was an important African American protest leader. He helped found the National Association for the Advancement of Colored People (NAACP) in 1909 to combat racial discrimination.

Scarlett, a sequel to *Gone with the Wind,* was published in September 1991. The author, Alexandra Ripley, was chosen by Mitchell's estate to continue the saga of Scarlett O'Hara. A television miniseries of the sequel aired in November 1994 and starred Joanne Whalley-Kilmer as Scarlett.

new forces such as industrialism and, following the Civil War, to mean-spirited radical Republicans. Mitchell contradicted this view, but only in part. She believed that the desire for money and power made the Old South tick, not noble ideals. Yet her view of African Americans was consistently negative.

Mitchell's novel, unlike the film, took issue with some prevailing ideas of her day about the South. Mitchell had little use for Southern women who were helpless, ready to swoon at the first crisis. She mocked fluffy females such as Aunt Pittypat. She also disliked the holier-than-thou views of the old guard, those offended by her risque Apache dance in 1921. In contrast, Mitchell admired tough characters such as Scarlett and Melanie. Rhett, the black sheep of his family and a person shunned by polite society, is, in the long run, a much stronger character than Ashley Wilkes, who is unable to adapt to a new world.

Yet *Gone with the Wind*—in its depiction of African Americans and in the way that white characters respond to them—disturbs many people today. The novel promotes the idea that slaves were contented, loyal, at a loss with freedom, and in need of a kindly guiding hand. Once free, former slaves are given to laziness and violence toward whites. The film, like other Hollywood creations of the time, reinforces many of these stereotypes.

Historical fiction mixes real events and stories about those events. So it is with *Gone with the Wind.* Written between 1926 and 1935 by a descendant of slaveholders, the novel reflects both the prejudices of the day and Mitchell's own limited vision. One could say that she was too close to her subject to see it clearly. As a result, despite her painstaking research, Mitchell was unaware of alternate histories of the South and the Civil War. Though W. E. B. Du Bois and others wrote of a different side of American history, she told the tale as she understood it. It is possible to forgive this quality and still find it objectionable.

A very readable novel set in Georgia at the same time is Margaret Walker's *Jubilee* (1966). Its main character, Vyry, is an intelligent kitchen slave on a Georgia plantation. She longs for freedom. The worlds of *Jubilee,* written by an African American, and *Gone with the Wind* could hardly be more different, however. Each is significant historical fiction, carefully researched, but the two convey very different understanding of the Civil War, Reconstruction, and those who experienced them.

Selected Bibliography

WORKS BY MARGARET MITCHELL

Oh! Lady Godiva (1926, unpublished)
Gone with the Wind (1936)
Lost Laysen (1996)

WORKS ABOUT MARGARET MITCHELL

Edwards, Anne. *Road to Tara: The Life of Margaret Mitchell.* New Haven, Conn.: Ticknor and Fields, 1983.

Emerson, Bo. "Writings of a Teenage Mitchell Found." Available on-line at *www.yall.com/culture/quill/mitchell/*

Pyron, Darden A. *Southern Daughter: The Life of Margaret Mitchell.* New York: Oxford University Press, 1991.

Taylor, Helen. *Scarlett's Women:* Gone with the Wind *and Its Female Fans.* New Brunswick, N.J.: Rutgers University Press, 1989.

Walker, Marianne. *Margaret Mitchell and John Marsh: The Love Story Behind* Gone with the Wind. Atlanta, Ga.: Peachtree Publishers, 1993.

You can visit the Margaret Mitchell House, which contains the apartment she affectionately called "the Dump," at
990 Peachtree Street
Atlanta, GA 30309

You can also visit the Margaret Mitchell House website at
www.gwtw.org

Kyoko Mori

(1957–)

by Barbara G. Samuels

Kyoko Mori says she "always loved to read and write." Like many other Japanese children in Kobe, Japan, where she was born, she started reading before she went to school. Her mother read to her all the time, and she absorbed simple lessons about story and language from those experiences. Once she started school and learned the phonetic signs of the Japanese alphabet, she could write her own compositions about her family, her home, and her friends. Mori wrote in her author profile for Ballantine Books that she also had two good models for writing. Her mother, Takako, wrote letters to her parents every week telling them about her garden, about recipes she had tried, and about Kyoko and her brother Jumpei. Mori's grandfather, a former schoolteacher, kept a journal. When Mori spent time in the summer with her grandparents, she saw him writing in his journal every day. She said in the author profile, "These two people in my family gave me the idea that writing was something we did everyday or even every week with enjoyment."

Quotations from Kyoko Mori that are not attributed to a published source are from a personal interview conducted by the author of this article on 24 February 1999 and are published here by permission of Kyoko Mori.

phonetic representing the sounds of speech

Although writing assignments in her Japanese classes involved traditional critical essays on authors or their works, in her high school English classes in Japan, Mori wrote essays about her family, friends, and dreams. Her English teachers, usually young women, encouraged her writing with comments on both form and content, and she looked forward to reading their comments. In her essay "School," in *Polite Lies: On Being a Woman Caught Between Cultures* (1997), Mori said "By the time I was a high school senior, I wanted to be a writer, and English was the only language I could write in" (p. 168). Real writing to Mori, a creative writing teacher, obviously means more than correct spelling or mechanics. "My public education in Japan prepared me to make the correct letters to spell out the correct sounds, but that is not the same as teaching me how to write" (p. 164).

When I asked Mori if she had any advice for teen writers, she talked about the value of keeping a journal or notebook. "They should note down what they see," she said, "and they should learn the names of things, common names of birds and flowers." She talked about the importance of developing observational skills. According to Mori, noticing detail is an important part of the writing process. Reading and noticing what authors do is also important training for a writer. Mori and other published writers go back and forth in time, following the natural progression of their minds. As one thing reminds them of something else, they follow the connections in their writing. She suggested that teens who are readers should pay attention to how authors provide cues to trigger the memory, then try to apply what they have learned to their own writing.

Mori's Books

memoir a literary work about personal experiences

protagonist the main character of a literary work

Kyoko Mori's two novels, a memoir, and a collection of essays focus on similar themes, and all reflect her own experiences. Mori's mother committed suicide when Mori was twelve years old. This tragic event in her life plays a major part in all her writings. Both of her novels for young adults, *Shizuko's Daughter* (1993) and *One Bird* (1995), are coming-of-age stories set in Japan. Both novels center on a young teen's loss of her mother and her consequent struggle with an emotionless father. Like her teen protagonists, Kyoko Mori learned about the plants and flowers of Japan from her mother. Like Yuki, Mori is a runner. She is a bird-watcher, and like Megumi, she has been a volunteer bird rehabilitator. In Mori's memoir, *The Dream of Water* (1995), she explores her feelings on her first journey back to Japan after thirteen years in the United States. On this trip, Mori confronted the tragedy of her childhood, the suicide of her mother when she was twelve and the brutality of her father and stepmother during her teen years. In fact, reality and fiction often merge in *Dream of Water, Shizuko's Daughter,* and *One Bird.* Mori's writing provides an example of the ways that authors fictionalize the truths of their own lives. In her author profile she wrote, "All the characters are reflections of some aspect of myself, but none of the characters are strictly myself. I think that the best thing about being a writer is that we get to make up things and tell the truth at the same time."

Mori's *Polite Lies: On Being a Woman Caught Between Cultures,* a collection of essays for adults, pulls together the threads of her novels and memoir. In twelve essays she discusses the ways in which Japanese and American cultures differ in their rules for communication. Her essays explain why she writes in English: "In Japanese, I don't have a voice for speaking my mind" (p. 16). Cultural rules in Japan forbid expressions of feelings in public "because to do so is rude, intrusive, and selfish" (p. 182). Weaving her own life story into her discussions of cultural differences, Mori considers women's roles in both societies. Japanese women are taught that their feelings are unimportant; their job is to serve their husbands and families. In Japan, men and women speak differently. Well-brought-up women use words which suggest that they are subservient to men. Even professional women and radio and TV announcers in Japan speak in high-pitched, childish voices. Mori explained that she writes in English because Japanese is too confining a language for a woman.

The role of women in Japanese society is a major theme in Mori's two young adult novels. Yuki's mother in *Shizuko's Daughter* kills herself because her husband has betrayed her with another woman and ignores his wife and daughter. She feels she has no other option besides suicide. Except for the wealthy, divorce is not accepted in Japan. Similarly, Megumi's mother in *One Bird* leaves her when she can no longer stand her husband's infidelity and absences. Although it doesn't make any sense to Megumi, in Japanese culture, "the woman must go to live with her parents for the rest of her life, giving up her children until they are old enough—full grown adults—to visit on their own; the father usually does not allow any visits" (p. 3).

rehabilitator one who helps restore health

subservient characterized by extreme obedience

After her mother's death in *Shizuko's Daughter,* Yuki is forced to live with a resentful stepmother who suffers her presence only because of what other people would say if she did not take care of her. The stepmother's attitude is part of what Mori refers to when she talks about "polite lies." Yuki tells Hanae, "When other people are around, you pretend that you like me. You pretend that we're all happy together. I don't pretend. I hate you" (p. 99). Hanae is an example of what is expected of Japanese women. She cleans her house thoroughly every day and complains about the fingerprints Yuki and her father leave on the refrigerator door because they never learned to hold the handle properly. She nags Yuki constantly about the way she does housework. Like Cinderella's wicked stepmother, Hanae is never satisfied with Yuki's work in the house.

> **"Whatever did your mother teach you?" Hanae had asked [Yuki] once. "She taught me things you wouldn't know about. . . . She taught me to draw and paint. She taught me the names of flowers and stories to tell from memory. She knew things no one else knew." (Pp. 89, 90)**

When Hanae complains that Yuki doesn't have manners, she replies, "What do I want with good manners? Why should I pretend to be nice to people when they don't like me and I don't like them? It's not honest" (p. 90).

Just as Yuki lives with a mean stepmother after her mother's death, Megumi ends up living with her father's mother, Grandmother Shimizu, when her mother moves away to live with Megumi's grandfather. Even though Japanese custom dictates that the child is left with the father, Megumi's father spends most of his time in Hiroshima with his girlfriend. Her grandmother loves her, but shows it by being gruff and critical of everything she does. She tries to convince Megumi's father to take her out of the supportive expensive private school she attends. And when she learns that Megumi has lied about going to church to spend Sundays with Toru, a twenty-year-old friend from her childhood who has also lost his mother, and has secretly received letters from her mother, her grandmother explodes with anger.

In both of Mori's novels, Japanese culture dictates the actions of the protagonists and their mothers, but Yuki and Megumi think freely. Megumi makes her own decision to stop attending church because she no longer believes in God after her mother leaves her. With Dr. Mizutani's support she also eventually stands up to her grandmother and father. Yuki, too, focuses on how she can reestablish connections with her mother's family when she is old enough to leave her father's house.

A Childhood in Japan

Like the teen protagonists in her novels, Mori remembers her mother as a gentle and sweet person. In *Polite Lies,* she says other people remember her "as I do, as a beautiful and sad woman. I loved her poise, her gracefulness. But I want to be different. I don't want grace or beauty if it means turning all my disappointments into something spare and elegant, an artful silence" (p. 100). The "polite lies" expected in Japanese culture mask true feelings and relationships. Throughout her essays, Mori compares the codes of behavior for American women and for Japanese women because she sees herself part of and yet separate from both cultures.

poise an easy, self-confident manner

Although her mother's suicide and her father's remarriage made her teen years miserable, Mori spent her early years with a wonderfully supportive and loving mother. For the five years between kindergarten and fourth grade, the family lived in a small apartment complex in the seaside neighborhood of Ashiya, the setting for *One Bird.* During those years her mother had many friends who got together to drink tea and knit and sew. Mori's mother was known for her warmth and cheerfulness. On weekends she often invited friends and their children to go on picnics and hikes. Together these women and children explored the natural beauty of Japan, admiring the plants and trees and appreciating the glory of the world around them. Mori's mother also often told her stories, and, as she grew up, reminded her of the pleasures they had shared together. During the summers Mori, her younger brother, and her mother spent weeks in a village in the country visiting her maternal grandparents. There the children collected eggs in the henhouse, swam in the river, and helped in the vegetable and flower gardens. Mori believes that these wonderful years with her mother gave her the strength to leave Japan and live her life in freedom. At the end of *Polite Lies,* Mori talks about leaving Japan and says, "I had left home, I was sure, not to forget about my mother but to be closer to her memory. . . . I speak her words though I speak them in another language" (p. 258).

setting the general time and place in which the events of a literary work take place

maternal related through the mother

As an older child, Mori knew her mother was a sad and lonely woman. Her father, Hiroshi, was rarely home, spending many nights away on "business trips." Although she didn't know it at the time, her father was spending much of his time with his mistress, who later became Mori's stepmother. Like the mother in *Shizuko's Daughter,* Mori's mother once asked her if she could go on living by herself if she died. Mori reports in *The Dream of Water* that she replied:

> "No, I don't want to die even if you were gone. But you are not going to die. I don't know why you keep talking about it. I wish you would stop." My voice sounded harsh, but I kept saying, "I want to go back to sleep. I'm so tired." I turned away from her and started crying.

> "I'm sorry," she said. "Maybe I'm going crazy. All I can think of is how I would be better off dead." (P. 8)

Mori knew also that her mother often cried herself to sleep. Later, when her mother committed suicide, Mori wondered if by saying she could go on living without her mother, she had, in effect, given her mother permission to take her own life. Mori repeated this same sequence in her novel *Shizuko's Daughter.*

After six years of mental and physical abuse while living in Kobe with her father and stepmother, in 1977, Mori escaped and came to spend her last year of high school in the United States. She then received her bachelor's degree from Rockford College in Illinois and her M.A. and Ph.D. from the University of Wisconsin at Milwaukee. Most of her adult life has been spent in Green Bay, Wisconsin, where she has taught creative writing at St. Norbert College. In the summer of 1999, Kyoko Mori began the Briggs-Copeland Lectureship in Creative Writing at Harvard University. She plans to teach at Harvard for the next five years.

Beauty in the Natural World

In addition to introducing Japanese culture, Mori's novels introduce the reader to the physical landscape and visual imagery of Japan. Although Mori is herself a bird-watcher and bird rehabilitation volunteer, she studied the birds of Japan to

include information about them in *One Bird.* In this novel,
Megumi finds strength and support in her relationship with
Dr. Mizutani, a female veterinarian who helps to rehabilitate
wild birds and also rejects the cultural system that diminishes
women. Megumi's situation when her mother leaves her is
parallel to that of the weak and injured wild baby birds she
helps care for. Megumi thinks, "Maybe I am like a lone bird. My
mother and I were two baby birds in the nest, and now she is
gone. I can think of her only in that way—as another helpless
baby—not as a mother bird returning with food in her beak"
(p. 65). She makes another connection between the birds and
her mother when she learns that the baby birds can drown if
too much water gets in their mouths. "My mother is a bird
whose mouth has become a big sea of tears. She had to leave
me to keep from drowning" (p. 65).

Megumi's mother is the source of Megumi's knowledge
about birds and nature. She tells Dr. Mizutani, "She didn't
want me to grow up knowing only sparrows, crows, and swal-
lows. It bothered her that people didn't know the birds, trees,
and flowers around them, so she used to take me on walks, to
show me things" (p. 39). Even though she is just a tenth
grader, Megumi writes an essay about her family in twenty-five
years—in the year 2000—that wins the school competition.
While she is writing, she hears the waxwing bird's sound,
which reminds her of the pampas grass at her grandmother's
house. She remembers walking in the pampas grass every August, "holding hands with my mother and Grandmother Kuri-
hara, listening to the crickets in the grass and the cicadas in
the trees above" (p. 44).

cicadas any of several
large insects with a
stout body, wide head,
and large, transparent
wings; male cicadas
produce the loudest
buzzing or humming
sounds of any insect

Flowers and plants are images that appear again and again
to support the action in *Shizuko's Daughter* as well. When
Yuki's family moves to their new house on the hill, Yuki and her
mother transplant chrysanthemums and other flowers, many of
which originally came from her grandmother's garden. While
digging in the flowers, Yuki's mother asks her if she could go on
without her. Two years later, after her mother's suicide, Yuki
looks at the flowers. "They were getting ready to blossom another year. Her mother had thought that Yuki, too, would go on
without her. Yuki had said so, two years ago, as they looked at
these same chrysanthemums and violas" (p. 42).

violas violets

At another time, when Yuki is feeling thrilled to have
begun a friendship with Sachiko, a runner from another
school, she notices the azalea bushes where Sachiko's mother

had been sitting. Yuki remembers that her mother had taught her how to make a trumpet from an azalea blossom and then taste the sweetness of the flower. "She wished she could eat the flowers, thousands of pink trumpets, and suffocate with their sweetness" (p. 56). Other images from nature support the action. The violas on her grandmother's doorstep are infested with spider mites that suck their juices just as Yuki's bitterness overflows in rudeness to her grandmother. Yuki frees the frogs that are to be killed and dissected in school. Her grandmother frees the tree frogs her little grandson has caught, and the cicada that she imagines is about to die begins to fly freely. This series of images of freedom reflects the escape Yuki will have from the narrow home with her father and stepmother as she recognizes the strength she has gotten from her past. At the same time, the images also reflect the freedom her grandmother will have as she moves along the cycle of life and eventually joins her husband and daughter in death.

Images such as these help make Kyoko Mori's writing particularly effective. The *Horn Book,* in its review of *Shizuko's Daughter,* notes, "Mori paints beautiful pictures with words, creating visual images that can be haunting and elliptical as poetry." Mori told me that she once thought she wanted to be an artist. She still has a sketchbook on which she draws things she wants to remember, although she confided that she wouldn't show her drawings to anyone but a close friend. It is the pictures she draws with her words that keep us coming back to read and reread her novels. Although she is working on a novel for adults, her young adult fans will continue to hope for more.

elliptical marked by few words in speech or writing

Selected Bibliography

WORKS BY KYOKO MORI

Novels for Young Adults
Shizuko's Daughter (1993)
One Bird (1995)

Books for Adults
Fallout (1994)
The Dream of Water: A Memoir (1995)
Polite Lies: On Being a Woman Caught Between Cultures (1997)

If you like Kyoko Mori's novels, you might also enjoy reading other coming-of-age novels about strong women, such as *Shabanu: Daughter of the Wind* and *Haveli* by Suzanne Fisher Staples and *I Know Why the Caged Bird Sings* by Maya Angelou.

Miscellaneous

Ballantine Author Profile. New York: Ballantine Books. Available on-line at *www.randomhouse.com/BB/teachers/bios/mori.html*

WORKS ABOUT KYOKO MORI

Parker, Jacqueline. *Ballantine Teacher's Guide for* Shizuko's Daughter. New York: Ballantine Books, 1993. Available on-line at *www.randomhouse.com/BB/teachers/tgs/Shisuko.html*

Pignatella, Ellen. " 'The Dream of Water': A Journey of Personal Discovery." *The Colby Echo,* 25 April 1996.

Vasilakis, Nancy. Review of *Shizuko's Daughter.* In *Horn Book,* September/October 1993, p. 603.

How to Write to the Author

Kyoko Mori
c/o Henry Holt and Company
115 West 18th Street
New York, NY 10011-4195

Donna Jo Napoli

(1948–)

by Patty Campbell

Imagine a beautiful dark-haired woman who is a professor of linguistics at Swarthmore, one of the most intellectual colleges in America, and who has published eight learned books on the subject and won many awards and grants. Now add in the fact that this woman also writes poetry, speaks and has taught Italian, and has degrees not only in Romance linguistics but also in mathematics. Next, take into account that this woman has five children. Finally, marvel that she is also the author of three picture books, nine lively and funny novels for middle grade readers, and eight magnificently original young adult novels, ranging from fairy-tale fantasies with a twist, to a contemporary love story set in Venice and a historical novel about the Nazi slave labor camps. Meet Donna Jo Napoli, Super Writer. How does she do it all? "Badly!" she jokes—a modest evaluation that is obviously far from the truth.

Quotations from Donna Jo Napoli that are not attributed to a published source are from personal interviews conducted by the author of this article on 18 January 1999 and are published here by permission of Donna Jo Napoli.

linguistics the study of human speech and all the parts of language

Romance of or referring to any language derived from Latin, such as French, Spanish, and Italian

217

Growing Up Italian in Miami

A **slave labor camp** is a form of concentration camp, usually for political prisoners. During World War II, many Jews (and members of other ethnic groups) were detained in these work camps, where prisoners were deliberately worked to death.

dialect a regional form of a language

Napoli's three sons and two daughters are also multitalented high achievers. Napoli herself had what she calls "a lousy teenagehood," but a good childhood. Donna Jo was born on 28 February 1948, the youngest of four in an Italian-American family. They lived in Miami, where her parents, she recalls, "were really pretty busy with their own problems and didn't notice me that much," so she was free to roam the nearby woods and smell the sea. All four grandparents had grown up in Italy (although one grandmother had been born in Egypt), and Napoli remembers sitting at the feet of her mother's mother and listening to her tell folktales in Calabrese, an Italian dialect. Napoli's father was a contractor who built houses, so the family was constantly moving into his various projects. "By the time I was thirteen we had lived in thirteen different places," she remembers. But this was not as disruptive as it sounds, because all of these houses were in the same area, and she had to change schools only once, although she missed having neighborhood friends. "That may be part of why I'm a writer," she says. "I really am a loner in a lot of ways. I'm happy with it though. My childhood was really extremely happy until I was thirteen. I was pretty oblivious, pretty unworried."

When she was thirteen, disaster struck. Her father was arrested for his part in what Napoli refers to as "a large-scale theft group," and the news was everywhere—on the television and in the headlines of the *Miami Herald.* Her school friends' parents would not allow her to play with them anymore, and overnight her life became dreadful. Eventually her father was sent to prison, and she settled into a dull role as a dutiful daughter. She worked very hard at school; she worked very hard at a grocery store in the evening; she studied all night; and on the weekends she had a job in a laundromat. "It was not a great life," she remembers. Her father came home from prison in her senior year, but by then she had won a full scholarship to Radcliffe, then the women's college of Harvard. Over his objections she went off to the university, and a whole new world of ideas and literature opened up for her.

Degrees and Babies

In her junior year at college she married law student Barry Furrow and continued to work toward a B.A. in mathematics in 1970 and a Ph.D. in linguistics. Shortly after she achieved her doctorate in 1973, their first child, Elena, was born, and Napoli knew she wanted many more children. A glimpse of her tender feelings toward babies appears in the novel *Changing Tunes* (1998), when ten-year-old Eileen is entranced with her neighbor's grandson. "She placed Jared on the center of the blanket like she always did. 'Hello, little funny face. How are you today?' She got on her hands and knees and nuzzled Jared's tummy" (p. 73).

Unfortunately, Napoli's next pregnancy ended in a miscarriage. In her grief, Napoli poured out her heart in letters to a friend, writing day after day for months. Eventually, after she had begun to heal, the friend brought the letters back to her. "I think you've got a novel here," he said. It was not, but in reading over what she had written, Napoli realized the potential power of her pen. She began to write—poetry, adult and children's fiction of all kinds—and kept at it during the next fourteen years, while four more babies were born, and her teaching jobs took the young couple to the University of North Carolina at Chapel Hill, Georgetown University, the University of Michigan, and finally to Swarthmore.

Napoli submitted her work to publishers and gathered armloads of rejection slips. But her family sustained her belief in herself. "I've always read them the first draft of every story," she says. "And they have been my most savage critics but also my biggest fans. They've always told me, 'We love it! This and this is wrong, but we love it!' I probably would have been in the loony bin long ago if it hadn't been for their support." Finally her talent was recognized by the editors of Carolrhoda Press, who bought Napoli's retelling of an Italian folktale, *The Hero of Barletta,* for a flat fee of $600 and published it in 1988.

> **miscarriage** the spontaneous ending of a pregnancy before the fetus is viable, or able to exist independent of the mother

Freckles and Frogs

This initial publication opened the door. Soon Dutton accepted her first novel, *Soccer Shock* (1991), a comical sports story for middle readers featuring a very peculiar plot about a boy who has conversations with his freckles. An outrageous idea, but in Napoli's competent hands it worked, and critics and readers loved it. Nevertheless, it was her next book, *The Prince of the Pond: Otherwise Known as De Fawg Pin* (1992), that really established her reputation as a writer. Hilariously, Napoli turned the prince-turns-into-a-frog fairy tale on its head

> **plot** the deliberate sequence of events in a literary work

amphibian animals and plants that are able to live both in and out of water, such as frogs and toads

garbling mixing up and distorting

The **Brothers Grimm** were two German brothers, Jakob Ludwig Grimm (1785–1863) and Wilhelm Karl Grimm (1786–1859). They were scholars who were best known for their collection of fairy tales.

theme central message about life in a literary work

redemption restoration to favor; salvation

abet to help

by telling the story from a frog's point of view. Jade, the lady frog who takes pity on the transformed prince's ineptness at amphibian life teaches him pond survival techniques. And what a clumsy one the Frog Prince is—getting tangled up in his long back legs and garbling words with his hinged-in-the-middle tongue so that his own name comes out "Fawg" and "Pin." However, he is brave and tender, too, as Jade realizes when he risks everything to save their hundreds of tadpole children. But one day a princess comes along and gives De Fawg Pin a kiss, and. . . .

Napoli took her editors by surprise with her next book, *The Magic Circle* (1993). This young adult novel is a serious and psychologically complex retelling of a story from the Brothers Grimm. It was very different in style and readership from the lighthearted stories that had preceded it, so much so that her editors asked if she would like to publish it under another name to separate the two kinds of writing. Napoli was tempted. "I didn't like the idea of a child who had just read *The Prince of the Pond* turning around and picking up *The Magic Circle,* thinking he was going to get the same sort of story. But then we decided that we'd just do it, and people would just have to trust the labeling—that it was really young adult."

The Other Point of View in Fairy Tales and Bible Scholarship

Napoli wove themes of love and redemption and pride and forgiveness into the dark tale of *The Magic Circle.* In savage medieval Europe, a hunchbacked Ugly Sorceress has been given the gift of healing because of her love for God. To abet her powers, she calls on demons, careful always to protect herself from them with a magic circle drawn on the ground. But one day they tempt her with a gold ring placed just outside the line. For one moment she thinks of herself as heavenly and deserving because of the good she has been granted to do; she reaches out and is seized by evil. The triumphant demon voices in her head command her to eat a human child. Horrified, she flees to the deep woods, where she remains in isolation, away from temptation, living in a house she builds herself and decorates with candy. Then one day there is someone nibbling on her roof, and we realize that we know this witch—even before the children introduce themselves as Hansel and Gretel. The story moves on to its inexorable conclusion in the fiery stove—but what a difference the point of view makes!

Zel (1996) is a third fairy tale told from unexpected viewpoints. This time Napoli mined the story of Rapunzel from the perspective of not only the long-haired girl herself, but also of the witch who has imprisoned her and the count who comes to woo and rescue her. By far the strongest voice is that of the witch, a woman drowning in the clutching excesses of motherly love. Rapunzel's charming innocence contrasts chillingly with the witch's feverish magic, and the great weight of the damsel's hair takes on its own identity in the plot. The count, as in the original, is brave but a bit dumb, caught in the crossfire of this mother-daughter conflict. As in all good fairy tales, the ending is suitably romantic: the lovers are reunited at last as Zel's happy tears heal the count's blinded eyes. Napoli set this story in medieval Switzerland, and to research the locale she went to the meadows and villages of that country. "I climbed and sat and just kind of wrapped myself up in where I was," she says.

This kind of immediate experience of a place is important to her. For *Song of the Magdalene* (1996), a novel set in New Testament times, she had planned to visit the Holy Land as a side trip from a speaking engagement at a university in Egypt. But political troubles and violence flared up in that part of the world, and "the U.S. government urged Americans not to go to Egypt or that area. So I cancelled my plans and did everything entirely by reading and talking with rabbis and religious scholars." While she found them wonderfully generous with their time, she also found that there are vehement disagreements among biblical experts about history and interpretation.

Nevertheless, Napoli forged ahead, and whenever she ran into a controversial area, she chose the version that best carried her story forward. "It's a tricky book," she admits, and in this absorbing story of the early life of Mary Magdalene, with its delicate and tactful introduction of Jesus as Joshua the Healer, Napoli feels she pleased neither conservative Jews nor fundamentalist Christians. Even her editor was uneasy, she remembers, although there was no controversy when the book finally appeared. This disappointed her a bit, because "I had hoped that people would get involved in it."

inexorable unable to be changed

Israel and the West Bank of the Jordan River make up most of the biblical **Holy Land,** where the religious and national identity of the Jews developed between 1800 B.C. and A.D. 100 and where Christianity had its origins.

vehement forceful and passionate

fundamentalist Christian member of a movement of Protestantism that stresses a literal interpretation of the Bible as the basis of Christian life and teaching

Italian Novels

Italy is a country that Napoli loves and has used as a setting in two novels: *For the Love of Venice* (1998) and *Stones in Water* (1997). She and her family have spent several summers living in Venice, where her children have become acclimated and learned to speak the local dialect—and to make fun of their mother for her standard Italian accent. Unlike Napoli's off-spring, Percy, 17, the main character in *For the Love of Venice,* speaks only English, and is hampered and clumsy in his efforts to romance beautiful Graziella. The city itself becomes the center of this contemporary love story, in which Percy represents the enemy—tourism and America—to Venetian political activist Graziella. The story rises to a rousing showdown in which Napoli makes good use of her insider knowledge of the political sore points in this beautiful canal city.

Another novel drawn from her Venetian experiences is *Stones in Water,* a Holocaust memoir and survival story. For the background of this book she is indebted to her friend Guido Fullin, who shared his terrible memories of the Nazi slave labor camps during World War II. Guido is one of a group of Venetians who come together now and then to sit in an outdoor Irish pub and talk over their war experiences. "They need to still talk to each other about it so many years later," says Napoli. She also drew on the archives of the International Red Cross in Geneva and diaries and letters she found in Venice to tell this story. The novel reveals the surprising historical fact that although the Italians were allies with the Germans, the Nazis preyed on the young men of Italy for slave labor. In the novel, teenager Roberto and his friends assemble at a local movie theater for the rare treat of an American Western, only to be rounded up by the Nazis and shipped to Ukraine. One of the boys, Samuele, is Jewish, and the others try to keep the guards from noticing that he is circumcised. In the terrible hardships at the labor camp, Samuele freezes to death, and Roberto escapes to make his way across Ukraine to safety.

In telling this grim story, Napoli lightened reality a bit to make it palatable for young readers. "Sometimes the things that happened to Guido were just too horrifying for me to be able to use them fairly. So when the train went from Italy and crossed the border, I made three boys on the train complain, and get taken out on the platform and shot in front of everyone. And I thought that was terrible enough. What really happened to Guido was that they went through the train and

The **Holocaust** was the mass murder of at least 11 million people, especially Jews, by the Nazis during World War II. The word "holocaust" means "through destruction by fire."

palatable acceptable to the mind

picked boys at random and took them out and shot them down. And after that all the boys completely obeyed."

But Napoli feels that to present the most horrible version is a risk, because readers may become anesthetized or turn away. "No matter what kind of story I write—and I write some pretty dark stories—I'm a hopeful person myself. I always want to leave my reader with the sense that you might not be able to change your world, but you can find something within yourself that allows you to live decently within your world."

anesthetize here, to lose one's feelings for the situation

Sirena and Beyond

Switching to more cheerful themes, *Sirena* (1998) draws on Greek mythology for the love story of a mermaid and a hero. Like her sister half-fishes, Sirena yearns for the immortality that the passion of a mortal man can give her, but not at the price of the terrible drownings the mermaids cause when they sing their seductive songs to sailors. She swims away to the island of Lemnos, where she spies Philoctetes, a hero wounded by a snake sent by the goddess Hera and abandoned by his shipmates. She heals him and they fall in love, and all is idyllic until he wants to return to the world of men and the inevitable question arises of whether honor or love will prevail.

idyllic lighthearted and carefree

In between her young adult novels, Napoli has written stories for middle readers and picture books and in 1999 was working on two picture books, a series for elementary school readers called Angel Wings, and a young adult novel set in Persia in 1500. She sums up her intentions with "I'm writing for kids who need stories that will make 'em laugh and make 'em cry, all in the same story. Kids know that life is wonderful and horrible at the same time. I want to keep them turning the pages, and I want to grab them by the heart!"

prevail to be triumphant through strength or superiority

Selected Bibliography

WORKS BY DONNA JO NAPOLI

Novels for Young Adults

The Magic Circle (1993)

Song of the Magdalene (1996)

Zel (1996)

Stones in Water (1997)

For the Love of Venice (1998)

If you like Donna Jo Napoli, you might also like Madeleine L'Engle.

Sirena (1998)

Crazy Jack (1999)

Spinners, with Richard Tchen (1999)

Novels for Middle and Elementary Readers

Soccer Shock (1991)

The Prince of the Pond: Otherwise Known as De Fawg Pin (1992)

Shark Shock (1994)

When the Water Closes Over My Head (1994)

The Bravest Thing (1995)

Jimmy, the Pickpocket of the Palace (1995)

On Guard (1997)

Trouble on the Tracks (1997)

Changing Tunes (1998)

Angel Wings series

Friends Everywhere (1999)

Little Creatures (1999)

One Leap Forward (1999)

On Her Own (1999)

Give and Take (2000)

No Fair (2000)

Playing Games (2000)

Spring Flowers (2000)

Short Stories

"Sweet Giongio." In *Diane Goode's Book of Silly Stories and Songs.* Illustrated by Diane Goode. New York: Dutton Children's Books, 1992.

"Little Lella." In *Diane Goode's Book of Giants and Little People.* Illustrated by Diane Goode. New York: Dutton Children's Books, 1997.

Picture Books

The Hero of Barletta (1988)

Albert (2000)

Flamingo Dream (2000)

How Hungry Are You?, with Richard Tchen (2001)

Rocky (2001)

Nonfiction for Adults

Elements of Tone, Stress, and Intonation, edited by Donna Jo Napoli (1978)

Syntactic Argumentation, with Emily Rando (1979)

Linguistic Symposium on Romance Languages, edited by Donna Jo Napoli and William Cressey (1981)

Predication Theory: A Case Study for Indexing Theory (1989)

Bridges Between Psychology and Linguistics: A Swarthmore Festschrift for Lila Gleitman, edited by Donna Jo Napoli and Judy Anne Kegl (1991)

Syntax: Theory and Problems (1993)

Phonological Factors in Historical Change: The Passage of the Latin Second Conjugation into Romance, with Stuart Davis (1994)

Linguistics: Theory and Problems (1996)

WORKS ABOUT DONNA JO NAPOLI

Book

Hedblad, Alan, ed. *Something About the Author.* Detroit: Gale Research, 1997, vol. 92, pp. 161–166.

Article

Campbell, Patty. "The Sand in the Oyster." *Horn Book,* November/December 1994, pp. 756–759.

Selected Reviews

Beck, Kathleen. Review of *Sirena.* In *Voice of Youth Advocates,* December 1998, p. 369.

Bergstrom, Libby. Review of *Song of the Magdalene.* In *Voice of Youth Advocates,* February 1997, p. 331.

Cooper, Ilene. Review of *Song of the Magdalene.* In *Booklist,* 1 October 1996, p. 833.

Dennis, Lisa. Review of *The Magic Circle.* In *School Library Journal,* August 1993, p. 186.

Edwards, Carol R. Review of *Changing Tunes.* In *School Library Journal,* August 1998, p. 164.

Fakolt, Jennifer R. Review of *For the Love of Venice.* In *School Library Journal,* June 1998, p. 148.

How to Write to the Author

Donna Jo Napoli
c/o Scholastic Press
555 Broadway
New York, NY 10012-3999

Hearne, Betsy. Review of *The Prince of the Pond.* In *Bulletin of the Center for Children's Books,* January 1993, p. 153.

Peters, John. Review of *Changing Tunes.* In *Booklist,* 15 May 1998, p. 1627.

Phillips, Marilyn Payne. Review of *Stones in Water.* In *School Library Journal,* November 1997, p. 122.

Rochman, Hazel. Review of *Stones in Water.* In *Booklist,* 1 October 1997, p. 333.

Rochman, Hazel. Review of *Zel.* In *Booklist,* 1 September 1996, p. 118.

Sutton, Roger. Review of *Zel.* In *Horn Book,* September/October 1996, p. 603.

Rodman Philbrick

(1951–)

by Bill Mollineaux

"I never had a brain until Freak came along and let me borrow his for a while, and that's the truth, the whole truth." These words not only begin an unforgettable and critically acclaimed novel, but catapulted Rodman Philbrick into the world of young adult literature. Prior to the publication of *Freak the Mighty* (1993), Philbrick was a successful writer of adult mysteries, thrillers, and detective stories. Writing a young adult novel never crossed his mind.

Searching for Success

As with most writers, success was hardly immediate. Philbrick was born in Boston, Massachusetts, on 22 January 1951 to William Rodman and Jane Elizabeth Merriman Philbrick. Beginning in the sixth grade in Rye Beach, New Hampshire, where he grew up, Philbrick started writing on his own, because he believed teachers did not think kids were capable of writing fiction. Of course, this writing had to be done secretly

Quotations from Rodman Philbrick that are not attributed to a published source are from personal interviews conducted by the author of this article on 20 January 1999 and 18 February 1999 and are published here by permission of Rodman Philbrick.

since it was not considered a "normal" activity. After all, most kids wanted to be "normal."

Philbrick's writing consisted of three-page short stories with trick endings patterned after O. Henry's, as well as science fiction inspired by Ray Bradbury. Upon completing a story, Philbrick would send the handwritten pages to a typing service, which charged him twenty-five cents a page. When he got the story back, he would submit it to magazines like *Amazing Stories, The Saturday Evening Post,* and *The New Yorker,* waiting weeks and sometimes months for the results, which were always rejections.

At the age of sixteen, when he told his father about his desire to be a writer, he was greeted with understandable concern from a father who did not want to see his son disappointed. What is significant, however, is that in his *ALAN Review* article "Finding a Voice," Philbrick says that his first novel, which was unpublished, was a "book-length series of anecdotal stories about two characters. The narrator is a boy who admires his best friend, who is a kind of genius, and the gifted friend eventually dies a tragic death. The two buddies hang out in the basement and share a series of adventures" (p. 3). Later this idea resurfaced in the writing of *Freak the Mighty.*

After graduating from Portsmouth High School in 1969, Philbrick enrolled at the University of New Hampshire as an English major. However, he dropped out in his sophomore year for what he thought would be only a semester (he never did go back). He and two friends borrowed some money from their parents and opened The Stone Church, which originally was to have been a coffeehouse. But in order to make it a success, they realized that they needed a beer license. Since none of the three was of age to drink legally, Philbrick's mother put the license in her name. The Stone Church is still there, but under different ownership.

At the age of twenty-seven, after writing eight or nine unpublished novels, Philbrick realized that all of them "had started out as ambitious attempts to astound the world by creating the great American novel but ended up as failed experiments" (p. 3). Although he considered the writing to be good, the storytelling was not. Tired of working a variety of jobs such as longshoreman, carpenter, boatbuilder, and mold maker as well as establishing a couple of businesses that went nowhere, Philbrick felt time was running out.

If he was going to make a living as a writer, he had to find a new approach. His decision was to write a genre novel, something he had despised as a young literary novelist. However, not only did he discover that he enjoyed his choice—writing suspense novels—but he was also able to support himself just by writing. Furthermore, he was successful—being nominated twice for a prestigious Shamus Award, which is presented by the Private Eye Writers of America, for the best paperback detective novel and finally winning one for his *Brothers and Sinners* (1993). Besides critical recognition, financially he was able to support himself through his writing—wintering in the Florida Keys, keeping an apartment in Kittery, Maine, smoking decent cigars, and spoiling a Maine Coon cat named Greta.

genre type of literature, such as science fiction or romance

Birth of a Young Adult Writer

Philbrick claims writing a young adult novel never crossed his mind. Although he read them as a kid, now he mainly reads writers he knows, such as Kathryn Lasky, David Klass, and Jerry Spinelli. In fact, he did not know *Freak the Mighty* would be characterized as a young adult novel. Philbrick states, "Personally, I always try to write a story that will appeal to adults as well as younger readers." He continues by adding, "I want it to be a book I'd enjoy myself, at the advanced age of 48."

There is an article about Kathryn Lasky in volume 2. There is an article about David Klass earlier in this volume. There is an article about Jerry Spinelli in volume 3.

However, here is where fate entered. An editor he knew was moved from adult mysteries to juvenile mysteries and asked him if he would be interested in writing a mystery for teens. While Philbrick's immediate reaction was negative, something clicked, but nothing that would interest an editor of juvenile mysteries.

As Philbrick was driving from New York City to Maine, a young voice suddenly popped into his head saying, "I never had a brain until Freak came along and lent me his for a while, and that's the truth, the whole truth." While *Freak the Mighty* is pure fiction, Philbrick does have a friend who had a child born with Morquio's Syndrome, a disease in which growth is stunted, resulting in severe medical problems. And, like Kevin in *Freak the Mighty,* he did manage to live longer than the doctors expected. Although Philbrick admired the boy's courage, he did not believe that it was something to write about. . . . until the voice of Max, a big awkward kid, entered his mind on that fateful drive to Maine.

When asked what inspired the character Max, Philbrick replied, "Max was inspired by the image of the big kid who used to ride the real 'Kevin' around on his shoulders. The personality of Max was invented, probably a composite of various people I've known or read about." As mentioned previously, Philbrick's first unpublished novel contained similarities to *Freak the Mighty.* According to Philbrick, it was not until he was writing "Finding a Voice" that he realized he was going back to old territory.

Novels

Thus, *Freak the Mighty* was born, a story about two boys with disabilities who become friends the summer before eighth grade. Maxwell Kane is learning-disabled, big for his age, and awkward, while brilliant, undersized Kevin suffers from a disease that has kept his body from growing to normal size. Both are mercilessly picked on by their peers, but when they combine their best parts—Kevin's mind and Max's brawn—they become Freak the Mighty, a partnership that helps each overcome his disabilities. Kevin is now able to participate in the happenings of the larger world, while Max, removed from the resource room, joins Kevin in his classes to help him get around, resulting in his proving he is intellectually more capable than anyone believed.

Inspired by the traditional Arthurian legends, of which Philbrick is a fan (the real "Kevin" also loved these tales as well as Dungeons & Dragons), the two engage in quests to promote good and to extinguish evil. Skillfully woven into the story is Kevin's belief that the armor of medieval knights makes them medieval robots, holding out hope for Kevin that his malformed body can be replaced and he will become the "first bionically improved human."

This situation turns sinister with the return of Killer Kane, Max's father, who is released from prison after serving a term for killing his wife, Max's mother. Kidnapped by his father and tied up, Max is heroically saved by none other than Kevin. Unfortunately, the inevitable comes: Kevin's death. But the story really is about a friendship that helps both slay their personal dragons, enabling Kevin to deal with progressing illness and Max to face the future with a positive attitude. After all, as Max says at the end of the book, "And now that I've written a book who knows, I might even read a few" (p. 160).

Arthurian legends are stories about King Arthur and his Knights of the Round Table. Passed down through the centuries, these stories of the great legendary king, may have been based on an actual British leader.

Dungeons & Dragons is a popular role-playing game. One person plays the Dungeon Master, who tells the other players what is happening as the story progresses. The players assume the roles of imaginary characters, such as fighters, wizards, and rogues.

When this winner of several state awards, an ALA Best Book for Young Adults, and an ALA Quick Pick for Reluctant Young Adult Readers was made into a movie called *The Mighty* (1998), Philbrick was elated. However, although it was greeted with a lot of positive reviews, "the audience never really showed up in large numbers. At which point Miramax essentially gave up on it."

Three years later, Philbrick's next young adult novel, *The Fire Pony* (1996), was released. Set on a horse ranch in the Southwest and narrated by eleven-year-old Roy, who was rescued from an unpleasant life in a foster home by his older half-brother, Joe Dilly, it is the story of how Roy finally finds a home at the Bar None Ranch. Highlights are Roy's breaking and keeping a wild pony, nursing the horse through a life-threatening fever, winning an exciting race at the rodeo against all odds, and being rescued from a fire by Joe Dilly, who starts it in an attempt to get even with a man who caused them trouble. Particularly touching are the scenes that show how pyromaniac "Joe Dilly tried so hard to fight the fire that burned inside him and kept making him do the wrong thing" (p. 175).

According to Philbrick, he got the idea for the story when he and his wife were driving from New England to California. It was the first time he had seen the Southwest, and he instantly knew that he wanted to write a story set in that landscape. Upon reaching California, the whole state seemed to be on fire, something he decided could be incorporated into a story. Although he never had a horse, one of his brothers worked on a horse ranch when he was college age. And one of his great-grandfathers raised Morgans in Vermont, which his mother, a horse-lover, never let her four boys forget. Research for the story consisted of taking a few riding lessons, hanging out with a blacksmith while he shod a couple of horses, and reading about horses.

After finishing *Freak the Mighty,* Philbrick assumed that he had heard the last from Maxwell Kane. However, letters from readers of *Freak the Mighty* were full of ideas for sequels. After one of these suggestions had the story end up on the moon, Philbrick decided, with so many rich imaginations at work, that he had better write the sequel before someone else beat him to it. Philbrick also wrote a sequel because he found himself wondering what would happen to Max after he recovered from Kevin's death.

The Mighty starred Kieran Culkin as Kevin, Sharon Stone as his mother, and Elden Ratliff as Max.

pyromaniac a person with an irresistible urge to start fires

sequel book that continues a story begun in an earlier book

So *Max the Mighty* (1998) was conceived. Picking up a year after Kevin's death, Max is understandably lonely. Max narrates this story in which Rachel, an eleven-year-old girl nicknamed Worm by the other kids because she is constantly reading, runs away from her abusive stepfather and seeks her real father in Chivalry, Montana. She is reluctantly aided by Max, who still is unsure of himself and who winds up having a $10,000 reward placed on his head by Worm's stepfather for kidnapping Worm. The two encounter a series of memorable characters on their way west. Throughout their journey, every time Worm finds herself in trouble, she counts on Max the Mighty, whom she regards as a character right out of the King Arthur era. Perhaps Max and his efforts are best summed up when Worm states, "It's all about fighting for honor and protecting the innocent and never giving up even if the whole world is against you" (p. 98).

In Chivalry (a word that so aptly characterizes knighthood), Max discovers that Worm's real father had been killed in a mine disaster years ago. However, the book ends happily after Max not only rescues Worm from being trapped in the mine but even saves the life of her dreaded stepfather. Once again, Philbrick has written a story that shows that there is a place in the world for people who discover that to be true to themselves they don't have to be "normal." Although Philbrick provides plenty of opportunity at the end of the novel for a sequel, he claims that there will be one only if he can come up with a good story.

Abduction (1998), Philbrick's latest young adult novel, was coauthored with Lynn Harnett, his wife of nineteen years, whom he met at a poker game arranged by a mutual friend. According to Philbrick, marrying Lynn was the best bet he ever made! Like her husband, Ms. Harnett's professional life revolves around writing, being an award-winning journalist and a founding editor of *Kidwriters Monthly*. Additionally, the two combined to write three series for younger readers—The House on Cherry Street, The Werewolf Chronicles, and The Visitors—which "were intended to be genre horror stories for readers slightly more sophisticated than Goosebumps fans." They wanted to write classic horror tales that included ghosts, werewolves, and invaders from Mars kind of things. Thrilling types of images and situations were for the most part recalled from B movies rather than from books. Readers of *Strange Invaders* (1997), the first volume in The Visitors series, should

The **Goosebumps** series is written by R. L. Stine. There is an article about him later in this volume.

B movie a cheaply produced movie

not be surprised to discover that it was inspired by films like *Invasion of the Body Snatchers, The Brain Stealers,* and *Invaders from Mars*—"movies that were pleasurably terrifying."

Abduction, (1998), a spellbinding page-turner, is a story about Luke Ingram and Mandy Durgin, two seventeen-year-olds living in a small rural town who thwart an alien takeover. As with *Max the Mighty,* opportunity is provided—and really expected—for at least one sequel.

According to Philbrick, the general idea of an alien abduction came from editor Jean Fiewel, who helped originate the Goosebumps series with R. L. Stine and who has an inexhaustible supply of ideas for popular books. Together, Harnett and Philbrick came up with a specific abduction story and decided to divide up the actual writing. While Philbrick wrote the story outline, Harnett wrote the chapters. Upon completion, each polished the story and incorporated editorial suggestions to improve it. Collaborating in this fashion—strictly defining who does what—is the key to their being able to work together. Philbrick believes it "saves a lot of argument."

Writing Habits and Thoughts About Writing

Like most writers, Philbrick is a voracious reader, something he inherited from his parents. Among his favorite writers are suspense novelists like Elmore Leonard; classic writers like Mark Twain, Joseph Conrad, Rudyard Kipling, and Herman Melville; and more recent authors like John Steinbeck, F. Scott Fitzgerald, Ernest Hemingway, and Patrick O'Brien, an author of seafaring tales.

As with many other writers, Philbrick does have someone read his work before he sends it to his editor. Not surprisingly, it is his wife who performs this task. And according to Philbrick, he always takes her advice seriously, because he feels "she's almost never wrong."

Each day Philbrick tries to write a few pages, mostly in the morning. This approach begins with making revisions, which to him is made so easy by using a computer that he tends to continually revise and improve as he goes along. When revising, he first looks for the extra stuff, "the repetitive description kind of thing." Favoring clean, spare writing, Philbrick tries "to get rid of anything extra, anything that doesn't specifically

voracious excessively eager; avid

There are articles about Mark Twain and John Steinbeck in volume 3. There is an article about Ernest Hemingway in volume 2.

advance the story or enhance the characters." Philbrick claims a writer needs to be brutal about self-editing, and that this is what makes a professional writer. Just because a sentence is well written doesn't mean it needs to be in the story. "You must stop loving the stuff and just whip it into shape, regardless of how pretty a sentence might be. If it's not required, out it goes." Philbrick feels that he learned to write by writing and reading the works of writers he admires. "There's talent involved, or a kind of a writer's imagination (which you may or may not be born with), but mostly getting better involves a lot of hard work." Just do it; write every day and then learn to improve what you've written by merciless editing.

After a morning of writing, Philbrick invariably spends his afternoons fishing—alone. Enjoying the silence and solitude, he thinks it helps clear his head for the next day's writing assignment.

Future Plans

As for the future, Philbrick plans to continue writing adult thrillers as well as young adult stories and novels. In the late 1990s he was working on *Spaz,* a young adult novel that he hoped to publish in 2001. Based on an idea described in a story called "The Last Book in the Universe," published in an anthology for Scholastic, *Spaz* is "set in the future, in a world ruined by humans, a 'Blade Runner' kind of future in which nobody reads, and therefore there are no writers—except one." As long as he continues to hear a young adult voice in his head talking and demanding that he write down his or her story, readers can count on exciting tales from this 6-foot, 48-year-old man with a great sense of humor, who understands and empathizes with young adults and who unabashedly admits that an important part of himself is still a 12-year-old boy.

Blade Runner is a 1982 science fiction film starring Harrison Ford. He plays a futuristic policeman who must hunt down and kill human clones.

If you like Rodman Philbrick, you might also like David Klass, Kathryn Lasky, and Jerry Spinelli, three of his favorite authors.

Selected Bibliography

WORKS BY RODMAN PHILBRICK

Novels for Young Adults

Freak the Mighty (1993)

The Fire Pony (1996)

Abduction, with Lynn Harnett (1998)

Max the Mighty (1998)

Novels for Younger Readers Written with Lynn Harnett

The House on Cherry Street series

The Final Nightmare: Book III (1995)

The Haunting: Book I (1995)

The Horror: Book II (1995)

The Werewolf Chronicles series

Children of the Wolf (1996)

Night Creature (1996)

The Wering (1996)

The Visitors series

Brain Stealers (1997)

Strange Invaders (1997)

Things (1997)

Novels for Adults Written as Rodman Philbrick or W. R. Philbrick

Shooting Star (1982)

Slow Dancer (1984)

Shadow Kills (1985)

Ice for the Eskimo (1986)

The Neon Flamingo (1987)

The Crystal Blue Persuasion (1988)

Paint It Black (1989)

Tough Enough (1989)

Walk on the Water (1991)

Brothers and Sinners (1993)

Novels for Adults Written Under the Pseudonym William R. Dantz

Pulse (1990)

The Seventh Sleeper (1991)

Hunger (1992)

Nine Levels Down (1995)

Short Stories for Adults

"The Empty Sleeve." In *Raymond Chandler's Philip Marlowe: A Centennial Celebration.* Edited by Byron Preiss. New York: Knopf, 1988.

"The Hungry Persian." In *The Black Moon.* Edited by Robert J. Randisi. New York: Lynx, 1989.

"Bad to the Bone." In *Justice for Hire: The Fourth Private Eye Writers' of America Anthology.* Edited by Robert J. Randisi. New York: Mysterious Press, 1990.

"Boogie Dead Men." In *New Crimes 3.* Edited by Maxim Jakubowski. New York: Carroll & Graf, 1991.

"The Dark Rising." In *The Ultimate Dracula.* Edited by Byron Preiss, David Keller, and Megan Miller. New York: Dell, 1991.

"The Cure." In *Dracula: Prince of Darkness.* Edited by Martin Harry Greenberg. New York: DAW Books, 1992.

Graphic Novel

The Big Chip (1990)

Article

"Finding a Voice." *The ALAN Review,* Spring 1996, pp. 2–5.

WORKS ABOUT RODMAN PHILBRICK

"A Mighty Interview with Rod Philbrick." *SeacoastNH.com, www.seacoastnh.com/film/mighty.html*

Robinson, J. Dennis. "Rod Philbrick: Portrait of a Writer." *SeacoastNH.com, www.seacoastnh.com/artists/philbrick/index.html*

Routhier, Ray. "Inner Kid Carries *Freak the Mighty. Maine Books Online, www.portland.com/books/about/freak.htm*

"Tale of a Small Boy Makes It to Big Screen." *Maine Books Online, www.portland.com/books/about/mighty.htm*

How to Write to the Author

Rodman Philbrick
c/o Scholastic Press
555 Broadway
New York, NY 10012-3999

You may also write to Rodman Philbrick at his e-mail address:
philbrick@earthlink.net

Christopher Pike

(1954–)

by Lawrence Baines

The *Star Trek* Connection

In an episode from the original *Star Trek* television series called "The Menagerie," Spock takes control of the *Enterprise* in what appears to be an act of mutiny against Captain Kirk. Eventually, Captain Kirk learns that Spock has risked his career in order to return his former captain, Christopher Pike, to a planet whose inhabitants manage to live their lives through an endless set of illusions. Captain Pike, whose face and body have been grossly disfigured by delta rays, is slowly and painfully dying. He is unable to move any part of his body and is completely dependent upon a machine for life support. Because he cannot speak, Pike can communicate only via a high-tech system that uses flashing lights. By the end of the show, Spock eventually manages to send Christopher Pike to the planet where he can live out his life through the power of illusions as if he were an active, normal human being again.

The original **Star Trek** television series ran from 1966 to 1969. Other series based on the original included *Star Trek* (the animated series), *Star Trek: Deep Space Nine*, *Star Trek: The Next Generation,* and *Star Trek Voyager.*

pseudonym fictitious or pen name

plot the deliberate sequence of events in a literary work

titillate to excite pleasurably

paraplegic one who is paralyzed from the waist down

nom de plume fictitious or pen name; pseudonym

In choosing a pseudonym, Kevin McFadden (writer Christopher Pike's real name) selected well, as his novels frequently feature outlandish plots, aliens from outer space, grisly mutilation, and near-death experiences. Like most television series, Pike's books are meant to titillate rather than educate.

It is also suitable that Captain Pike is a paraplegic, dependent upon a life-support system, as author Pike includes a character with some kind of disability in many of his stories—a nerd-genius dying of AIDS (Seymour in *The Last Vampire* [1994]), a brilliant teen with cancer who goes over the edge (Neil in *Chain Letter* [1986]), an affable and brainy, wheelchair-bound buddy (Rick in *Scavenger Hunt* [1989]). In general, if a character is crippled, sickly, or dying in one of Pike's books, you can rest assured that the individual could easily qualify as a National Merit Scholar without even filling out the application. So, on a number of levels, it seems appropriate that McFadden would choose Christopher Pike as his nom de plume. "Christopher Pike" certainly sounds much cooler—and much more like a writer of horror fiction—than Kevin McFadden." Another reason an author might choose to write under a different name is to avoid the commotion that often comes with the life of a public figure.

Making Contact with Pike

There can be little doubt that Christopher Pike goes to a great deal of trouble to ensure his privacy. On one of the Pike fan club sites on the World Wide Web (called Starlight Crystal), a member reveals that he discovered that Pike's e-mail address was *cpike2@aol.com*. Shortly after he tried to contact Pike via e-mail, the member reported that it no longer worked. Another member of the Starlight Crystal Club reported that he read a posting by Pike on America Online which said that he was working on a twelve volume saga tentatively called *The Fallen*.

At the back of *The Howling Ghost* (1995), among several of the Spookville series of books, it is written:

> Little is known about Christopher Pike, although he is supposed to be a strange man. . . . No one really knows what he looks like, or how old he is. It is pos-

sible that he is not a real person, but an eccentric creature visiting from another world. When he is not writing, he sits and stares at the walls of his huge haunted house. A short, ugly troll wanders around him in the dark and whispers scary stories in his ear. (P. 117)

One of the few published photos of Pike appeared on the inside back cover of *Sati* (1990) along with the following biographical comments:

Pike was born in Brooklyn, New York, but grew up in Los Angeles, where he lives to this day. Prior to becoming a writer, he worked in a factory, painted houses, and programmed computers. His hobbies include astronomy, running, Transcendental Meditation, and playing with his nieces and nephews.

Although *Contemporary Authors* lists Pike's birthday as sometime in 1961, other sources indicate that Pike was born on 12 November 1954. As a college dropout, he began dabbling in horror and thrillers when his first few attempts at writing science fiction for adults failed. Eventually, the novel *Slumber Party* (1985) was accepted for publication, soon followed by *Chain Letter* and *Weekend* (1986). Over the past fifteen years, Pike has had almost one hundred books published. Many of his older books have also been re-released or combined into "collector's editions." Although the eleven books Pike penned in 1995 might seem impressive, he wrote eighteen during the following year of 1997, or roughly one book every three weeks.

Popularity Among Preteens and Teens

Representative of the allegiance of his readers is a fan club on the World Wide Web that includes "pikegod" as part of its website address. Indeed, as a former English teacher, I remember well how my students would smuggle Pike novels in their backpacks and drag them out though I had actually assigned them *Where the Red Fern Grows, The Pearl,* or *Sounder.* For young readers, Pike's novels are deliciously decadent entertainments

transcendental meditation a method of contemplation or reflection in which one chants a word or phrase in order to foster calm, creativity, and spiritual well-being

Where the Red Fern Grows (1961) was written by Wilson Rawls. ***Sounder*** (1969) was written by William Howard Armstrong. ***The Pearl*** (1947) was written by John Steinbeck. There is an article about Steinbeck in volume 3.

innuendo an indirect hint or reference, often insulting

protagonist the main character of a literary work

libido sexual drive

with high body counts, intricately detailed violence, and maximal sexual innuendo. His books are absolutely bereft of what most parents would consider "redeeming value." In his review of *Gimme a Kiss* (1991) in the *Bulletin of the Center for Children's Books,* Roger Sutton described Pike's style as "straightforward lowmindedness." A reader waiting for an evil character to receive her/his comeuppance will be sorely disappointed with the works of Pike: his protagonists murder, get murdered, lust, and lie without regard for the quality of their character.

Undeniably, most of the characters in Pike's novels have very active libidos, especially the females. Although he occasionally writes from the male perspective, the most common narrator for a Pike novel is an anxious, beautiful sixteen-year-old girl with little carnal experience. In either case, a reader does not have to wait long before it becomes evident that sex will play a major role in the story line. In *Bury Me Deep* (1991), Jean is a sixteen-year-old girl traveling on an airplane by herself to meet two teenage friends in Hawaii. On the airplane, she dreams about having sex with some older boys she might meet during her trip. "Jean might not have wanted to lose her virginity in Hawaii, but she wanted to come close" (p. 5). When Jean asks her friend Mandy about the third member of their party, a pretty blonde named Michele, Mandy informs her that Michele is already sleeping with a man. "They're probably doing it as we talk," Mandy says. About Mandy's sexual drive, Pike writes, "Mandy was another virgin, rich in fantasy but lacking in experience" (p. 28).

Like the teenagers in Pike's young adolescent fiction, the preteen characters in the Spookville series, written for ages five to ten, give in at times to lust, jealousy, and love. In *The Howling Ghost,* when a boy named Adam is thought to have drowned, ten-year-old Sally confesses that "I will risk my life to save Adam because my love for him is more powerful than my fear of death." Indeed, one student reviewer on the Amazon Books website commented,

> **Chris Pike is a wonderful author, but he writes about sex all the time. I mean ALL THE TIME, even in books about space and aliens. Choose one book that hasn't got sex in it. I bet you won't find one. It is in no way necessary to discuss intercourse in every book.**

But sex is often fraught with difficulties in Pike's complex plots. For example, in the popular Last Vampire series, the main character, Sita, appears to be an eighteen-year-old blonde, blue-eyed beauty queen, though she is really a 5,000-year-old bisexual vampire who must kill living creatures, especially humans, in order to survive. First, in *The Last Vampire,* Sita ruthlessly murders detective Mike Riley:

> **I hear the bones crack as he topples backward onto the floor. . . . gasping for breath, blood pouring out of his mouth. I have crushed the walls of his heart as well as the bones of his chest, and he is going to die. . . . His grimacing teeth tear into his lower lip, and more blood messes his face. He draws in a breath that is more a shovel of mud on his coffin. He makes a series of sick wet sounds. Then, his eyes roll back in his head, and he goes limp in my arms. (Pp. 13–15)**

Next she enrolls in a high school, where she meets and falls in love with Mike Riley's son, Ray. Although Ray is a wholesome boy with a long-time steady girlfriend, Sita seduces him anyway. Then she kills a few more innocent people, cures a male friend of AIDS, and then seduces Ray again.

After sex, Sita confesses to Ray that she murdered his father. Ray is momentarily shocked but quickly recovers. Briefly, Sita wrestles with the question of whether or not she should transform Ray into a vampire. Not surprisingly, she ends up giving Ray a blood transfusion near the end of the first book in the series, and they hedonistically cavort and kill together through parts of subsequent volumes in the vampire series.

On Starlight Crystal, one website dedicated to Pike, a girl named Diana writes, "Sita is the best character in the whole world." Another teen reader of the vampire series comments on the Amazon Books website: "Reading Pike's books makes me wish I was just like Sita. Pike rules!"

hedonistically in a manner that assumes pleasure and happiness are the most important goals

Violence as a Response to Problems

If a dilemma involves love, sex, or reputation, Pike's characters readily turn to violent behavior in order to deal with it. In fact,

empathetic having sincere concern and understanding

garroted strangled, as with a wire

omnipotent all-powerful

in Pike's novels, violence is often the only solution that ever seems to have any effect at all. In *The Last Vampire,* Sita doesn't get her man Ray until after she kills his father, blasts her former lover with a nuclear bomb, and offs several other folks in equally elaborate fashion. In *Chain Letter,* the psychotic character Neil is completely ignored by his friends until he ties them all up with handcuffs, Jeffrey Dahmer style, in an abandoned house, and plunges a needle full of who knows what into the calf of sweet, young, empathetic Allison. In *Scavenger Hunt* (1989), the male protagonist Carl runs into a church to escape some lizard people. Instead of finding protection, Carl inadvertently ushers the priest out of the safety of his confessional, where the priest is promptly garroted by the lizards-in-pursuit.

In *Sati,* one of Pike's adult novels, the main character is a young, sensuous teenage girl who claims to be God. A 32-year-old truck driver named Michael picks her up because he fancies that he might want to have sex with her. Later, Michael comes to believe that Sati might be divine, but his friend David seems to have his doubts. Finally, figuring that if Sati were truly omnipotent, she could not be killed, David poisons her drink as a test of her divine powers.

Michael makes David walk back through twenty miles of desert, but otherwise forgives him. Still Michael thinks, "I couldn't kill him not now, even though I might have done so a few days earlier" (p. 202). In Pike's books, murder is one of an array of options that seem to come up quickly for many of his characters.

To be sure, one unique attribute of Pike's novels is that characters often perish, even if their deaths are not necessary for the development of the plot. For example, the grisly mutilation of the priest in *Scavenger Hunt* could have just as easily been handled by knocking the priest unconscious. In *Bury Me Deep,* Jean's friend Mandy, whose only sin might have been a little overeating, is thrown out of the fifth floor of a hotel building by Jean's psychotic killer boyfriend, for no apparent reason. Of course, Pike describes Mandy's death in excruciating detail nevertheless:

> **Mandy must have landed on top of her head. The crown of her skull was crushed flat. The delicate bones that made up her pleasant expression were shattered. There was blood everywhere. But it was**

still good old Mandy. Jean could see that even from five stories up. (P. 165)

Familiar Terrain

Whether a reader likes to read Pike's novels or not, one must admit that the man has an ear for dialogue and a sense of what might appeal to teenagers and preteens. For example, in *Chain Letter,* after seven teenagers crowd into a Ford Maverick, head out on a dark two-lane road, and begin to guzzle innumerable beers, they listen to a cassette tape of the high school football coach supposedly seducing one of his students. ". . . Clothes rustled and stretched through the car's speakers. Zippers slowly pulled down. This was *soo bitchin'!"* (p. 33).

When faithful readers of Pike's books are asked about his most common plot devices, many are quick to concede that predictability is not necessarily a negative attribute of his books. One twelve-year-old female reader told me that what she liked best about the books was that "you know Pike's characters are going to end up chopping each other up somehow. You know that there will be lots of blood, that someone is going to get naked, but that's why you read them."

Some other common elements of Pike's books are dreams that foretell the future, excursions to libraries to examine newspapers of yesteryear that help explain supernatural phenomena of the present, and characters once thought dead who come back to life. For example, in *Bury Me Deep,* Jean dreams a bloody dream about a drowned young man, only to awaken and find a ketchup bottle inexplicably broken in her bathtub. The characters in *Chain Letter, Scavenger Hunt, The Howling Ghost,* and many other novels head for the newspaper archives to search for answers that have so far managed to elude them. Somehow, despite having to rifle through hundreds of newspapers, these characters always seem to find precisely the answers they need.

phenomena observable events or facts

The phenomenon of dead people coming back to life is found in so many Pike novels that it is more difficult to think of plots that don't involve a resurrection of some kind. In *Scavenger Hunt,* the character of Tom is actually the dead Joe, who has come back to life to harm his best friend. However, the lizard people help brainwash all the characters in the story so that they think that Tom is really a longtime friend, though he has actually come on the scene only since Joe's death.

abhor to hate

There is an article about R. L. Stine later in this volume.

The ***Sweet Valley High*** series is written by Francine Pascal. The series focuses on identical twins Jessica and Elizabeth and their friends.

If you like Christopher Pike, you might also like R. L. Stine.

Starlight Crystal (1996) is another book about the lizard people, but this phrase is also uttered by Sati ("I am the starlight crystal"), is the name of the computer game Mark plays in *See You Later* (1990), and is the name of the story Shari told in *Remember Me 3: The Last Story* (1995). Reptilian races are a theme of *Scavenger Hunt, The Season of Passage* (1992), *The Listeners* (1994), and *Starlight Crystal* (1996). Although Pike often travels terrain quite familiar to his frequent readers, many seem to relish rather than abhor the repetition. Two of Pike's most popular heroines have similar names—Sati and Sita (from the Last Vampire series)—that sound suspiciously like "Satan."

Few teens or adults could read a novel by Christopher Pike without stopping to consider the works of R. L. Stine, who works a similar territory, but who sells many more books than Pike (and most other authors on the face of the planet). The Pike/Stine rivalry is evident even in the bylaws of the Pike Fan Club, which discourages discussion of Stine altogether (The Midnight Club website, 7 October 1998). When I asked a dozen or so middle school readers of horror fiction about the differences between Pike and Stine, the consensus seemed to be that Stine includes much less sex in his novels but creates more believable plots and seems to surprise the reader more with his endings.

Over the past decade, Christopher Pike has become one of the best-selling author for young adults of all time. Pike appeals to young female readers who used to read romances and the Sweet Valley High series and boys who used to read adventures and sports stories. Like the Jerry Springer television show, Pike's stories are never boring, though they aren't particularly enlightening either. While some readers obviously enjoy the titillating mix of sex, violence, outrageous plots, and "sworn to fun, loyal to none" mentality of most of Pike's characters, many other young people will eventually grow weary of the formula and look elsewhere.

Selected Bibliography

WORKS BY CHRISTOPHER PIKE

Getting Even (1985)

Slumber Party (1985)

Chain Letter (1986)

The Tachyon Web (1986)

Weekend (1986)

Thrills, Chills, and Nightmares (1987)

The Dance (1988)

Gimme a Kiss (1988)

Last Act (1988)

Spellbound (1988; also published as *Precious Ingredient*)

The Graduation (1989)

The Party (1989)

Remember Me (1989)

Scavenger Hunt (1989)

Fall into Darkness (1990)

Sati (1990)

See You Later (1990)

Witch (1990)

Bury Me Deep (1991)

Die Softly (1991)

Whisper of Death (1991)

Chain Letter 2: The Ancient Evil (1992)

Master of Murder (1992)

Monster (1992)

The Season of Passage (1992)

The Eternal Enemy (1993)

The Immortal (1993)

Road to Nowhere (1993)

The Wicked Heart (1993)

The Last Vampire (1994)

The Last Vampire 2: Black Blood (1994)

The Listeners (1994)

The Midnight Club (1994)

Remember Me 2: The Return (1994)

The Cold One (1995)

The Haunted Cave (1995)

The Howling Ghost (1995)

The Last Story (1995)

The Lost Mind (1995)

The Last Vampire 3: Red Dice (1995)

Remember Me 3: The Last Story (1995)

Secret Path (1995)

The Visitor (1995)

Aliens in the Sky (1996)

The Cold People (1996)

Creature in the Teacher (1996)

The Last Vampire 6: Creatures of Forever (1996)

The Dark Corner (1996)

The Deadly Past (1996)

The Last Vampire 5: Evil Thirst (1996)

The Hidden Beast (1996)

The Last Vampire 4: Phantom (1996)

The Little People (1996)

The Starlight Crystal (1996)

The Wicked Cat (1996)

The Wishing Stone (1996)

The Witch's Revenge (1996)

Attack of the Killer Crabs (1997)

Christopher Pike's Tales of Terror (1997)

The Dangerous Quest (1997)

The Evil House (1997)

Execution of Innocence (1997)

Invasion of the No-Ones (1997)

Night of the Vampire (1997)

The Star Group (1997)

The Thing in the Closet (1997)

Time Terror (1997)

Christopher Pike's Tales of Terror: Volume 2 (1998)

The Creepy Creature (1998)

The Hollow Skull (1998)

Living Dead (1998)

Magic Fire (1998)

Phone Fear (1998)

The Witch's Gift (1999)

WORKS ABOUT CHRISTOPHER PIKE

Alderdice, Kit. "Archway Launches Christopher Pike Novels in Multi-Book Contract." *Publishers Weekly,* 29 April 1988, p. 49.

Drew, Bernard, ed. "Christopher Pike." *The 100 Most Popular Young Adult Authors: Biographical Sketches and Bibliographies.* Detroit: Libraries Unlimited, 1997.

Harris, Laurie, ed. "Christopher Pike." *Biography Today, 1996 Annual Cumulation: Profiles of People of Interest to Young Readers.* Detroit: Omnigraphics, 1997, vol. 2.

Hile, Kevin, ed. "Christopher Pike." *Something About the Author,* New York: Gale Research, 1992, vol. 68.

Hubbard, Andrea. *An Analysis of the Incidence of Havighurst's Developmental Tasks in the Adolescent Horror Novels of R. L. Stine and Christopher Pike.* Thesis, University of North Carolina at Chapel Hill, 1994.

Jones, Daniel, and John D. Jorgenson, eds. "McFadden, Kevin Christopher." *Contemporary Authors, New Revision Series.* Detroit: Gale Research, 1998, vol. 66, pp. 316–320.

Senick, Gerald, ed. "Christopher Pike." *Children's Literature Review,* New York: Gale Research, 1993, vol. 29, pp. 168–175.

Sutton, Roger (1988, October). Review of *Gimme a Kiss. Bulletin of the Center for Children's Books,* 42 (2), p. 50.

Websites

The Midnight Club, *www.geocities.com/Athens/7887/midnightclub.html*

Starlight Crystal, *www.geocities.com/Athens/Parthenon/3765/mainl.html*

Amazon Books, *www.amazon.com*

Reader's Choice, *www.thegrid.net/adkaiser/books/horror/pikechri.htm*

How to Write to the Author

Christopher Pike
c/o Simon & Schuster
1230 Avenue of the Americas
New York, NY 10020

Philip Pullman

(1946–)

by Elizabeth A. Poe and Judith Volc

When Philip Pullman accepted England's prestigious Carnegie Medal for *The Golden Compass* (1995), he told the audience, "There's a hunger for stories in all of us." Pullman has been satisfying that hunger by telling stories since he was a child. As a young boy, he was an outcast who gained acceptance by telling other children stories. As a teacher, he enthralled his students by retelling classic tales of adventure. Now as a writer of stories, he captivates readers of all ages.

Pullman's young adult novels fall into three general categories: historical fiction, contemporary fiction, and fantasy. Set in Victorian London, *The Ruby in the Smoke* (1985), *Shadow in the North* (1988), and *The Tiger in the Well* (1990) form the Sally Lockhart trilogy. These intriguing mystery/adventure/thrillers begin in Sally Lockhart's teenage years and end in her early adulthood. The complex mysteries in which she is involved often show the unsavory side of London and England during the late nineteenth century. Although not part of the trilogy itself, *The Tin Princess* (1994) takes place a generation

enthralled captivated

Victorian referring to the period of the reign of Queen Victoria of England (1837–1901)

trilogy a series of three literary works that are closely related and share a single theme

unsavory morally offensive; distasteful

249

intrigue secret plot or scheme that arouses curiosity

voodoo African religion involving ancestor worship and the use of charms and spells

apprentice one who learns by experience under the direction of a skilled craftsperson

after the Sally Lockhart books, with Sally appearing briefly. In this companion novel, the children have become adults and find themselves targets in political intrigues.

Pullman's contemporary novels include *The Broken Bridge* (1990) and *The White Mercedes* (1992), both of which contain complex plots and multilayered characters. *The Broken Bridge,* set in Wales, is the story of sixteen-year-old Ginny, whose contented life with her single-parent father is disrupted when she discovers she has a half brother whom she never knew existed. The novel deals with an array of sophisticated social issues, including family relationships, sexual orientation, child abuse, race, adoption, and voodoo, all within the context of an engaging story about a likeable character. Set in Oxford, England, *The White Mercedes,* which also includes sophisticated subject matter concerning sexuality, sexual abuse, drugs, robbery, and murder, is a fast-paced thriller about seventeen-year-old Chris's psychological journey from innocence to self-knowledge.

Pullman's fantasy, or as he calls it, stark realism, is just as engaging, sophisticated, and complex as his historical and contemporary fiction. *The Golden Compass* and *The Subtle Knife* (1997) comprise the first two books in Pullman's His Dark Materials trilogy. In these books, Lyra discovers that her father and mother quarreled; her father murdered her mother's lover and was consequently stripped of his wealth and power. But he has rebuilt his power and, in a fight between good and evil, both parents seek access to alternate worlds, a feat that would ensure greater power for her and an opportunity for him to re-create the struggle between God and the Devil or Angels. Readers all over the globe now breathlessly await the final book in the His Dark Materials trilogy. In the meantime an American publisher has issued Pullman's *Clockwork: Or All Wound Up,* (1996) a tale set in Germany about a storyteller and an apprentice clockwork maker whose lives become entwined.

Born in Norwich, England, on 19 October 1946, Philip Pullman spent various portions of his childhood living in Rhodesia, England, Wales, and Australia. He graduated with a B.A. from Oxford University in 1968 and was a teacher at Ivanhoe, Bishop Kirk, and Marston middle schools in Oxford, England, from 1972 to 1988. He worked as a part-time senior lecturer in English at Westminster College, Oxford, teaching courses on the Victorian novel, the traditional tale, and creative writing from 1988 to 1996.

The Story at the Heart of All Stories

Pullman's extensive work with stories has led him to conclude that there is really only one story at the heart of all stories: the Quest for the Holy Grail. The Holy Grail represents happiness, freedom, vengeance, love, or whatever is sought above all else by the protagonist. The story begins with the awareness of what is missing, and everything else becomes relatively unimportant until it is found. The story ends when the quest is over. It is not surprising that Pullman's stories are generally quests. For example, Sally Lockhart is driven to solve the mystery of her father's death in *The Ruby in the Smoke,* to expose the evilness of a powerful and unscrupulous businessman in *The Shadow in the North,* and to recover her kidnapped daughter in *The Tiger in the Well.* In *The Broken Bridge,* Ginny is determined to uncover the truth about her identity, and Chris, of *The White Mercedes,* searches for the girl he loves. Lyra, too, has a quest in Pullman's His Dark Materials books. She must discover the secret of Dust and help free the world from a sinister power. Other characters—Lyra's parents, the Bears, Witches, and other groups—all pursue their own quests as well, as they choose sides in this battle of good versus evil played out so brilliantly in His Dark Materials.

Although Pullman believes the Quest for the Holy Grail to be the archetypal story, he has identified ten plots representing various types of quests. These he considers to be the only ten plots in the world; all stories therefore fit into these plots in one way or another. Following are the basic plots that Pullman originally mentioned in a speech given at an NCTE conference and then published in a 1997/1998 *SIGNAL Journal* article titled "Myths, Folktales, and Fiction."

protagonist the main character of a literary work

archetypal basic or original (after which other forms are patterned)

plot the deliberate sequence of events in a literary work

The Only Ten Plots in the World

Cinderella. This is the story of "every under-regarded, overlooked, downtrodden girl or boy who overcomes all the odds and comes out transformed, a winner." Examples include *The Tortoise and the Hare, David and Goliath, The Ugly Duckling, Pinocchio,* and *Oliver Twist.*

Little Red Riding Hood, or *Will You Step into My Parlour? said the Spider to the Fly.* This "story of seduction of innocence, which might not end happily," occurs between Circe

Oliver Twist was written by Charles Dickens. There is an article about Dickens in volume 1.

seduction the act of leading one astray by false promises or persuasion

and Odysseus, Iago and Othello, or it can be found in Richard of Gloucester's seduction of Lady Ann in *Richard III.*

Beauty and the Beast, which is *Little Red Riding Hood* in reverse. In this case, "the great ugly threatening monster is transformed by the love of the pure innocent one." This happens in *Jane Eyre, Pollyanna,* and probably *Heidi.*

Romeo and Juliet. This is the classic story of boy meets girl, boy loses girl, boy finds girl (or boy/boy or girl/girl, of course). There is no love triangle here, and whether the story ends happily or not usually depends on luck.

Tristram and Iseult, or Tristan and Isolde. This is *Romeo and Juliet* with the addition of an extra character, making it a love triangle. Because there are three lovers, not two, it ends unhappily for at least one of them.

Shane. This is the story of an incorruptible avenger who comes out of nowhere, kills the bad guys, and moves on. It is a very common plot in film westerns and stories.

Psycho. In this case, a horrible thing comes out of the dark, "bursting into normal everyday life without warning and sometimes without explanation," as in *Nightmare on Elm Street, Night of the Living Dead, Jaws,* and so on.

Orpheus and Eurydice. This sequence centers around whatever a character feels is missing and must be obtained: "the lost beautiful thing which is always sought for and never found. Or never quite found. Or when regained has changed beyond recognition."

Achilles. The "great protagonist is brought low by his (usually his) one weakness," known as a Fatal Flaw. This happens in practically every tragedy ever written.

Faust. This is the story of the Fatal Bargain or the Debt That Must Be Paid. *Frankenstein, Jurassic Park, Picture of Dorian Gray,* and the story of the fall of Adam and Eve all exemplify this story line.

The Ten Plots as They Occur in Pullman's Stories

With these plots in mind, readers can see how Pullman uses them in his own stories. The story of Cinderella occurs in both the Sally Lockhart and His Dark Materials trilogies. Sally Lockhart is underregarded in her career and must prove herself. Lyra is abandoned at Jordan College, untended as a child, and only given attention when her mother wants to use her. Lyra also follows the Little Red Riding Hood pattern when she innocently carries the alethiometer, the golden compass that detects truth, to her father/uncle. Beauty and the Beast is the basis of the plot or interaction between Lyra and Lorek, the bear. Lyra transforms the monstrous Lorek by helping him regain his armor, which represents his soul or the true and good part of him. Restored, he saves Lyra's life and advances her quest. *The White Mercedes,* in which Chris tries desperately to reconnect with his lost love, is clearly a modern Romeo and Juliet tale. Tristam and Iseult come to mind in *The Broken Bridge,* when Ginny is attracted to Andy, who is involved in a homosexual relationship with Dafydd. This parallels her father's falling in love with Ginny's mother though he was already married.

The Shane plot is replayed when Sally Lockhart, an incorruptible avenger, restores money and position to her clients. Lyra, because she must remain innocent of the crucial role she plays in saving the cosmos, also fits this pattern. Psycho, or the horrible surprise sequence, appears most obviously in *The Broken Bridge,* as Ginny learns one truth after another: she has a half brother, her mother is not dead, the boy she loves is gay, and her father has lied to her over and over. *Clockwork* takes Psycho another step in having the plot appear twice: first, when Dr. Kalmenius arrives with his mechanical knight and then when the reader learns that human hearts have been used in the manufacture of mechanical figures.

Elements of Opheus and Eurydice come into play briefly in *The White Mercedes,* when Chris assumes Jenny has been sexually involved with his boss, Barry. The Achilles scenario occurs in the Sally Lockhart stories repeatedly, as her Achilles heel is her feminine gender just as Lord Asriel's is his arrogance. The Faust plot is played out twice in *Clockwork*—once when the storyteller sells his soul to the Devil and again when the clockmaker's apprentice does the same. Both Sally Lockhart and Lyra seem to fit into the Shane role because Sally takes care of her clients and then goes on to something else. Lyra literally goes from one world to another, thwarting evil where only she in her innocence can prevail.

Ways of Linking Stories

According to Pullman, there are two ways of linking stories to form a chain of episodes that can contain one or several of the ten plots. He calls the first the Flying Dutchman approach. In

Achilles was one of the Greek heroes of the Trojan War. His mother had dipped Achilles into the River Styx as a baby. The water made him invulnerable but did not touch his heel, which became his only vulnerable spot. He died after being shot by an arrow in that heel.

tragedy a serious drama with a sorrowful or disastrous conclusion

Faust, a German astrologer and magician, lived from about 1480 to 1540. In 1587, an unknown author produced a legendary biography that tells of Faust selling his soul to the devil. This story was retold in Christopher Marlowe's *The Tragical History of Doctor Faustus,* written about 1588.

Picture of Dorian Gray (1890) was Oscar Wilde's only novel. It describes a man whose portrait grows old and hideous as a reflection of his moral corruption, though his appearance remains youthful and handsome.

The Fugitive ran from 1963 to 1967 and starred David Janssen as Dr. Richard Kimble. A 1993 movie remake featured Harrison Ford as the doctor.

Sherlock Holmes is the main character of many stories written by Sir Arthur Conan Doyle. There is an article about Doyle in volume 1.

subplot a secondary series of events that is less important than the plot

superficial lacking depth or substance

narrating telling a story

setting the general time and place in which the events of a literary work take place

these stories, the hero, having done something wrong, is condemned to wander forever searching for redemption. Because each adventure ends with the poor hero having to move on, there are endless possibilities for adventures. The old TV series *The Fugitive* is a perfect example of this form. Pullman calls the comic version of the Flying Dutchman the Dennis the Menace approach. Superman, Robin Hood, and Sherlock Holmes stories fall into this category; this time each adventure ends happily, with the hero triumphant. And like the Flying Dutchman, they could go on in an endless series.

Depending on whether one sees His Dark Materials trilogy as comic or tragic, Lyra could be either the Flying Dutchman or Dennis the Menace. Lyra is certainly comic in the mud wars she organizes among the children of Oxford. Things become much more serious, however, both when she meets the Goblers, while trying to get Roger back, and again when she tricks the evil bear king and restores the good bear, Lorek Byrinson, to his throne. With her series of misadventures over the course of three books, Sally—who is a female Sherlock Holmes— seems more like Dennis the Menace.

Story Mutations

In "Myths, Folktales, and Fiction" (pp. 15–18), Pullman goes on to suggest that "stories can mutate into one another, and endless variations are possible within each of the forms. So a Flying Dutchman episode could be a Tristan story, or Romeo and Juliet include a subplot about the seduction of innocence. Or combine *Psycho* with *Shane,* take it back 1,300 years and write it in Anglo-Saxon, and you've got *Beowulf.*" Stories can mutate in superficial ways by changing the narrating voice, the point of view, the protagonist (making the Prince the central character in Cinderella), the setting (situating Cinderella in modern New York), or the medium (changing words to pictures, prose to verse). Stories can also mutate in fundamental ways by addition—adding a new character who has a real function in the story (What if a poor young man loves Cinderella before the Prince does?); by substraction—taking away one of the fundamental elements (What would the story be like without Cinderella's sisters?); by contradiction—reversing one of the structural elements (What if a fairy godmother comes not to help but to hinder Cinderella?); or by changing the order of events (What if Cinderella and the Prince meet and fall in love before the ball?).

Pullman, it would seem, enjoys the particular "superficial mutation" of having his protagonist be a female. In his Sally Lockhart mysteries, Sally is a female detective and business-woman in the 1800s, a time when respectable women married and raised children. Only desperation would drive a woman to take a job. But Sally makes her own choices and sets herself up in business even though she is often hard pressed to survive on several levels. Likewise, Ginny of *The Broken Bridge,* risks bodily harm when she waits to question a thug in a dark bed-room. Although this is *not* a situation that any sane female would create for herself, sixteen-year-old Ginny succeeds in gaining the upper hand in this instance. Lyra also encounters much danger as she ventures from one world to another trying to save the cosmos from destruction. Pullman's female charac-ters from Sally to Lyra are not only intrepid, they also prevail.

intrepid fearless

prevail to be tri-umphant through strength or superiority

Animal Daemons

As a master storyteller, Pullman re-imagines, combines, and changes the ten plots to create a marvelous variety of fascinat-ing stories. One of his embellishments is the use of daemons, or animal counterparts serving as the embodiment of one's soul, to define characters in His Dark Materials trilogy. Every-one has a daemon, and with one exception, the daemons are all the opposite sex of the human to whom they are con-nected. Daemons of children can shift shapes to suit the mood of the child, but the settling of one's daemon signals adulthood and self-knowledge. This device enables Pullman to draw complex characters as well as highlight action within the story. Lyra's daemon is often a moth so that he won't be no-ticeable as he lends her advice. He turns into a ferret to warm her when she is cold, a mouse or cat when she reads the alethiometer, a bird to scout ahead when she is running, a fish or sea bird when she is at sea, and so on. He is also the perfect confidant because Lyra can trust her daemon totally. However, separation from her daemon would mean Lyra's destruction.

A person's daemon cannot be chosen, but when an inter-viewer for an article in the January 1999 issue of the *Lion and the Unicorn* asked Pullman what his daemon would be if he *could* choose, he answered: "It would probably be a raven, be-cause that's the Native American image of the trickster, and a storyteller is a trickster and can persuade people of something that isn't true. I like that idea. The raven is the great Creator spirit." A raven seems to be a fitting daemon for Pullman, an extraordinary literary trickster who creates stories that entertain, probe, inspire, and most of all satisfy. The complexity of his stories speaks to his respect for his audience and his high regard for the literary traditions that undergird his creations, all of which, of course, are delicious variations within the rich tradition of storytelling that has been nurturing readers and listeners throughout the ages.

If you like the works of Philip Pullman, you might also like the works of Lloyd Alexander, Charles Dickens, Sir Arthur Conan Doyle, Ursula K. Le Guin, Madaleine L'Engle, and J. R. R. Tolkien.

Selected Bibliography

WORKS BY PHILIP PULLMAN

Novels for Young Adults

The Ruby in the Smoke (1985)

The Shadow in the Plate (1987); published in the United States as *The Shadow in the North* (1988)

Spring-Heeled Jack, illustrated by David Mostyn (1989; 1991)

The Broken Bridge (1990; 1992)

The Tiger in the Well (1990)

The White Mercedes (1992)

The Tin Princess (1994)

Northern Lights (1995); published in United States as *The Golden Compass* (1996)

The Subtle Knife (1997)

Clockwork: Or All Wound Up (1996), illustrated by Leonid Gore (1998)

Novel for Adults

Galatea (1978; 1979)

Children's Books

Ancient Civilizations, illustrated by G. Long (1978)

Count Karlstein (1982), illustrated by Patrice Agg (1991)

How to Be Cool (1987)

Penny Dreadful (1989)

Plays

Sherlock Holmes and the Adventure of the Sumation Devil (1985)

The Three Musketeers (1986)

Frankenstein (1988)

Articles

"Gotterdammerung or Bust." *Horn Book,* January 1999, pp. 31–33.

"Myths, Folktales, and Fiction." *SIGNAL Journal,* fall 1997/ winter 1998, pp. 15–18.

Television Adaptation

How to Be Cool (1988)

Speech

"Carnegie Medal Acceptance Speech." NCTE Conference, Detroit, 20 November 1997. Available on-line at *www. randomhouse.com/goldencompass/subtleknife/seams/ speech.html*

Edited Work

Detective Stories (1998)

WORKS ABOUT PHILIP PULLMAN

"Achuka Interview: Philip Pullman." *www.achuka.co.uk/ ppint.htm*

Commire, Anne, ed. *Something About the Author.* Detroit: Gale Research, 1994, vol. 65, pp. 170–171.

Forman, Jack. "Philip Pullman." In *Twentieth-Century Young Adult Writers.* Edited by Laura Standley Berger. Detroit: St. James, 1994, pp. 543–544.

Gallo, Donald R., ed. Essay in *Speaking for Ourselves, Too: More Autobiographical Sketches by Notable Authors of Books for Young Adults.* Urbana, Ill: National Council of Teachers of English, 1993, pp. 162–163.

Jones, Nicolette. "What Shall We Tell the Children: Profile: Philip Pullman." *Times of London,* 18 July 1996.

Parsons, Wendy, and Catriona Nicholson. "Talking to Philip Pullman: An Interview." *Lion and the Unicorn: Contemporary British Children's Literature,* January 1999, pp. 116–134.

"Philip Pullman." In *Children's Books and Their Creators: An Invitation to the Feast of Twentieth-Century Children's Literature.* Edited by Anita Silvey. Boston: Houghton Mifflin, 1995, p. 544.

"Pullman, Philip" In *Contemporary Authors.* Edited by Pamela S. Dear. Detroit: Gale Research, vol. 50, 1996, pp. 365–367.

How to Write to the Author

Philip Pullman
24 Templar Road
Oxford OX2 8LT
England

Cynthia Rylant

(1954–)

by Colleen P. Gilrane

Has something happened to you that you wish had turned out differently? While growing up, Cynthia Rylant experienced some events that were difficult for her, and she believes that has influenced her writing and her decision to become a writer. In her autobiography, *But I'll Be Back Again: An Album* (1989), she says,

autobiography the story of one's own life

> I think maybe some children who have suffered a loss too great for words grow up into writers who are always trying to find those words, trying to find a meaning for the way they have lived. Painters do that. And composers. . . . Writing stories has given me the power to change things I could not change as a child. I can make boys into doctors. I can make fathers stop drinking. I can make mothers stay. (Pp. 5, 10)

In her writing, Rylant has changed things to be the way she wished they were when she was a child. She has also celebrated the things that were wonderful about her childhood in West Virginia, as well as her love of animals and her love of art.

Early Childhood in the Mountains

Cynthia Rylant was born on 6 June 1954 on an army base in Hopewell, Virginia. Her father, John, was an army sergeant, and for the first four years of her life, she and her parents moved around the country, living at different military bases. Her parents' marriage was unhappy, in part because of her father's drinking problem, and when Cynthia was four, her mother, Leatrel, decided to leave him. Cynthia was taken to her grandparents' home in West Virginia to live, while her mother went away to nursing school so that she would be able to work as a nurse and support herself and Cynthia.

Even though she missed her parents, Rylant loved living in her grandparents' house with her two cousins and several aunts and uncles. She reminisced about this time in her first book, *When I Was Young in the Mountains* (1982), which is dedicated to her grandparents, Elda and Ferrell Rylant. Other people and events from that time in her life have shown up in her writing as well. Her Uncle Joe, who was her hero and who fought in the Vietnam War, was the inspiration for Ellie's Uncle Joe in *A Blue-Eyed Daisy* (1985) and was probably on her mind as she wrote *I Had Seen Castles* (1993).

Rylant's disappointment at not receiving a nurse's kit as a child was turned into Frankie's disappointment at not receiving a doctor's kit, year after year, in the story "Silver Packages" in *Children of Christmas* (1987). However, in her writing, Rylant was able to create a happy ending for this story: Frankie grew up to become a doctor and to have a real doctor's kit!

In her writing, Rylant has returned time and time again to growing up in the mountains. *The Relatives Came* (1985) allows readers to imagine the fun and the love in that house full of grandparents, aunts, uncles, and cousins. If you read *Night in the Country* (1986), you will know what young Cynthia Rylant heard and thought when she lay awake at night: "Far over the hill you hear someone open and close a creaking screen door. You wonder who is up so late" (p. 9). In her nonfiction picture book *Appalachia: The Voices of Sleeping Birds* (1991), Rylant describes the homes and the lives and the work of the people she grew up with. Barry Moser, who illustrated this

In the **Vietnam War** (1957–1975), Communist-ruled North Vietnam fought to take over South Vietnam. From 1965 to 1969, the United States tried to stop the advancement of North Vietnam but failed. In 1975, South Vietnam surrendered to North Vietnam.

book, also grew up in Appalachia, and included his brother Tommy and the porch of his Grandpa Haggard's store in his illustrations for this book. (When I read *Appalachia: The Voices of Sleeping Birds* to my college students at the University of Tennessee-Knoxville, the ones who grew up in Appalachia tell me that it portrays their lives exactly. Some of them even cry.)

Cynthia Rylant won the Newbery Award for her 1992 novel, *Missing May,* in which six-year-old orphan Summer, unwanted by any other relatives, is taken in by her aunt and uncle. Perhaps the love she felt in her grandparents' house helped Rylant write this description of Summer's feelings:

> **Then Uncle Ob and Aunt May from West Virginia visited, and they knew an angel when they saw her, and they took her on home.**
>
> **Home was, still is, a rusty old trailer stuck on the face of a mountain in Deep Water, in the heart of Fayette County. It looked to me, the first time, like a toy that God had been playing with and accidentally dropped out of heaven. Down and down and down it came and landed, thunk, on this mountain . . .**
>
> **That first night in it with Ob and May was as close to paradise as I may ever come in my life. Paradise because these two old people—who never dreamed they'd be bringing a little girl back from their visit with the relatives in Ohio—started, from the minute we pulled up in Ob's old Valiant, to turn their rusty, falling-down place into a house just meant for a child. (P. 5)**

Her love of the mountains and her love for her family appear again in Rylant's 1997 book, *The Blue Hill Meadows.* In its four stories, Willie Meadows experiences adventures with different members of his family while the four seasons of the year bring changes to Blue Hill, Virginia.

Growing Up in Town

When Rylant was eight years old, her mother finished nursing school, and the two of them went to live in Beaver, West Virginia, where her mother worked as a nurse. They lived in an

Appalachia refers to an area of the eastern United States that includes the Appalachian Mountains. This covers part of New York, most of Pennsylvania, and the mountainous regions of Virginia, West Virginia, Kentucky, Tennessee, North Carolina, South Carolina, Alabama, and Georgia.

apartment, and Rylant began attending third grade in a new school and "learning to live with a mother I was thrilled to have again but whom I really did not know" (*But I'll Be Back Again,* p. 14). In 1985 she wrote an article, "Thank You, Miss Evans," in which she said this about her third grade teacher:

> I had this third grade teacher named Miss Evans back in Beaver, West Virginia. She was a short little woman with jet-black hair, tomato-red lipstick, and black-rimmed glasses. I was the new kid in school that year, which is perhaps why my memory of her physical appearance is so vivid. I never took my eyes off her that first terrifying week.
>
> Miss Evans was the first, and last, person who ever told me stories. I don't mean the reading aloud of books. I mean the spinning of tales. Let me tell you what this very short woman in Beaver, West Virginia, created.
>
> It was an ongoing saga entitled *The Journey.* The main characters in *The Journey* were the twenty-five of us sitting in her classroom. Once a week, Miss Evans led us on an adventure into the jungles of Africa or the glaciers of the Antarctic or some equally harrowing place, and she narrated, in a tense, mysterious, breathless voice, the epic battles we won, together and individually.
>
> One time in the Sahara Desert, I was bitten by a rattlesnake. And Randy Meadows carried me to a safe place, slit my flesh into an X, and sucked the poison from my foot. Sitting at my desk, I was nearly overcome with nervous exhaustion before Miss Evans finished this particular installment.
>
> And you know, Randy Meadows and I would spend nine more years together in school. . . . And in those nine years, I never once lost that feeling of immense gratitude toward Randy for saving me from certain death by snakebite, though he sat only three desks away during the entire ordeal.
>
> *That* is the power of what a story can do to you.
> (P. 460)

harrowing disturbing; distressing

narrate to tell a story

epic heroic

Rylant did not write stories in Beaver, but her writing includes the stories from her childhood and teenage years there. She did not like being poor and having a mother who had to go to work instead of participating in the PTA, as the mothers of her schoolmates did. Her book *Waiting to Waltz: A Childhood* (1984) is a collection of poems about her life in Beaver, and in one of the poems, "PTA" (p. 32), she laments the fact that all of the other mothers are active at school events and she wishes her mom were too—until something happens that makes her mother's being a nurse more important. The poem ends this way:

> Until one day a boy
> fainted
> in class
> and everyone turned to me
> and said
> what do we do?
> Because my mom
> was a nurse
> and they knew it, and she might never
> pop popcorn at halftime
> but she could
> sure
> save their lives, boy.
> PTA could just
> keep her
> on call.

Boyfriends were an important part of Rylant's teenage years as she describes them in *But I'll Be Back Again.* Her first kiss, with Harold Treadway, was the inspiration for "A Lovely Night," the chapter in which Ellie experiences her first kiss in *A Blue-Eyed Daisy.* Rylant also fell in love with the Beatles, which you will figure out quickly if you read her autobiography. Its title, *But I'll Be Back Again,* is a line from a Beatles song, and other song lyrics are included in the book, as well as the fact that Cynthia spent part of her young adulthood walking around Beaver with a guitar slung across her back to emulate her favorite Beatle, Paul McCartney.

Soda Jerk (1990) is a collection of poems spoken by a high school boy who has a part-time job as the soda jerk in Maywell's

The **Beatles** were the most popular rock group in history. The band and its four members, Paul McCartney, John Lennon, George Harrison, and Ringo Starr, were enormously popular during the 1960s. The line "But I'll be back again" is from the song "I'll Be Back," which appeared on the soundtrack for the 1964 Beatles movie, *A Hard Day's Night.*

emulate to try to equal by imitating

soda jerk a person who mixes and serves carbonated drinks and ice cream at a soda fountain

Drugstore in the small town of Cheston, Virginia. The reader comes to know this young man and his secret desires, including the one to leave Cheston, which he believes will never be fulfilled:

> My good friend Bob and me
> we talk about
> what we'll do after graduation,
> and we talk like
> we've got all the choices in the world,
> but who are we kidding? . . . Truth is, Cheston is Cheston.
> And we've never learned a thing
> about dreams here,
> much less making them come true. (Pp. 44–45)

Teenaged Cynthia Rylant had experienced glimpses of the world beyond Beaver through visits from the New Orleans Symphony Orchestra and from presidential candidate Robert F. Kennedy. She never believed she would leave, though, figuring she would become someone's wife and live there forever. However, her father's military service allowed her to attend college paid for by the G. I. Bill, so after high school she left Beaver to become a student at Morris Harvey College (now the University of Charleston), majoring in English. In *Speaking for Ourselves, Too* (1993), she describes the experience this way:

> I loved college. I loved reading Langston Hughes and James Agee. I loved the boys in flannel shirts who made pottery and smelled like patchouli. I loved the girls in the dorm who popped popcorn at 4:00 A.M. and dyed their hair green. College was one long wonderful Hollywood movie.
>
> After college I happened into the children's room of a public library (for the first time) and, at twenty-four, I found out what I wanted to do. I wanted to write. (P. 178)

Religion and Art

Rylant grew up hearing the preachers in church tell her she was doomed to hellfire if she did not walk down the aisle to the front of the church and confess that she was a sinner.

Eventually, her fear won out over her embarrassment, and she did. As an adult, she looked back on that Sunday feeling as if she'd been tricked into something. In *But I'll Be Back Again,* she notes: "If you had to scare somebody into loving you, would you think you were loved for who you were? . . . It took me until I was grown up to realize I'd gone about religion in all the wrong way, and I had to figure out God all over again" (p. 30). Some of the figuring out takes place in her writing. In the poem "Saved" in *Waiting to Waltz* (p. 42), she evokes for the reader her mother's dismay at the confession:

evoke to call to mind

> After church all of us shaking hands, tears pouring,
> and my mother embarrassed,
> surely wishing she'd stayed in bed,
> for she'd never liked preachers
> who yelled people to the Cross.
> Dismayed her daughter could be so duped.

dupe to deceive

Thirteen-year-old Pete, the main character in Rylant's 1986 novel, *A Fine White Dust,* is also duped, by a traveling evangelist who comes to his town for a revival. Deeply religious, Pete feels he is being called by God to leave his home, his family, and his best friend, Rufus, to follow the traveling preacher and join in his ministry. Pete secretly packs a bag to meet the preacher at their rendezvous point—10:00 P.M. at the filling station—and waits. When the preacher does not show up by 1:00 A.M., Pete admits to himself that the preacher is not coming and allows Rufus, who has been hiding in the bushes nearby, to lead him home. By the time he narrates the story, Pete has figured some things out about God, religion, and relationships:

evangelist a person who preaches the gospel with militant or crusading enthusiasm

revival a highly emotional evangelistic religious meeting or series of meetings

> One thing I can see now that I couldn't see last summer is that after the revival is over, the world is a place that isn't anything like the inside of a church on a hot summer night. It's a world where the good guys like Rufus are happy atheists, and nice folks like my parents don't care much about church, and spiritual people like me wander around on earth wishing it was heaven.
>   . . . [E]ven though I don't go to church as much—I'm still trying to figure church out—even

atheist one who does not believe in the existence of God

though I don't seem to need church as much, I know I need God.

I just don't know how to get Him. And fit Him in with the other folks I need. (Pp. 104–105)

Rylant now seems more comfortable with God. In her 1993 children's book, *The Dreamer,* God is a daydreaming artist who decides to make everything he dreams. Page after page, he cuts out and paints and sculpts and draws the world and everything in it, including new artists who also love to daydream: "Living among blue water and green grass, they have daydreamed the most beautiful things in the world. The first young artist, still a dreamer, has always called them his children. And they, in turn, have always called him God" (pp. 20–24).

In *Dog Heaven* (1995), God gives dogs fields and fields and fields because he knows they love to run best of all, and he fills Dog Heaven with children because dogs love to play with them. God lets all the cats in *Cat Heaven* (1997) lie on his bed or sleep on his head while he walks in the garden. *Bless Us All* (1998) is a collection of twelve blessings for children, one for each month of the year. *The Heavenly Village* (1999) is about God loving all his people so much that he has created a special place where people who do not feel as if they want to go to heaven yet can spend some time getting ready.

Rylant has become a self-taught painter and has illustrated several of her own books, including *Dog Heaven, Cat Heaven,* and *Bless Us All.* Her folk paintings have been exhibited at the Society of Illustrators in New York City. Anne Becker, an artist who exhibits her work in New York, is one of the main characters in Rylant's novel *A Kindness* (1989). Becker and her son Chip live in Seattle, Washington, while Rylant and her son live in Oregon.

Selected Bibliography

WORKS BY CYNTHIA RYLANT

Novels for Young Adults

    A Blue-Eyed Daisy (1985)

    A Fine White Dust (1986)

    A Kindness (1989)

    Missing May (1992)

If you like the work of Cynthia Rylant, you might also like the work of Betsy Byars and Katherine Paterson.

I Had Seen Castles (1993)

The Van Gogh Cafe (1995)

The Islander (1998)

The Heavenly Village (1999)

Short Stories

Every Living Thing, illustrated by Stephen D. Schindler (1985)

Children of Christmas, illustrated by Stephen D. Schindler (1987)

A Couple of Kooks: And Other Stories About Love (1990)

The Blue Hill Meadows (1997)

Picture Books

When I Was Young in the Mountains, illustrated by Diane Goode (1982)

Miss Maggie, illustrated by Thomas di Grazia (1983)

This Year's Garden, illustrated by Mary Szilagyi (1984)

The Relatives Came, illustrated by Stephen Gammell (1985)

Night in the Country, illustrated by Mary Szilagyi (1986)

Birthday Presents, illustrated by Sucie Stevenson (1987)

All I See, illustrated by Peter Catalonotto (1988)

Mr. Griggs' Work, illustrated by Julie Downing (1989)

An Angel for Solomon Singer, illustrated by Peter Catalonotto (1992)

The Dreamer (1993)

Dog Heaven (1995)

Cat Heaven (1997)

The Bird House (1998)

Poetry

Waiting to Waltz: A Childhood, illustrated by Stephen Gammell (1984)

Soda Jerk, illustrated by Peter Catalonotto (1990)

Something Permanent (1994)

Nonfiction

"Thank You, Miss Evans." *Language Arts,* September 1985, pp. 460–462.

But I'll Be Back Again: An Album (1989) [Autobiography.]

Appalachia: The Voices of Sleeping Birds, illustrated by Barry Moser (1991)

Best Wishes (1992) [Autobiography.]

Bless Us All (1998) [Prayers.]

Children's Books

The Mr. Putter and Tabby series

The Henry and Mudge series

In Aunt Lucy's Kitchen (1998)

A Little Shopping (1998)

WORKS ABOUT CYNTHIA RYLANT

Gallo, Donald R., ed. *Speaking for Ourselves, Too: More Autobiographical Sketches by Notable Authors of Books for Young Adults.* Urbana, Ill.: National Council of Teachers of English, 1993, pp. 177–179.

Senick, Gerard J., ed. *Children's Literature Review.* Detroit: Gale Research, 1988, vol. 15, pp. 167–174.

Telgen, Diane, ed. *Something About the Author.* Detroit: Gale Research, 1994, vol. 76, pp. 193–199.

Trosky, Susan M., ed. *Contemporary Authors.* Detroit: Gale Research, 1992, vol. 136, pp. 357–360.

How to Write to the Author

Cynthia Rylant
c/o Blue Sky Press/
Scholastic, Inc.
555 Broadway
New York, NY 10012-3999

Louis Sachar

(1954–)

by Kevin Sue Bailey

To get a handle on Louis Sachar, you would have to go to the nineteenth floor of Wayside School (which doesn't exist) and talk to Miss Zarves (who doesn't exist). If this sounds like a paradoxical mission, then you are beginning to get the picture. Sachar's work abounds with paradox and ironic twists, which he uses skillfully to develop the plot, when there is one, and masterfully to create humor, which always exists in his stories.

His work ranges from the bizarre fantasy of *Sideways Stories from Wayside School* (1998) to the realistic fiction of *There's a Boy in the Girls' Bathroom* (1987) and *Holes* (1998). But in the quest to find the real Sachar, steer clear of reality and go directly to fantasy.

In the Beginning

To say it all started with Wayside School is more concise than such a general statement might first convey. Both Sachar's

Quotations from Louis Sachar that are not attributed to a published source are from a personal interview conducted by the author of this article on 11 February 1999 and are published here by permission of Louis Sachar.

paradoxical with contradictory qualities

ironic marked by a contrast between what is said and what is actually meant; sarcastic

plot the deliberate sequence of events in a literary work

writing debut and his personal appearance in one of his novels did start with Wayside School. *Sideways Stories from Wayside School* is a novel about an elementary school that is thirty stories high with one classroom on each floor, except for the nineteenth floor, which, of course, does not exist. Actually, the story is about the teachers and students at the school. In fact, each chapter in the book describes a different character, starting with Mrs. Gorf, the long-tongued, pointy-eared teacher who wiggles her ears and turns students into apples. When Mrs. Gorf falls victim to her own spell and becomes an apple, Louis, the yard teacher, appears for the first time in the story. Hungry from yard duty, Louis eats the apple. So ends Mrs. Gorf and begins the story of the children on the thirtieth floor of Wayside School and their new teacher, Mrs. Jewls.

The peculiarities of Wayside School extend well beyond its architecture. Each book chapter features a different student who adds a new dimension to the strange tale, all introduced with Sachar's paradoxical twist. Todd, the only student who thinks before he speaks, is sent home daily at noon on the kindergarten bus for talking in class. Myron, the class president, whose job it is to turn the classroom lights on and off each day, loses his job after the first day because he stops to save the life of a classmate's dog and is late getting the lights turned on. John is the smartest kid in the class but can only read upside down, and Rondi is known for her beautiful two front teeth, which, of course, are missing. When the students are not in class practicing arithmetic by counting Dana's mosquito bites or Joe's hair, they are sent outside under the watchful eye of Louis, the yard teacher, whose job it is to make sure they don't have too much fun. At the end of the book, there is a blizzard in June, and Louis goes to Mrs. Jewls' class to entertain the children with a story about a school much like their own. Only in his story, the classrooms are all built on the ground floor, none of the children has ever been turned into an apple, no one reads upside down, and arithmetic is not taught with mosquito bites. When the children become frightened by the absurdity of the tale, Mrs. Jewls assures them it is only a story.

Reality or Fiction?

Is it possible that a story this wacky could have any basis in reality or that an author such as Sachar could have any connection with such a school? Sachar attests that Louis "the yard teacher" is his autobiographical counterpart. In fact, when Sachar was enrolled at the University of California at Berkeley in 1973, he majored in economics while studying creative writing. He registered for what he expected to be an easy three-hour course serving as a teacher's aide at an elementary school near the campus.

As an aide, he was assigned to Mrs. Jukes, the Wayside equivalent of Mrs. Jewls, and was soon offered a part-time job as "the yard teacher," supervising the children during recess. The children described in *Sideways Stories* are named after the children he met as yard teacher in that Berkeley elementary school.

Lawyer or Writer?

You might think that is an odd enough twist to capture your interest in Sachar, but the irony in his life story goes on to parallel the irony in his work. Sachar was born 20 March 1954 in East Meadow, New York, to Robert and Ruth Sachar. He graduated from Berkeley with a B.A. in economics and started writing *Sideways Stories.* While writing, he worked as a middle manager in a sweater warehouse, a job that bore none of the excitement of the school yard. After eight months, he finished the book, lost his job, started looking for a publisher, and decided to pursue a law degree. In 1976, during his first week of law school at the University of California at San Francisco, he heard from Follett Press that it intended to publish *Sideways Stories.* The book went on to sell nearly 10,000 copies and won the 1979 Children's Choice Award from the International Reading Association and the Children's Book Council.

In 1990 Sachar graduated from the University of California at San Francisco, with a degree in law. By that time he had written *Johnny's in the Basement* (1981) and *Someday Angeline* (1983). These works presented a move to realistic fiction, each dealing with adolescents as outsiders who rely on friendship to help them through their personal crises. During this time, Sachar was experiencing his own personal crisis: lawyer versus writer. He was writing in the morning and working as a lawyer in the afternoon on cases referred to him by friends and former classmates. Follett was no longer publishing trade books, so he found himself starting over. Avon eventually agreed to publish *Johnny's in the Basement* and *Someday Angeline* but

autobiographical related to the author's own life

trade books books intended for general readership

point of view the position or perspective from which the story is told

turned down his fourth book, *There's a Boy in the Girls' Bathroom.* Sachar admitted that there was too much shifting in point of view in the original version of the manuscript.

Sachar hit a slump at this point in his career. He found himself struggling to get published at a time when he most wanted to turn to writing as his full-time career. He recalls, "The thing that kept me going was that even though *Sideways Stories from Wayside School* sold less than 10,000 copies, I got a tremendous amount of fan mail from it. Wherever I went I got letters that said it was voted the favorite book at their school, so I knew that there was something there."

This affirmation from his fans kept him pursuing a new publisher. His luck began to change all at once when an editor who had worked for his original publisher agreed to accept *There's a Boy in the Girls' Bathroom* if he revised the manuscript. At the same time, Sachar got the rights back to *Sideways Stories from Wayside School.* He remembers trying to get Avon to publish *Sideways Stories,* but the company was taking a long time to make a decision. He recalls, "After a while I just kept forwarding all of the fan letters that I kept getting. They finally agreed to publish it." He goes on to remember, "Two events happened all at once, *Sideways Stories* getting back into print and *There's a Boy in the Girls' Bathroom* getting published. My career took off after that."

Even this part of Sachar's life is not without an ironic spin. When he finally met with the editor who had agreed to publish *There's a Boy in the Girls' Bathroom,* she took him out to lunch and invited along one of her other authors, Mavis Jukes. Sachar's thoughts immediately turned to that Berkeley elementary school. He asked if by chance she had a relative who taught school at Berkeley and found himself face-to-face with Mrs. Juke's daughter. He said, "Well, I wrote a book about your mother." Since nine years had passed between his days at the school and the publication of the book, the children never knew he had written about them. This chance meeting with Mavis did enable him to send a copy to Mrs. Jukes. Sachar adds, "That's why in the new *Wayside School Gets a Little Stranger* (1995), Mrs. Jewls has a baby and the baby's name is Mavis."

Mavis Jukes (1947–) is an American children's book author. Her books include *Like Jake and Me* (1984) and *Blackberries in the Dark* (1985).

Emotion, Cliques, and Tricks

Sachar confesses that the fight to get *There's a Boy in the Girls' Bathroom* published marked the longest struggle of his career. "It took three years from when I first thought I had finished writing *There's a Boy in the Girls' Bathroom* to find a publisher and two more years before it was published." But in the true Sachar style of expecting the unexpected, this is his most popular book and the one that has won the most awards. Any adolescent or anyone who has struggled to survive that period feels pangs of kinship in the opening lines: "Bradley Chalkers sat at his desk in the back of the room—last seat, last row. No one sat at the desk next to him or at the one in front of him. He was an island" (p. 3).

In fact, Sachar's novels consistently tug the reader back and forth between the free-spirited humor of their childish side and the poignant recognition of their adolescent self. This emotional tug-of-war is clearly set in motion in *Sixth Grade Secrets* (1987). When feisty, long-haired Laura dons a red cap with the silver letters "Pig City" emblazoned on the front, the battle lines are drawn. This garage sale treasure quickly becomes the icon for a club. Implicit in the formation of a club is membership, belonging or not belonging, the ever-present adolescent battle. Clique #1 leads to clique #2, Monkey Town. War ensues with a strategic attack on the clubhouse and comical but challenging messages left on the chalkboard at school. The skirmish comes to an abrupt halt when rival club members cut Laura's hair. The mean-spirited attack results in a truce between Laura and Gabriel, her wanna-be boyfriend from the other side.

Cliques and scapegoating also add adolescent reality to *The Boy Who Lost His Face* (1989). David competes with the "popular guys" for the friendship of his childhood buddy, Scott. In an attempt to fit in, David participates in a devious trick on the elderly Mrs. Bayfield, long rumored to be a witch. His guilt sends him reeling into a series of embarrassing mishaps that he is convinced are a result of her curse. With the help of a couple of true friends and a new ally, Tori Williams, David returns to Mrs. Bayfield's to make amends. The fantastical curse is lifted, but not before Tori and her aunt, Mrs. Bayfield, play one last trick on David.

Kindness and Warmth

A *Publisher's Weekly* review of *The Boy Who Lost His Face* stated, "Sachar captures awkward junior high experiences with humor and sensitivity." Sachar admits that he tries to create stories that are "fun, thoughtful, and thought provoking," a

poignant touching or moving

clique an exclusive group

skirmish a minor dispute

scapegoating blaming an individual for the wrongdoing of others

phrase he says he came up with to describe his intention as a writer.

> **With all of my books, the first thing I'm trying to do is make them fun to read. That goes for *Holes* to the *Wayside School*. Every once in a while the reviewer will talk about the warmth and kindness of Wayside School. I always love it when they mention that instead of saying it's wacky. It says to me, 'They got it! They got what I was trying to say!'**

Sachar feels that although the kids who read his books may not talk about the underlying kindness and warmth, it is that kindness and warmth that really attracts them more than the wackiness. And they are attracted. Not only did the fan mail persuade the publisher to reprint *Sideways Stories,* but it was the letters from kids that inspired sequels. Sachar admits, "It was never intended to be a series."

He did respond to his readers' interest in 1989 with *Wayside School Is Falling Down.* Sachar picks up where he left off with the characters that he developed in *Sideways Stories* and dedicates each chapter to adventures that could only happen at Wayside School. He went on to write *Sideways Arithmetic from Wayside School* (1989) and *Wayside School Gets a Little Stranger.*

Once Sachar caught on to the popularity of series books, he moved on to master the art. *Marvin Redpost: Kidnapped at Birth?* (1992) represents the launch of a new Sachar series. Readers capture blue-eyed, red-haired Marvin in mishap after mishap from nose picking, in *Why Pick on Me?* (1993), to dog sitting his teacher's pet in *Alone in His Teacher's House* (1994). The good-hearted Marvin finds himself in predicaments that are sure to leave nine-year-olds asking for more.

Flexibility as a Writer

While Sachar has had great success with his series, he is most interested in stretching himself as a writer. "If I was only interested in making money, I would only write the Wayside School books. But I've always wanted to try lots of different things. That's why I wanted to be a writer, just to push myself."

And push himself he does—all the way to the Texas sun. The 1999 Newbery winner, *Holes,* leaves little doubt about Sachar's flexibility. This is Sachar spinning at its finest. Using paradox and palindromes, Sachar has fun with the story and with the reader. Because nothing Sachar is ever what it seems, don't be fooled at the outset by the harsh sentencing of teenager Stanley Yelnats to a drought-ridden detention camp in the blistering Texas sun. After all, he gives you a clue that illusion will prevail in the first line of the book when he writes, "There is no lake at Camp Green Lake" (p. 3). From this paradox, he turns to palindrome naming the main character Stanley Yelnats (Stanley spelled backward). This is not the only reversal. The story itself cannot move forward without moving backward into the history of the characters and the setting.

It is through Sachar's snapshots of the past that we get a picture of the present. Stanley's "no-good-dirty-rotten-pig-stealing-great-great-grandfather" had been cursed by Madame Zeroni, fellow inmate Zero's ancestor. Likewise, flashbacks reveal that Green Lake had been a lake and a prosperous, peach-growing community until landowner Trout Walker unjustly took revenge against Katherine Barlow (later described as bank robber Kissin' Kate), who rejected his affection. The resulting curse is so powerful that the rain stops falling, the lake goes dry, and the Walker land becomes worthless, except as a detention camp. It is at this very camp where Stanley finds himself under the watchful eye of the venom-toting Warden, Walker's evil descendant. The story that ensues is one of atonement for crimes and curses, past and present.

The Author's Craft

The adage "Tall oaks from little acorns grow" seems to capture the craft of Sachar's writing. He usually begins with a small idea, a colorful character, or a place and just sees where it takes him. In the case of *Holes,* the long, hot Texas summer was the initial spark. The heat led to the idea of Camp Green Lake. He immediately thought of buried treasure. Simultaneously came flashes of Kissin' Kate, the Warden with rattlesnake fingernails, and yellow-spotted lizards (though he admits he didn't know what he would do with those). "My idea all along was not to write a grim story, but I thought of an intriguing setting to write a fun adventure story."

palindrome a word, verse, sentence, or number that reads the same backward or forward

A **detention camp** is a place where juvenile offenders may be sent while awaiting trial or as punishment. The goal of a detention camp is to rehabilitate youthful offenders through a disciplined program of exercise, therapy, classes, and other activities.

atonement actions taken to rectify an offense or injury

adage a saying that often metaphorically describes a common observation

When Sachar begins to write, he does not know where the story is going. The initial idea develops and transforms over a year or a year and a half. With *Holes,* he knew how it was going to end but was challenged by trying to create the history. It was almost backward. "I knew how it was going to come together at the end. The hard part was building a whole history that didn't exist."

Advice From the Author

The best tip that Sachar offers is "rewrite." He first got serious about rewriting when he was in a high school creative writing class and noticed how rewriting caused his work to get better. Still today he says his first drafts of his books are terrible. The initial draft is just to get ideas on paper, to get the basic story down. "The first draft is not wrong; it's just not done yet."

Author as Award Winner

Sachar has numerous awards to his credit, over a dozen for *There's a Boy in the Girl's Bathroom.* Until 1998 that was his most recognized book, but 1998 gave Sachar something even bigger to celebrate. In November of that year, he was awarded the National Book Award for *Holes.* Since the coveted award is usually given for adult literature, the recognition was especially meaningful to Sachar. "The National Book Award was especially nice because it treated children's literature as part of literature." Sachar hardly had time to relish the first award for *Holes* before he won the prestigious 1999 Newbery Award for most distinguished contribution to American literature for children. Sachar admits that the Newbery is one that people will see at the top of his resume. Other awards for *Holes* include the following: American Library Association Best Book for Young Adults, American Library Association Quick Pick for Young Adults, *Bulletin of the Center for Children's Books* Blue Ribbon Book, the *Horn Book* Fanfare Honor List, *School Library Journal* Best Book of the Year, and *Publisher's Weekly* Best Book of the Year.

Although the list is long and sure to get longer, Sachar enjoys each of his works for the feeling of artistic accomplishment that he experiences. "None of them equals the feeling I get myself when I finish a book and I've done as well as I can on the book. The greatest reward is doing something you're proud of."

coveted strongly desired

Selected Bibliography

WORKS BY LOUIS SACHAR

Sideways Stories from Wayside School (1978)

Johnny's in the Basement (1981)

Someday Angeline (1983)

Sixth Grade Secrets (1987)

There's a Boy in the Girls' Bathroom (1987)

The Boy Who Lost His Face (1989)

Sideways Arithmetic from Wayside School (1989)

Wayside School Is Falling Down (1989)

Dogs Don't Tell Jokes (1992)

Marvin Redpost: Kidnapped at Birth? (1992)

Marvin Redpost: Is He a Girl? (1993)

Marvin Redpost: Why Pick on Me? (1993)

Marvin Redpost: Alone in His Teacher's House (1994)

Wayside School Gets a Little Stranger (1995)

Holes (1998)

Marvin Redpost: Class President (1999)

Marvin Redpost: A Flying Birthday Cake (1999)

Marvin Redpost: Super Fast, Out of Control (2000)

WORKS ABOUT LOUIS SACHAR

Brown, Jennifer M. Review of *Holes*. In *Publisher's Weekly.* 27 July 1998, p. 78.

Commire, Anne, ed. *Something About the Author.* Detroit: Gale Research, 1991, vol. 63, pp. 137–140.

Follos, Alison. Review of *Holes*. In *School Library Journal.* September 1998, p. 210.

Holtze, Sally Holmes, ed. *Seventh Book of Authors and Illustrators.* New York: H. W. Wilson, 1996, pp. 274–276.

Lesniak, James, ed. *Contemporary Authors.* Detroit: Gale Research, 1991, vol. 33, p. 386.

Sutton, Roger. Review of *Holes*. In *Horn Book.* September/October 1998, pp. 593–595.

If you like the works of Louis Sachar, you might also like the works of Judy Blume, Chris Crutcher, Paula Danziger, Phyllis Reynolds Naylor, Jerry Spinelli, and Paul Zindel.

How to Write to the Author

Louis Sachar
c/o Children's Marketing
Farrar, Straus & Giroux
19 Union Square West
New York, NY 10003

Suzanne Fisher Staples

(1945–)

by Jinx Stapleton Watson

Once upon a time, not so long ago, a girl lived in a village not so far away. And when she turned eighteen, the girl announced she would marry her prince. Her father, displeased with the news, pronounced that she was too young, that she should wait to be married and if it were meant to be, it would be. Crushed by her father's proclamation, but dutiful, the girl obeyed and separated from her love for more than thirty years, until by chance they found each other and married and lived happily ever after.

Sound like a fairy tale? Suzanne Fisher Staples loves to make up stories, but this one, her own, is true. She has not yet written this story because even she cannot believe she finally married her true love. However, when you read Staples' writing closely, you can find many of the themes of her own fairy tale working in the lives of her characters as their values grow out

Quotations from Suzanne Fisher Staples that are not attributed to a published source are from personal interviews conducted by the author of this article on 9 December 1998 and 13 January 1999 and are published here by permission of Suzanne Fisher Staples.

theme central message about life in a literary work

of, match, and conflict with the values of their families. Her stories span continents and cultures. They assert that all teenagers feel, universally, the same emotions, despite differences in their particular ethnicity, religion, or social-economic class. In her stories you can meet, among others, Shabanu, nomad daughter of the Cholistan Desert in Pakistan, (*Shabanu: Daughter of the Wind,* 1989; and *Haveli,* 1993), and Buck, white landowners' son, far away in the Chesapeake Bay area (*Dangerous Skies,* 1996). Although their families are very different, both try to find out what they believe is right while remaining faithful to their families.

Chesapeake Bay is located in southern Maryland and northern Virginia.

Growing Up

Suzanne Fisher Staples was born in Philadelphia, Pennsylvania, on 27 August 1945 to Helen and Robert Fisher. The second of four children, she was nine years old when her family moved twelve miles north of Scranton, Pennsylvania, to a house in the country by a lake. Like Buck and Tunes in *Dangerous Skies,* she grew to love fishing and walking in the woods, discovering and caring for raccoons, turtles, frogs, rabbits and birds, as well as her family's dogs. Though her dad continued to commute to the city for his business and did not farm, Staples always wanted to be a farmer and to have animals. Today in Chattanooga, Tennessee, she has found a home in the woods, just five minutes from the city's center, where she and her husband care for their two standard poodles, Bogie and Mango, and feed the squirrels and the birds.

Staples' family influenced her early love of stories. Her parents always read to Suzanne, her sister Karen, and her brothers Robert and Charles, taking them weekly to the library. "My Grandmother, a big storyteller, lived with us. She would get us to wash dishes or weed her garden by promising to tell a story," Staples recounts. "The Grimm Brothers tales scared us witless!" She says she loves the feeling she still gets when she hears a good storyteller. Her vision seems to narrow so that all she can see is the story, and nothing intrudes on the image she creates as she listens. She says, "I just *love* stories more than anything."

The early comforts of rural life and storytelling offered Staples positive ways to handle her own feeling of being an anomaly in her family. She says that she always felt different from her parents and siblings, different in beliefs, different in ways

anomaly different from the standard

that she figured and sorted out how the world works. Although she knew her parents were decent, thoughtful, and kind people, she wrestled with the big questions of religion and politics on her own because she disagreed with their points of view. After being sent away from the dinner table a number of times for challenging an opinion of her parents or grandparents, she learned that, to keep the peace, she had to figure out things for herself. Staples' Aunt Edith, her grandmother's sister and the first professional woman in the family, served as a touchstone for the family's thinking about Suzanne. She can still hear her mother saying, "Well, you're just like your Aunt Edith." And Staples would wonder if she meant, "You're just impossible and we don't understand you!"

touchstone standard by which something's qualities are tested

Even her sister, just one year younger, seemed so different from Suzanne. Although they shared a room, they did not hang out together. Suzanne was always outdoors, fishing and walking, while her sister stayed in doors, enjoying fingernail polish and dolls. Nevertheless, her sister still calls Suzanne "Miss Practically Perfect" because she didn't ever want to be in trouble. She wanted to be left alone, choosing to spend time by herself in the woods and by the lake.

Throughout school, Staples had one close friend, but they were not perceived as being in the mainstream or popular. She loved classical music and played the trombone until she got embarrassed carrying it around and turned fully to singing in an a capella choir and the district, regional, and state choruses. She still loves music and attends the symphony today.

a cappella without instrumental accompaniment

Leaving Home

When she turned eighteen, Suzanne Fisher Staples met and fell in love with Wayne, a college graduate about to begin his own career. Her father did not encourage the romantic involvement. Heartbroken, Suzanne went off, as planned, to Cedar Crest College in Allentown, Pennsylvania, perceiving that her parents felt that this was one last chance to "civilize" her. She says that she would compare anybody else she was ever interested in to Wayne and her feelings for him. For the rest of her adult life, she believed that this kind of love only happens once. Though each married and divorced another in the intervening thirty years, Suzanne and Wayne finally found each other and continue to appreciate their blessings.

Hinduism is the dominant religion of India, also practiced in parts of Pakistan, Bangladesh, Sri Lanka, and Nepal. Hinduism incorporates all forms of belief and worship, including rituals, reincarnation, and karma—the idea that previous acts determine in what form a person will be reborn.

retrospect view of past events

Majoring in literature and minoring in politics, Staples remembers studying Hinduism and thinking she wanted to learn more about it some day. Her fourth book for young adults, *Shiva's Fire* (1999), explores Hinduism. Although her father encouraged her to become a teacher as a way to become gainfully employed after graduation, Staples told him she wanted to become a writer. A shy person at the time, she was terrified of the idea of getting up in front of people and speaking, though she thinks in retrospect that she might have enjoyed a teaching career. Nevertheless, her father told her then that he did not believe that anyone made a living writing. She likes to tell young people now that it is important to have dreams and to work in the direction of something you want to do. "Although you may not go exactly where you want to go, you'll be closer to where you want to be than if you just knuckle under and do the practical thing," and, she adds laughingly, "I'm sure parents and teachers hate it when I say this!"

An International Career

After graduation, still determined to become a writer, Staples took a job writing economic and political analyses for multinational corporations. Then she accepted an opportunity to work in Hong Kong, where she spent the next six years, chiefly as a United Press International (UPI) journalist. Staples subsequently took over the position of bureau chief in South Asia, based in New Delhi, India. She loved to travel on her breaks from news assignments. She visited the old princely palaces of India and traveled to see traditional, classical dance performances that might go on into the early hours of the morning.

Staples says that some of her most extraordinary stories of that period come out of covering the war in Afghanistan (1979–1989) between the USSR and Afghanistan. "So many children were involved. Sirens would come on, searchlights played over the city buildings, wild dogs started howling and you could hear shouting and machine-gunfire." Memories of a gentle and beautiful people so repressed politically still trouble her.

Upon her return to the United States, where she wrote for the *Washington Post,* Staples contemplated writing fiction but found no time: "Writing news is all-consuming; you can work twenty-four hours a day and not do everything that there is to do." Eager to return to Asia, Staples accepted a "joint package" position with her first husband to work with U.S. Aid for International Development (USAID) in Pakistan. Her contract to conduct a study on women in rural Pakistan offered her language training in Urdu, the national language. She learned that although USAID had a history of building schools for villagers, few teachers wanted to live in isolated places such as the Cholistan Desert. So she participated in a literacy project that "was just wonderful, wonderful, where they took women from villages and trained them to train the other women in their village to read."

Staples feels lucky to have traveled in such an adventurous way. The first time she went to Cholistan, it was the first time anybody she worked with there had seen a westerner. On her early trips out to the desert, she had to go with a desert ranger who felt that, because she was a westerner, she ought to travel by Jeep rather than by camel. However, with no roads in the desert, the Jeeps would get stuck, so they would often arrive twelve hours or more later than planned. Nevertheless, the entire village would be there to welcome Staples and her party with touching speeches.

Staples, always the journalist, kept detailed notebooks and journals throughout her Pakistani assignment. *Shabanu: Daughter of the Wind* comes from stories told to her during her stay there. "Everything in *Shabanu* is a true story that was told to me. I didn't make any of it up." After her Pakistani assignment and armed with a lifetime of journals and notebooks, Staples returned to the United States, moving first to the Chesapeake Bay area (Virginia), next to Florida, and then to Tennessee, where she writes fiction for young adults.

The war in **Afghanistan** began in 1978 with a hostile takeover of the government. The new government received aid from the Soviet Union. When fighting broke out between the government and resistance fighters, the Soviet Union invaded with thousands of troops. Although the Soviet Union withdrew in 1989, the fighting continued for many years.

Key Issues and Themes in Staples' Fiction

Finding Out You're Different from Your Family

With no brothers in her family, Staples' character, Shabanu, enjoys the full attention and teachings of her father. She learns to listen to the wind, to make camp, and to find water in the Cholistan Desert. Shabanu's father takes pride in her training of Gulaband, her pet dancing camel. But, although he's promised he never will, Shabanu's father sells her beloved Gulaband for an irresistible offer at the annual market. Heartbroken, Shabanu feels betrayed by her own father. Later, when he

Muslim word commonly used to describe people who follow the teachings of Muhammad

protagonist the main character of a literary work

implicate to involve by some incriminating connection

ostracize to exclude someone by common agreement

unencumbered free from burdens

negotiates an ancient contract of marriage for her, Shabanu cannot appreciate her father's sense of honor but feels only another betrayal. As she gains understanding of their world and culture, Shabanu begins to comprehend that she does not share all the values and thinking of her parents. A thoughtful but high-spirited young woman, she wrestles with her own notions of independence and justice, caught in the ancient and proud traditions of her nomadic Muslim tribe.

Trapped, too, is Buck Smith, the protagonist of *Dangerous Skies* whose beliefs about racial justice do not mirror those of his family and neighbors. For nearly three centuries, since the early 1700s, whites and blacks have worked the land and fished the waters of the Chesapeake Bay, Virginia, in an unequal partnership. Striving to find justice for his life-long friend, Tunes, who is implicated in a murder, thirteen-year-old Buck is perceived as only a child when he challenges ideas the community believes are right. Because he "bucks" a system rarely questioned by others, he works alone for racial justice, enjoying no support from his kind but silent family.

Staples feels that gaining the insight that your parents are not perfect reveals itself in different ways to young people. At the same time, all of her protagonists share a kind of loneliness when they question traditions and customs within their cultures. In *Haveli* Shabanu remains ostracized from all of her husband's other wives. Staples reveals that Pravati, the main character in *Shiva's Fire,* "has supernatural powers that make people frightened of her and so she doesn't really have any friends." Staples, too, remembers feeling alone in her ideas yet wanting to be heard as she sorted out the twin attractions of duty and choice.

Duty and Choice

No matter what the cultural strictures, Staples believes that individuals have some capacity for personal choices. What is interesting for Staples is to learn how cultures differ in what they perceive as important. For example, Staples reflects that "to Hindus, duty is a much more important concept than it is to us. And yet it's an issue that we face. A lot of times we can do what want to do or we can do what our duty is. And growing up is learning about these choices." Staples made a choice by following her father's direction to go on to college unencumbered by serious romance. Shabanu honors her father's contract to marry Rahim, the elderly landowner, but figures out ways to protect her heart and stimulate her mind. Buck, because of his age and the law, loses his political battles but continues to grow in moral courage and appreciation for life. And in *Shiva's Fire,* Pravati wrestles with the complication of knowing that "her destiny is to become a dancer" even as she is falling in love with the son of the maharajah. Each of these life stories, though set in a particular culture, reflects surprisingly universal issues. However, can a writer from another culture have enough authentic knowledge and understanding, or will he or she always be an outsider?

maharaja a Hindu prince

Writing from Experience

A few readers and critics are troubled because Staples is not a Muslim, nor is she from Pakistan, much less a member of the nomadic tribe in the Cholistan Desert, which she portrays in *Shabanu: Daughter of the Wind* and *Haveli.* She is not from India, yet she writes about Hindi customs and beliefs in *Shiva's Fire.* "I think that when writing about other cultures you have to do an enormous amount of research because you have to get it right," Staples suggests. Thirteen scholars and others who know the Cholistan Desert geographic area and culture read the manuscript for *Shabanu* for accuracy. As a former journalist, Staples is tuned in to the need for accurate details for making a story sound true, possible, and plausible. She knows that without those details she cannot make a story come alive for readers. Her boxes and boxes of notebooks remind her of the sights, smells, tastes, sounds, and feelings she notes throughout her travels and interviews. She has a collection of city maps from around the world for street names and intersections; she has a knowledge of several languages and an appreciation for customs, traditions, and ceremonies celebrated throughout the areas where she lived and of which she writes. Finally, she understands that writing about characters in distinctive and recognizable cultures and religions creates emotionally charged issues because readers fear being represented by an author who is not a member of their group. Sensitive to the issues of proprietorship because she lived and worked overseas for so many years, reading news stories portraying the United States, Staples is keenly aware of being seen as an outsider when writing about other cultures. But for Staples, as she notes in the fall 1997 issue of *Bookbird,* "story is

plausible appearing worthy of belief

proprietorship the exclusive rights to something

very particular. It speaks only for the author and the characters the author creates. Its power lies in its focus on the human heart, illumination and connection. It is not meant to represent or instruct about or speak for any group of people."

In her Tennessee home in the woods, curled up against her dozens of embroidered pillows and bolsters from Afghanistan, India, and Pakistan, Suzanne Fisher Staples continues to listen for good stories that come from experience and her heart. Her writing cultivates the memories of growing up in a loving family while discovering the complex outside world. The recollections seem to echo the universal themes of many young adults' coming of age, no matter their culture or setting.

cultivate to foster the growth of something

Selected Biography

WORKS BY SUZANNE FISHER STAPLES

Novels for Young Adults

Shabanu: Daughter of the Wind (1989)

Haveli (1993)

Dangerous Skies (1996)

Shiva's Fire (1999)

Nonfiction

"Writing About the Islamic World: An American Author's Thoughts on Authenticity." *Bookbird,* fall 1997, pp. 17–20.

"What Johnny Can't Read: Censorship in American Libraries 1996." *ALAN Review,* winter 1996.

WORKS ABOUT SUZANNE FISHER STAPLES

How to Write to the Author

Suzanne Fisher Staples
c/o Farrar, Straus & Giroux
19 Union Square West
New York, NY 10003

Greever, E., and P. Austin. "Suzanne Fisher Staples: From Journalist to Novelist." *Teaching and Learning Literature,* November/December 1997, pp. 43–55.

Sawyer, W., and J. Sawyer. "A Discussion with Suzanne Fisher Staples: The Author as Writer and Cultural Observer." *New Advocate,* summer 1993, pp. 159–169.

R. L. Stine

(1943–)

by Richard F. Abrahamson

In 1978, Robert Lawrence Stine arrived at a bookstore to sign copies of his first book for young people—*How to Be Funny*. Because it was a humorous book, he decided to wear bunny ears on his head as he sat at the autograph table. All afternoon young people and adults alike avoided the grown man sporting the bunny ears. Stine sold only one book at that first signing.

Fast-forward to 1995, when the famous author of the Fear Street books and the Goosebumps series showed up at a book signing in a mall near Washington, D.C. While several hundred fans were expected, no one was prepared for more than five thousand. Stine describes the scene in his 1997 autobiography, *It Came from Ohio! My Life as a Writer.* "They had to turn off all the escalators so that no one would get crushed. Security guards and local police officers had to be called in. I had to climb up on a bench and shout through a megaphone: Thank you for coming! But I cannot meet you all today. Please go home!" (pp. 124–125).

autobiography the story of one's own life

Without question, R. L. Stine has come a long way from that first book signing fiasco to becoming one of America's all-time best-selling authors.

An Attic and a Typewriter: The Early Years

Robert Lawrence Stine was born on 8 October 1943 to Lewis and Anne Stine in Columbus, Ohio, and grew up with his sister Pam and his brother Bill in the suburb of Bexley. One of Stine's earliest recollections is that he and his younger brother, Bill, were forbidden to enter the third floor attic. In *Ohio* Stine says, "That attic from my childhood is also one of the reasons why I write Goosebumps and Fear Street today. I used to lie in my bed at night and stare at the ceiling. *What terrible thing is up there in the attic?*" (p. 2).

When he wasn't scaring himself with his active imagination, he was scaring himself listening to spooky radio shows and terrifying his brother by making up ghost stories at bedtime. He'd tell tales of monsters chasing a boy who just happened to resemble his brother. Just as the monster was about to grab the boy, Stine would shut off the light, leaving his brother begging for the story's end. A grown-up Stine says in *Ohio,* "Today in my scary books, I do the same trick at the end of every chapter. I try to leave my readers in the same state of shock and suspense that I left my brother in, all those years ago" (p. 10). Stine attributes his interest in scary things to the fact that he was a fearful child who saw the real world as scary and preferred sitting in his room writing.

One day he was adventurous enough, however, to forget his mother's admonition, and he climbed the steps to the attic. Disappointment greeted young Bob because all he found at first were some old clothes. But way in a corner was a dust-covered black case. He opened it to find a typewriter, a treasure for this budding writer. Stine learned to type with one finger and to this day cranks out each of his more than 250 books with his one-finger typing technique. At age nine, Bob was not ready to write novels, but he was ready to write the kinds of things he enjoyed reading: magazines and comics. *Mad Magazine, Tales from the Crypt,* and *Vault of Horror* were some of his favorites. The first magazine he wrote was *The All New Bob Stine Giggle Book,* a ten-page magazine in a

admonition mild word of caution

3-by-4-inch format. Other little magazines followed. "I was a weird kid," he writes in *Ohio.* "I spent so many hours—such a large part of my childhood—alone in my room, typing . . . typing . . . typing . . . *just as I do today!*" (p. 26).

Writing, for Stine, became his way of being accepted. Growing up, he was the kid no one picked to play sports. In the rich suburb of Bexley, he felt out of place. "I always seemed to be standing away from the crowd, watching everyone. I became an *observer,* which is part of what a writer does" (*Ohio,* p. 43). In his last year in high school, Stine wrote the senior skit. The audience roared with laughter. They were laughing at his words. For a while, at least, he was accepted by his peers.

After high school graduation, Stine moved on to Ohio State University with a goal of writing for the campus humor magazine, the *Sundial.* He served as editor for three years and dubbed himself Jovial Bob. Jovial Bob kept the students at Ohio State laughing, and Stine made some of his best friends during those years. But college ends, and Jovial Bob needed a job.

Teaching, the Beatles, and *Bananas:* Stine's Jobs

"Scarier than the scariest walk down Fear Street!" is how R. L. Stine describes his first job out of college as a substitute teacher (*Ohio,* p. 64). After a few months, he was given his own class, and he made a deal with the students. If they behaved Monday through Thursday, Friday would be Free Reading Day: they could bring in anything they wanted to read, even comic books. One Friday the principal arrived in Stine's classroom to find the teacher catching up on the latest edition of *Spider Man.* The principal let Stine stay until the end of the school year; while Stine maintains it was the toughest job he ever had, he says in *Ohio,* "Teaching gave me time to watch kids in action. I was able to listen to what they said and the way they said it. I think my characters' conversations in Fear Street and Goosebumps are more true to life because of my real-life year in the classroom" (p. 66). Teaching also gave him some of the money he needed to leave Ohio and rent an apartment in his dream city of New York.

The year 1966 found Stine in his New York apartment, trying to find a job, pay the bills, and eat. He lasted one day

Glen Campbell
(1936–) is an American musician. His first hit single was "Rhinestone Cowboy" in the mid-1970s. The **Beatles,** a 1960s British band, were the most popular rock group in history. The **Rolling Stones** are a British rock group who first emerged in the 1960s and are still popular today. The **Jacksons** are an American rhythm and blues group. They were called the Jackson 5 until 1976.

bogus fake

prolific marked by producing many works

working for a magazine called *Institutional Investor.* He quickly found another writing job working for an editor of six teen fan magazines. Stine's job was to write interviews with popular music stars of the day, such as Glen Campbell, the Beatles, the Rolling Stones, and the Jacksons. He was pretty excited about the prospect until he realized that he would never meet any of these singers. His job as a writer was to make up the entire interview. During his month of employment, Stine estimates that he wrote more than one hundred bogus interviews. When those magazines went out of business, he found himself writing articles about bottle caps and soda for *Soft Drink Industry* magazine. The job might not have been inspiring, but during this time he met his future wife, Jane Waldhorn.

In 1968, Stine's job changed, and so did his life, when he became a staff writer for *Junior Scholastic* magazine. He and Jane both landed jobs at Scholastic, Inc., where Stine stayed for sixteen years. The hectic pace of putting out a weekly magazine appealed to him. People often cannot imagine how Stine writes so fast. "They can't believe I write two books a month," Stine states in *Ohio.* "Magazine writing was the perfect training for me. I learned to write fast—and move on to the next piece. I've always been able to write quickly, and it usually comes out the way I want it on the first try" (p. 84).

When Scholastic asked Stine to start a humor magazine for teens, he couldn't refuse. All those years creating humor magazines on the old typewriter as a kid and his time as editor of the *Sundial* at Ohio State all came together to make Jovial Bob Stine's dream come true—in the form of *Bananas.*

One day while working on *Bananas,* Stine received a call from a children's book editor. She liked *Bananas* and told him she thought he could write funny books for children. His first children's book was *How to Be Funny.* It was a kind of guidebook on how to tell jokes and make bumbling entrances into classrooms. Its publication led to that infamous bunny-ear book signing, where only one book was sold. Still, Stine's life was changing.

Jane and Bob's son, Matt, was born on 7 June 1980. Several years later, *Bananas* magazine went out of business, so Stine stayed home and became a full-time writer of books for children and young adults. As always, Stine was prolific in his output, writing bubblegum cards and Indiana Jones and James Bond "Find-Your-Fate" books that featured multiple endings that readers could choose from. G.I. Joe novels and Mighty Mouse coloring books all came from the one-finger typist.

The Horror Luncheon that Led to Fear Street

One afternoon, I had lunch with Jean Feiwel. Jean is my friend and the associate publisher at Scholastic. Near the end of the lunch, she leaned across the table and asked, "Did you ever think of writing a YA horror novel?"

"Huh? A *what?*" I replied.

"A horror novel for teenagers," she repeated.

"Well . . . I've always *liked* horror," I told her. "But I never thought of writing it."

"Well, why don't you give it a try?" she suggested. "Go home and write a novel called *Blind Date,*" (*Ohio*, p. 107)

In five months *Blind Date* (1986) was outlined, written, and revised. This story about a boy who gets mysterious calls from a girl who he later finds out has been dead for three years was a best-seller right away. Then came *Twisted* (1987) and The *Baby-Sitter* (1989). When all three made the best-seller category, Bob's wife, Jane, suggested he write a series of scary books. By this time Jane had her own publishing company called Parachute Press, so husband and wife began work on the series project. A search for the series title began because a book's title is everything to Stine. "For as long as I have written books, I always start the same way—with a title. If I know the title of the story, coming up with the story itself isn't hard for me" (*Ohio*, p. 110). Suddenly the name Fear Street came to him. When he suggested the title to Jane, she said, "Fear Street, where your worst nightmares live" (*Ohio*, p. 112). The title was set.

The Fear Street books are an important departure from other series books. Most series books focus on one set of characters who remain the same from book to book, such as Nancy Drew or the Hardy Boys. Stine's new direction involved

Indiana Jones is a fictional archaeologist and professor who has many adventures. Harrison Ford played Indiana Jones in three movies. Secret agent **James Bond** is a character in a series of books written by Ian Fleming and in nearly 20 movies. Based on the American infantryman and on a 1945 movie, the **G. I. Joe** character became the first action figure in 1964. **Mighty Mouse** was the star of the first Saturday morning cartoon, which began in 1955.

The **Nancy Drew** and **Hardy Boys** series were created by Edward Stratemeyer. There is an article about him in volume 3.

using different characters in each book, but what remains constant is the town where all the action takes place. When Jane took the idea to Pocket Book publishers, they bought three Fear Street books and shortly after three more. Starting with *The New Girl* in 1989, in no time Fear Street was the most popular young adult book series in the United States, and R. L. Stine was writing a new Fear Street novel every month.

The Fear Street Formula

One of the reasons readers love series books such as the Fear Street novels is that they know what they are getting. While they certainly don't know what horrible things will happen in each book, they do expect some common elements. In his book *What's So Scary About R. L. Stine?* (1998), librarian and critic Patrick Jones lays out the Fear Street pattern.

red herring something that distracts attention from the main issue

paranoia excessive suspiciousness and distrust of others

> Although Stine would certainly add (and subtract) some elements, all the building blocks are in the first Fear Street. The evil of Fear Street, the cliff-hanger chapter endings, the constant threats and pranks, the mix of fake scares with real ones, the red herrings, the twisting relationships between teenagers, the groups of teens who share a job or a certain setting, cars and phones as major props, a sense of paranoia and danger, obsessive thoughts and actions, quick dramatic action told in short one-sentence paragraphs, simple vocabulary, lots of sentence fragments, lots of teen dialogue that sounds authentic without being laced with slang, lots of recognizable settings like pizza places, some violence but more "gross outs" than "gore outs," and finally the trick ending involving a confused identity to explain what seems unexplainable. Every Fear Street book is different—yet they are all the same because they work from this formula. (Pp. 86–87)

Whether you examine the first Fear Street book, *The New Girl,* or Stine's latest installment in the new Fear Street series, *Seniors,* you'll see Stine playing with the elements Jones has listed.

Fear Street Gives Readers Goosebumps

Seeing the success of each succeeding Fear Street title, Jane Stine's business partner at Parachute Press called Stine in for a meeting. "Maybe younger kids would like to be scared too," Joan suggested. "Maybe you could write a series of scary books that are also funny. You know. Plenty of thrills and chills, without the gore and the blood." (*Ohio,* p. 114) Again the search for a series title began. While Stine was paging through *TV Guide,* he saw an ad announcing a week of scary movies on one of the channels: "GOOSEBUMPS Week on Channel 11!" Today the Goosebumps books have become "the best-selling book series of all time" (*Ohio,* p. 116). The Goosebumps phenomenon has led to a television show, videos, T-shirts, and even an attraction at Walt Disney World. It also means Stine writes at least two books per month (one Fear Street and one Goosebumps) and receives more than two thousand letters a week.

Goosebumps, the television show, premiered in 1995 on the Fox network.

Fear Street Critics: A Horror Story

As R. L. Stine busily works six days a week churning out at least fifteen pages a day—two novels a month—some parents, teachers, librarians, and book critics have been busily declaring war on Stine's popular books. Teen readers show their support by buying millions of Stine novels, but some adults worry about the teens' choice of reading. In Patrick Jones's book, young adult literature critic Patty Campbell says of Stine, "I think he is extremely destructive. He preys on the absolute worst instincts of the human soul. He's also an extremely bad writer. If any of his books were turned in as a 5th grade essay, he would get a D minus."

Diana West is even stronger in her criticism. In an article reprinted in the fall 1995 issue of *American Educator,* West writes that after reading what she calls shock fiction books,

pornographic using a sensationalist depiction of events in order to gain an intense emotional reaction

There is an article about Edgar Allan Poe in volume 3.

> I could not help but perceive an unmistakably porno-graphic pattern of means and ends. As graphic, hor-rific, and exciting as Edgar Allan Poe's stories may be, for example, the act of reading them requires a mental engagement with language, with character, with the author's interpretation of events that trans-forms the action and elevates it above the cheap

rap sheet a list of criminal offenses a person has been charged with, found in official police records

Here, **deathless prose** refers to immortal (deathless) writing without regular rhythm (prose). West is implying that Stine's writing is ordinary, that it will never last, and that Stine's books have little chance of ever being considered classics like Poe's.

perennial always existing

appalling provoking horror or disgust

thrills of a rap sheet. But in shock fiction, a raw catalogue of horrors and grotesqueries is used—not interpreted, not stylized, not in any way transformed by a writer for good or bad—to charge the nerve endings of young readers. In less than deathless (indeed, less than grammatical) prose, shock writers deliver fix after blunt fix to shock (in other words, satisfy) their audience.

West, and other critics like her, believe that Stine's books are a bad influence on teenagers' morals and developing literary tastes. Other adults praise Stine for writing books teens will read. They argue that at least teens are reading something, becoming better readers, and spending less time watching television or playing video games. Stine, himself, is especially pleased at the success he has had motivating both girls and boys to read. In an interview with *Publishers Weekly* writer Kit Alderdice, Stine says, "But the really amazing thing is that the series—Goosebumps and Fear Street—are the first ones ever to have equal numbers of girls and boys reading them. We got boys to read. That's the difference."

As to the perennial appeal of horror, Stine sees nothing changing in the new millennium. In his 1998 *Newsweek* magazine article, "Lurking in the Dark," he tells us that we will always be afraid of the dark.

When I was the age of the kids who now read my books, I discovered the EC Horror comics, titles such as "Tales from the Crypt" and "The Vault of Horror." They featured gruesome stories and art: lots of blood and gore, decapitations, hideous ghouls, vampires, swamp creatures, butcher-shop customers shoved through meat grinders to make hamburger. I loved them because they were appalling—frightening and funny at the same time.

My mother said the comics were "trash."

Nearly fifty years later, these stories are still popular.

Why do kids like scary stories so much? Like fictional monsters, many kids sometimes feel like outsiders: different, ugly, out of control, frightened by their angry feelings. Don't we all have times when we feel like ranting and raging and stepping on Tokyo or Washington, D.C.?

Stephen King once wrote, "We make up horrors to help us cope with the real ones." We also make up monsters because we *are* them. (P. 66)

There is an article about Stephen King earlier in this volume.

Selected Bibliography

If you like the works of R. L. Stine, you might also like the works of Christopher Pike.

WORKS BY R. L. STINE

Stine has written more than 250 books. Space limitations do not allow for a listing of all of them. What follows is a list of books and articles mentioned in this essay as well as a list of the first books in Stine's new Fear Street series titled Seniors.

Books for Young Adults

How to Be Funny (written as Jovial Bob Stine) (1978)

Blind Date (1986)

Twisted (1987)

The Baby-Sitter (1989)

The New Girl (1989)

Fear Street Seniors series

Let's Party! (1998; Seniors #1)

In Too Deep (1998; Seniors #2)

The Thirst (1998; Seniors #3)

No Answer (1998; Seniors #4)

Last Chance (1998; Seniors #5)

The Gift (1998; Seniors #6)

Fight, Team, Fight! (1999; Seniors #7)

Autobiography

It Came from Ohio: My Life as a Writer, as told to Joe Arthur (1997)

Article

"Lurking in the Dark." *Newsweek,* 2 November 1998, p. 66.

How to Write to the Author

R. L. Stine
c/o Scholastic, Inc.
555 Broadway
New York, NY 10012-3999

You can also visit the Fear Street website at *www.fearstreet.com*

WORKS ABOUT R. L. STINE

Alderdice, Kit. "R. L. Stine: 90 Million Spooky Adventures." *Publishers Weekly,* 17 July 1995, p. 208.

Jones, Patrick. *What's So Scary About R. L. Stine?* Lanham, Md.: Scarecrow Press, 1998.

West, Diana. "The Horror of R. L. Stine." *American Educator,* fall 1995, p. 40.

Shelley Stoehr

(1969–)

by David Gill

A teenage girl has a razor blade and she's in pain, so she cuts herself to make everything better. Another girl runs from her genius reputation and ends up dancing nude in sleazy clubs. A third teenager gets in trouble with the Mafia, and still another finds herself falling in love with her boyfriend's sister. These girls are all lost souls, and they lead scary lives.

Shelly Stoehr writes scary stories. These aren't books about homicidal maniacs in masks or supernatural creatures running amok in the night. Reality is Stoehr's forte, and she writes about it in a straightforward, grimly honest way. Part of a new generation of authors for young adults that includes such in-your-face writers as Rob Thomas and Francesca Lia Block, she writes about teenagers who face the problems of drugs, self-mutilation ("cutting"), dysfunctional adults, and prostitution with the same casual attitude that youths in the 1970s talked about what television show to watch.

What makes Stoehr and her peer writers different is that they are not sensationalizing teenagers' problems. Instead,

Quotations from Shelley Stoehr that are not attributed to a published source are from personal interviews conducted by the author of this article on 8 January 1999 and 19 January 1999 and are published here by permission of Shelley Stoehr.

forte strength; what one is good at

There is an article about Rob Thomas later in this volume. There is an article about Francesca Lia Block in volume 1.

dysfunctional characterized by impaired or abnormal functioning

they look at contemporary adolescents with a journalist's eye, reporting what they see. Shelley Stoehr, author of some of the most controversial novels of the 1990s, has the ability to see many things, very few of them pretty.

Influences and Life as a Writer

Stoehr wasn't far removed from adolescence when her first novel appeared in 1991. Born on 31 January 1969 in the Pennsylvania town of Sellersville, she is the daughter of parents who made sure there were plenty of books in the house. Later the family moved to Long Island, New York.

literate educated; cultured

Surrounded by books and literate people, Stoehr knew at an early age that she wanted to be an artist of some kind, whether it was a writer or a painter. Her grandmother often took young Shelley to art classes to foster her talent. In high school she won art awards such as the Congressional Art Competition. For awhile, Stoehr says in one of the interviews she has given over the past few years, she thought of combining her love of words and of painting. Before she went to Connecticut College, however, she realized that she "could represent something very well on paper, but . . . never really could 'create' it. . . . Once [she] went to college and started meeting people who represented themselves with paint and paper," she realized her artistic ability lay in other areas.

At first she majored in English in college, expecting to devote her energy to writing, which came honestly to her. Her father wrote for pleasure, and her mother was a teacher. Both of

nurture to further the development of something or someone

them nurtured their daughter's writing ability. They also, Stoehr says, were "very good critics." They edited her earliest stories, making suggestions for revisions. Although it wasn't always easy to accept their critiques, she would revise with their suggestions in mind. At some point in college, however, Stoehr found that dance was also an avenue of expression for her. She had been interested in dance since childhood. When she rediscovered it as an adult, she "just threw [herself] at dance and started majoring in it and . . . got involved with choreography."

This love for dance is nowhere more apparent than in her novel *Weird on the Outside* (1995), the story of a teenage runaway who dances in New York City strip clubs. Her description of the dancing was so realistic that many readers (and some critics) wondered if she had ever been a stripper (she hadn't).

After graduating from college, she lived for awhile in New York and performed with a dance troupe. Later she trained as a massage therapist and moved to San Francisco.

All the while, she was still writing, a passion that began as early as seventh grade, when she started sending out stories to the prestigious *New Yorker* magazine. Her work was rejected, but her motto, she says, was "aim for the top, and work your way down." She was mature enough to listen to the comments on the rejection slips: "They always sent things back"; she admits, "I never liked criticism, but I would always take it, once I calmed down and stopped being self-righteous." Her maturity and her willingness to revise material led to her first published novel, *Crosses* (1991).

Like many writers, Stoehr is influenced by writers whose work has "jumped out and grabbed" her. For themes, she reads the work of Mona Simpson, Tama Janowitz, Judy Blume, and Robert Cormier. To look at style, she studies the above writers and others such as Roger Zelazny and Francesca Lia Block. Not all of her influences are writers for young adults because Stoehr believes that "great writing surpasses genre distinctions."

Not Your Mother's Young Adult Fiction: Stoehr's Controversial Novels

Crosses

Stoehr's *Crosses* started out as an assignment for a college creative writing class. Surrounded by older students and a professor initially unimpressed with her work, she struggled to keep pace. That changed when she wrote the story that would later become *Crosses*. Her professor liked it, so she expanded it into a novel. After revisions suggested by her professor, she sent it off to Delacorte's First Young Adult Novel contest. Delacorte rejected the novel, explaining that it lacked an ending. Stoehr, more determined than ever, rewrote the ending and sent it out again. To her surprise, it was accepted and then named an honor book for the eighth Annual Delacorte Press Prize for a first young adult novel. She was a published writer before graduating from college.

Critics and readers didn't know what to think of *Crosses*. Here was the story of Nancy Byer, a high school freshman and self-proclaimed "good girl," who intentionally cuts herself.

prestigious honored or well-known

theme central message about life in a literary work

Mona Simpson is an American novelist. Her novel Anywhere But Here was made into a movie starring Susan Sarandon in 1999.
Tama Janowitz is also a novelist. Her novels include *By the Shores of Gitchee Gumee* (1996) and *Slaves of New York* (1986).
Roger Zelazny is an American science fiction writer.

There are articles about Judy Blume and Robert Cormier in volume 1.

genre a particular style or form of writing

binge drinking unrestrained and often excessive drinking

This act of self-mutilation, one she learned from best friend Katie Meenan, is meant to give her power. But Nancy can't stop cutting herself. She starts using drugs and binge drinking, and she can't stop doing that either.

Stoehr got the idea for *Crosses* from a research study about victims of self-inflicted injuries. As a teenager herself, she had known others who had performed these rituals, so she thought it would make an intriguing story for young adults. No one, as far as she knew, had ever written about it. *Crosses* became an overnight sensation. Stoehr had accomplished a great feat. She had written about a pertinent issue in the lives of teenagers, and she had done it using brilliant prose characterized by descriptions so vivid that many readers wondered if Stoehr herself was carving up her own skin (she wasn't).

pertinent clearly relevant

prose writing without regular rhythm; ordinary writing

Sometimes critical attention has its drawbacks, however. If some readers admired Stoehr for her frank treatment of a real problem in society, others criticized her for the characters' use of profanity and casual attitudes about sex and drugs. This in some ways echoes the criticism often heaped on writers of young adult fiction who try to portray today's youth realistically. Robert Cormier, for example, was routinely condemned for the "dark" ending of his story *The Chocolate War* (1974). Stoehr's *Crosses* likewise ends darkly. Lost in their depravity and drug abuse, Nancy and Katie see only one way out—to commit suicide. Tragically, Katie succeeds. There is no fairy tale ending; there are no heroes, no bad guys in black hats. There are only victims.

depravity corruption

Stoehr, in an article in the winter 1997 issue of the *ALAN Review*, responds to critics' complaints about the language in her books by saying: "Yes, my characters use foul language, often to excess. . . . Many authors don't use foul language and still create beautiful, meaningful young adult novels. It happens not to be the way I write, and more importantly, it's not the way my characters talk" (p. 4).

Weird on the Outside

niche place or position best suited to a person

For Stoehr, her subject matter is a double-edged sword. Her desire to show the stark reality of some adolescents' lives has carved a niche for her work in the young adult world. Because of this commitment, however, her sales are limited. Librarians and teachers are hesitant to put her work on the shelves for fear of criticism and censorship. Her second novel, *Weird on the Outside,* was every bit as controversial as her first.

It is the story of Tracey Bascombe, the sassy genius child of an MIT professor and a working-class manicurist (now divorced, of course). Tracey has her mother's looks, her father's intelligence, and a rebellious attitude that causes her to run away to New York. At first she tries to play it straight, but the need for food, shelter, and money forces her to become a dancer in a seedy strip club. She sinks fast, drinking too much and abusing drugs. It all comes to a frightening end when a strip club customer follows Tracey home and savagely attacks her.

Weird on the Outside changed the definition of young adult fiction. Tracey is not a particularly nice person, and her desire to gain independence from her controlling father leads her down a dangerous path. However, even after being beaten so badly that she has to return home, she does not regret her decisions. In fact, she is convinced that being a stripper has made her a woman. Some readers want characters to feel regret about their behavior, but Tracey doesn't feel bad at all. This lack of remorse, even more than the language and graphic descriptions, may be the most controversial part of the novel.

Wannabe

Stoehr's next novel, *Wannabe* (1997), is the story of Catherine (Cat) Tavarelli, a wanna-be writer whose brother, Mickey, is a wannabe gangster. They live in New York's Little Italy, where Mickey sells drugs for the Mafia. At first Cat is angry about Mickey's dealing, but soon she begins abusing cocaine and other drugs. The novel is more than a story about two teenagers getting in over their heads with gangsters. It is also about a brother and a sister and the bond that keeps them together. They watch each other, protect each other, and when their addictions begin to destroy them, Cat and Mickey are able to clean up their lives.

Like Stoehr's other novels, *Wannabe* shocked some critics when it was published, and reviews were mixed. Here were casual drug use, cursing, and seemingly no consequence for characters' actions. Unlike *Crosses* and *Weird on the Outside,* it did not seem to have the same evocative subject matter. No one else had written a novel about self-mutilation or about stripping as a rite of passage, but the Mafia was a fairly common

censorship the suppression of something that one finds objectionable

seedy poor; shabby

evocative tending to bring an emotional response

rite of passage a ceremonial act or procedure associated with a crisis or change in status of a person (such as marriage, death, or illness)

convoluted intricate; involved

narration telling of a story

Audrey Hepburn (1929–1993) was a Belgian-born actress who won an Academy Award for her role in *Roman Holiday* (1953).

credible believable

subject. One reviewer in *Kirkus Reviews* wrote that Mickey and Cat "aren't likable, even when they are believable." Others complained about the convoluted plot, which tends to wander at times. They also said that the resolution happens too quickly to be believable.

Despite the criticism, *Wannabe* shows that Stoehr's writing ability had grown. Her vivid descriptions of Little Italy are remarkable. Her choice of narrative technique—alternating narration seamlessly between Cat and Mickey—gives the novel an unusual dual perspective that allows the reader to enjoy the thoughts of both Cat and Mickey almost simultaneously.

Tomorrow Wendy: A Love Story

Stoehr's next novel quickly re-established her reputation as an excellent storyteller, while reconfirming her willingness to tackle subjects considered taboo. In *Tomorrow Wendy: A Love Story* (1998), Cary is a student at Long Island's Babylon High School. Her boyfriend is Danny, a good-looking kid who can provide all sorts of extracurricular entertainment. The relationship sours when Cary becomes obsessed with Danny's sister, Wendy. Cary begins stealing things from Wendy's room and having sexual thoughts about her. She attempts to mask her feelings by abusing alcohol and dancing to the point of exhaustion at teenage clubs, but it doesn't work. After trying to seduce Wendy, Cary admits her feelings to Danny, who dumps her. The only person who understands is Rad, Cary's imaginary friend.

Tomorrow Wendy: A Love Story is a coarse, unromantic look at teen sexuality, but it treats sensitively Cary's need for acceptance. She tries to keep up a good face, going so far as to mimic the looks of actress Audrey Hepburn, but she can't hide forever. Stoehr creates a memorable character who makes a small, credible step toward self-honesty.

Inside the Writer

All four of Stoehr's novels are controversial; she wouldn't have it any other way. She enjoys reading reviews of her work, especially "good reviews," saying that she is "generally . . . not much affected by bad reviews." More often, she is surprised when critics seem to miss the point of a novel or target small details—such as a character's language or setting—for criticism. It would be easy for her to write less honest stories, ones where characters didn't curse, didn't use drugs, and didn't have sexual relations. But as Stoehr says, "Young adults shouldn't read in a vacuum."

Stoehr claims that she creates characters before she creates plots: "What I do is first write a sort of character outline, before I start a book, just to sketch out where I think the characters might go and to begin to see how they will interact and influence each other." She likes to climb into such a newly born person's head and see where it takes her. Then, as a novel starts to unfold, she writes "short summaries of the upcoming chapters—about a paragraph per chapter—about three to four chapters in advance." She does not plan too far in advance because either she doesn't use the summaries or the chapters have a "forced" feel to them. She does not like to revise, preferring to get it right the first time. Research is not her forte, but she does like to listen to music or watch videotapes to help understand her characters better. She also uses props such as photographs to help form a mental image of a character "just to stay focused. The characters still tend to make a lot of their own decisions. I just try to guide their actions, pulling out the scenes I think are most interesting or relevant."

Stoehr is hard at work on what she calls the most difficult book of her career. Called *Zine,* it may be the first installment in a series of novels set in the El Cerrita/Corona, California, area. She plans on intertwining the stories in the series, having minor characters in one book become main characters in others. It is an ambitious project, an unusual type of series in the young adult market. But Stoehr has made a career of changing the view of what young adult literature is, even though she never planned to write in the genre: "When I initially wrote *Crosses,* I didn't have aspirations of being a YA novelist. I just wanted to be published, but I didn't know as what. Now that I'm involved with the YA market, I think it's really exciting, and I want to keep with it as long as I can."

Selected Bibliography

WORKS BY SHELLEY STOEHR

Novels for Young Adults

Crosses (1991)

plot the deliberate sequence of events in a literary work

If you like the works of Shelley Stoehr, you might also like the works of Francesca Lia Block, Robert Cormier, Chris Lynch, and Rob Thomas.

Weird on the Outside (1995)

Wannabe (1997)

Tomorrow Wendy: A Love Story (1998)

Article

"Controversial Issues in the Lives of Contemporary Young Adults." *ALAN Review,* winter 1997, pp. 3–5.

WORKS ABOUT SHELLEY STOEHR

Budin, Mirlam Lang. *"Tomorrow Wendy: A Love Story."* *School Library Journal,* March 1998, p. 224.

Campbell, Patty. "The Sand in the Oyster." *Horn Book,* July 1995, pp. 495–499.

Cole, Margaret. *"Weird on the Outside* by Shelley Stoehr." *School Library Journal,* February 1995, pp. 112–115.

Devereaux, Elizabeth, and Diane Roback. "Children's Books—*Weird on the Outside* by Shelley Stoehr." *Publishers Weekly,* 12 December 1994, p. 63.

Dillon, Brooke Selby. "Fiction—*Weird on the Outside* by Shelley Stoehr." *Book Report,* March 1995, pp. 41–42.

Gordon, Lee Diane. "Fiction—*Crosses* by Shelley Stoehr." *Book Report,* May 1992, pp. 46–47.

Hofmann, Mary. Review of *Wannabe.* In *Book Report,* May 1997, pp. 37–38.

Jenkinson, Dave. "Portraits: Shelley Stoehr." *Emergency Librarian,* September 1995, pp. 61–64.

Lesesne, Teri S., and Kylene Beers. *"Tomorrow Wendy: A Love Story."* *Journal of Adolescent & Adult Literacy,* May 1998, p. 696.

————; Rosemary Chance; and Lois Buckman. "Books for Adolescents—*Weird on the Outside* by Shelley Stoehr." *Journal of Adolescent & Adult Literacy,* September 1995, pp. 88–89.

Richmond, Gail. "Fiction—*Crosses* by Shelley Stoehr." *School Library Journal,* October 1991, p. 148.

Roback, Diane; Jennifer M. Brown; and Cindi Di Marzo. Review of *Tomorrow Wendy: A Love Story.* In *Publishers Weekly,* 1 December 1997, p. 54.

————, and Richard Donahue. "Children's Books—*Crosses* by Shelley Stoehr." *Publishers Weekly,* 15 November 1991, p. 74.

Shoemaker, Joel. Review of *Wannabe.* In *School Library Journal,* January 1997, p. 116.

How to Write to the Author

Shelley Stoehr
c/o Bantam Doubleday Dell
Publicity Department
201 East 50th Street
New York, NY 10022

Rob Thomas

(1965–)

by Kylene Beers and Teri S. Lesesne

T he main characters in the novels of Rob Thomas all share one common trait: they are facing challenges not totally of their own making. Yet they shoulder the responsibility for their actions as they fight for what they believe is true and right. On the surface, this might make the novels of Rob Thomas seem tense, sobering tales. Certainly those characteristics are in evidence. However, the hallmark of a book by Rob Thomas is the omnipresence of great good-natured humor. Rob Thomas has the knack for finding the humor in serious situations. Though each of his books tackles a serious topic, the comic element serves to relieve tension, to underscore the irony of an action, and occasionally to make the conflict worse.

Born in Sunnyside, Washington on 15 August 1965, Thomas moved to San Marcos, Texas, at the age of ten. There he moved from high school on to the University of Texas at Austin, graduating with a B.A. in history in 1987. Thomas taught high school journalism for several years, served as adviser for the University

omnipresence the quality of being present in all places at all times

irony a situation in which the actual outcome is opposite or contrary to what was expected

307

Dawson's Creek is a popular teen drama starring James Van Der Beek, Katie Holmes, Joshua Jackson, and Michelle Williams. The show began in 1998. **Cupid** was a romantic comedy that ran for most of the 1998–1999 television season before being canceled. Jeremy Piven starred as a man who believed he was Cupid, the Roman god of love.

levity excessive frivolity

sterile lacking in emotion or intellectual quality

cynicism distrust; pessimism

narrative a story told in fiction, nonfiction, poetry, or drama

of Texas student magazine, and worked for Channel One before his first novel, *Rats Saw God,* was published in 1996. Within a few very short years, the film and television industries recognized his ability to grab the attention of older teens and made him a part of that world. He left Texas and headed west for California to be a staff writer for *Dawson's Creek.* Additionally, he was creator, producer, and writer for the ABC series *Cupid,* and has completed two screenplays for movies in production.

Whether he is working on a young adult novel, a television pilot, or a screenplay, one thing is always evident from Rob Thomas: his ability to present tough characters against a backdrop of levity. Indeed, as one Houston area teen reported about Thomas, "I don't know if I shiver more or laugh more when I read Rob Thomas." A look at each of his novels reveals that blend he has mastered.

Rats Saw God

Steve York has a problem. To the casual observer it might seem that Steve's problem stems from his use of marijuana, his lack of interest in school, or his rather strange friends, but the problem goes much deeper as readers learn in Thomas' first novel, *Rats Saw God.* Steve York is hauled into the counselor's office one afternoon and asked to explain how it is possible that he is failing his senior English class at the same time the school is notified that he is a National Merit Scholarship finalist. Steve tries to offer excuses; however, his counselor, Mr. DeMouy, is not buying any of them. Instead, Mr. DeMouy informs Steve that summer school looms as a distinct possibility in his future. When Steve pleads for some assistance, DeMouy offers a deal: if Steve turns in some serious writing (one hundred typewritten pages, no less), the counselor will help him out. At first Steve tries to keep his writing sterile. After all, he is under no obligation to entertain Mr. DeMouy; he can write anything he desires. His early attempts to handle this assignment with his typical cynicism fail. Soon the truth of why Steve seeks escape through drugs begins to seep into the narrative. The story flashes back and forth between Steve's senior year in San Diego, California, and his sophomore year in Houston, Texas.

Steve York has lived in the very powerful shadow of his father, Alan York, whom Steve refers to as "The Astronaut." Steve's parents divorce, and Steve elects to live with his father, a decision that surprises even Steve himself since Alan York maintains a rather impersonal relationship with his son. Steve covers up his feelings and matches this icy demeanor until "Dub" comes into his life and thaws his heart with her candid and winning ways. Love is grand, Steve discovers, at least at the beginning of a relationship. Dub is friend, lover, adviser, and parent to Steve. However, love does not last, and Steve becomes disillusioned. He flees Texas and "The Astronaut," seeking escape with his mother and sister in San Diego. There no one will know the awful truth about Dub and the breakup. Steve can take further asylum in the haze created by smoking pot. He can steel himself against any further hurt simply by avoiding any further relationships. Eventually Steve's actions begin to make more sense when readers are able to view the raw emotions that threaten to overpower Steve and render him helpless to change his life. Ultimately the hopeful ending leaves readers satisfied that Steve will be able to reassemble the fragments of his family and personal life and face the challenges of the future.

demeanor outward manner

asylum protection

Rarely does a first novel create such a stir. Thomas' ability to tackle the serious topics of first love, lost love, and problems with parents created a book that demanded attention. Thomas gave readers a character who makes some smart choices and some dumb choices, but he also gave them a character who lives the pains and joys they live. Moreover, because Steve is a graduating senior, Thomas gave older teens a book that gained their attention. This voice of the older teen, one on the brink of adulthood, is a voice that had not been heard in the pages of a young adult novel for some time. Rob Thomas' characters were "hip"; they offered the mature reader alternatives to adult best-sellers and too childish young adult novels. Here was a writer with a bold approach. Critics and readers responded alike: the book was a winner. But winning first novels, in many cases, can spell disaster for the book to follow. What could Thomas possibly do to fulfill the expectations of all of the fans of *Rats Saw God*? That question was answered with his even more powerful second novel, *Slave Day* (1997).

Slave Day

Slave Day is a time-honored tradition at Robert E. Lee High School. Despite Keene Davenport's efforts to organize a boycott, especially among the African American students, once

boycott the refusal to deal or associate with someone or something

racist referring to hatred for or intolerance of another race

myriad a great number; countless

point of view the position or perspective from which the story is told

more teachers and students are auctioned as "slaves" for the day. However, the slave day captured in Thomas' novel will be one not easily forgotten by eight very different characters: four "slaves" and four "masters." From the hapless teacher Mr. Twilley, purchased by a student who did not do very well in his class last year, to Tiffany, the rich girl who buys the services of the one of the biggest geeks in the school, to Keene himself, who purchases the services of the Student Council president, hoping to drive home his point about the racist root of the slave day tradition, this cast of characters provides readers with multiple perspectives and powerful insights into the thoughts and feelings of a variety of the myriad inhabitants of a typical school.

As Thomas proved so ably in his first novel, realistic characters change in gradual steps during the course of a story. Here are eight characters who learn a bit more about themselves, perhaps rethink their attitudes and behavior as a result of their participation in the slave day. Are there miraculous turnarounds? Does everyone get a happy ending? No. Thomas allows his characters to begin their growth toward a deeper awareness of who they are and how either they are becoming their own person or they are simply living within the shadow of "everyone else is doing it" behavior. Told from eight points of view, by the end of the novel, readers learn that not everyone is changed dramatically; some characters triumph over their challenges. Others are made more aware of the need to make changes, and a few remain unchanged. Just as in real life, there is no magic pill or spell that can tie the ending into a perfect bow and complete each story line with a "happily ever after." Thomas leaves readers secure in the knowledge that the unlikely hero, Keene Davenport, will go on to fight other battles against what he perceives is wrong; however, there is a price to pay. How often he might be willing to have payment exacted is not as clear. Keene is, after all, quite human and will continue to grow and change.

Perhaps this is another commonality shared by Thomas' books: they present characters who learn not to take themselves quite so seriously while grappling with the most serious of issues. Possessing a sense of humor, it seems, is an essential tool for future success and happiness. Thomas' books also focus on the so-called absolutes: truth, justice, honesty, and love, to name but a few. Characters in Thomas' works eventually come to understand that there are no absolutes in life. Life is not a series of black and white decisions to make; the gray, shady areas of ethics and morality are tough to navigate. In many ways, Keene is both like and unlike Steve from *Rats Saw God.* Like Steve, Keene's acts of civil disobedience serve to point out some of the absurdities that masquerade as rules in schools. However, Keene and Steve are quite different in their passions, in what drives each to act. One might easily imagine, though, that the two could be friends if they were ever to meet.

With *Rats Saw God* and *Slave Day,* Rob Thomas has served up two delicious stories that deal with everyday kind of characters caught up in conflicts without ready solutions. This formula carries him on into book three.

Doing Time: Notes from the Undergrad

Just when one might think there is nothing more to plumb in a school setting, Thomas delivers his third book, *Doing Time: Notes from the Undergrad* (1997), a collection of individual stories about nine students who must perform two hundred hours of community service in order to graduate from high school. At the end of the service, the students are required to write an account of their activities. A college student enrolled in a sociology course is assigned these reports to read. He is also told to follow up each report with an interview. However, as readers learn in the opening story, this college student has had his own experience with community service, which colors his perspective. He decides to read each of the reports to see if any of the high school students benefited from their experiences. This ingenious twist, having a student read the reports of the high school students, allows Thomas (and the reader) to examine how the lives of several individuals are altered during the course of their community service involvement.

Though each story is able to stand on its own, the forced volunteerism of the students provides a framework to make the separate stories seem more like chapters in a novel. The experiences of each of the characters are as different as the effects that their involvement has on their lives. Some are changed by their community involvement, leaving behind self-centered absorption for a more global view of how interconnected we are. Not everyone, though, comes away from the service projects changed for the better. As Thomas demonstrated in *Slave Day,* some tigers do not change their stripes; some people will not change. Although some characters come

civil disobedience a refusal to obey the commands of an authority in order to gain concessions

ingenious clever

empathize to understand, by being aware of and sensitive to, another's feelings, without actually experiencing those feelings

chagrin distress caused by disappointment, failure, or humiliation

demographics the statistical characteristics of a human population used to identify a market, usually by age or income

plot the deliberate sequence of events in a literary work

stereotype universal type; character that conforms to a preconceived and often oversimplified notion about a person or group

to empathize with the hurts and fears of other people, others see the service project as something to get done and leave behind. For them, there is no lesson about the interdependency of society; there is just a need to complete the project, file the report, and graduate. Thomas once again shows readers that powerful endings reflect the complexity and confusion of life.

Satellite Down

Thomas drew upon his own experience with Channel One to tell the story of a young man from Texas tapped by a Channel One type of station as a reporter. In *Satellite Down* (1998) Patrick Sheridan's life has gone from humdrum to hotshot in the past few years as he has moved from being a nobody to becoming a local reporter. Now his career is about to take off in an entirely new direction as he travels from Doggett, Texas, to Los Angeles, California. Patrick goes to L.A. excited about the prospect of honing his journalism skills. Much to his chagrin, he discovers that he has not been selected as one of the newest members of Channel One because of his journalistic expertise. Instead, Patrick is just a "pretty face" who fits the right demographics needed to sell Channel One (and its sponsors' products) to the captive teen market in the schools that receive the broadcasts. Patrick quickly learns to bend to the will of those who run the station; if he is to continue leading this heady and head-swelling life, he has to surrender some of his principles, right? Patrick's life, already radically changed by his move from Texas to California, gets yet another jolt when a family secret is revealed and Patrick learns more about himself and the people he thought to be his parents. Unable to deal with the messy truth, Patrick opts to run away to Ireland. He eventually realizes that running away cannot solve problems. Like Steve, Patrick comes to understand that he must confront his demons if he is ever to return to Texas and resume the life he wishes to lead.

Satellite Down explores some territory already familiar to readers of previous books by Rob Thomas. However, the plot, characters, and conflicts are far from predictable. Just because the territory may not be new does not mean there is nothing left to discover. Plot twists keep the reader guessing about Patrick's ultimate decision; characters are once again fully realized; what may seem to be stereotypes are actually fully fleshed-out characters waiting for the opportunity to unmask in front of the reader and reveal their true thoughts and feelings. While Patrick's family appears on the surface to be strong and solid, too many secrets have been kept over the years. As those secrets are revealed, Patrick's family is thrown into crisis, leaving him bereft. As Steve from *Rats Saw God* and Keene from *Slave Day* did, Patrick discovers that answers about his life, his pain, and his joys can't be found in friends, in parents, or in the world. Instead, answers about things that matter most must come from within. Ultimately that is one of the defining characteristics of a Rob Thomas hero, the ability to find answers not from outside sources but from within. Readers aware of Thomas' own move from Austin, Texas, to Hollywood, California, and his shift from novel writer to screenwriter will enjoy guessing about the reality in this piece of realistic fiction.

Green Thumb

The next of Rob Thomas' books—*Green Thumb*—is also a first: his first for middle-grade readers. Once again, the main character is a young man who is facing both tremendous opportunities and some fairly big obstacles in his life. For Grady Jacobs, science is serious business. He has his own hothouse where experiments are in bloom; he has won many awards for his previous efforts in the area of botany. So when he has the chance to spend the summer working with a prestigious scientist in the rain forest, Grady applies for an internship. When the scientist discovers his new intern is barely thirteen years old, Grady finds himself relegated to kitchen detail. This young scientist, however, refuses to be left out of the experiments and soon discovers that he can control the movement of trees. This discovery may just save Grady's life when he is chased by natives with blow guns.

Eventually, the poisonous darts of some of the forest tribes seem less threatening than Dr. Carter, especially when Grady uncovers data the good doctor would like to keep hidden from his funding sources. Grady must learn how to survive in the rain forest if he is to complete his experiment.

Though Grady may be years younger than the protagonists of Thomas' previous books, he is a young teen with a nicely self-deprecating sense of humor like that of Steve York and Patrick Sheridan. The laugh-out-loud manner with which Grady dispatches the bullies at school (a scene that involves spitballs and depilatory) and the gradual growth toward

hothouse a greenhouse maintained at a high temperature for the cultivation of tropical plants

prestigious honored or well-known

protagonist the main character of a literary work

self-deprecating playing down or discrediting oneself; belittling oneself

depilatory a lotion or cream used for hair removal

self-confidence Grady experiences during his jungle adventure are again prime traits readers have come to expect from Thomas' books. They will not be disappointed.

School Stories? Not quite!

ludicrous ridiculous; absurd

capricious impulsive; inconstant

Labeling Rob Thomas' works school stories is as ludicrous as calling Shakespeare's plays court dramas or Chris Crutcher's books sports stories. Though each of Thomas' novels is set at least partially in a school, there is much more to each story. The school setting does allow Thomas to explore the sometimes irrational world of education, to poke more than occasional fun at rules that seem capricious. Ultimately, however, Rob Thomas' books are about everyday kinds of people who find themselves dealing with everyday kinds of problems: family conflicts, school bullies, lost loves, career decisions. The characters in his books come to some understanding of what it takes to survive in school and in the "real" world beyond school. They are changed in some ways by their experiences, but they know there is much more to come. Rob Thomas' works leave readers feeling as though they too have survived, that they too can deal with the sometimes painful curves life throws. More importantly, Thomas writes to an overlooked audience, that older male teen who wants characters who reflect his needs, questions, and more-adult-than-kid lifestyle, who wants serious issues discussed against the backdrop of humor, who wants a writer who understands that life is more than history tests and English papers. While doing just that, Thomas' novels go a step further and do what good fiction is supposed to do: they reflect life with all its bumps and imperfections while giving readers the courage to keep looking around the next bend.

If you like the works of Rob Thomas, you might also like the works of Alden R. Carter, Chris Crutcher, David Klass, Gordon Korman, Chris Lynch, and Todd Strasser.

How to Write to the Author

Rob Thomas
c/o Simon and Schuster Books
for Young Readers
1230 Avenue of the Americas
New York, NY 10020

You can also find out
more about Rob Thomas
at his website:
www.mediacomp.com/robt

Selected Bibliography

WORKS BY ROB THOMAS

Rats Saw God (1996)

Doing Time: Notes from the Undergrad (1997)

Slave Day (1997)

Satellite Down (1998)

Green Thumb (1999)

Stephanie S. Tolan

(1942–)

by Lynne Alvine

"Writing and reading were my twin favorite activities when I was growing up," says Stephanie Tolan, author of more than twenty novels for children and young adults. "I was always reading and writing, writing and reading. I read and wrote inside. I read and wrote outside. I also loved to ride horses. You know, I never tried reading or writing on horseback, but I read and wrote most of the rest of the time. I even read books while sitting up in trees."

Like many avid readers, Stephanie Tolan took a flashlight to bed with her so that she could read under the covers after the lights were out. As early as fourth grade, she had begun to think of herself as a writer. She has continued to write throughout her life although, from time to time, "real world" jobs have kept her writing on a back burner. Tolan gave up university teaching and turned to writing full-time several years ago and notes that it "turned out to be a wonderful choice. I'm awfully glad I did it."

Quotations from Stephanie S. Tolan that are not attributed to a published source are from a personal interview conducted by the author of this article on 26 January 1999 and are published here by permission of Stephanie S. Tolan.

avid very eager

A Basic Philosophical Question

In contrast to the serious, often disturbing issues dealt with in Stephanie Tolan's works for adolescents, she has written a series of junior novels that are, in her words, "just for fun." These are the Great Skinner books, in which the older daughter Jenny Skinner relates the various adventures of her family of six. (Full titles of all four Great Skinner novels are listed at the end of this article.) When Tolan was struggling with the writing of one of these lighter books, she realized that she was having trouble because she had not clarified its basic philosophical question. It seemed unusual to her to think of a book written "just for fun" as having such a thing as a basic philosophical question, but when she identified that book's key issue, "it all fell into place." In her words:

> Of course I write to entertain readers, but that is not enough. I can't spend a year of my life on a book unless it has a philosophical issue that I am deeply interested in. Thus, I think all of my books have such backbones. Each one has an intense psychological, emotional, or philosophical question. It must have that for me to deal with it for the length of time it takes to write a book.

Someone once told Tolan that all of her books have the same issue at the base: they are grounded in the belief that all young people have the right to be who they are, to be fully accepted for themselves, and to be allowed to believe in themselves. Indeed, those are recurring themes in her novels, and those themes have emerged from and been shaped by Tolan's life experiences.

The Author's Early Life, Education, and Early Career

Stephanie Stein (Tolan) was born in Canton, Ohio, on 25 October 1942 to Joseph Edward and Mary Stein. She completed a bachelor of arts degree in 1964 and a master of arts degree in 1967, both at Purdue University in Indiana. In 1964, she

philosophical relating to the basic beliefs and values of an individual or group

theme central message about life in a literary work

married Robert W. Tolan, a managing director of a theater. Her early career included serving as an instructor in continuing education at Purdue University from 1966 to 1970. During those years, Tolan was also a lecturer at Indiana University. From 1970 to 1971, she worked as an actress, performing with Curtain Call, Co. She was a faculty member in speech and theater at the State University of New York at Buffalo in 1972. From 1973 to 1975, Tolan served as a faculty member in English at Franklin and Marshall College in Lancaster, Pennsylvania. She was also coordinator of continuing education there from 1974 to 1975. Since 1975, Tolan has worked full-time as a writer.

During the 1970s, Stephanie Tolan also worked in various federally funded arts programs, including serving as a Poet-in-the-Schools and later as an Artist-in-the-Schools in Pennsylvania and Ohio. Today she frequently responds to invitations to visit schools where children have read her novels as part of their assigned reading. She talks about the craft of writing and about her characters and their stories.

Advocate for Gifted Children

For many years, Tolan has been an outspoken advocate for exceptionally gifted children. She has written numerous articles on the problems and needs of the highly gifted and has traveled widely serving as a speaker and consultant to parents and schools. Her co-authored *Guiding the Gifted Child: A Practical Source for Parents and Teachers* (1982) is still being used as a reference in educating the gifted. Tolan acknowledges that she became aware of many of the problems gifted children face in school and with peers because she raised a son who was exceptionally bright.

In writing *Welcome to the Ark* (1996), she was able to put two important aspects of her life and career together. She notes:

> I combined my self as a consultant to parents of highly gifted kids with my self as a writer when I wrote that book. It finally occurred to me that I could tell people more about these kids and their needs by writing a novel about them than I could by

advocate one who defends or maintains a cause

continuing only to write scholarly articles about the gifted.

Once, when she worked with six young people ages eight to thirteen whose mean IQ was above 200, she witnessed their ability to communicate psychically. They were having a discussion and then stopped talking. When the talk resumed, they had moved further along in the discussion—only no one had spoken. Tolan refers to the phenomenon as "mind melding." Because she included children with similar psychic abilities in *Welcome to the Ark,* many readers have referred to the novel, which is set in the near future, as "science fiction." Tolan objects to that designation: "I tend not to think of it as science fiction. It is fiction, yes, but it is not about the impossible or even the improbable."

unabashedly without apology

Though she is aware that authors typically claim not to have a favorite among their "children," Tolan unabashedly claims *Welcome to the Ark* as her personal favorite of all the books she has written. It is special because it is the novel that has helped her integrate her intense interest in writing and her intense interest in helping the gifted children of the world have the support they need.

integrate to blend together

It is a favorite also, perhaps, because it has prompted the most interesting response from readers. Tolan describes the letters and phone calls she has received in response to *Welcome to the Ark* as "simply astonishing." Sometimes adults phone her and say that they recognize themselves in the novel. Once a parent called to say that her child would not go to bed until she phoned Tolan to tell her how much the book meant to the child.

One reader found Tolan's e-mail address and wrote to her saying that *Guiding the Gifted Child* had "saved his life." His parents had read it and finally had someone who knew what they were going through. He also said that reading *Welcome to the Ark* was even more important to him because he had never seen himself on the pages of a book before. The young man had gone on to connect with other young people like himself on the Internet and had decided to devote part of his time to making those connections available for other gifted children around the world. With this kind of evidence that the book has made such a powerful impact on readers who needed to read it, it is not surprising that *Welcome to the Ark* is Tolan's favorite "child."

Notes on Selected Books for Young Adults

A Good Courage

In *A Good Courage* (1988), Tolan tackles the subject of adolescent life within a religious cult. Fourteen-year-old Tie-Dye Rainey has followed his mother, Jasmine, from one utopian community to another in her search for refuge from a harsh world. On their way to a cult in Florida, she is drawn to the Kingdom of Yahweh, led by charismatic Brother Daniel. At first, their symbolic taking of new names (Jordana and Tobias) is only a minor annoyance to Ty. Then he becomes aware that he and his mother are being systematically separated. When he is tied to a tree all night in the freezing cold, for the "sin" of comforting a child who has had a nightmare, Ty realizes that the world within the Kingdom of Yahweh is harsh for the children and youths who have not yet become "The Chosen." Along with his friend Samara (and with the assistance of Brother Benjamin), Ty manages to escape from the Kingdom and find his stepfather, who takes in both young people. In doing so, Ty must sort out his responsibilities to himself and to others, as he realizes that he must leave his mother behind.

The novel has been praised for presenting underlying tensions between faith and fanaticism (*Horn Book,* July 1988) and for its gripping, unexpected, and well-handled ending (*Booklist,* March 1988). *A Good Courage* was selected as a Best Young Adult Book by the *School Library Journal* in 1988. It was a Dorothy Canfield Fisher Award nominee in Vermont in 1990, and it was one of the Virginia Young Readers Best Choices for 1990–1991.

cult a religious group that follows a living leader who promotes unusual teachings or practices

utopian resembling the ideal of a perfect society

charismatic possessing extraordinary personal charm

Plague Year

Bran Slocum, the "new kid" in school, is different from the other teens. He looks different. He acts different. But then Bran Slocum's father has been charged as a serial killer—and Bran is trying to find his own identity when he arrives to attend high school in the small town where his aunt and uncle live. When word gets out about Bran's father, prejudice and ignorance take over, and hysteria is the result. *Plague Year* (1990), the Stephanie Tolan young adult novel that is most widely assigned in schools, offers students and teachers an opportunity to explore together issues of difference and tolerance. This novel was a Virginia Young Readers Best Choice winner in 1992–1993. It won the Nevada Young Readers Award in 1993–1994, and was a Sequoyah Young Adult Book Award nominee in 1992–1993.

Save Halloween!

Stephanie Tolan's 1993 *Save Halloween!* also takes on the subject of religion. This time it is sixth grader Johanna Flikins who is caught in an ironic dilemma. She has written the script for the school Halloween play, *Devil's Holiday,* but her evangelist Uncle T. T. has come to town to crusade against the play. This work was cited in the August 1993 issue of *Kirkus Reviews* for its "nicely realized characters of quiet courage, [who are] refreshingly committed to their faith." *Save Halloween!* was a Young Adult Library Services Association (YALSA) Best Book in 1994 and a Sequoyah Young Adult Book Award nominee in 1993. Tolan has written a prequel to *Save Halloween!* It is titled *Ordinary Miracles,* and it was published in 1999.

Welcome to the Ark

In writing *Welcome to the Ark,* Tolan has drawn on her extensive knowledge of the characteristics and needs of highly intelligent adolescents to tell the story of four such teens who are a part of an experimental "group home" for the troubled gifted. Fifteen-year-old Miranda created her own language when she was three; ten-year-old Taryn is psychic; eight-year-old Elijah is clairvoyant; and seventeen-year-old Doug is a computer genius. These four children, whom no one knows what to do with, wind up in the Laurel Mountain Research Center in an experiment run by Dr. Turnbull, the director, whose need for control sabotages the project. The four reach out to other teenagers around the world, first on the Internet, then using their psychic powers, in an effort to turn the world away from violent solutions to problems. Though they are thwarted, they reunite four years later and pledge to continue their efforts for global unity.

The form used in this novel is quite different from that used in Tolan's other works. She tells this story by interspersing bits of narrative with e-mail messages, notes, memos, hospital records, journal entries, and poetry. Though the story

---

ironic marked by a contrast between what is said and what is actually meant; sarcastic

evangelist a person who preaches the gospel with militant or crusading enthusiasm

prequel a dramatic work in which the story takes place before that of an earlier work

clairvoyant unusually perceptive

narrative a story told in fiction, nonfiction, poetry, or drama

line may be difficult for some young readers to grasp at first, the unconventional form and the compelling subject matter will pull them into the novel for a fast-paced reading experience. *Welcome to the Ark* was written as the first of three related novels.

The Face in the Mirror

Tolan's *The Face in the Mirror* (1998) is the result of her finally drawing on her lifelong link with the theater. Though her husband and son both work in the theater and though she herself has been a college faculty member of theater departments and a member of the Actors' Equity Association, she had not set any of her previous novels in the theater. *The Face in the Mirror* is also her second attempt at telling a ghost story. After her readers responded so positively to *Who's There?* (1994), Tolan's editor encouraged her to summon another ghost character to appear in one of her books. *The Face in the Mirror* features the ghost of nineteenth-century tragic actor Garrick Marsden, who has haunted an abandoned theater in a small town in Ohio for more than a hundred years. It is the story of a family-run theatrical company that reopens the theater and makes the acquaintance of Marsden's ghost. It is, more importantly, the story of fifteen-year-old Jared Kingsley, who must join the family of his natural father until the grandfather who raised him has recovered from a stroke. Jared is willing to share his newly found parents with their son Tad, but his half-brother is unwilling to share anything. The company is doing Shakespeare's *Richard III,* and Tad and Jared must get along well enough to play the diabolical Richard's ill-fated nephews.

Though some reviewers have criticized this novel as having one-dimensional characters, another, in the September 1998 issue of *Booklist,* suggests that Tolan's "seamless and exciting integration of *Richard III* may even tempt readers to search out the original." And so it has. In a school visit, Tolan talked with seventh and eighth graders who had just read *The Face in the Mirror* and who indicated to her that they were eager to read *Richard III.*

stroke a sudden loss of consciousness because of an obstruction of an artery leading to the brain

There is an article about William Shakespeare in volume 3.

diabolical characteristic of the devil

Conclusion

Young readers want to see themselves in the stories they read. They want to have an emotional connection to characters who are sorting out problems similar to those they face. Adolescent readers searching for their own identities will find a connection with the main characters in these five Stephanie Tolan novels.

Like Ty Rainey, they may live with a mother who is incapable of meeting their emotional needs. Like Bran Slocum, they may have to face the irrational prejudice and cruelty of peers. Like Johanna Filkins, they may be torn between the religious expectations of their family and their own desires to fit in with friends. Like the four children of the Ark, they may have needs or talents that make it difficult for them to relate to family members or to their peers. Or like Jared Kinglsey, they may have a jealous sibling or step-sibling who is unwilling to share his or her parents' time and affection. These books and others by author Stephanie Tolan offer readers emotional connection with characters who struggle to be allowed to be who they are—to be fully accepted as they are and to believe in themselves—without apology or erasure of self-esteem.

If you like Stephanie Tolan, you might also like Madeleine L'Engle, Lois Lowry, and Margaret Mahy.

Selected Bibliography

WORKS BY STEPHANIE S. TOLAN

Novels for Children and Young Adults
Grandpa—and Me (1978)
The Last of Eden (1980)
The Liberation of Tansy Warner (1980)
A Time to Fly Free (1980)
No Safe Harbors (1981)
The Great Skinner Strike (1983)
The Great Skinner Enterprise (1986)
Pride of the Peacock (1986)
The Great Skinner Getaway (1987)
A Good Courage (1988)
The Great Skinner Homestead (1988)
Plague Year (1990)
Marcy Hooper and the Greatest Treasure on Earth (1991)
Sophie and the Sidewalk Man (1992)
The Witch of Maple Park (1992)

Save Halloween! (1993)

Who's There? (1994)

Welcome to the Ark (1996)

The Face in the Mirror (1998)

Nonfiction Book

Guiding the Gifted Child: A Practical Source for Parents and Teachers, with James T. Webb and Elizabeth A. Meckstroth (1982)

Articles and Essays

"Stop Accepting, Start Demanding!" *Gifted Child Monthly,* January 1985, p. 6.

"Stuck in Another Dimension: The Exceptionally Gifted Child in School." *G/C/T,* November/December 1985, pp. 22–26.

"Young Adult Books: A Writer's Response to 'Members of the Last Generation.'" *Horn Book,* May/June 1986, pp. 358–362.

"Parents and 'Professionals', A Question of Priorities." *Roeper Review,* February 1987, pp. 184–187.

"Happily Ever After." *New Advocate,* December 1989, pp. 9–14.

"The Reading Room" [regular column]. *Understanding Our Gifted,* 1988–1995.

"From Production to Nurturing: Hollingworth and Parental Perspectives Today." *Roeper Review,* March 1990, pp. 203–207.

"Special Problems of the Highly Gifted." *Understanding Our Gifted,* May 1989, pp. 7–10.

"Helping Your Highly Gifted Child." ERIC Flyer File on Gifted Students, 1990, p. 5.

"Parents vs. Theorists: Dealing with the Exceptionally Gifted." *Roeper Review,* September 1992, pp. 14–18.

"A Parent and Writer's Response to the Federal Report on Gifted Education." *Roeper Review,* June/July 1994, pp. 230–231.

"Ridi Pagliaccio." In *The Day My Father Died: Women Share Their Stories of Love, Loss, and Life.* Philadelphia: Running Press, 1994.

"Discovering the Gifted Ex-Child." *Roeper Review,* August 1994; *Journal of Advanced Development,* 1996, pp. 134–138.

"Is It a Cheetah?" *Highly Gifted Child,* spring 1997; *OAGC Newsletter,* fall 1996. Available on-line at *www.gtworld.org/cheetah.html*

Plays

The Ledge (1968)

Not I Said the Little Red Hen. Produced by Enchanted Hills Playhouse, Elkhart, Ind., 1970; York Theater Company, New York, 1971.

Bridge to Terabithia, a play with music, adapted with Katherine Paterson from her novel of the same name; music composed by Steve Liebman (1992). First professional production by Stage One, Louisville, Ky., 1990; national tour 1991–1992.

The Tale of the Mandarin Ducks, a play with music, adapted with Katherine Paterson from her novel of the same name; music composed by Steve Liebman. First professional production by Stage One, Louisville, Ky., 1995.

A Tale of Jemima Puddle-Duck, a musical based on Beatrix Potter's story of the same name, with Katherine Paterson; music composed by Steve Liebman. First professional production by Stage One, Louisville, Ky., 1998.

WORKS ABOUT STEPHANIE S. TOLAN

Hile, Kevin S., ed. *Something About the Author.* Detroit: Gale Research, 1994, vol. 78, pp. 218–220.

Lesniak, James, ed. *Contemporary Authors: New Revision Series.* Detroit: Gale Research, 1991, vol. 34, p. 451.

Locher, Frances Carol, ed. *Contemporary Authors.* Detroit: Gale Research, 1979, vols. 77–80, pp. 550–551.

Metzger, Linda, ed. *Contemporary Authors: New Revision Series.* Detroit: Gale Research, 1985, vol. 15, p. 430.

How to Write to the Author

Stephanie S. Tolan
c/o Children's Book
Marketing Agent
William Morrow Company
1350 Avenue of the Americas
New York, NY 10019

Will Weaver

(1950–)

by Jean E. Brown

It is often difficult to see what is right in front of us. Sometimes we have to leave a place to gain a perspective about it, to understand what it is really like, and even more importantly to begin to realize the hold that a place has on us. This is especially true of how difficult it is to see home and what it is like. Will Weaver experienced this reaction when he left rural Minnesota for California after college. According to Ronald Barron, writing in the fall 1996 *ALAN Review,* Weaver has said, "From the vantage point of California I could see clearly, for the first time, the American Midwest where I had grown up. That perspective provided him with a sense of place that shapes all of his novels in an interwoven fabric of Midwestern sights, sound, and values.

Some people describe Will Weaver as a writer of sports books; others say he is a spokesman of traditional rural life; some say he is a master of characterization; and still others call him a great storyteller. They are all correct. Each of the elements is part of the totality that makes Weaver one of the

Quotations from Will Weaver that are not attributed to a published source are from a personal telephone interview conducted by the author of this article in January 1999 and a personal e-mail interview with Jeanice Caverly and Laurie Hoggard in November 1998 and are published here by permission of Will Weaver.

characterization
method by which a writer creates and develops the appearance and personality of a character

strongest emerging voices in the field of young adult literature. After two highly acclaimed books for adults—a novel titled *Red Earth, White Earth* (1986) and a collection of short stories, *A Gravestone Made of Wheat* (1989)—Weaver turned his attention to writing for young adults. These books along with his three young adult novels share the northern Minnesota farm country setting.

Accidental Careers

William Weller Weaver was born on 19 January 1950 and grew up in the northern Minnesota farmlands of his books. His father was a dairy farmer in Park Rapids, a few miles from the White Earth Indian reservation. Senior class president in high school, he was also a successful athlete. He was captain of the basketball team and a member of both the baseball and cross-country teams. After high school he attended St. Cloud State University before transferring to the University of Minnesota, where he graduated *magna cum laude* with a degree in English.

> I took a straight B.A. in English from the University of Minnesota, Minneapolis, with no creative writing classes. It wasn't until I was out of college a couple of years and thinking of an M.A. that I considered fiction writing. This was in California, and with a small deer-hunting story and lots of luck, I was accepted into the Stanford Writing Program.

Weaver graduated from college in 1972 in the waning days of the Vietnam War. He was a conscientious objector who applied for alternative service in California, where he managed a company that manufactured circuit boards. He left that job when he entered Stanford University, earning a master's degree in English and creative writing in 1979. Weaver was in the program at Stanford with another young adult author, Terry Davis.

Weaver then returned to Minnesota, where he taught writing part-time for several years while he operated the family dairy farm after his father retired. In 1981, he turned to full-time teaching at Bemidji State University. During this period, he began a two-track career as a successful author and as a

---

setting the general time and place in which the events of a literary work take place

magna cum laude Latin for "with great distinction"

In the **Vietnam War** (1957–1975), Communist-ruled North Vietnam fought to take over South Vietnam. From 1965 to 1969, the United States tried to stop the advancement of North Vietnam but failed. In 1975, South Vietnam surrendered to North Vietnam. A **conscientious objector** is someone who refuses to serve in the armed services for moral or religious reasons.

There is an article about Terry Davis in volume 1.

professor of English who teaches mostly creative writing courses. He did not plan either career; in fact, he refers to himself as "an accidental professor." Nor was writing a career he planned to pursue. "I never planned to be a writer. I only knew [in college] that I liked literature classes. . . . There [at Stanford] I really learned a lot and eventually returned to the Midwest, where I began to publish my short stories. I firmly believe that, for fiction writers, the short story is the place to start."

It is no coincidence that Weaver's success as an author began when he returned to Minnesota, where the farmlands he knew growing up inspired a sense of place for all his books. Again according to Barron, Weaver has said that going home allowed him "to be closer to my subject matter."

Transition to Young Adult Fiction

While Weaver did not consciously make the decision to write for a youthful audience, he believes "that it suits me, I think, and I'm very happy to make a contribution. If we can keep a few more kids reading in spite of the great pressures on them now from our nonreading society, I feel good about that." After he began writing young adult fiction, he looked back on his first two books and realized that "some of my best writing in my so-called adult books was fiction that worked for young adults, including the first half of *Red Earth, White Earth* and several stories from *A Gravestone Made of Wheat*. . . . I think that there is a built-in affinity for young adults."

Weaver also feels that writing young adult fiction helps him connect with his own daughter and son. Barron quoted Weaver as saying: "I think it validates for them that I am interested in their lives, their dilemmas. On the other hand, they now 'accuse' me (mostly in jest) of stealing all the good lines they come up with or hear at school. For sure it has brought us closer as a family."

affinity feeling of preference or connection

The Saga of Billy Baggs

Weaver characterizes his work: "I write realism, with a lot of material coming from my life, my observations, and Midwestern setting. . . . All my best stories have a really strong moral dilemma at their hearts." Certainly, adolescence is a time of resolving a number of dilemmas and making choices, as he demonstrates in his three novels, *Striking Out* (1993), *Farm Team* (1995), and *Hard Ball* (1998). These novels present the evolving story of Billy Baggs, a farm boy with a talent for and love of baseball. Weaver also returns to his heritage of rural northern Minnesota farm country to create the Baggs dairy farm, twenty miles from the fictional town of Flint, population 2,001.

In *Striking Out,* Weaver introduces us to Billy at thirteen. His world is a narrow one composed of long hours of chores on the farm, a twenty-mile school bus ride morning and night, and school itself. He has little time for anything else except pitching an old baseball against the barn wall. The first chapter of the book begins with the following portrait of Billy's life:

> **Billy Baggs was thirteen and he had never played baseball. Never, that is, on a team with other boys. Never in uniform with black stirrups over white socks and a jersey with a number all his own. He had never even owned a real baseball glove or a Minnesota Twins cap. There were lots of nevers in Billy's life. (P. 1)**

reclusive marked by a withdrawal from society

Billy's life is hard, filled with long hours of physical labor. His world is populated by his reclusive, bitter father, Abner, and his resourceful mother, Mavis. Yet there is a fourth member of the Baggs family, an older son, Robert, killed in a farming accident five years before, though his ghost embraces the farm and has an impact on each member of his family. "Their pain and grief is unresolved and resides like an uninvited guest that they try to pretend isn't there except on birthdays and anniversaries when it breaks through their consciousness" (*Signal,* 1996, p. 11).

balk to refuse abruptly

Coach Anderson of the town baseball team recognizes Billy's talent for baseball and wants him to play for the team. While Abner balks at the possibility of Billy wasting time away from the farm when he should be working, Mavis believes that Billy should have a chance to have a life away from the farm. Mavis knows that they must get on with their lives, so she gets a job in town and encourages Billy to play baseball. Billy practices with the town team and plays in their last game of the season. While his coach, Ozzie Anderson, recognizes Billy's raw talent, Billy faces new challenges of rivalry, and he remains an outsider with the town youth.

In the next two novels, we experience Billy's growth as he encounters new challenges. When his father is sent to jail, Billy assumes responsibility for running the farm. While his extra duties keep him from participating in the town baseball league, his mother encourages a "come one, come all" Friday evening baseball game at the Baggs farm. As he works to prepare the field, Billy feels his brother's presence. For the first time, he shares his memories of Robert with his mother, thus helping both of them deal with their pain. Billy's relationship with his father remains difficult and unresolved, however. His relationship with the town teenagers also continues to be difficult. As he has gained confidence in himself and in his skills as a pitcher, he has become a threat to King Kenwood, the star pitcher for the town team. He and Billy are rivals as pitchers as well as rivals for the affection of Suzy Langen. So Billy is faced with challenges both at home and in town.

Weaver says that he likes to think of the development of his characters as "movement in which they evolve from an earlier position." This accurately describes the changes that Billy undergoes throughout these three novels. Billy emerges from a self-conscious, gawky youth to become an athlete who grows far more confident when he puts on the team uniform and plays in his first game. The change in Billy occurs as he continues to erase the "nevers" in his life. In each book, he faces new challenges and responsibilities as he juggles his farm responsibilities with finding out who he is. It is through baseball and his other activities that Billy grows and tests himself.

Unifying Elements

The Rural Setting

The evolution of the Billy Baggs novels juxtaposes the playing field with the planting field. While baseball is a release and a hope he dreams, farming is the daily reality he lives. Throughout these novels the role of the rural farm setting has a significant impact on the characters and their actions. Weaver is an eloquent voice of rural America. He makes the Baggs farm come alive. The hardships of farm work and rural poverty shape the characters of Billy, Abner, and Mavis, as well as a number of minor characters.

juxtapose to place side by side

Weaver's accurate portrayal of farming life reflects his growing up on a dairy farm. He believes that it is important to chronicle the way of life on a small farm as it was in the early 1970s.

> That [the descriptions of farming and farm life] is a calculated aspect of my Midwestern fiction. I like to insert, as much as I can, the texture and reality of the small farm in the Midwest. . . . If you look closely at each of the three Billy Baggs novels, I attend to different aspects of farming, whether putting up hay or filling silos or that sort of thing because I want to capture that before it goes away. The small farms are rapidly disappearing.

The Sports Novel

The Billy Baggs novels far transcend the traditional sports novel. Chris Crowe, in his article in the fall 1996 issue of *Signal,* acknowledges this and coins the term "sportlerroman," which he defines as "a form of the traditional apprenticeship novel where the protagonist is an athlete struggling to maturity." Crowe makes a case for the intertwining of sports as one vehicle through which youths can respond and confront the dilemmas they face. Certainly this is true of Billy as he seeks to make his own way and handle difficulties along that way.

For Weaver, the sports novel, while it reflects an interest of his, provides a bridge to readers. He says, "I'm not obsessed with baseball; rather, it makes a nice 'hook' for boy readers in particular, and then I try to squeeze in the most literary value I can."

Humor

Contributing to the richness of Weaver's novels is his use of humor. It is manifested in subtle ways through the comments of the characters or in more outrageous ways such as Abner's solution to Mavis's car problems, or "Uncle Dan's" introduction to a social worker, or Abner and Billy's unique way of paying a fine.

Weaver also uses humorous bantering between the characters to reveal what they are like. For example, Gina Erickson

chronicle to record historical events in the order in which they occur without analysis or interruption

transcend to rise above

apprenticeship a period of work during which one learns a skill or trade from an expert

manifested revealed or shown

bantering speech characterized by wit or teasing

has a smart and often suggestive response for everything. But she is a wry observer and the barometer of adolescent sexuality in the Billy Baggs novels. It is Gina who notices that Suzy's fall in the barn must have been serious since it rearranged how her blouse was buttoned. Speaking of his use of humor, Weaver notes: "I think there is more humor in my books than first appears. It's fun to work with undercurrents of wit and wryness. Good readers pick that up and it's their reward to see ironies and be amused."

barometer something that indicates fluctuations

Other Works

In addition to his novels, Weaver has written three stories that have been included in young adult anthologies. "Stealing for Girls" (in *Ultimate Sports,* 1995) is the story of a father and his basketball-playing daughter. Weaver says he liked writing this story because "it let me broaden my base by paying attention to young girls and athletes." Weaver's daughter, a high school basketball player, suggested to him when he was working on a Billy Baggs book that he should write something for girls. Thus began a collaboration between father and daughter. He and his daughter, Caitlin, worked together for a summer crafting the first draft of a novel about girls' basketball, titled *Nothing But Net.* "It was a wonderful experience, a true collaboration," says Weaver. "We wrote in adjoining rooms and went back and forth. I would keep the plot from spinning off too far, and she was providing stunning texture, detail, and imagery that I was not privy to." While his editor was interested in the manuscript and proposed that father and daughter collaborate on a trilogy, the project stalled and remains on hold.

imagery words or phrases that appeal to one or more of the five senses in order to create a mental picture

The second short story is "The Photograph" (in *No Easy Answers,* 1997). This is a powerful story of peer pressure, bad choices, and unfortunate implications, as a student photographer is drafted by two football players to get a picture of an attractive young teacher skinny-dipping. The photographer gets more than he expected in the photograph he takes, and it initiates a series of dire consequences. This story, like Weaver's next novel, is not about sports.

trilogy a series of three literary works that are closely related and share a single theme

The third short story, "Bootleg Summer," is set in the 1920s. It appears in *Time Capsule: Short Stories About Teenagers Throughout the Twentieth Century* (1999), an anthology of ten stories by different authors with each story focusing on a different decade of the twentieth century.

Weaver is completing his fourth novel, *Memory Boy*, which is totally different from anything he has written before. It is a story of a brother and sister who confront a changing world. "It's, as they say in Hollywood, a high concept book. It takes place after a natural disaster of world-class proportions and when there is global cooling and life changes. I'm working with a family that has to relearn some lessons about surviving."

While Weaver felt the need to explore other stories and take a break from Billy and his friends (in fact he suspects that he "had gotten tired of me"), he plans to return to the Billy Baggs saga in the future so that readers can look forward to catching up with them. Perhaps the best news is that Weaver plans to reduce his teaching to half-time soon so that he will be able to spend more time writing. He believes that dividing his time more equally will provide a better balance between his love of teaching and of writing.

If you like the works of Will Weaver, you might also like the works of Chris Crutcher, Terry Davis, and, David Klass.

Selected Bibliography

WORKS BY WILL WEAVER

Novels for Young Adults

Striking Out (1993)

Farm Team (1995)

Hard Ball (1998)

SHORT STORIES

"Stealing for Girls." In *Ultimate Sports: Short Stories by Outstanding Writers for Young Adults.* Edited by Donald R. Gallo. New York: Delacorte Press, 1995, pp. 93–115.

"The Photograph." In *No Easy Answers: Short Stories About Teenagers Making Tough Choices.* Edited by Donald R. Gallo. New York: Delacorte Press, 1997, pp. 3–24.

"Bootleg Summer." In *Time Capsule: Short Stories About Teenagers Throughout the Twentieth Century.* Edited by Donald R. Gallo. New York: Bantam Doubleday Dell, 1999.

Books for Adults

Red Earth, White Earth (1986; novel)

A Gravestone Made of Wheat (1989; short stories)

WORKS ABOUT WILL WEAVER

Barron, Ronald. "Will Weaver: A Grand Slam in His First At-Bat." *ALAN Review,* winter 1996.

Brown, Jean E. "Some Musings on Our National Pastime: Baseball in Young Adult Literature." *Signal,* fall 1996, pp. 11–14.

Crowe, Chris. "Sportlerroman: Coming of Age on the Playing Field." *Signal,* fall 1996, pp. 11–14.

How to Write to the Author

Will Weaver
English Department
Bemidji State University
1500 Birchmont Drive, NE
Bemidji, MN 56601-2699

You can also e-mail
Will Weaver at
weaverww@vax1.bemidji.msus.edu

Walt Whitman

(1819–1892)

by Mike Angelotti

Camerado, this is no book,
Who touches this touches a man,
(Is it night? are we here together alone?)
It is I you hold and who holds you,
I spring from the pages into your arms—decease calls me
    forth.
("So Long!", 1881, ll. 53–57, *Leaves of Grass*)

I n 1855 Walt Whitman self-published *Leaves of Grass,* a
book of twelve poems printed by Rome Brothers of
Brooklyn, New York, to mixed reviews, some quite negative. Sales of only a few hundred were disappointing to a
writer whose ambition was to be "absorbed" by the masses.
Whittier reportedly threw his complimentary copy into the
fire. Longfellow and Lowell criticized it severely. Emerson, almost alone among American writers, praised the book. In it,
Whitman, always the free thinker, challenged an American literary establishment that he believed was too influenced by
Old World literary tradition. He characterized his poetry as

Dates for poems in this essay
reflect final revision dates.

John Greenleaf **Whit-
tier** (1807–1892) was
an American poet.
Henry Wadsworth
Longfellow
(1807–1882) was a
widely published
American poet of the
1800s. James Russell
Lowell (1819–1891)
was an American poet
and diplomat.
Ralph Waldo **Emerson**
(1803–1882) was an
American writer who
believed that knowl-
edge of the physical
world was secondary
to pure knowledge of
a spiritual world.

335

experimental, termed his poetic mission "a war," and fought the battle to establish a body of truly American poetry—one that featured American language, American life, an American vision, and musical free verse—to his dying breath. He did it by revising, expanding, and promoting that one book, *Leaves of Grass,* through nine editions over his lifetime, concluding his work with the publication of his so-called "deathbed edition" in 1891–1892. Now, more than a century after his death, Walt Whitman is known throughout the world primarily for that one collection of poetry and prose, commonly thought to be the most influential work on the development of a unique American poetry in the history of the United States to date.

How is it that this seemingly mainstream newspaperman, fiction writer, and poet from Brooklyn, New York, could produce such a unique and powerful book as *Leaves of Grass* in 1855 in a style and voice so different from his previously published work? What was there about his life prior to 1855 that prepared him to become America's poet?

Life and Writing to 1855

Walt Whitman was the second child in a family of nine children. He was born in rural West Hills, near Huntington, Long Island, on 31 May 1819. His father, Walter, was a blunt-speaking and freethinking (he claimed Thomas Paine as a friend) farmer and carpenter of English descent; his mother, Louisa, was lively, imaginative, and a good storyteller of Dutch origin. The family fell on hard times and moved to Brooklyn to improve their situation when Walt was four. He completed five years of schooling and then worked primarily as a printer, teacher, fiction writer, and journalist in the New York area until he published the first *Leaves of Grass.* Politically, Whitman became a loyal Democrat in the highly charged Tammany Hall political atmosphere of New York City and Brooklyn (then separate cities) in the 1840s and 1850s, and he often wrote editorials, sometimes as satiric or biting poems typical of the times. He was often fired, only to move on to another newspaper, or to establish his own.

While writing countless journalistic pieces, Whitman also experimented with the popular dark, sensationalistic, and moral forms of the day, publishing, according to David Reynolds in his *Walt Whitman's America* (1995), twenty-four pieces of fiction and nineteen poems. Reynolds points out, ironically, that Whitman's only novel, *Franklin Evans; or The*

---

free verse poetry that does not follow traditional forms, meters, or rhyme schemes

prose writing without regular rhythm; ordinary writing

Tammany Hall was the headquarters and nickname for the Society of Tammany, which became a political machine with vast powers of the Democratic Party. Many scandals have occurred during its history. Tammany Hall dominated New York City politics until 1933.

satiric ridiculing through sarcasm and irony

sensationalistic shocking, intense, and disturbing (such emotional responses are often achieved by using gruesome details)

ironically marked by a contrast between what is said and what is actually meant

Inebriate, A Tale of the Times (1842), was his "most popular work during his lifetime (it sold some twenty thousand copies)" (p. 94). Although in these early writings he had not yet crystalized the style that was to dominate *Leaves,* Whitman was continuously experimenting with it in his notebooks.

Influences

Reynolds suggests in his book that by examining the culture surrounding Whitman's life one can better understand the influences on the evolution of Whitman's poetry. He discusses among the social elements that attracted Whitman the character of his parents, liberal philosophies and the fiery politics of the day, progressive education, and evangelical preachers. There also were Whitman's prolific writing practice and the works of other writers, particularly Sir Walter Scott and MacDonald Clarke, "the so-called Mad Poet of Broadway." Reynolds' point of view, in fact, is consistent with Whitman's own sense that his personal history significantly shaped his writing. Whitman's intention, as I read it, was to "sing" as a representative American the culture and events of his American experience. As will be shown later, for example, he was very much moved by the American Civil War ("the secession outbreak" as he called it) and explored it extensively in prose and poetry at a very personal level. One key to understanding Whitman, then, is to understand the culture that shaped him. But how is one to understand a culture more than a century in the past?

evangelical referring to a person who preaches the gospel with militant or crusading enthusiasm

prolific producing a large amount

Sir Walter Scott (1771–1832) was a Scottish writer, famous for his works of historical fiction such as *Ivanhoe* and *The Talisman.*

Purposes

One place to begin such a study is with a cultural biography such as that written by David Reynolds. Another, and foremost, is with Walt Whitman's interpretations of his own century and its connections to his purposes for writing. In "A Backward Glance O'er Travel'd Roads" (1889), the poet, then seventy, wrote what he wanted to be his final essay on *Leaves.*

To explore Whitman's purpose and provide background for later discussions of particular poems, selected excerpts from "Backward Glance" are here presented as printed in Small, Maynard, and Company's 1907 edition of *Leaves*—a faithful reprint of Walt Whitman's personally revised final version of *Leaves of Grass,* the 1891–1892 edition.

ardor eagerness or passion

motif situation or theme

verse here, poetry

genesis-motive a reason for the creation of a work

theme central message about life in a literary work

Perhaps this in brief, or suggests, all I have sought to do. . . . "Leaves of Grass" is, or seeks to be, simply a faithful and doubtless self-will'd record. In the midst of all, it gives one man's—the author's—identity, ardors, observations, faiths, and thoughts, color'd hardly at all with any decided coloring from other faiths or other identities. . . . quite solely with reference to America and to-day [p. 435]. . . . In the centre of all, and object of all, stands the Human Being, towards whose heroic and spiritual evolution poems and everything directly or indirectly tend, Old World or New [p. 440]. . . . I have allow'd the stress of my poems from beginning to end to bear upon American individuality. . . . I avowedly chant "the great pride of man in himself," and permit it to be more or less a *motif* of nearly all my verse [p. 443]. . . . Without yielding an inch the working-man and working-woman were to be in my pages from first to last. . . . the poems of women entirely as much as men [pp. 443–444]. . . . One main genesis-motive of the "Leaves" was my conviction (just as strong to-day as ever) that the crowning growth of the United States is to be spiritual and heroic. To help start and favor that growth—or even to call attention to it, or the need of it—is the beginning, middle and final purpose of the poems. [P. 445]

Leaves of Grass

Did Walt Whitman fulfill his promises by the evidence of his poems? Clearly so. Whitman was so focused on his main themes of individualism, love, America, democracy, union, the soul, death (immortality), and nature that one could choose a page of *Leaves* virtually at random and find most or all of them.

In the first three lines of one of the best known of his poems, "Song of Myself" (1881), for example, he celebrates at once individualism and the union of all human beings:

I CELEBRATE myself, and sing myself,
And what I assume, you shall assume,

For every atom belonging to me as good belongs to you.

(ll. 1–3, part 1)

Interpretation of the "I" as used by Whitman in *Leaves of Grass* is both unique and initially problematic for the reader. Whitman intended that his narrative voice represent Whitman as himself and all Americans of his time as a kind of conglomerate first person addressing the reader directly. Further, he also includes the reader in the "I" so that in these lines, for example, the reader joins the first person and sings of himself or herself, "I CELEBRATE myself." The point is that Whitman in exemplifying his ideal democracy is inviting the reader to become one with him through his poems, to join him in chanting "the great pride of man in himself."

narrative related to the telling of a story

conglomerate made from many different parts

In addition, he wrote the entire volume of *Leaves* as one poem, making each poem within it part of the whole, so that the full meaning of the first poem is not accessible until the last is read, and so on through multiple readings. In the end, *Leaves of Grass* becomes his book and the reader's book and the book of all humankind. For deeper discussions of Walt Whitman's own interpretations of *Leaves* and selected individual poems, please see Richard Maurice Bucke's *Walt Whitman* (1883). That book, like a number of others written about *Leaves* during that period, was written under the close supervision and revision of the poet himself, and therefore its interpretations ring with a certain authenticity that those written after his death cannot.

The first edition of *Leaves of Grass* featured twelve poems and the famous preface of 1855. The last edition revised and recommended by the poet was the 1891–1892 edition. During the intervening years, Whitman added, deleted, revised, rearranged poems and thematic sections, and shifted parts of poems from one poem to another. In general, he worked incessantly to bring his vision of *Leaves* to fruition by his own hand only, ending with a single unified poem titled *Leaves of Grass* and composed of a number of thematic sections.

preface the introductory remarks of an author

incessantly without interruption

So many different poems and sections have been preferred over the years, and the overall quality of work is so high, that it is difficult to point to one or another as superior. For example, the sections "Calamus" and "Drum-Taps" have both been recognized for their excellence.

"Calamus" explores the themes of democracy and comradeship through a number of poems, particularly in "Song of the Open Road" (1881).

I give you my love more precious than money, . . .
Will you give me yourself? will you come travel with me?
Shall we stick by each other as long as we live? (ll. 8,
    10–11, part 15)

"Drum-Taps" is a study of a nation at war with, as Whitman promised, a focus on the individuals affected, whose personal stories are often omitted from war records and news reports that become generalized accounts of battles and armies. Whitman nursed wounded soldiers through most of the Civil War and captured much of its personal horror in his notebooks, which were published as part of *Specimens and Collect.* Particular notebook entries often formed the substance of poems that later appeared in *Leaves.* One example is "The Wound-Dresser" (1881). In it, he writes:

From the stump of the arm, the amputated hand,
I undo the clotted lint, remove the slough, wash off the
    matter and blood,
Back on his pillow the soldier bends with curv'd neck and
    side-falling head,
His eyes are closed, his face is pale, he dares not look on
    the bloody stump,
And has not yet look'd on it. (ll. 7–11, part 3)

Closely related to and immediately following, "Drum-Taps" is a section titled "Memories of President Lincoln," which features one of Whitman's best-known poems, "When Lilacs Last in the Dooryard Bloom'd" (1881), an elegy to the president that followed the journey of his coffin from Washington to its burial place in Illinois. It begins:

When lilacs last in the dooryard bloom'd,
And the great star early droop'd in the western sky in the
    night,
I mourn'd, and yet shall mourn with ever-returning
    spring. (ll. 1–3, part 1)

Final Thoughts

What is it that so characterized Whitman's poetry that it should be held in such high regard today? His skillfulness with his chosen poetic form? Command of American English? Willingness to experiment? Timing? Artist's eye? Choices of subject matter? His energy, freedom of spirit, arrogance, single-mindedness, genius, enthusiasm, voice? Absolute belief in his aims? For world-renowned poet Galway Kinnell, in his essay "Walt Whitman's Indicative Words" (1973), reprinted in *Walt Whitman's Autograph Revision of the Analysis of* Leaves of Grass (1974), it is Whitman's musical line, "what I can only call the mystic music of his voice. . . . No one before him had thrust his presence and actual voice so boldly onto the written page. . . . The music seems to flow from a source deeper even than its words" (p. 54).

Walt Whitman left a rich treasure of his life, his times, and his writing. There are his own books, letters, articles, notebooks, fragments—he threw very little away. He had faithful friends and editors who kept every scrap of his work that they could capture. Some of these contemporaries collaborated with him to write favorable books under their own names. Chief among them were those who became his literary executors: Richard M. Bucke, whose analytical *Walt Whitman* has already been mentioned; Thomas B. Harned; and Horace L. Traubel. Today they are all gone, and his work stands on its own merit. Their legacy (and Whitman's) is that we can literally follow in detail, from his own hand, the development of his poems (and his writer's mind) over more than thirty years of revisions, his thinking about particular poems and poetry in general, and his approaches to writing from idea to finished poem.

For all of his effort Walt Whitman, although finally recognized by the American literary community in his later years, was only modestly appreciated by the masses he coveted, and he seldom earned enough money from his poetry to keep himself above the poverty level. He was overlooked for a long time after his death by twentieth-century American literary figures. About this point, Galway Kinnell wrote:

> For [Ezra] Pound, [T.S.] Eliot, [Robert] Frost, and [William Carlos] Williams, Whitman meant very little. Whitman's return to American poetry, if we can set a date, did not come until 101 years after the appearance of *Leaves of Grass,* with the publication of [Allen] Ginsberg's Howl in 1956. . . . Only now is Whitman accepted as our greatest native master, the bearer of the American tradition. (P. 54)

Galway Kinnell (1927–) is an American poet. He won the Pulitzer Prize for American Poetry for his Selected Poems in 1983.

Ezra Pound (1885–1972), **T. S. Eliot** (1888–1965), **Robert Frost** (1874–1963), and **William Carlos Williams** (1883–1963) were important American poets of the 1900s. There is an article about Robert Frost in volume 2. **Allen Ginsburg** (1926–) is another American poet. **"Howl"** is one of his most famous poems.

effuse to pour out

bequeath to give or leave something, as by a will

Walt Whitman's belief in himself and his poetry was unshakable. He believed that *Leaves of Grass* would make its mark on future generations. He never lost sight of the indivisible union of his poetry, his soul, and his immortality, so present in "Song of Myself":

> I depart as air, I shake my white locks at the runaway sun,
> I effuse my flesh in eddies, and drift it in lacy jags.

> I bequeath myself to the dirt to grow from the grass I
>   love,
> If you want me again look for me under your boot-soles.
>   (ll. 7–10, part 52)

At 6:43 P.M. on 26 March 1892, Walt Whitman died of bronchial pneumonia in his own bed at 328 Wickle Street, Camden, New Jersey, not long after proposing to friends a new edition of *Leaves of Grass* for children.

If you like Walt Whitman, you might also like Stephen Crane, Emily Dickinson, Edgar Allan Poe, and Mark Twain, contemporaries of Whitman with very different approaches to writing poetry. You might also enjoy Carl Sandburg, a poet of the early twentieth century whose style was very much influenced by Whitman, and Maya Angelou, a modern poet whose strong voice also resonates among Americans.

Selected Bibliography

WORKS BY WALT WHITMAN

Poetry

Leaves of Grass: Including Sands at Seventy, Good Bye My Fancy, Old Age Echoes, and A Backward Glance O'er Travel'd Roads. Boston: Small, Maynard & Company, 1907. A faithful reprinting of Whitman's preferred and recommended version of his 1891–1892 so-called "deathbed edition" of *Leaves of Grass,* personally revised by the poet. The 1891–1892 edition includes virtually all of Whitman's completed poems as he last revised them.

Walt Whitman's Blue Book: The 1860–1861 Leaves of Grass Containing His Manuscript Additions and Revisions. Volume I: Facsimile of the unique copy in the Oscar Lion Collection of The New York Public Library. New York: New York Public Library, 1968. The more serious researcher is interested in reviewing primary sources, those representing exactly, or as closely as we have on record, the written words of Walt Whitman. For example, facsimile copies of Whitman's famous "Blue Book" edition, his personal copy of the 1860 third edition of *Leaves,* is readily available in most university and large public libraries. In it you will find handwritten revisions of many of the poems that appeared in his 1867 fourth edition of *Leaves of Grass.*

Walt Whitman. Leaves of Grass: Comprehensive Reader's Edition. (Including the annexes, the prefaces, *A Backward Glance O'er Travel'd Roads, Old Age Echoes,* The Excluded Poems and Fragments, and The Uncollected Poems and Fragments) Blodgett, Harold and Bradley, Scully, ed. New York: New York University Press, 1967. Not only claims "to present in one volume and in accurate text the whole body of Walt Whitman's poems" but also includes a detailed introduction to the poet's work as well as historical and literary notes for most of the poems included.

Prose

Franklin Evans; or The Inebriate, A Tale of the Times. New York: The New World Extra Series, 1842. A "temperance" novel first published serially in the weekly newspaper *The New World.* Franklin Evans was Whitman's best selling work (about 20,000 copies) during his lifetime. In his later years he called it "damned rot." The novel was later reprinted in the *Brooklyn Daily Eagle* under the nontemperance title of *Fortunes of a Country-Boy; Incidents in Town—and His Adventures at the South.*

Specimen Days & Collect. New York: Dover, 1995. A complete and unabridged republication of the book as originally issued by David McKay, Philadelphia, and Wilson & McCormick, Glasgow, 1882–1883. Includes *Specimen Days* (day to day notebook entries) & *Collect* (essays, prefaces to editions of *Leaves* and other prose; fiction and other pieces "from early youth"). Important to the researcher interested in autobiographical information and source material for Whitman's poems. Written and edited by the poet.

Poetry and Prose

Complete Poems and Prose of Walt Whitman, 1855–1888/ Authenticated and Personal Book. Philadelphia: Ferguson Brothers, 1888. Includes poetry to that time as well as *November Boughs* and other prose. Edited by the poet.

Walt Whitman, Leaves of Grass: A Selection of Poems and Prose. The New-York Public Library's Collector's Edition. New York: Doubleday, 1997. Provides an excellent introduction to Whitman, a sampling of his works, and brief discussions of current scholarship. Especially useful to the beginning researcher is the "Suggestions For Further Reading" section (431–438) that presents annotated listings of biographies, criticism, and books "of related interest," some of which are referenced in this essay. Throughout the book proper are photographs and facimiles that bring the reader a step closer to Walt Whitman and his nineteenth century America.

Letters

Miller, Edwin Haviland, ed. *Selected Letters of Walt Whitman.* Iowa City: University of Iowa Press, 1990.

WORKS ABOUT WALT WHITMAN

Allen, Gay Wilson, and Ed Folsom, eds. *Walt Whitman & the World.* Iowa City: University of Iowa Press, 1995. More than 100 international writers and scholars discuss how Whitman has been absorbed into cultures from around the world for more than a century—a fascinating world's view of Whitman.

Hindus, Milton, ed. *Walt Whitman: The Critical Heritage.* London: Routledge & Kegan Paul, 1971. Commentaries, often personal, by Whitman contemporaries and others.

Krieg, Joann P. *A Whitman Chronology.* Iowa City: University of Iowa Press, 1998.

Lawrence, D. H. "Whitman." *Studies in Classic American Literature.* New York: Doubleday, 1953. Reprint of 1923 original edition. A second version of this essay by Lawrence appears in Armin, Arnold, ed. *D. H. Lawrence: The Symbolic Meaning (The uncollected versions of Studies in Classic American Literature).* Fontwell, Arundel, England: Centaur Press, 1962.

Loving, Jerome. *Walt Whitman: The Song of Himself.* Berkeley, Calif.: University of California Press, 1999.

Murphy, Francis, ed. *Walt Whitman: A Critical Anthology.* Harmondsworth, England: Penguin Books, 1970. Includes reviews by Henry James, William Carlos Williams, and Amy Lowell, among others, and by Whitman himself.

Perlman, Jim; Ed Folsom; and Dan Campion, eds. *Walt Whitman: The Measure of His Song.* Minneapolis: Holy Cow Press, 1981. Poets respond critically to Walt Whitman. Includes Ezra Pound, Langston Hughes, Allen Ginsberg, Robert Bly, and Pablo Neruda.

Reynolds, David S. *Walt Whitman's America: A Cultural Biography.* New York: Vintage Books, 1996. In Reynolds' words, his purpose was to compose a "recreation of Walt Whitman's life and art in the historical context of his culture, the way he experienced it as a vital, sensitive journalist and poet." Describes in well-researched and corroborated detail the cultural influences on Walt Whitman and his work.

Traubel, Horace. *With Walt Whitman in Camden.* Seven vols. Vol. 1, Boston: Small, Maynard & Co., 1906; vol. 2, New York: D. Appleton, 1908; vol. 3, New York: Mitchell, Kennerly, 1914; vol. 4, Philadelphia: University of Pennsylvania Press, 1953; vol. 5–7, Carbondale, IL: Southern Illinois University Press, 1964, 1982, 1992. A day-to-day record of conversations between Traubel and Whitman during the last four years of Whitman's life.

Walt Whitman's Autograph Revision of the Analysis of Leaves of Grass *(For Dr. R. M. Bucke's Walt Whitman).* Includes two critical essays: "Whitman's New Man" by Quentin Anderson; "Walt Whitman's Indicative Words" by Galway Kinnell, reprinted from *American Poetry Review,* March/April 1973; text notes by Stephen Railton; thirty-five facsimile pages of the manuscript; final two chapters and appendix of R. M. Bucke's *Walt Whitman.* New York: New York University Press, 1974. An important resource because Bucke's analysis of *Leaves* was reviewed, revised, and approved by Whitman himself before publication, providing the reader-researcher with an authentic source of the poet's intent.

Zweig, Paul. *Walt Whitman: The Making of the Poet.* New York: Basic Books, Inc., 1984.

The Walt Whitman Cultural Arts Center, located in Camden, New Jersey, is a nonprofit, multicultural center for the arts dedicated to continuing the legacy of its namesake. You can write to or visit the center at:

Walt Whitman
Cultural Arts Center, Inc.
Johnson Park
2nd and Cooper Streets
Camden, NJ 08102

You can also visit
the website at
www.waltwhitmancenter.org

Thornton Wilder

(1897–1975)

by Jeffrey S. Kaplan

A Writer for All Times

In my family, no writer is more revered than Thornton Wilder. Why? His wonderful play *Our Town* (1938). In my lifetime, my family and I must have seen nearly a dozen productions of *Our Town,* and whether the performance is a local high school or a Broadway production, I am always moved. The sheer simplicity of this carefully constructed masterpiece about life in a small town always grabs me like no other work of literature. Perhaps it is the sheer theatricality of showing small pleasures in a dramatic fashion or the underlying meaning of how everyone's life, no matter how small or large, does really matter. I am always affected.

Today high schools, community theaters, college drama departments, and professional acting companies continue to tackle *Our Town,* a seemingly simple but deceptively difficult play. This story of two families in a small New England town and their living and dying captures the essence of what it means to be alive. Young people coming of age, middle-aged

refrain a regularly repeated phrase or verse

couples, and retired folk settling into their remaining years can relate to this drama's powerful statement about the virtues of simple pleasures. I am particularly taken by its haunting refrain that everything in life is precious and that, in our hurried existence, we rarely remember to stop and give thanks.

Thornton Wilder is the only author to receive the Pulitzer Prize for both drama and fiction. His novel *The Bridge of San Luis Rey* (1927) and his two plays, *Our Town* and *The Skin of Our Teeth* (1942), are his best-known works, and they reaffirm his optimistic and life-affirming philosophy. Yet they cannot be more different in style and tone. Each work promotes Wilder's deeply believed set of values—Christian morality, community, family, and the appreciation of life's simple moments—but his methods, especially in his plays, are unorthodox. For his time and place, Thornton Wilder was a very different writer, and his desire to be seen as unique—as a man who has something important to say and in a way that makes readers and audiences sit up and listen—is what makes him most distinct in American literature.

optimistic tendency to look on the bright side of things

unorthodox not conforming to established doctrine

Thornton Wilder will always be remembered as not just a philosopher—but an innovator. He will be written about years hence as someone who helped shaped the way we look at our world and made a difference in how we perceive ourselves. His attention to the inside of human beings—the ways people feel in the most delicate and difficult of circumstances—has long stood the test of time, and continues to intrigue and delight new generations of young readers. Wilder's novels and plays are read and performed in high schools across the world, for each reading and rendition brings to light something that we have not seen before. Each new look at this author's funny and moving accounts of the human condition tells us something that we had not seen before in our own lives. And, I suppose, that is why I continue to seek out performances of *Our Town* and revisit Wilder's writings. Thornton Wilder is a writer for all times.

Thornton Wilder—His Life

Thornton Wilder came from a family of writers. His father, Amos Parker Wilder, was a newspaper owner and editor and U.S. consul general for Hong Kong and Shanghai. His brother, Amos Niven Wilder, was a highly acclaimed professor of New Testament scholarship and a noted poet. His sister Isabel

Wilder was the author of three popular novels and curator of the Yale theater archive. Another sister, Charlotte Wilder, was a professor of English and an award-winning poet. The youngest Wilder, Janet Wilder Dakin, was a professor of biology and a respected environmentalist. To be sure, the Wilder family made its mark across many generations and in many fields.

Thornton Niven Wilder began life in Madison, Wisconsin, on 17 April 1897, the son of Amos Parker and Isabella Thornton Niven Wilder. His father brought his family to Wisconsin when he became owner and editor of the *Wisconsin State Journal.* The Wilders were members of the First Congregational Church, a place that figures prominently in many of his novels and plays. The family stayed in Wisconsin until 1906, when Wilder's father, Amos, was appointed U.S. consul general to Hong Kong. There his family stayed until they returned to the United States, and Thornton was able to complete high school in Berkeley, California.

After high school, Wilder attended Oberlin College for two years, then transferred to Yale University, where he completed his bachelor's degree. At Yale he published his first full-length play, *The Trumpet Shall Sound,* in the *Yale Literary Magazine* in 1919. After graduation, Wilder traveled to Rome, where he spent a year studying, of all things, archaeology. This experience is credited with shaping his deep interest in the human condition and the passage of time—certainly, a theme reflected often in his works.

theme central message about life in a literary work

Upon returning to the United States, Wilder set out to become a teacher, first teaching French at the Lawrenceville School in New Jersey. He left Lawrenceville four years later to attend Princeton University, where he received his master's degree in French in 1926. Still, Wilder kept his dream alive to become a writer, supplementing his income by writing silent film scripts. In the same year that he finished Princeton, he completed his first novel. This novel, *The Cabala* (1926), is the story of a young American student's firsthand experience of living in Europe and joining a mysterious social group called, aptly, "the Cabala." In this story, Wilder establishes his reputation as a writer to be watched.

Wilder's literary reputation was established, though, with the publication of his second novel, *The Bridge of San Luis Rey,* for which he won the Pulitzer Prize. Set in 1700 Peru, Wilder portrays a priest's desperate quest to discover a theological meaning for the accidental death of five people when a

theological relating to the study of God and God's relation to the world

charismatic possessing extraordinary personal charm

landmark of unusual historical or aesthetic interest

bridge collapses. This haunting and enduring work cemented Wilder's recognition for what in life is most enduring—family, friends, and faith.

With his writing ability recognized, Wilder and his sister Isabel began a tour of Europe in 1928 to study stage production techniques in various countries. His love for the theater, nurtured at his parents' feet and evident in his early plays, came to full bloom as he now felt more secure about himself and his life as a writer. Returning to the United States, he taught at the University of Chicago during the 1930s and lectured widely throughout the United States. Well known as an inspiring and charismatic speaker, Wilder was not content to rest on his laurels, and he continued his adventure into playwrighting. In 1938, his landmark play, *Our Town,* was produced at the McCarter Theater at Princeton University, but it received poor reviews. Still, Wilder believed deeply in his new work, and he made a creative suggestion to the director—he wanted the props and scenery removed. Upon seeing his play performed, Wilder had realized that "getting rid of the real walls and hand properties," would reveal the true essence of the play—the simplicity of the human condition. And of course, he was right. *Our Town* became a 1938 Broadway success, and Thornton Wilder received his second Pulitzer Prize.

During World War II, Wilder served in the U.S. Air Force, but that did not stop his creativity. He received his third Pulitzer Prize for *The Skin of Our Teeth,* a play about how people from all walks of life (and time periods) share the same thoughts and feelings. Thus, by the 1950s, Wilder had solidly established himself as a major figure in American literature. He was the Charles Eliot Norton Professor of Poetry at Harvard from 1951 to 1952, on the cover of *Time* magazine on 12 January 1953, and was awarded the Presidential Medal of Freedom in 1963. During his later years, Wilder continued to write, producing most notably *The Eighth Day* (1967), for which he won the National Book Award.

Wilder spent his later years in Hamden, Connecticut, where he died on 7 December 1975. He was 78 years old. He never married.

Thornton Wilder—His Writings

There is possibly not a night in any year when *Our Town* is not being played somewhere in the world. Audiences feel a special connection with the play, often feeling that it was written just for them. Yet when all is said and done, Wilder is equally remembered for his other literary creations—a collection of writings that spans many kinds and styles.

Wilder published his best-known novel, *The Bridge of San Luis Rey,* at the tender age of thirty, in 1927. With this spare and elegant work, Wilder established his reputation as a writer of great depth and artistry. The story is about the collapse of a bridge that, without warning or meaning, kills five of the novel's half-dozen characters. Only his second novel, this work is set in eighteenth-century Peru and portrays a priest's quest to discover a religious meaning for the accidental death of five people when a bridge collapses. The Jesuit priest, Brother Juniper, wonders: Was the bridge falling and the death of five people accidental, or divine intervention? Brother Juniper thinks divine intervention, but Wilder does not say. He knows that it is the readers' job to come to their own conclusion about why this bridge, at this time, carrying these five souls, has collapsed. Wilder understates his questions about the role of fate and religion with simple sentences and deep thoughts.

Jesuit a member of the Roman Catholic Society of Jesus, which is devoted to missionary and educational work

Wilder's characters on the bridge are filled with the same sweet sadness that underline his novel. There are the sweet old duchess who loves her grown daughter but does not feel loved in return; a beautiful, but unfortunate genius of an actress who after a life of raucous behavior, suddenly decides to become a nun; a tutor who is a jolly old rogue but a true worshiper of literature; and finally, two strange brothers who love each other with a deep and abiding passion. These are the characters who fall to their death when the San Luis Rey bridge collapses beneath them, and these are the people who haunt the mind of Brother Juniper. Brother Juniper's attempt to reconcile their sudden and horrifying death is the crux of this Pulitzer Prize–winning book.

raucous loud and disorderly

rogue mischievous person

crux essential point requiring resolution

I suppose Wilder's work is so widely read and well received by young adults because after years of scientific advancement, people still pay tribute to the uncertainty of chance. From praying to knocking on wood, people everywhere harbor their own doubts and leaps of faith. *The Bridge of San Luis Rey* raises again the eternal question: Do events happen by accident or design? Wilder poses this philosophical dilemma, only to conclude that no matter what your answer is, love and loving others in the moment is the only salvation in the face of such horror. Whether by design or accident, the fate of those who perish is forever entwined with the fate of the living.

The Bridge of San Luis Rey also continues to be popular because of Wilder's economy of style. Written in simple sentences and a third the length of an average novel, this book still packs a large wallop and manages to excite even the most reluctant readers.

Two plays, *Our Town* and *The Skin of Our Teeth,* are Wilder's best-known theatrical creations. His other plays include *The Long Christmas Dinner* (1931), a wonderful and haunting one-act play about one family's Christmas dinner as seen over the span of ninety years, and *The Matchmaker* (1957), a light comedy about love and marriage in Yonkers, New York, which was later made into the international musical *Hello Dolly!*

High schools perform *The Long Christmas Dinner* and *Our Town* with stunning regularity. The simplicity of theme and set make for easy productions and much discussion. And the special quality of Wilder's writing—simple declarative sentences—provides an avenue for easy access for readers of all ages and abilities.

Our Town focuses on life in early 1900s Grover's Corners, a small New Hampshire town, and is presented in three acts titled "Daily Life," "Love and Marriage," and "Death." Each act depicts another life event in the ordinary lives of the citizens of Grover's Corners and in particular two families, the Gibbs and the Webbs. Their comings and goings and the marriage of their two children, George Gibb and Emily Webb, are the focus of the play's clear and simple action. The play is held together by an omniscient stage manager who narrates the drama. His presence is meant to interweave the story and characters so the unfolding events can be seen in some grand context. In the play's third act, Emily Webb, who has by now married George Gibb and unfortunately died in childbirth, is granted the opportunity to relive her twelfth birthday. On a bare stage, with only chairs representing graves, Emily descends into the "real world," and learns firsthand how "precious life really is." Her moving return to relive her life is Wilder's cautionary reminder that we should never forget how wonderful life is in even the ordinary detail of the day.

Hello Dolly! was made into a film starring Barbra Streisand in 1969.

omniscient having complete knowledge

narrate to tell a story

context environment; setting

The power of *Our Town* rests in answering profound questions in simple fashion. By showing characters living ordinary lives, Wilder resists high drama to make his point. Elegantly and movingly, he shows how even ordinary events can be viewed as exceptional moments of significance and thus are filled with a dignity all their own. *Our Town* continues to be performed around the world because it presents the fragility of the human life in quiet terms.

On the other hand, *The Skin of Our Teeth* is Thornton Wilder's tip of the hat to just plain fun. Like his other works, *The Skin of Our Teeth* asks hard questions about the human condition: How do human beings survive in the face of great tragedy? What inspires people to prevail—despite everything? Yet in this two-act play, Wilder uses farce to demonstrate humankind's struggle to survive.

In this zany work, Wilder manipulates time so that events from different time periods seem to occur simultaneously. For instance, in Act I, a 1940s family from Excelsior, New Jersey, faces the bizarre and incomprehensible peril of the "ice age." In Act II, and Atlantic City beauty pageant takes place amidst preparations for the Great Flood. Truly, this strange and whimsical tale is made all the more fantastic by characters stepping in and out of character to share "their true feelings" with the audience. To add misery to misery, a pretend stage crew steps in every so often to fill in for actors who have become ill. This farce communicates Wilder's belief that the human will to survive is more powerful than any known disaster.

During the 1940s, Wilder served in World War II as a military intelligence officer and published little. During the 1950s, his work consisted primarily of revivals and revisions. Still, he did receive the American Academy of Arts and Letters' Gold Medal in 1952 for distinguished work in fiction. Wilder enjoyed great success with his novel *The Eighth Day* (1967), the story of a man who is falsely convicted of murdering his neighbor, is sent to prison, and then escapes and lives as a fugitive. The book won the National Book Award.

Thornton Niven Wilder was a novelist, playwright, essayist, screenwriter, translator, musician, and scholar. He was a man of many talents, and a creative and talented innovator of the theater. Above all, he was a writer who spoke of simple beauty in simple words. He was a writer my family will always remember.

Our Town has been made into several movies. A made-for-television version in 1989 starred Eric Stoltz as George and Penelope Ann Miller as Emily.

farce a light dramatic composition characterized by broad satirical comedy and a highly improbable plot

whimsical oddly humorous or fanciful

If you like Thornton Wilden's works, you might also like Sue Ellen Bridgers' *All Together Now* and Maureen Daly's *Sixteen and Other Stories.*

Selected Bibliography

WORKS BY THORNTON WILDER

Novels

The Cabala (1926)

The Bridge of San Luis Rey (1927)

The Woman of Andros (1930)

Heaven's My Destination (1934)

Ides of March (1948)

The Eighth Day (1967)

Theophilus North (1973)

The Alcestiad, or A Life in the Sun (1977)

Plays

The Trumpet Shall Sound (1919)

The Angel That Troubled the Waters and Other Plays (1928)

The Long Christmas Dinner and Other Plays in One Act (1931)

Our Town (1938)

Merchant of Yonkers (1939)

The Skin of Our Teeth (1942)

The Matchmaker (1955) [Revision of Merchant of Yonkers.]

Childhood (1960)

Infancy (1960)

WORKS ABOUT THORNTON WILDER

Burbank, Rex J. *Thornton Wilder.* New York: Twayne Publishers, 1978.

Castronovo, David. *Thornton Wilder.* New York: Ungar, 1986.

Goldstone, Richard Henry, and Gary Anderson. *Thornton Wilder: An Annotated Bibliography of Works by and About Thornton Wilder.* New York: AMS Press, 1982.

Gretzemer, Bernard. *Thornton Wilder.* Minneapolis: University of Minnesota Press, 1964.

Haberman, Donald C. *Our Town: An American Play.* Boston: Twayne Publishers, 1989.

Harrison, Gilbert A. *The Enthusiast: A Life of Thornton Wilder.* New Haven, Conn.: Ticknor and Fields, 1983.

Lifton, Paul. *Vast Encyclopedia: The Theater of Thornton Wilder.* Westport, Conn.: Greenwood Press, 1995.

Marowski, Daniel G., ed. *Contemporary Literary Criticism.* Detroit: Gale Research, 1994. vol. 82, pp. 336–393.

The Thornton Wilder Page. *www.sky.net/~emily/thornton. html*

Walsh, Claudette. *Thornton Wilder: A Reference Guide: 1926–1990.* New York: G. K. Hall, 1993.

Wilder, Amos Niven. *Thornton Wilder and His Public.* Philadelphia: Fortress Press, 1980.

Wilson, Lawrence. "The Question of Wilder." *Sewanee Review,* winter, 1987, pp. 162–168.

Thornton Wilder was once a resident of the MacDowell Colony in Peterborough, New Hampshire. This artists' colony, created to provide an environment in which creative artists are free to pursue their work without distraction, was founded in 1907. You can find out more about this colony at *www.nhptv. org/kn/itv/mcd/mcdabt.htm*

Carol Lynch Williams

(1959–)

by Chris Crowe

arol Lynch Williams has a great sense of humor. She has
to. She has a husband who travels all over, working on
Internet security, and she has five daughters.

Five.

Five daughters who do not go to school. Five daughters
who stay home everyday. All day. And Williams is their teacher.
And their mother. When she is not teaching or mothering, she
writes young adult novels: seven so far, with more on the way.
Without a sense of humor, she would never survive.

When you first meet her, though, you wouldn't guess that
she is the mother of five girls as well as a famous author who's
known for her funny streak. She looks younger than she really
is. Her light brown hair hangs straight to her shoulders, and
the dash of freckles across her nose and her ready smile make
her seem more like a girlfriend from school than a writer your
mother's age. At first, she is quiet, even a little shy. Her voice is
soft and earnest, with just a hint of Southern flavor in it. Once
you get her talking, she tells you about her daughters or her
husband or her home in Springville, Utah. You wouldn't know

Quotations from Carol Lynch
Williams that are not attributed
to a published source are from
personal interviews conducted
by the author of this article in
December 1998 and January
1999 and an unpublished autobiographical sketch dated 23
November 1998 and are published here by permission of
Carol Lynch Williams.

357

that she writes books, books that are sometimes funny and sometimes sad, or that she likes to laugh or that she hates violence or that she can use American Sign Language and served an LDS (Mormon) church mission to a deaf program in North Carolina.

After you talk with her a while, however, maybe after she trusts you, she is willing to talk about her books—and herself. That's when her sense of humor reveals itself. It is a droll humor; one-liners are delivered without a smile. Okay, maybe a mischievous smirk that lets you know she's trying to be funny. Her humor comes from real life, from funny situations, from surprising things that belong in the "truth is stranger than fiction" category.

Williams' Home Life

Of course, Williams' sense of humor also comes from living and working with five young girls. If you call her home during the day, the phone will be answered by Elise, the oldest. She's twelve, full of spunk and intelligence. While you're talking to Elise, eight-year-old Kyra bangs out "Minuet" on the piano in the background. Laura, ten, shouts something at Caitlynne, five. As Elise talks, you hear an occasional coo from one-year-old Carolina who's riding on Elise's hip. The room seems filled with noise and activity. It's not exactly chaos, but you can't think of a better word to describe it at the moment.

This is where Williams lives, sleeps, works, and writes.

You ask Elise what it's like having a mother who's a writer. "It's fun," she says, "'cause she gets to work at home. She sits at her computer upstairs in her office and writes, sometimes even in her pajamas. She writes mostly in the morning or later at night when we're in bed so she can get her writing done." Elise pauses: "—Hold on, I've got to go kill my sister. . . ." The phone clatters on a tabletop, but in a moment, she's back. "Mom doesn't like having us come into her office and ask her questions while she's writing, but we can get in there sometimes if she's been working all day and her neck hurts. We help her by rubbing her neck."

It's clear that these girls love their mother and love having her at home. They also love their mother's books, mainly because "her writing's funny." *My Angelica* (1999) is the girls' favorite because it is their mother's funniest novel.

Mormons are members of The Church of Jesus Christ of Latter-day Saints **(LDS)**. They believe that the church as established by Jesus Christ did not survive and was restored in modern times by a prophet, Joseph Smith. They consider theirs to be the true and complete church of Jesus Christ restored on Earth. Church headquarters are in Salt Lake City, Utah. There are more than ten million Latter-day Saints in the world; nearly two million members live in Utah.

droll oddly humorous

Her daughters willingly share the phone to talk about Mom. They tell you what she likes (breakfast in bed, chocolate caramel, See's candy) and what she hates (sharks, violent movies), what she does (dances in the kitchen with Dad) and what she can't do (rollerblade). There's lots of laughter as the phone is passed from one sister to the next. Eventually, after much giggling, they tell you Mom's not home but you can talk to her later if you want.

Williams Herself

When you finally get to sit down with Williams, she grins when you tell about your phone call and asks to set the record straight. About what she hates:

> Shopping malls, spending money, screaming and hollering, flying in airplanes, anything that might kill me or anyone I know. I'm afraid of heights. I'm paranoid of pain, of death in unusual ways. Okay, death period. I don't want to fall off anything. I don't want to burn to death. I don't want to be stabbed. I don't want to be in labor for the rest of my life, and I don't want to be in an elevator during an earthquake.

paranoid extremely fearful

She keeps talking, sometimes with a lopsided grin, about her family, her life, and her books. You settle down, taking notes as fast as you can. It's fun listening to Carol Lynch Williams, as much fun as reading her books.

Williams' Life

Born in Lincoln, Nebraska on 28 September 1959, Williams moved with her family to Florida, her mother's home state, soon after her birth. While she was still young, her father, a member of the U.S. Air Force, was transferred to England, taking Williams and her mother with him. Soon after her sister, Samantha, was born, the family moved back to Florida, and after a few years there, her parents divorced, when Williams was nine. She has little to say about her family life except, "Sam and I grew up in the typical dysfunctional home."

prominent widely
known

Though her home life may not have been what she had hoped for, Williams found other avenues of pleasure and security. She often lost herself in books, all kinds of books, but especially those by prominent Southern writers. She also enjoyed Florida life: fishing, swimming, playing outside with friends. Her years in Florida were important ones for her, so important that Florida has become the setting for nearly all her novels. "I've never gotten out of that Florida era," she says. "That's where I joined the [LDS] Church, and that's where family was: my aunts, my cousin and best friend, Kelly, and Nana."

Her grandmother, Nana, provided the family connection Williams longed for.

> **She loved us no matter what. When we stayed with her, she took us to the library, let me check out as many books as I wanted, let me climb into bed and read them. I don't remember my nana ever being mad at me, though I'm sure she had reasons to. She was kind and loving and a chain smoker, a card player, a beer drinker, but I never heard a swear word from her. There was nothing fake about Nana; she loved all her grandkids.**

Williams pauses for a moment, and her smile fades. "She died a few years ago, and still I miss her."

Though Williams loved learning, she never liked school. "School probably saved my life, but I hated it. I hated the way I felt, the way people treated me, the way I looked. We were always poor, so my clothes weren't what everyone else was wearing. I never had money for lunch, for anything. I hated it." When she was a teenager, her schools were battling over desegregation. "The tensions were unbearable, and I was afraid, so I dropped out of school when I was fifteen." She enrolled in an alternative school, took all the rest of her credits in a single year, and graduated from high school at sixteen. It was a "jam-packed year, but I loved the alternative school. I didn't feel stupid; they treated us more like adults than the other schools did."

At sixteen Williams enrolled at Seminole Community College. When she was seventeen, she joined the LDS church, and except for her eighteen-month church mission to North Carolina, she remained in Florida until she was twenty-three. "I wanted to marry in my religion, and there weren't many Mor-

desegregation the process of ending segregation, the separation of a race, class, or ethnic group by discriminatory means

mon guys in Florida, so I decided to move to Utah." In Utah she held a variety of jobs, including working as an interpreter for deaf students in local schools. She later met her husband at a church talent show; they married when she was almost twenty-six. Williams continued to work until her first daughter was born. Since then, she's been a stay-at-home mother—and writer.

Williams' Writing Career

An avid reader from the moment she learned to read, Williams fell in love with writing at an early age and wrote her first story when she was five or six. In an unpublished autobiographical sketch, she explained that it took her that long to have an experience worth writing about.

autobiographical related to the author's own life

> My cousin Kelly (who is the character base in my first book, *Kelly and Me* [1993], and hates the fact that the character dies at the end of the book) and I were walking in the woods out behind her home. There we saw a snake. I am terrified of snakes. I screamed my guts out and ran all the way back to my cousin's house.
>
> When I went home I began my first story, called "The Snake." I described what Kelly and I were wearing that day, why we were headed out into the woods (to see if a witch lived in the small shack that was out there) and described the fear of seeing the snake. I wrote and rewrote that story. I don't know how many versions I did, but I can imagine that there were a lot and that they were all very similar.

After "The Snake," Williams starting writing plays, scripts that nearly always had an alcoholic character in them. When she was twelve, she began writing stories for teen magazines but never mailed any of her manuscripts, except one to a contest sponsored by *The New Era*. She didn't win.

Writing Influences

An important influence in Williams' writing career was Bruce Aufhammer, her creative writing instructor at Seminole Community College. As a sixteen-year-old college student, Williams

Louise Plummer is another LDS writer for young adults and an English professor at Brigham Young University. Her books include *The Unlikely Romance of Kate Bjorkman* (1995) and *My Name Is Sus5an Smith. The 5 Is Silent* (1991).

There are articles about Betsy Byars and Bill and Vera Cleaver in volume 1; an article about Lois Lowry in volume 2; and articles about Richard Peck, Jerry Spinelli, and Theodore Taylor in volume 3.

Rick Walton is the author of more than thirty books for children. His books include the picture books *Bullfrog Pops* (1999), *So Many Bunnies* (1998), and *Once There Was a Bull . . . frog* (1995).

indispensable absolutely necessary

was unsure about her writing ability, but Aufhammer convinced her she had the potential to be a successful writer. "He loved everything I wrote," she recalls, "except for one really bad poem about grandmothers." Inspired by her teacher, Williams wrote steadily for the next fourteen years.

Her big break came when she took a correspondence creative writing course from young adult novelist Louise Plummer. For one assignment, Williams submitted a collection of short stories titled *Me and Kelly* that she had been working on since she was sixteen, and Plummer urged her to submit the stories to Delacorte Press's annual young adult novel contest. Buoyed by Plummer's encouragement, Williams changed her characters' ages from preteens to teenagers and sent off the manuscript. An editor at Delacorte told her that her characters were too old for the story, so Williams changed them back to their original ages and revised the short stories into novel form. The manuscript didn't win any prizes, but Delacorte decided to publish it. That success launched her writing career. Since then, she has published six other young adult novels and more than nine series books for middle graders.

In addition to Bruce Aufhammer and Louise Plummer, Williams has been influenced by the books of Betsy Byars, Lois Lowry, Claudia Mills, Theodore Taylor, Jerry Spinelli, Bill and Vera Cleaver, and Richard Peck. Even though she is a busy writer, Williams remains an avid reader; the work of other talented authors inspires her to keep writing. One of her most consistent influences is her writing group, headed by children's book author Rick Walton. Williams has met regularly with this group for nearly a decade; their support and feedback have been indispensable, so indispensable that *My Angelica* is dedicated to them. Her steadiest supporter is her husband, Drew. "He's always encouraged me to write, and he has faith in my work. He doesn't always like what I write, but he will tell me if the writing's good."

Williams' Books

Williams' first novel, *Kelly and Me,* grew out of her desire to become a published writer. It is based on her Florida childhood and captures the feelings of a contented childhood, perhaps the childhood Williams wishes she had experienced. This novel established patterns that would emerge in nearly all her books: a Florida setting, a grandparent as a key character, and the close relationship of two young girls, often sisters, who confront obstacles together.

Adeline Street (1995), the sequel to *Kelly and Me,* continues the story of Leah Orton after the death of her sister, Kelly. Leah is still grieving, but with the help of her loving grandfather and a new friend, Vickie, she learns to get on with life without Kelly. This novel maintains the warm and secure family tone that began in *Kelly and Me* but hints at the theme of abuse that would surface prominently in her next novel.

The True Colors of Caitlynne Jackson (1997) continues the pattern of a strong pair of sisters but reverses the family circumstances. Caitlynne and her sister, Cara, rely on each other for survival. As in *Kelly and Me,* these sisters are each other's best friend and enjoy spending time together in their Florida neighborhood, but they are raised by a single mother, a violent and cruel woman who physically and emotionally abuses them. Thanks to their grandmother, the girls eventually escape their mother's dominance. *True Colors* is a stark departure from Williams' previous books, but it captures a feeling Williams wanted to express: the longing for a safe and loving home and the relief that comes when it's finally achieved.

Her fourth novel, *If I Forget, You Remember* (1998), exchanges the Florida setting for Utah but returns to the gentler circumstances of Williams' first novels. Initially, Elyse Donaldson does not get along with her older sister, but she overcomes the sibling rivalry when the two of them must face their beloved grandmother's decline into Alzheimer's disease. Elyse's crush on Bruce A., a sixth grade classmate, introduces a new plot angle in Williams' books: a romantic encounter. This scenario would be expanded in comic ways in her next novel.

Perhaps as a release from the seriousness of the two previous books, *My Angelica* is a romantic comedy and the only Williams' novel in which siblings, parents, and grandparents play no significant roles. The novel's co-protagonist, Sage Oliver, is an aspiring romance novelist with a fierce crush on her friend George Blandford. George likes Sage just as fiercely, but he can't stand her sappy romance stories. By using Sage and George as alternating narrators, Williams makes full use of dramatic irony: two lovers separated by barriers of their own making. This book is pure fun.

Williams returns to more serious themes in *Carolina Autumn* (2000). Once again she is trying to capture a feeling with

Alzheimer's disease a disease of the central nervous system, often involving senility or a loss of mental faculties

protagonist the main character of a literary work

narrator a speaker or character who tells a story

dramatic irony a situation in a literary work in which a character unknowingly makes a remark that the audience knows to be ironic, or in contradiction to the full truth

her story, in this case a combination of "that awful, yucky feeling" and "the happy, good feeling" that results from family tragedy and the healing a nurturing family provides: Carolina and her mother are left alone in Florida when her father and sister die in a plane crash.

Williams' seventh novel, tentatively titled *Christmas in Heaven* (2000), deals with a spiritual tragedy. Afraid of death and afraid that she cannot be spiritually saved, Honey must confront her fears. She is helped along the way by a new and odd friend, Christmas, but ultimately resolves her conflict with the help of her parents and her grandfather.

Williams' Themes

abhor to hate

Williams values family relationships, especially the involvement of sisters, parents, and grandparents. She abhors abuse: "I don't think kids should go through that. I think they need to know there's a way out," which is the message implied in both *Adeline Street* and *The True Colors of Caitlynne Jackson*. She thinks death is "a really crummy deal" and explores that theme in *If I Forget, You Remember* and more explicitly in *Christmas in Heaven* and *Carolina Autumn*.

Perhaps the most general themes that run through Williams' books are the importance of healthy families and the importance of savoring life. Her characters thrive—or suffer— because of their family circumstances, and in all her books, young women, even those in difficult situations, are full of life. As Williams says, "As crummy as life can be, young people should love it. There's something immobilizing about being afraid of everything. Love life, because the next thing you know, you're old." The young characters in Carol Lynch Williams' novels do love life, and their love of life combined with the love of important adults in their lives helps them overcome the obstacles they face.

Selected Bibliography

If you like the works of Carol Lynch Williams, you might also enjoy the works of Norma Fox Mazer and Cynthia Voigt.

WORKS BY CAROL LYNCH WILLIAMS

Novels for Young Adults

Kelly and Me (1993)

Adeline Street (1995)

The True Colors of Caitlynne Jackson (1997)

If I Forget, You Remember (1998)

My Angelica (1999)

Carolina Autumn (2000)

Christmas in Heaven (2000)

Latter-day Daughters Series

Anna's Gift (1995)

Laurel's Flight (1995)

Sarah's Quest (1995)

Catherine's Remembrance (1996)

Esther's Celebration (1996)

Marciea's Melody (1996)

Caroline's Secret (1997)

Victoria's Courage (1998)

Short Story

"A Harbor of My Own." In *From the Outside Looking in: Short Stories for LDS Teenagers.* Edited by Chris Crowe. Salt Lake City, Utah: Bookcraft, 1998, pp. 22–29.

WORKS ABOUT CAROL LYNCH WILLIAMS

Jaffee, Cyrisse. Review of *If I Forget, You Remember.* In *School Library Journal,* March 1998, p. 226.

Lempke, Susan Dove. Review of *The True Colors of Caitlynne Jackson.* In *Booklist,* 1 March 1997, p. 1155.

Nichols, C. Allen. Review of *Kelly and Me.* In *VOYA,* October 1993, p. 220.

Noah, Carolyn. Review of *Kelly and Me.* In *School Library Journal,* September 1993, p. 236.

———. Review of *The True Colors of Caitlynne Jackson.* In *School Library Journal,* fall 1997, p. 106.

Orlando, Marie. Review of *Adeline Street.* In *School Library Journal,* July 1995, p. 82.

Review of *Adeline Street.* In *Publishers Weekly,* 23 January 1995, p. 70.

Review of *Adeline Street.* In *Kirkus Reviews,* 15 February 1995, p. 235.

Review of *If I Forget, You Remember.* In *Kirkus Reviews,* 15 December 1997, p. 1844.

Review of *If I Forget, You Remember.* In *Publishers Weekly,* 5 January 1998, p. 68.

Review of *Kelly and Me.* In *Publishers Weekly,* 6 September 1993, p. 98.

Review of *Kelly and Me.* In *Kirkus Reviews,* 1 November 1993, p. 1400.

Review of *The True Colors of Caitlynne Jackson.* In *Kirkus Reviews,* 1 November 1996, p. 1610.

Review of *The True Colors of Caitlynne Jackson.* In *Publishers Weekly,* 16 December 1996, p. 60.

Stevenson, Deborah. Review of *Adeline Street.* In *Bulletin of the Center on Children's Books,* April 1995, p. 289.

———. Review of *Kelly and Me.* In *Bulletin of the Center on Children's Books,* March 1994, p. 238.

———. Review of *The True Colors of Caitlynne Jackson.* In *Bulletin of the Center on Children's Books,* fall 1997, p. 226.

Weisman, Kay. Review of *Adeline Street. Booklist,* 1 April 1995, p. 1393.

How to Write to the Author

Carol Lynch Williams
543 S. 1700 East
Springville, UT 84663

Rita Williams-Garcia

(1957–)

by Marshall A. George

When asked about her writing, Rita Williams-Garcia's whole face lights up, and a normally quiet, shy woman suddenly becomes very animated and has a great deal to say.

> I've always loved to write. When I was in kindergarten, and my classmates were finger painting, I asked permission to sit at my desk so I could practice making the letters of the alphabet and try putting them together to form words. In elementary school, I spent recess by myself writing stories and poems. I made my first sale, a short story, to *Highlights Magazine* when I was fourteen years old. Even today, I sit huddled on a New York City subway every day going from my office in Manhattan to my home in Jamaica, Queens, revising and editing my next novel. I don't think a day has passed since kindergarten that I haven't written for my own pleasure.

Quotations from Rita Williams-Garcia that are not attributed to a published source are from a personal interview conducted by the author of this article on 13 January 1999 and are published here by permission of Rita Williams-Garcia.

A native New Yorker, Rita Williams-Garcia has made a childhood dream come true: she is a successful writer of novels and short stories. She is also a manager of software distribution and production for a marketing services company. Her works have been awarded such citations as Coretta Scott King Honor Book (1996), American Library Association Best Book (1991), PEN/Norma Klein Award (1997), and School Library Journal Best Book (1995) just to name a few. However, she did not set out to be a writer of books for young people. That happened by accident!

A sister in the Alpha Kappa Alpha sorority at Hofstra University, twenty-year-old Williams-Garcia was involved in a community outreach literacy program, which allowed her the opportunity to tutor four inner-city high school girls who read below the fourth grade level. The girls in her tutorial hated the literature they were reading in their high school English class, so Williams-Garcia went to the library and bookstore to find books that the young African American girls in her group might find more interesting and relevant to their own lives. She was frustrated to discover that the shelves held almost nothing that she felt would "speak" to these young women; so, she began writing dialogue and vignettes based on the conversations of teenagers with whom she came into contact. The girls responded so enthusiastically to the story that was developing, that Williams-Garcia wrote a chapter a week about the experiences of her newly created fictional character, Joyce Collins.

That same semester, the aspiring author was in a university-sponsored writer's workshop, so she was able to get feedback from her writing teacher and colleagues as well. (Williams-Garcia admits that she hated it when her colleagues and teacher criticized anything she had written.) From this came a manuscript that would, after a string of rejections from several publishers and many revisions, become her first published novel, *Blue Tights* (1988). Young readers in this country, along with readers in other countries, have had the same reaction to this novel that the young girls for whom it was originally conceived did—they love it!

Blue Tights

Joyce Collins, the central character in *Blue Tights,* is a fifteen-year old African American girl in Queens, New York, who knows what she wants out of life. First, she needs to be

There is an article about Norma Klein in volume 2.

vignette short episode or anecdote

aspiring seeking to reach a particular goal

cool—cool enough to hang out with girls in her school dance class like Cindi and Jay Jay. Even more, she wants to have the most gorgeous guy in school, Andre Miller, as her very own boyfriend, but most importantly, Joyce aspires to be a successful ballet dancer, just like her mother, Minnie, had been in her youth.

Rita Williams-Garcia states, "I like for my characters to be responsible for their behavior. They have to confront their problems and affect changes in their own lives. I won't let a knight in shining armor save them. They have to save themselves." Indeed, Joyce certainly has her share of problems. She faces a major setback when, to the delight of the in-crowd in her dance class, her insensitive high school ballet teacher tells her that because of her large butt, Joyce will not dance in the school's dance production. At first, Joyce retreats from her family and friends as she broods over her disappointment. Eventually, she joins an African dance troupe, whose members and director not only accept her as a dancer but also give her the lead role in their spring show. Her experience in the dance troupe not only teaches her about her cultural heritage, but it also enables her to begin building self-confidence. Joyce gradually accepts who she is and is proud of both her body and her dance abilities. *Blue Tights* is a fast-paced, realistic portrayal of important issues in the life of an urban teenage girl. In her review of the book in the September/October 1992 *Horn Book,* critic Rudine Sims Bishop suggests that, "Williams-Garcia has created in Joyce a credible teenager—headstrong, confused, self-absorbed, but capable of positive growth and change" (p. 617).

Although Rita Williams-Garcia wrote *Blue Tights* for a very specific audience, urban teenage African American girls, she reports receiving letters from boys and girls alike, of varying cultural backgrounds, in which they praise the novel, suggesting that Joyce's experience speaks to them. One boy, who admitted to being a "girl teaser," commented, "When I saw how the kids' picking on Joyce made her feel, I realized what it's like to be a girl who gets teased because of her body. I won't do that anymore." Another reader, a young immigrant girl from China, writes, "The book may be about an African American girl, but the same thing happened to me in China. I can't believe how much this story is like my own." Although Williams-Garcia had thought that *Blue Tights* would be her first and last book for young adult audiences, comments like

"I like for my characters to be responsible for their behavior. They have to confront their problems and affect changes in their own lives. I won't let a knight in shining armor save them. They have to save themselves."

troupe a group of theatrical performers

credible believable

these and hundreds of others she has received from fans encouraged her to consider writing a second novel for adolescents.

Fast Talk on a Slow Track

One afternoon, as she walked into a fast food place for lunch with her young daughter, Rita Williams-Garcia recognized the manager behind the counter as one of her college classmates. "This guy had been big man on campus: student body president, student senator, and a pre-law major. He had it all! He was supposed to be in a midtown Manhattan law firm, not a fast food restaurant in Queens!" This experience made Williams-Garcia start thinking about the many young people who have so much potential but waste it and give up their dreams, often out of a fear of failure.

Fast Talk on a Slow Track (1991) is a story of one such person. Dinizulu (Denzel) Watson who, it appears to his friends, family, and community, "has it made." The self-confident and talented class valedictorian is bound for the prestigious halls of Princeton University. However, he must first complete a summer program for minority students. Much to his surprise, Denzel discovers that his charm, wit, and outgoing personality will not impress people at Princeton as they had in his high school. Frustrated by his dissatisfying experience and humiliating near failure in the summer program, Denzel returns home to Queens, with no intention of returning to Princeton in the fall. His biggest problem, he thinks, is how to tell his proud parents that their dreams for him will never be realized.

This compelling story tells of the events of those summer months between high school graduation and the beginning of his freshman year in college. Denzel returns to New York and begins selling candy door-to-door, a summer job that allows him to feel the confidence that he lacked in the summer program at Princeton. Just like his high school experience, this job gives Denzel the opportunity to be successful (he's the top salesman of the summer) without having to work very hard.

Fast Talk on a Slow Track shows that Rita Williams-Garcia can get inside the heads of a male character as convincingly as she does female ones. In her review of this book in the July/August 1991 *Horn Book,* Nancy Vasilakis commented,

prestigious honored or well-known

"Williams-Garcia writes just as authoritatively about teenage boys as she did about girls in her first novel, *Blue Tights*. She understands the forces and fears driving a young man in search of his true self. . . . This engrossing, fast-moving novel resounds with authenticity" (p. 466). When asked if it was difficult to write from the perspective of a young man, Williams-Garcia replied, "No. Even though Denzel is a male character, he is facing a universal experience. When young people go off to college, they are faced with the fact that they are starting from scratch. You get to redefine yourself in college. For some, that is a good thing. For others, like Denzel, they think it is going to be terrible. They are afraid of their new life." After all, Denzel loves who he is in high school and does not like the preview he gets of himself in college during the summer program.

engrossing absorbing

Like many teenage boys, Denzel is a victim of his own image. He has a huge ego, and because of the events that occur in the novel, his ego is deflated. Readers, in letters to the author about the novel, suggest that they often have a love-hate relationship with this character. In some ways he is so admirable; he has gifts, family support, values, and resources. Yet he squanders them. When readers reach a scene in which Denzel is badly beaten by his friend and rival Carmello (Williams-Garcia's favorite character in the novel), they report that they are glad that the cocky Denzel finally gets the attitude adjustment he needs! Although her readers and critics have responded positively to the ending of the book, Williams-Garcia says she has never been satisfied with it and wishes she had the opportunity to do it over.

squander to lose through carelessness

Like Sisters on the Homefront

Although her first two novels were well received, Rita Williams-Garcia considers her third book, *Like Sisters on the Homefront* (1995), to be her breakthrough novel. The idea for this story also grew out of a visit to a fast food restaurant. As she waited in line one day, Williams-Garcia noticed a five-year-old girl taking care of her infant brother, feeding him, wiping his mouth, and burping him. "I was struck by the fact that this child, like so many other African American girls, was having an aborted childhood. By that I mean that so many of our girls skip from *childhood* to *motherhood* without ever experiencing the carefree days of *girlhood*. This five-year-old girl had an

blasé unconcerned

> *"I am writing about characters. They may face very serious issues in their lives, but ultimately it is the growth and change that occurs in the teen characters as a result of the issues that I want to address—not the issues themselves."*

matriarch female head of a family

adult's job to do, and she was doing it, very matter-of-factly, like a grown-up." This incident brought back memories to the author of walking down a street in her neighborhood in Jamaica, Queens, and seeing the younger sister of one of her classmates with a baby on her hip. When Williams-Garcia approached the twelve-year-old girl to compliment her on what she assumed to be her baby brother, the girl responded in a very blasé manner that the child was her own. When the author expressed surprise, the girl "got attitude," saying that having a baby was "no big deal." These two experiences led to Gayle, the main character in *Like Sisters on the Homefront,* being conceived in Rita Williams-Garcia's mind.

This novel begins with fourteen-year-old Gayle's second pregnancy. When her mother discovers that Gayle, who already has a seven-month-old child, is pregnant again, she insists that her daughter get an abortion, and sends her to Georgia to live with her conservative, religious relatives. Gayle is furious about her exile to the South. On her trip to Georgia, when a flight attendant asks her if she is comfortable, Gayle thinks, "Stomach still cramp from the abortion. Side still smarting from tussling with Mama. Back still sore from hauling the baby around. Cut off from Troy and the girls, being sold to slavery" (p. 23). No, she is neither happy nor comfortable, and is filled with anger at having to leave the action of her beloved New York City.

Yes, this novel explores serious issues such as teen pregnancy and abortion, but Williams-Garcia insists that when she writes, she is not writing about issues. "I am writing about characters. They may face very serious issues in their lives, but ultimately it is the growth and change that occurs in the teen characters as a *result* of the issues that I want to address—not the issues themselves."

In this award-winning novel (it is a 1996 Coretta Scott King Honor Book), Gayle learns what it is to be a mother and a woman. It is not from her culturally aware, intellectual, college-professor aunt, Virginia, that she learns who she is. Rather, Gayle comes to understand African American womanhood, and more importantly, the significance of family, from "Great," the family matriarch, whose stories of the past begin to change how Gayle sees her own future.

Rita Williams-Garcia says that the most frequently asked question when she visits classrooms where students have read *Blue Tights* and *Like Sisters on the Homefront* is if the two protagonists, Joyce and Gayle, are anything like the author herself. "Absolutely not," she always replies. A quiet, shy, self-proclaimed nerd, Williams-Garcia has spent most of her life in Jamaica, Queens, where Joyce and Gayle grew up. However, she was always a good student, well-mannered, and respectful of her teachers, parents, and classmates. "I was a Martian, though," she claims. "A real misfit. My classmates thought I was weird. I didn't like being a girl and was angered by the unwanted attention my body brought me. So I do have that in common with Joyce in *Blue Tights;* but unlike the two girls, I was a high-achieving brain." Williams-Garcia was born in Jamaica in Queens, New York, on 13 April 1957. Her parents, James and Essie Williams, raised Rita, her sister, and her brother in a loving home. She did well in school, though her family moved around a great deal when she was in elementary school. Because of her father's military career, (he was away from the family for two years when he served in the Vietnam War) her family moved to California when she was a small child. Before the age of twelve, she had moved eight times and attended several different elementary schools.

The Williams family moved back to New York when she was in junior high school, which Williams-Garcia claims caused her culture shock. "I had lived the life of a black Brady Bunch family in small town California and was suddenly thrown into an inner city junior high school where there were regular police drug raids, violence, and even a murder once." During those years, the teenage Rita Williams found solace in the St. Alban's Public Library, where she checked out her two favorite books, *The Writer's Handbook* and *The Writer's Market* every single week. At the age of twelve she began sending out stories to magazines on a regular basis. Despite many rejections, she never quit trying. Her persistence finally paid off, and today Rita Williams-Garcia is an important writer of novels for young adults. Rudine Sims Bishop, of *Horn Book,* says that Rita Williams-Garcia is part of a small group that "may well turn out to be the most prominent African American literary artists of the next generation" (p. 616).

She has two books in progress. The first, *Every Time . . . A Rainbow Dies* (2000), is a novel about a boy who retreats into solitude when his mother dies. One day, he witnesses a rape attempt, and befriends the rape victim, eventually falling in love with her. In addition, Williams-Garcia's first picture book for children, *Chasing the Wild Waiuuzee,* is in the revision process.

protagonist the main character of a literary work

In the **Vietnam War** (1957–1975), Communist-ruled North Vietnam fought to take over South Vietnam. From 1965 to 1969, the United States tried to stop the advancement of North Vietnam but failed. In 1975, South Vietnam surrendered to North Vietnam.

Fans of Rita Williams-Garcia will be pleased to know that production has begun on a screen version of *Like Sisters on the Homefront.* Rita Williams-Garcia, a writer who says she is not sure which she loves more, her characters or her readers, lives in Queens, New York, with her husband and two daughters.

If you like Rita Williams-Garcia, you might also like Maya Angelou, Robert Lipsyte, Walter Dean Myers, Virginia Euwer Wolff, and Jacqueline Woodson.

Selected Bibliography

WORKS BY RITA WILLIAMS-GARCIA

Novels for Young Adults

Blue Tights (1988)

Fast Talk on a Slow Track (1991)

Like Sisters on the Homefront (1995)

Every Time . . . A Rainbow Dies (2000)

Short Stories

"Into the Game." In *Join In: Multiethnic Stories by Outstanding Writers for Young Adults.* Edited by Donald R. Gallo. New York: Delacorte Press, 1993.

"Chalkman." In *Twelve Shots: Outstanding Short Stories About Guns.* Edited by Harry Mazer. New York: Delacorte Press, 1997.

"Crazy as a Daisy." In *Stay True: Stories of Strong Girls.* Edited by Marilyn Singer. New York: Scholastic, 1997.

"Wishing It Away." In *No Easy Answers: Short Stories About Teenagers Making Tough Choices.* Edited by Donald R. Gallo. New York: Bantam, 1997.

"About Russell." In *Dirty Laundry: Stories About Family Secrets.* Edited by Lisa Rowe Fraustino. New York: Viking, 1998.

"Cross Over." In *Trapped!* Edited by Lois Duncan. New York: Simon & Schuster, 1998.

"Food from the Outside." In *When I Was Your Age, Volume II: Original Stories About Growing Up.* Edited by Amy Ehrlich. Cambridge, Mass.: Candlewick Press, 1999.

WORKS ABOUT RITA WILLIAMS-GARCIA

Bishop, Rudine Sims. "Books from Parallel Cultures: New African-American Voices" *Horn Book,* September/October 1992, pp. 616–620.

Kutenplon, D., and Olmstead, E. *Young Adult Fiction by African-American Writers, 1968–1993: A Critical and Annotated Guide.* New York: Garland, pp. 313–316.

Larson, Gerry. "Blue Tights." *School Library Journal.* June/July 1988, p. 120.

Senick, Gerard and Hedblad, Alan (1995). "Rita Williams-Garcia." In *Children's Literature Review.* Detroit: Gale Research, 1995, vol. 36, pp. 202–206.

Vasilakis, Nancy. Review of *Fast Talk on a Slow Track.* In *Horn Book,* July/August 1991.

How to Write to the Author

Rita Williams-Garcia
P.O. Box 2277
New York, NY 10185

You can also e-mail
Rita Williams-Garcia at
ritawg@aol.com

Jacqueline Woodson

(1963–)

by Judith A. Hayn

How would you react if your seventh grade English teacher returned your first story and commented, "You are the real thing"? In an unpublished speech given to the Michigan Council of Teachers in the fall of 1998, Jacqueline Woodson described the impact Mr. Miller's words had on her even though she still doesn't understand what he meant. It was he, and others like him, who started her on her path as a reader and a writer.

Since that first story written as an English class assignment, Woodson has extended her writing talents beyond the days of her fifth grade experience as the literary editor of her school's magazine. She continued to hone those initial efforts with her first publications in 1990, for this is when she began the trilogy of Margaret and Maizon, two African American girls, who are best friends growing up in Brooklyn. Woodson draws on her familiarity with this section of New York City as she spent her own adolescence splitting residences between there and South Carolina.

Quotations from Jacqueline Woodson that are not attributed to a published source are from a personal interview conducted by the author of this article on 19 December 1998 and are published here by permission of Jacqueline Woodson.

Richard Nixon (1913–1994) was the 37th president of the United States. After the investigation of a burglary and wiretapping of Democratic Party headquarters, Nixon faced probable impeachment. Rather than endure a trial, Nixon resigned in 1974. **George McGovern** (1922–) was a Democratic senator from South Dakota who made an unsuccessful attempt for the U.S. presidency in 1972.

In the **Vietnam War** (1957–1975), Communist-ruled North Vietnam fought to take over South Vietnam. From 1965 to 1969, the United States tried to stop the advancement of North Vietnam but failed. In 1975, South Vietnam surrendered.

James Baldwin (1924–1987) was an African American novelist, essayist, and playwright. **Toni Cade Bambara** (1939–1995) was an African American writer, civil rights activist, and teacher. **Langston Hughes** (1902–1967) was an African American poet.

trilogy a series of three literary works that are closely related and share a single theme

Perhaps this continual switching of homes contributes to the sense of searching for a place to belong so evident in her works for young adults. Yet Woodson revealed in a telephone interview that her books are "not about my personal past, but rather deal with a question of identity" and "the shackles society puts around us." In a 1995 *Horn Book* article, she elaborates on the realization that concern for this issue of powerlessness came early when she was a preteen. She had just witnessed Richard Nixon's downfall, the destruction generated by the Vietnam War, and the inadequacies of the civil rights movement when George McGovern failed in his bid for the presidency. "The world became a place that didn't welcome me and the people I loved, and in response I stepped outside of the world. From this vantage point, I watched and took note" (p. 7).

What she read guided her growing awareness of the inequities in the world around her. Jacqueline Woodson was born on 12 February 1964 in Columbus, Ohio. As an African American girl growing up in the seventies, Woodson discovered the works of James Baldwin, Toni Cade Bambara, and Langston Hughes. In 1994 she chose excerpts from the works of these writers and others for a powerful collection she edited, *A Way Out of No Way: Writings About Growing Up Black in America* (1996). She reveals in her introduction that the writings continue to inspire her even now as her memory "fills with the spirits of these writers offering anyone who reads their words, a way out of no way: pointing a beautiful black finger toward a holy, holy place" (p. 3).

Friends and Families

Woodson acknowledges in the same *Horn Book* article that when she chooses more conventional themes as she did in her earlier novels, she feels she experiences more acceptance by librarians and teachers. She calls these her "good," or "nice" books. The trilogy that generates her evaluation begins with *Last Summer with Maizon* (1990), where Margaret and Maizon are introduced. Woodson excels at describing young girls, their language, their yearnings, their despair; she further explains: "I write about black girls because this world would like to keep us invisible. I write about all girls because I know what happens to self-esteem when we turn twelve, and I hope to show readers the number of ways in which we are strong" (p. 10).

The success of her intent permeates her planned trilogy. In the first book, Margaret's father dies from a heart attack, and Maizon leaves her friend and their Brooklyn neighborhood to attend an elite boarding school on scholarship. Margaret is the quieter one, and during Maizon's absence, she finds comfort in writing, much as Woodson did as a child. The words of her anguish in a poem generate admiration and attention from teachers and classmates: "It's funny how we never know/exactly how our life will go/It's funny how a dream can fade/With the break of day" (p. 67). Her family also provides support during this troubled time. Meanwhile, Maizon returns from the Connecticut school after only three months, and the two are reunited as both enroll in a local school for the gifted.

The pains of growing up continue in *Maizon at Blue Hill* (1992) where Maizon's experiences at an exclusive boarding school unfold. Although she enjoys the academic challenges, she fails to find a comfortable place socially. Most of the other girls are white and either racist or elitist toward her or her scholarship status; the small clique of black girls are equally as intolerant. Maizon leaves for the security and familiarity of her home with Grandmother Singh back in Brooklyn.

Between Madison and Palmetto (1993), which are the names of two streets in Brooklyn, contains the completion of the story amid the uncertainties of adolescent friendship and the challenges of family connections for the now eighth grade protagonists. As the neighborhood begins to integrate, Margaret struggles with an eating disorder and a potential boyfriend while dealing with Maizon's emerging friendship with a fellow student, Caroline, who is white. Maizon's father, who abandoned her as a child, also reappears and tries to establish connections with his daughter.

Woodson's abilities to delineate character development continue as the girls grow from eleven to thirteen in the saga. The warmth and closeness between the two is developed in a poetic, eloquent narrative voice; the third-person point of view in the first story focuses on Margaret, while Maizon tells the second in first person. In the final book, Woodson returns to third person, perhaps to highlight the rift the girls experience in their relationship. The plot lines of all three novels also address the adult concerns Woodson says drive her writing: racism, self-esteem in young adolescent girls, death, giftedness, and, most importantly, identity.

---

permeate to penetrate or diffuse through something

protagonist the main character of a literary work

third-person point of view the position or perspective of someone outside the story

first person the position or perspective of someone inside the story, using the pronoun "I"

racism hatred for or intolerance of another race

Differences and the Unfamiliar

plot the deliberate sequence of events in a literary work

When Woodson deviates from what she feels is a more comfortable friendship plot line, she feels the controversies surrounding her choices of subject matter—alcoholism, abuse, teen pregnancy, homosexuality, biracial dating, interracial marriage, and violence—influence the decisions of librarians and teachers about what is "appropriate" for young adolescents to read. She maintains in a *Horn Book* article in 1998 that "every story I've written. . . . is my story. . . . most of all, like the characters in my story, I have felt a sense of powerlessness in my lifetime. And this is the room into which I can walk and join them. This sense of being on the outside of things, of feeling misunderstood and invisible, is the experience I bring to the story" (pp. 36–37). The characters who meet her definition are those Woodson refers to in her Michigan speech as "something different, something unfamiliar."

The differences emerging in *The Dear One* (1991) affect twelve-year-old Afeni, whose name means "dear one" in Swahili. Her comfortable, upper-middle-class life with her single mother in an affluent, black suburb in Pennsylvania changes dramatically, when a pregnant, unwed, openly hostile teen, the daughter of her mother's college friend, arrives from Harlem. The presence of a lesbian couple, one a teacher at Feni's private school, adds another jarring note; yet it is clear that Marion and Bernadette and their stable relationship, coupled with their understanding words of wisdom, augment the patient support Feni receives from her mother.

augment to supplement

In *I Hadn't Meant to Tell You This* (1994), the inequities of economic class continue as Marie, the daughter of a single father who is a college professor living in an all-black suburb in Ohio, meets Lena. The new girl in the eighth-grade narrator's school is decidedly "white trash," and Marie's father and friends warn her to avoid her. Yet the two have a strong bond in common; both live with only their fathers, as Marie's mother has abandoned her family while Lena's mother has died from cancer. Lena shares the terrible secret she hides from everyone else: her father molests her, and she fears for her younger sister's fate. Marie's reaction, at first of disbelief and denial, leaves a powerful lesson for the young reader.

The companion to this multiple award-winning novel is *Lena* (1999), beginning with the conclusion to Marie's story. Lena has taken her younger sister Dion and run away; they plan to find their mother's Kentucky home in the hopes that someone will want them. A kind, gentle, intuitive, African American woman, Miz Lily, points them back to Marie, whose friendship and love could provide the home Lena wants for herself and her sister.

After graduating with a B.A. in English, Woodson became a drama therapist for runaways and homeless children in New York City. She is now a full-time writer. Her experiences undoubtedly create the sense of believability and gritty realism in the adventures Lena and Dion encounter.

Nevertheless, Woodson herself acknowledges that her biggest risk-taking occurs when she continues to delve into other areas of diversity. She is quoted in teaching materials provided by Bantam Doubleday Dell: "There are all kinds of people in the world, and I want to help introduce readers to the kinds of people they might not otherwise meet." Certainly that concern became clear with the publication of *From the Notebooks of Melanin Sun* in 1995. This time her protagonist is a thirteen-year-old African American male, Melanin Sun.

Living a stable, normal life with his single mother in Brooklyn, Mel worries about his male friends, the opposite sex, school, basketball, and acceptance—all chronicled in his private notebooks. When his mother reveals her love for a white woman, Mel's world shatters; gossip ravages the familiar neighborhood, and some of his friends desert him. Hazel S. Moore, in the October 1997 *Voice of Youth Advocates* wrote that "Woodson has addressed with care and skill the sensitive issue of homosexuality within the family. . . ." (p. 227).

chronicle to record historical events in the order in which they occur without analysis or interruption

Moving her subject matter deeper into the confusion adolescents feel about their own sexuality, Woodson introduces Staggerlee in *The House You Pass on the Way* (1997). Having explored this theme in "Slipping Away," a short story published in Marion Dane Bauer's collection, *Am I Blue? Coming Out from the Silence* (1994), the author uses summer vacation relationships for two girls to grapple with desires and yearnings not understood by others around them. In Staggerlee's case, she is already set apart as the daughter of a racially mixed marriage and the grandchild of talented, artistic grandparents martyred by a bomb explosion during the civil rights demonstrations.

martyr to suffer or die for a cause or a religious belief

The protagonist looks back to the stillness of winter to remember the feelings she confronted in her longing for her adopted cousin Trout. A letter from Trout tells Staggerlee that though the summer was special, she now has a boyfriend and has moved in another direction. Staggerlee wonders if someday there will be—"Someone she could whisper her life to. Someone she could take to a party, walk off the edge of the world with" (pp. 98–99). Readers can become the recipients of those whispers and enter the poignant thoughts of this sensitive, intelligent girl whose worries about being gay are revealed as another part of finding an identity.

From interracial marriage and its complications for children, Woodson moves to the story of a romance between a white, upper-middle-class, Jewish girl and an African American male classmate in *If You Come Softly* (1998). Ellie has just enrolled in Percy, an elite prep school in New York City, and in her prologue she writes of impending heartbreak: "I close my eyes again. And remember what I can" (p. 2). As the story unfolds, the author switches from Ellie's first person narrative point of view to a third person perspective for Jeremiah's tale. Both are effective at revealing the impending doom of this relationship as the reader realizes that the outcome will be tragic.

Her Lyrical Voice

Nearly all who critique Woodson's works write of her lyrical prose style as her characters either reveal themselves or are seen through the eyes of others. Her dialogue authenticates the language of her characters, both young and old. She has written for *Horn Book,* asking "Who Can Tell My Story?" (1998), where she draws on the language heard in her grandmother's house in South Carolina.

> It tell its own story, our language does, and woven through it are all the places we've been, all that we've seen, experiences held close, good and bad. . . . I have come to love all aspects of the English language—have come to love sitting down with the writings of [Henry] James and [Ezra] Pound as much as I love sitting down to Sunday dinner at my grandmother's house. Each event is buttered thick with experience and language. . . . And by this means, through the different, complicated elements of language and experience, through being and reading and listening and re-creating, I have

Henry James (1843–1916) was an American novelist. He wrote *The Portrait of a Lady* (1881). **Ezra Pound** (1885–1972) was an American poet and essayist. He was one of the most influential literary figures of his time.

come to understand the world around me—and my-self as a writer. (P. 35)

Listen to her characters speak. Lena asserts to Marie, "White, black—it shouldn't make no difference. We all just people here" (p. 59). Jeremiah's father tells him, "Thing about white people. . . . they know what everybody else is, but they don't know they're white" (p. 134). Maizon confides to her white roommate at Blue Hill before she decides to leave, "I hate this place. . . . I don't belong here" (p. 102). Melanin Sun writes in his notebook, "Some days I wear alone like a coat, like a hood draping from my head that first warm day of spring, like socks bunching up inside my sneakers" (p. 27). Woodson finds the voices to combat racism, injustice, cruelty, loneliness—the powerlessness her characters encounter—with careful choice of language.

The voices of her adolescent girls resonate perhaps most effectively, however, as they reveal themselves in their own words. This is important to Woodson, for as she says on her Bantam website: "Girls rarely get discussed in books and films, and I want to do 'girl stories' that show strong, independent people. I think girls are often disregarded in this society and taught to be dependent. I want to show young people that there are other ways to be."

resonate to sound loudly

Language is her vehicle, and her girls speak lyrically of their struggles. Listen to Ellie in *If You Come Softly* as she describes her ordeal of tragedy, growth, and triumph when she concludes:

This is how the time moves—an hour here, a day somewhere, and then it's night and then it's morning. A clock ticking on a shelf. A small child running to school, a father coming home.

Time moves over us and past us, and the feeling of lips pressed against lips fades into memory. A picture yellows at its edges. A phone rings in an empty room. . . .

Time comes to us softly, slowly. It sits beside us for a while.

Then, long before we are ready, it moves on. (Pp. 180–181)

With her control of language, the poetic quality of her prose, Jacqueline Woodson continues in a personal quest, as she states in "A *Sign* of *Having* Been *Here*" in the November 1995 *Horn Book,* "to change the way the world thinks, one reader at a time."

If you like Jacqueline Woodson, you might also like Virginia Hamilton, Carolyn Meyer, Mildred Delois Taylor, and Rita Williams-Garcia.

Selected Bibliography

WORKS BY JACQUELINE WOODSON

Novels for Young Adults

Last Summer with Maizon (1990)

The Dear One (1991)

Maizon at Blue Hill (1992)

Between Madison and Palmetto (1993)

I Hadn't Meant to Tell You This (1994)

From the Notebooks of Melanin Sun (1995)

The House You Pass on the Way (1997)

If You Come Softly (1998)

Lena (1999)

Novel for Adults

Autobiography of a Family Photo (1994)

Short Story

"Slipping Away." In *Am I Blue? Coming Out from the Silence.* Edited by Marion Dane Bauer. New York: Harper Trophy, 1994.

Children's Books

Martin Luther King, Jr. and His Birthday, illustrated by Floyd Cooper (1990)

We Had a Picnic This Sunday Past, illustrated by Diane Greenseid (1997)

Collected Work

A Way Out of No Way: Writings About Growing Up Black in America, edited by Jacqueline Woodson (1996)

Audiovisual Material

Among Good Christian Peoples. Video with Catherine Saalfield. San Francisco, Calif.: Frameline, 1991.

Articles

"A *Sign* of *Having* Been *Here*." *Horn Book,* November/December 1995, pp. 7–11.

"Who Can Tell My Story?" *Horn Book,* January/February 1998, pp. 34–35.

Speech

Unpublished Speech, Michigan Council of Teachers of English, fall 1998.

WORKS ABOUT JACQUELINE WOODSON

BDD Teacher's Resource Center on the Internet at *www. bdd.com/teachers*

Bishop, Rudine Sims. "Books from Parallel Cultures: New African-American Voices," *Horn Book.* September 1992, pp. 616–620.

Bloom, Susan P. Review of *The House You Pass on the Way.* In *Horn Book,* September/October 1997, p. 583.

Cart, Michael. "Jacqueline Woodson." In *Twentieth-Century Children's Writers.* Edited by Laura Standley Berger. Detroit: St. James Press, 1995, pp. 1042–1043.

Hile, Janet L. "Jacqueline Woodson." In *Authors & Artists for Young Adults.* Edited by Thomas McMahor. Detroit: Gale Research, 1989, vol. 21, pp. 211–217.

Moore, Hazel S. Review of *The Dear One.* In *Voice of Youth Advocates,* October 1991, p. 236.

Teacher's Resource Center on the Internet at *www. randomhouse.com/teachers*

How to Write to the Author

Jacqueline Woodson
c/o Penguin Putnam Books
for Young Readers
345 Hudson Street, 14th Floor
New York, NY 10014

Contributors

Professor Richard F. Abrahamson
University of Houston
R. L. STINE

Professor Lynne Alvine
Indiana University of Pennsylvania
STEPHANIE S. TOLAN

Professor Mike Angelotti
University of Oklahoma
WALT WHITMAN

Dr. Kevin Sue Bailey
Indiana University, Southeast Campus,
New Albany, NY
LOUIS SACHAR

Professor Lawrence Baines
Berry College
CHRISTOPHER PIKE

Professor Rebecca Barnhouse
Youngstown State University
KAREN CUSHMAN

Dr. Kylene Beers
University of Houston
ROB THOMAS

Mr. Jim Blasingame
University of Kansas
SHARON CREECH

Professor James M. Brewbaker
Columbus State University
MARGARET MITCHELL

Professor Jean E. Brown
Rhode Island College
WILL WEAVER

Professor John H. Bushman
University of Kansas
SHARON CREECH

Ms. Patty Campbell
Amazon.com
Horn Book Magazine
Scarecrow Press
MICHAEL CADNUM, DONNA JO NAPOLI

Professor Pamela Sissi Carroll
Florida State University
ANNE C. LEMIEUX

Mr. Michael Cart
Booklist Magazine
ADELE GRIFFIN

Professor Betty Carter
Texas Woman's University
CAROLYN MEYER

Professor Leila Christenbury
Virginia Commonwealth University
ARTHUR MILLER

Dr. Pam B. Cole
Kennesaw State University
PAUL FLEISCHMAN

Professor Chris Crowe
Brigham Young University
CAROL LYNCH WILLIAMS

Dr. Patricia L. Daniel
University of South Florida Liaison to
Weightman Middle School
STEPHEN KING

Professor Marshall A. George
Fordham University
RITA WILLIAMS-GARCIA

Dr. Sam D. Gill
University of North Carolina, Wilmington
SHELLEY STOEHR, K. A. APPLEGATE

Professor Colleen P. Gilrane
University of Tennessee, Knoxville
CYNTHIA RYLANT

Professor Judith A. Hayn
Auburn University, Auburn, Alabama
JACQUELINE WOODSON

Professor Jeffrey S. Kaplan
University of Central Florida
THORNTON WILDER

Dr. Joan F. Kaywell
University of South Florida
NANCY GARDEN

Professor Patricia P. Kelly
Virginia Polytechnic Institute and
State University
RONALD KOERTGE

Dean Donald J. Kenney
Virginia Polytechnic Institute and
State University
LOU KASSEM

Professor Teri S. Lesesne
Sam Houston State University
MEL GLENN, ROB THOMAS

387

Ms. Amy B. Maupin
University of Tennessee, Knoxville
JANE AUSTEN

Mr. Bill Mollineaux
Sedgwick Middle School, West Hartford,
Connecticut
RODMAN PHILBRICK

Professor Alleen Pace Nilsen
Arizona State University
ANNETTE CURTIS KLAUSE

Dr. Elizabeth A. Poe
West Virginia University
PHILIP PULLMAN

Professor Suzanne Elizabeth Reid
Emory and Henry College, Emory, Virginia
JIM HASKINS

Professor Barbara G. Samuels
University of Houston, Clear Lake
KYOKO MORI

Dean Robert C. Small, Jr.
Radford University
LOU KASSEM

Dr. Elaine C. Stephens
Saginaw Valley State University
DAVID KLASS

Professor Lois T. Stover
St. Mary's College of Maryland
KAREN HESSE

Ms. Judith Volc
Boulder Public Library
PHILIP PULLMAN

Dr. Jinx Stapleton Watson
University of Tennessee, Knoxville
SUZANNE FISHER STAPLES

Professor Connie S. Zitlow
Ohio Wesleyan University
TRUDY KRISHER

Category Index

Page numbers in boldface refer to the main discussion of the subject.

Index

Page numbers in boldface refer to the main discussion of the subject.